WALLACE STEVENS: THE CRITICAL HERITAGE

THE CRITICAL HERITAGE SERIES

GENERAL EDITOR: B. C. SOUTHAM, M.A., B.LITT. (OXON.)
Formerly Department of English, Westfield College, University of London

---

For a list of books in the series see the back end paper

WALLACE STEVENS

THE CRITICAL HERITAGE

Edited by

CHARLES DOYLE

Professor of English
University of Victoria, British Columbia

ROUTLEDGE & KEGAN PAUL
LONDON, BOSTON AND HENLEY

First published in 1985
by Routledge & Kegan Paul plc
14 Leicester Square, London WC2H 7PH, England
9 Park Street, Boston, Mass. 02108, USA, and
Broadway House, Newton Road,
Henley on Thames, Oxon RG9 1EN, England

Set in 11 on 12 pt. Bembo
by Thomson Press (India) Ltd.
and printed in Great Britain
by The Thetford Press Ltd.
Thetford, Norfolk

Library of Congress Cataloging in Publication Data

Wallace Stevens, the critical heritage.
Bibliography: p.
Includes index.
1. Stevens, Wallace, 1879–1955—Criticism and
interpretation—Addresses, essays, lectures.
I. Doyle, Charles, 1928-
PS3537.T4753Z882 1985   811'.52   84–24858

British Library CIP data available

ISBN 0–7100–9647–X

General Editor's Preface

The reception given to a writer by his contemporaries and near-contemporaries is evidence of considerable value to the student of literature. On one side we learn a great deal about the state of criticism at large and in particular about the development of critical attitudes towards a single writer; at the same time, thought private comments in letters, journals or marginalia, we gain an insight upon the tastes and literary thought of individual readers of the period. Evidence of this kind helps us to understand the writer's historical situation, the nature of his immediate reading-public, and his response to these pressures.

The separate volumes in the *Critical Heritage Series* present a record of this early criticism. Clearly, for many of the highly productive and lengthily reviewed nineteenth- and twentieth-century writers, there exists an enormous body of material; and in these cases the volume editors have made a selection of the most important views, significant for their intrinsic critical worth or for their representative quality – perhaps even registering incomprehension!

For earlier writers, notably pre-eighteenth century, the materials are much scarcer and the historical period has been extended, sometimes far beyond the writer's lifetime, in order to show the inception and growth of critical views which were initially slow to appear.

In each volume the documents are headed by an Introduction, discussing the material assembled and relating the early stages of the author's reception to what we have come to identify as the critical tradition. The volumes will make available much material which would otherwise be difficult of access and it is hoped that the modern reader will be thereby helped towards an informed understanding of the ways in which literature has been read and judged.

B.C.S.

Contents

CONTENTS

CONTENTS

CONTENTS

CONTENTS

CONTENTS

Acknowledgments

Every effort has been made to locate copyright holders, but the editor and publishers regret that it has proved impossible to locate some of them. We wish to thank the following for permission to reprint copyright material: *Birmingham Post* for No. 116; Brandt & Brandt Literary Agents, Inc., for No. 4; *Commonweal* for No. 27; *Dallas Morning News* for No. 87; Donald Davie and Carcanet Press for No. 95, from Donald Davie, *The Poet in the Imaginary Museum: Essays of Two Decades,* ed. Barry Alpert (Carcanet, Manchester, 1977); Farrar, Straus & Giroux, Inc., for No. 106, from *The Third Book of Criticism* by Randall Jarrell (Copyright © 1955 by Mrs Randall Jarrell, © 1963, 1965 by Randall Jarrell); Lawrence Ferlinghetti for No. 102; Edwin Honig for No. 89; Irving Howe for No. 113; *The Hudson Review* for No. 114, reprinted by permission from *The Hudson Review,* vol. X, no. 4 (Winter 1957–8) (Copyright © 1958 by The Hudson Review, Inc.); I.H.T. Corporation for Nos 3, 32, 39, 44, 74 and 85 (© I.H.T. Corporation); *Irish Times* for No. 117; *Journal of Philosophy* for No. 72; Ruth Limmer, Literary Executor of the Estate of Louise Bogan, for Nos 52 and 67, originally published in the *New Yorker,* 10 October 1942 and 3 May 1947, and for No. 76, from Louise Bogan, *A Poet's Alphabet: Reflections on the Literary Art and Vocation* (McGraw-Hill, 1970), and originally published in the *New Yorker,* 28 October 1950; *London Magazine* for No. 121; Louis L. Martz for No. 64; *The Nation* for Nos 9, 25, 41, 55, 65, 88, 100 and 112, New Directions Publishing Corporation for Nos 45 and 98 by William Carlos Williams, which first appeared in *The New Republic,* November 1937 (Copyright 1937 by William Carlos Williams), and in *Trinity Review,* May 1954 (Copyright 1954 by William Carlos Williams); *The New Republic* for Nos 51, 80 and 101 (© 1942, 1951, 1954 The New Republic, Inc.); *New York Times* for Nos 2, 24, 40, 43, 56, 66, 99 and 111 (© 1917, 1931, 1936, 1937, 1942, 1947, 1954, 1957 by the New York Times Company. Reprinted by permission): *North American Review* for No. 38; The Ohio University Press, Athens, Ohio, for No. 60; *Partisan Review* for No. 49 (© *Partisan Review,* vol. IV, no. 3, 1938), No. 58 (© *Partisan Review,* vol. X, no. 3, 1943), No. 62 (© *Partisan Review,* vol. XIII, no. 1, 1946), No. 69 (© *Partisan Review,* vol. XIV, no. 5, 1947), No. 75 (© *Partisan Review,* vol. XVI, no. 9, 1949), No. 81 (© *Partisan Review,* vol. XVIII, no. 3, 1951), and No. 107 (© *Partisan Review,* vol. XXII, no. 2, 1955); *Poetry* for Nos 7, 8, 11, 15, 31, 54, 63, 71, and 77 (Copyright 1920, 1922, 1923,

1924, 1935, 1942, 1946, 1948, 1950 by The Modern Poetry Association); *Poetry* and Hayden Carruth for No. 104 (Copyright 1955 by The Modern Poetry Association); *Poetry* and Clive E. Driver, Literary Executor of the Estate of Marianne C. Moore, for No. 42 (Copyright 1937 by The Modern Poetry Association): *Poetry* and Robert Fitzgerald for No. 46 (Copyright 1937 by The Modern Poetry Association); *Poetry* and Mrs Alta M. Sutton for No. 26 (Copyright 1931 by The Modern Poetry Association); *Providence Sunday Journal* for No. 84; *The Sewanee Review* for No. 82 (Copyright 1951, 1979 by the University of the South); *Shenandoah* for No. 108 (Copyright 1955 by Washington and Lee University); The Society of Authors as the literary representative of the Estate of Llewelyn Powys for No. 17; *Southern Review* for Nos 29 and 37; *Spectator* for Nos 92, 109, and 115; The Statesman and Nation Publishing Co., Ltd, for Nos 93 and 123, from the *New Statesman*; Julian Symons for No. 50; Times Newspapers Ltd for Nos 96, 118 and 122, from the *Times Literary Supplement*; *Virginia Quarterly Review* for No. 35; *The Yale Review* for Nos 18, 34, 70 and 91 (Copyright Yale University); Yale University Press for No. 23, from *Selected Letters of Conrad Aiken,* ed. Joseph Killorin.

Introduction

Wallace Stevens, as is well known, was a late starter in putting his poetry before the public. That first 'damned serious affair' *Harmonium* did not appear until 1923 when its author was forty-four years old. Fortunately, in Holly Stevens' *Souvenirs and Prophecies: The Young Wallace Stevens* we have an exploration of the poet's life and the progress of his literary maturation up to 1915, his thirty-sixth year.[1] Otherwise, probably aided by his wife, Stevens seems to have been at some pains to cover his early tracks.

The first known criticism of his poetry appeared in print in 1916, when the *Minaret* for 16 February (see No. 1 below) included a notice of the 'war number' of *Poetry*,[2] production of which had been delayed especially to include Stevens' last-minute submission. A little over a month later, George Soule, in the *New Republic* for 25 March 1916, indicated the element of the fantastic and the delicacy of touch in Stevens' 'Peter Quince at the Clavier', printed in William Stanley Braithwaite's *Anthology of Magazine Verse for 1915*.[3] After a further eighteen months, a staging of Stevens' 'Carlos Among the Candles' was greeted with some bemusement by the New York drama critics (Nos 2 and 3).

A belated and not particularly auspicious beginning – but by 1919 Stevens had become enough part of the literary scene to figure incidentally in a squabble between Conrad Aiken and Louis Untermeyer, the then influential anthologist. Immediate occasion of the spat was Untermeyer's *The New Era in American Poetry*,[4] and the book is an episode in the long-continuing debate between indigenous and international, a controversy which was to persist at least to the end of the career of William Carlos Williams in the 1960s. Untermeyer championed what he thought of as 'realism', particularly as represented by Chicago poets such as Edgar Lee Masters and Carl Sandburg, and attacked the very recent intrusion of internationalism in the form of French

I

influence,[5] including Stevens incidentally among his targets. In reviewing *The New Era in American Poetry* (No. 6) Aiken scoffed at what he saw as Untermeyer's narrowly-based moralism, citing Stevens as a poet pure and by no means simple. Stevens was not then a major figure in the argument, nor was he especially singled out, but it is noteworthy that both Aiken and Untermeyer readily labelled him an aesthete, Aiken finding that a condition sufficient unto itself while Untermeyer deplored it.[6]

Although Maxwell Bodenheim, poet and fellow member of the Grantwood colony, in 1920 included Stevens among those who were attempting 'to unearth an inner reality which often conflicts with the surface plausibility and visual falseness which men have ever called "reality"',[7] Untermeyer's judgments set the tone for Stevens' critical reception during what Samuel French Morse categorizes as the *Harmonium* years, 1914–30.[8] It was Untermeyer who attached the 'hedonist' tag to Stevens, and who dismissively charged him with deliberate obfuscation, preciosity and slightness – in sum, pigeon-holing him as a minor, if amusing, entertainer.[9] Many reviewers appeared to take their cue from this attitude, overlooking for the moment the incidental remark of the twenty-one-year-old Yvor Winters, in reviewing Edwin Arlington Robinson's poems, that the 'cool master', Stevens, was the 'greatest of living and of American poets' (No. 8).

Reviewers of *Harmonium* took note of its verbal wit, refinement and lushness, gaudiness, exoticism, sensuousness. Matthew Josephson (No. 10) was impressed by the poet's 'personality', as were Harriet Monroe and Llewelyn Powys, though others seemed to feel rather Stevens' detachment or aloofness, his stance of poet as philosopher, and Edmund Wilson, more severely, detected an ironic chilliness and dissociation from life (No. 16). Powys, however, has quite a different kind of philosopher in mind when he gushes that Stevens' poetry is 'beyond good and evil, beyond hope and despair' (No. 17), though he risks the reader's mirth in adding 'beyond thought of any kind'. Yet he touches upon a subliminal element in finding Stevens 'obscure and yet objective' and has a point (mimetically, too), which Stevens himself might well have appreciated, when he transforms the poet's 'stately pleasure-dome' into a dagoba. Behind most of the critics, with the likely exception of Stevens' lifelong ally and friend Marianne Moore (No. 13), one half suspects ambivalence of judgment. What Powys considered, happily, 'beyond thought', Untermeyer deplored as 'determined obscurity'.

As Riddel points out, the most influential or trend-setting review of *Harmonium* was Gorham B. Munson's (No. 20). Munson successfully attached the 'dandyist' label to Stevens and, while admiring the poet's adroitness, deplored his escapism. Stevens' speculative or dialectical stance seems to Munson a tactic for evasions, behind which Stevens is able to rest in comfort and security. Enigmatically, Stevens is at once a romantic and a materialist, a contented observer at the circus of life, set in the 'easy posture' of an onlooker. It is not so much an unfavourable assessment as a circumscription.

For the remainder of the 1920s nothing was heard from him – at least there was no new book – a circumstance which might seem to demonstrate the correctness of Wilson and others in judging that Stevens' aesthetic *mundo* was limited and self-limiting. Yet Riddel seems to read too much into Tate's comments on 'undoubtedly the most finished poet of the age' (No. 21), when he suggests that Tate discerned the exhaustion of over-refinement in Stevens' work. Writing at the same time (1929) René Taupin also places Stevens in the (Baudelaire–Laforgue) dandyist line, which he associates with colour and music, as well as 'elegance and nuance'.[10] Alfred Kreymborg (No. 22) in his wordy way is more down to earth than most about Stevens, whose work he obviously admires. He provides what at first seems an eminently commonsense reason for the post-*Harmonium* silence: 'Comparatively few copies sold; the rest were remaindered.' Holly Stevens seems to confirm this, noting that 'the book was received rather indifferently by the public and the critics',[11] but leaves one with a question. If Kreymborg is correct, why publish a new edition in 1931 (admittedly with fourteen new poems)? For Kreymborg, diffidence and fastidiousness are dominant Stevens characteristics and the years of silence which followed 'The Grand Poem: Preliminary Minutiae' (a title the poet proposed to Alfred Knopf for this first book) are partly to be explained by the circumstance that he was settling into the insurance business, but also by his fastidiousness. Just before *Harmonium* was published Stevens had looked upon his works with some disgust and expressed to Harriet Monroe the desire 'to keep on dabbling and to be as obscure as possible until I have perfected an authentic and fluent speech for myself'.[12] Momentarily, at least, the poems seemed to him like 'abortive insects'.

When the new edition of *Harmonium* appeared in 1931, Horace Gregory could say of Stevens: 'Since the publication of his collected poems in 1923 his subterranean reputation has been steadily growing';[13] but the key critical document in advancing Stevens' reputation is R.P. Blackmur's brilliant and extended 'Examples of Wallace Stevens' in the Winter 1932 number of *Hound and Horn* (No. 28). Blackmur attributes Stevens' strength to his deployment of language, not merely musically but as an instrument of exact communication, even down to the precise management of ambiguities. Blackmur, in fact, greets Stevens as one who can overcome what Eliot termed 'the dissociation of sensibility', or at least one who is aware enough to attempt persistently 'to transform what is felt with the senses and what is thought in the mind – if we can still distinguish the two – into that realm of being, which we call poetry, where what is thought is felt and what is felt has the strict point of poetry'. Thus is refuted Munson's charge of mere dandyism, with the support of Walton, Zabel (Nos 25 and 26) and others. Each sees in Stevens a moral dimension, though on this matter we may turn back to Horace Gregory, who concludes that 'Wallace Stevens is the perfect example of the civilised artist thrust head first into modern society, he is not merely a connoisseur of fine rhythms and the precise nuances of the lyrical line, but a trained observer who gazes with an intelligent eye upon the decadence that follows the rapid acquisition of wealth and power'.

THE 1930s AND THE ORDER OF THINGS

Most often the 1930s are perceived as transitional (in some

minds, from a great early period to a great late period), a time of revaluation in Stevens' career. Beginning with the augmented edition of *Harmonium* (1931), the decade was also launched on Stevens' part by repeated professions of diffidence or hesitancy, as is clearly demonstrable from his letters. In April 1931, for example, he told Lincoln Kirstein: 'Nothing short of a coup d'etat would make it possible for me to write poetry now'.[14] Over a year later, in August 1932, we find him excusing himself to Harriet Monroe, 'Whatever else I do, I do not write poetry now'[15], though he does enclose one 'scrap' for her editorial consideration. The following March he admitted to some writing, but groused, 'I do not much like the new things that I write'.[16] Meantime he had chosen an old poem, 'The Emperor of Ice Cream', for William Rose Benét's compilation, *Fifty Poets: An American Auto-Anthology*,[17] providing as his own critique the observation that the poem 'wears a commonplace costume, and yet seems to me to contain something of the essential gaudiness of poetry; that is the reason why I like it'.[18]

By late 1934, the situation and Stevens' outlook had begun to change, possibly influenced by the mysterious J. Ronald Lane Latimer, Stevens' major correspondent in the late 1930s, until he disappeared completely from the scene. Latimer, who edited the periodical *Alcestis* and published volumes of poetry under the imprint of the Alcestis Press, was important to both Stevens and William Carlos Williams. 'One of the essential conditions to the writing of poetry', Stevens now told Latimer,[19] 'is impetus. That is a reason for thinking that to be a poet at all one ought to be a poet constantly. It was a great loss to poetry when people began to think that the professional poet was an outlaw or an exile. Writing poetry is a conscious activity. While poems may very well occur, they had very much better be caused.' Stevens' view of the making of poetry was itself orderly, then, and from sending Latimer poems and gatherings of poems he quite quickly proceeded to the possibility of a new book, to be titled *Ideas of Order*.

Both terms of this title are important in clarifying the direction now to be taken by Stevens' work and the development of his reputation. We may refer once more to the correspondence with Latimer where Stevens, obviously stung by the suggestion that 'gaudiness', hedonism and aestheticism were what he had to offer, protests: 'Here in Hartford... people who speak about the thing at all speak of my verse as aesthetic. But I don't like any labels, because I am not doing one thing all the time; it may look very like one thing, just as it seems to be entirely without ideas, which, from my point of view, is ridiculously wrong'.[20] He believes in change, however, and admits that he does not 'have ideas that are permanently fixed'.

One of his dominant and persistent ideas was that poetry is an activity of very high order, essential to a true ordering of the world. In the early 1930s, feeling his way towards a somewhat different quality of poetry, less obviously flamboyant, he was, however (in the course of a review furthering his admiration for Marianne Moore), ready enough to declare: 'It is absurd to wince at being called a romantic poet. Unless one is that, one is not a poet at all. That, of course, does not mean banyans and frangipani; and it cannot for long mean no banyans and no frangipani.'[21] After *Harmonium* his work was temporarily less energetic, less 'brilliant', though the general nature of his language and images did not change much and what change there was led to no magnanimous recognition of his intentions, as witness Geoffrey Grigson's grumpy catalogue in 'The Stuffed Goldfinch', reviewing *Ideas of Order* – 'less panache, periwinkle, cantilene, fewer melons and peacocks, but still the finicking privateer, prosy Herrick, Klee without rhythm, observing nothing, single artificer of his own world of mannerism'.[22] But the most prominent review of the book (it has become part of Stevens' biography) was Stanley Burnshaw's, in *New Masses* in October 1935 (No. 30).

Burnshaw, in effect, treated Stevens as a facile aesthete fiddling away in the midst of a collapsing world, or one who had lost his bearings at the centre of turmoil. Stevens' first recorded reaction is contained in a letter to Latimer written a week or so after the review appeared:

The review in *Masses* was a most interesting review, because it placed me in a new setting. I hope I am headed left, but there are lefts and lefts, and certainly I am not headed for the ghastly left of

Masses. The rich man and the comfortable man of the imagination of people like Mr. Burnshaw are not nearly so rich nor nearly so comfortable as he believes them to be. And what is more, his poor men are not nearly so poor. These professionals lament in a way that would have given Job a fever.[23]

At best, this is a question-begging rejoinder. At a deeper level, Stevens believed that human order must be sought for and found in and through the imagination. As proponent of a then intellectually modish Marxism, Burnshaw believed not so much in the individual as in an ideology. His attack on Stevens' political and social complacency served to awaken in the poet some measure of ideological consciousness. Stevens reacted by writing 'Mr. Burnshaw and the Statue',[24] part of the title sequence of *Owl's Clover* (1936). Excluded from *Collected Poems*, but published in the omnium gatherum of *Opus Posthumous*, the sequence is not nicely calculated to clarify the issues raised by Burnshaw, whose conception of art, Stevens seems to imply, is 'a thing from Schwarz's, a thing/of the dank imagination'. Stevens repudiates the notion of

> A time in which the poets' politics
> Will rule in a poets' world. Yet that will be
> A world impossible for poets....

While some critics catch sight only of the old aestheticist Stevens, Harriet Monroe (No. 31) seems inadvertently to confirm Burnshaw's doubts about him when she declares that even 'a revolution, even communism or fascism, will never disturb the firm foundations of his philosophy'. Otherwise, reactions were mixed. Roethke (No. 36) blames Stevens for being out of touch with the world; Howard Baker at somewhat unnecessary length praises his psychological depth (No. 29); John Holmes, in a curiously toned notice (No. 35), says 'recent moods of the real world have affected him, and they show in this book'; a patient ideologue, F. O. Matthiessen, in a nice irony of circumstance, simultaneously reviews Burnshaw's poetry *The Iron Land*, but finds it wanting, and asserts that Stevens' *Ideas of Order* yields 'a mature apprehension of actual society' (No. 34).

7

'William Carlos Williams could remark that Stevens "of late has turned definitely to the left"', Joseph N. Riddel informs us;[25] but Williams, himself at that period flirting coyly with *New Masses*, was far from thinking so. His actual statement, which shows a capacity for intelligent objectivity, is to quite opposite effect: 'The story is that Stevens has turned of late definitely to the left. I should say not, from anything in this book [*The Man with the Blue Guitar* – see No. 45.] He's merely older and as an artist infinitely more accomplished'. In March 1936, Stevens could follow up his remark 'I hope I am headed left', tossed off to Latimer, with the explanation, or qualifications: 'For my own part, I believe in social reform and not in social revolution. From the point of view of social revolution, *Ideas of Order* is a book of the most otiose prettiness; and it is probably quite inadequate from any social point of view. However, I am not a propagandist'.[26]

Yet if Matthiessen has a point, and *Ideas of Order* can be claimed as offering a mature apprehension of actual society, this apprehension, as most reviewers seemed to realize, is not deepened in *Owl's Clover*, even though that work is intended directly as a more socially pointed act. Stevens adheres to his conviction that art – poetry – is socially valid and important in its own right, but he does make some attempt to respond to Burnshaw's strictures. The problem is that his characteristic manner is unsuited to a direct polemic or an exchange of social ideas and Stevens, of course, could not (happily, if one looks at the case in a broader perspective) all at once discard the manner so assiduously cultivated over a thirty-year period. Eda Lou Walton (No. 40) and others saw the difficulty for what it was. One effect of the clash between Stevens' manner and the current political demands emanates from the work as some sense of dislocation or a feeling of self-parody. *Owl's Clover* has an air of lame self-consciousness.

As Williams was quick to recognize, matters were soon put right with *The Man with the Blue Guitar* (1937). More generally, Riddel is to the point in observing that Stevens' 'verse in the thirties was preoccupied mainly with the preservation of poetry as a vital act in an anti-poetic age'.[27]

As to his political commitment, it is perhaps fair to allow Stevens himself the final word. 'I am in the long run interested in pure poetry', he told his friend Henry Church in June 1939. 'No doubt from a Marxian point of view this sort of thing is incredible, but pure poetry is rather older and tougher than Marx and will remain so. My own way out towards the future involves a confidence in the spiritual role of the poet ....'[28] This last point chimes in with Ben Belitt's attempt to summarize the purpose of the sequence 'The Man with the Blue Guitar' as 'the search for artistic identity at a time when the poet is compelled to examine that identity critically, in terms of a changing world-spirit'.[29]

Williams acutely, and in pursuit of his own ideology, attributes the let-down of *Owl's Clover* to employment of a five-beat pseudo-iambic measure, but on the other hand Yvor Winters in *Primitivism and Decadence* (1937) labelled Stevens one of 'the masters of free verse', and Stevens came out of the 1930s with his poetic reputation greatly enhanced. The reviewers of *The Man with the Blue Guitar*, with one or two exceptions, generally responded with delight and respect. As one of them, Robert Fitzgerald, put it, he found himself surprised to realize the 'eminence' of Stevens' poetry, and to recognize 'a passionate sharpness of authority which I do not remember having felt before' (No. 46). Yvor Winters, in the above-mentioned book, subtitled 'A Study of American Experimental Poetry', reiterated his claim of fifteen years earlier, dubbing Stevens 'probably the greatest poet of his generation'.

THE 1940s

The beginning of the new decade brought several substantial gestures of recognition for Stevens' poetry, at least one of them of lasting importance.

A special number of the *Harvard Advocate* in December 1940 showed, at least, that his work had become respected in the academies, and its pages included testimonials from Harry Levin, F. O. Matthiessen, Marianne Moore, Allen Tate and Cleanth Brooks, among others. Matthiessen notes again, and admires, Stevens' 'deepening preoccupation with the problems of social order'.[30] He feels this concern has made Stevens as poet less dazzling, though with enhanced literary dignity, more prolific and more resourceful. But, immediately following Matthiessen, Marianne Moore appears to rejoice in the original aesthetic Stevens, who continues 'to live in an unspoiled cosmos of his own'. Following Moore, Allen Tate offers her oblique support, regretting 'somewhat that Stevens' recent books have shown a developing indignation', but making obeisance none the less to 'one of the best poets alive'.

One *Advocate* contributor, Hi Simons, in agreement with the high valuation set upon Stevens' work by Tate, Moore, Winters and others, had embarked on a full-scale study of the poetry, publishing in the *Southern Review* in this same year a seminal explicatory essay on 'The Comedian as the Letter C'.[31] Simons followed up his review, 'The Humanism of Wallace Stevens' (No. 54), with two other important, more extended pieces. 'The Genre of Wallace Stevens' (*Southern Review*, Autumn 1945) is an elaboration of the present review and a rebuttal of Horace Gregory's opinions (No. 53) and Mary Colum's (No. 56), as well as, by implication, repudiating Winters' charge of mere hedonism (No. 60). Simons, who might possibly have produced the first serious book-length study devoted to Stevens, died in the spring of 1945, and there was only one further contribution from him, an essay on Stevens and Mallarmé, published in 1946.[32]

Just before the *Advocate* special number appeared, Julian Symons' 'A Short View of Wallace Stevens' (No. 50) was published in London. Symons is condescending about *Harmonium* and the early work generally, perhaps rather too readily seeing Stevens' gaudiness as flippancy; but he is respectful of 'The Man with the Blue Guitar', valuing it as 'one of the most notable poetic achievements of the past twenty years'. Despite this he returns, in conclusion, to asserting Stevens' flippancy, rejecting as false one of Stevens' major themes, that 'Poetry is the subject of the poem' (which also happens to be, in variants deriving from a broad spectrum of arts, a central motif of Modernism.) At least one British publisher, if we go by Stevens' letters, had shown interest before this date in publishing a volume of his poetry,[33] but Symons' conclusions cannot have much helped Stevens' reputation in Britain.

Symons doubted if it were possible for poetry in Stevens' manner to accommodate philosophical reflection. A succession of reviewers of *Parts of a World* (1942), having been able to grasp from the spareness of texture in *The Man with the Blue Guitar* the dialectic of relationship between things-as-they-are and imagination, were disappointed in the later book. Many expressed uncertainty about it, though Hi Simons declared it Stevens' 'most deeply imagined work'. An old adversary, Louis Untermeyer, stated the continuing reservations magnanimously in praising Stevens' poetry of comedy and his comic use of language (No. 57).

Alongside this generally lukewarm public response to his work, and traceable in his 1942 lecture 'The Noble Rider and the Sound of Words', Stevens was meditating upon the role of the poet in modern, demythified society, and was strengthening his conviction that it is the poet who 'gives life to the supreme fictions', which are essential to the full reality of our human life.[34] The following year, in 'The Figure of the Youth as Virile Poet', he speaks of poetry as 'the unofficial view of being'.[35] But to these cool appraisals should be added a remark in a 1943 letter to Henry Church: 'The belief in poetry is a magnificent fury, or it is nothing'.[36]

At this moment, in *The Anatomy of Nonsense* (1943), Yvor Winters weighed in with a major assessment, 'Wallace Stevens, or the Hedonist's Progress' (No. 60). Evaluating 'Sunday Morning' (1915) as 'probably the greatest American poem of the twentieth-century', he none the less finds in it the seeds of decadence and suggests that from the early poems onward Stevens' career was a decline rather than a progress. After Stevens' death, Winters, in a postscript to his essay, suggests that a much later poem, 'The Course of a Particular'[37] (omitted from the *Collected Poems* in error),[38] which he interprets as a belated renunciation of hedonism, is perhaps 'the greatest' in the canon.

Despite an air of positive respect for Stevens' work, Winters through a detailed examination of several poems accuses him of verbal imprecision, irrationalism, triviality and decadent hedonism. Stevens' published letters suggest that he refused to become embroiled in any debate and even to read Winters (though half a dozen years later he endorsed Winters' nomination for membership of the National Institute of Arts and Letters).[39] Despite a jibe or two at Blackmur's prolixity, Stevens thought his a better mind than Winters', and certainly, in an extended review of *Notes Toward a Supreme Fiction* (No. 58), Blackmur comes closer to the 'philosophical' Stevens by considering him positively, as a poet of epistemological process.

The young Robert Lowell, who had just won the Pulitzer Prize for his second book *Lord Weary's Castle* (1946), here enters the picture (No. 65), to state a magisterial preference for Blackmur's 'masterpiece of imaginative elucidation' (i.e. No. 28, 'The Examples of Wallace Stevens') over Winters' 'overdone' dismissal of Stevens' later poetry. The latter he felt, however, was a good corrective to Blackmur. Lowell himself found in *Transport to Summer* some of Stevens' best work since *Harmonium*, though he voices a common complaint in a pointed phrase, suggesting that 'one feels that tolerance and serenity are a little too blandly appropriated.' Yet his overall evaluation of Stevens is high and while he finds 'Notes Toward a Supreme Fiction' unsuccessful as a whole, he judges 'Esthétique du Mal' 'about as good and important a poem as T. S. Eliot's *Four Quartets* or "Ash Wednesday"'.

Blackmur and Winters had both approached Stevens through his language and with the separate publication of *Esthétique du Mal* (1945) another voice, that of Wylie Sypher (No. 62), chimed in to declare that 'Stevens has demonstrated the uses of imprecision'. For this he could perhaps have cited Stevens' own authority, the famous sentence from 'Man Carrying Thing': 'The poem must resist the intelligence/ Almost successfully';[40] or even the question in 'Notes Toward a Supreme Fiction'—'Is there a poem that never reaches words...?'[41] The point is deliberately taken up by Louis Martz in 'Wallace Stevens: The Romance of the Precise' (No. 64), wherein Martz engages Hi Simons, but chiefly Sypher, to say in effect that what Sypher terms 'imprecision' is a more profound and elaborate precision. Several sentences in Martz's essay are incidentally an effective answer to Winters' charge of hedonism and support the general position stated by Blackmur in 'An Abstraction Blooded' (No. 58):

Mr. Sypher's main difficulty lies in a central misunderstanding: he does not see the unifying theme which permeates Stevens' poetry. Emptied of its theme, any writing will appear imprecise and fractured. Stevens' central problem has always been the same: the adjustment of man to a universe from which the supernatural and mythical have been drained, and in which the human imagination is consequently starving.

A trickle of complaints continued, as when Louise Bogan greeted *Transport to Summer* with the grumble that the later Stevens has 'elaborated a style and an attitude that almost entirely destroy the possibility of any sustained emotion or idea'.[42] Yet the book manifests a deepened attention to the nature of poetry and Stevens was widely reviewed as a 'philosophical' poet, even favourably so by a professional in the *Journal of Philosophy* (No. 72). Apart from pursuing his concern for poetry as theme, Stevens continued coaxing the epistemological imagination, or, as Martz expresses it:

The 'transport to summer' consists in seizing with the imagination some pleasurable physical object, and then, by metaphor, clarifying it and relating it to other objects, until one has formed an integrated composition of the 'ideal' and the 'real'. By such man-made 'credences' we dominate and enjoy our environment, though such domination cannot be sustained for long, and must be vigilantly re-established from moment to moment. (No. 70)

The 1940s concluded with two substantial evaluations of Stevens – by J. V. Cunningham and Marius Bewley respectively. A Winters ephebe, Cunningham, in 'The Poetry of Wallace Stevens',[43] follows the master in his high regard for 'Sunday Morning' and the early poetry and places Stevens in the Romantic tradition, in effect as a descendant of Wordsworth. Bewley (excerpted, No. 75) in contrast suggests that Stevens' early work has been overvalued at the expense of his later. Attempting to place Stevens in the American Transcendentalist tradition, Bewley finds a coherent development from the first, leading up to the pre-eminent *Transport to*

Summer, a collection which incorporates that 'great achievement' 'Notes Towards a Supreme Fiction'.

THE 1950s AND AFTER

Though the career-long plaint about his obscurity of
expression and/or superficiality of thought continued as a
minor note (best sustained, perhaps, by Louise Bogan in the
New Yorker), the growth of Stevens' reputation in the 1950s
may be traced in a series of well-defined steps.

The Auroras of Autumn (1950) and the first, American
edition of *The Necessary Angel: Essays on Reality and the
Imagination* (1951) may be regarded as one major step;
Collected Poems (1954; English edition 1955) and Stevens'
death in 1955 may be taken as another. Reception of the
American edition of *Opus Posthumous* (1957) may be seen as a
little stutter-step following the second. The third step is the
wave of reviews which greeted British editions of *Opus
Posthumous* (1959) and *The Necessary Angel* (1960).

To the first of these steps may be added William Van
O'Connor's now largely superseded book-length study *The
Shaping Spirit* (1950), and a landmark in the academic
appraisal of Stevens' development as a poet, Roy Harvey
Pearce's 'Wallace Stevens: The Life of the Imagination'
(*PMLA*, September 1951), which was inculcated into a major
chapter of *The Continuity of American Poetry* (Princeton,
1961). A few months after Pearce's essay, Cid Corman's
Origin (First Series, no. V, Spring 1952) carried an overview
of Stevens' career by Samuel French Morse, who was to
become a Stevens scholar of some substance, perhaps most
notably as editor of *Opus Posthumous*.

An influential counterweight to these was Randall Jarrell's
'Reflections on Wallace Stevens' (No. 81). Just as he sketched
what he perceived to be the declining curve of Williams'
Paterson, Jarrell traces a progressive weakening from *Harmonium* to *The Auroras of Autumn*. Jarrell, of course, had a gift
for the incisive or lapidary phrase or aphoristic sentence and
not a few of them occur here, including the often-quoted
closing statement: 'A good poet is someone who manages, in
a lifetime of standing out in thunderstorms, to be struck by

lightning five or six times; a dozen or two dozen times and he is great.' Jarrell makes it by no means clear whether he considers Stevens to belong to the latter group. Along the way to his conclusion, he voices some cogent reservations: of *Harmonium*, that 'there was nothing really unusual in what Stevens felt', and that, in effect, Stevens' 'home-truths' were 'acquitted on the grounds that they were incomprehensible'. Jarrell appears to follow Yvor Winters' line in judging 'Sunday Morning' 'as perfect, in its calm transparency, as the best of Wordsworth'; but Stevens seemed to Jarrell to have become increasingly detached from life in a way which eventually produced 'so abstract, so monotonous, so overwhelmingly *characteristic* a book' as *The Auroras of Autumn*. It's as if he half-consciously felt that the older poet had lapsed into repetitive self-parody.

Seen in this light, Stevens' besetting weakness, one that grew and was particularly disastrous for a poet, was the habit not only of generalizing, but of seeing every particular as illustrating a generalization, so that 'a fossil imprisoned in the rock of himself', Stevens 'needs to be possessed by subjects to be shaken out of himself'. Because he writes so well, one is always tempted to quote Jarrell rather than to summarize him. What he says here is quite finely balanced between indictment and praise, so that his own mastery of style allows him to make exceptionally tough judgments about Stevens and yet pay a due measure of tribute to a master. Stevens, had he paid much attention to such things, might have consoled himself with Conrad's sardonic observation, 'I do not read reviews, I measure them', or he might have taken note of the declaration of his compeer, William Carlos Williams, who wrote of '*The Auroras of Autumn* where his stature as a major poet has reached the full' (No. 98).

American reviews of *The Necessary Angel* were, on the whole, undistinguished, with many reviewers resorting to the device of summarizing Stevens' ideas on the interaction between imagination and reality. Several accorded recognition to the fact that the book was comprised of occasional papers written to be spoken. One categorized them as 'a body of notes rather than a systematic *ars poetica*' (No. 86), but this writer and others conceded that *The Necessary Angel* is larded with keen practical insights into the nature of modern poetry. In sum, Stevens' first prose book was received respectfully enough, but without undue excitement.

Although not decisive, a spate of British reviews in 1953 began adding a new dimension to Stevens' reputation. Twenty years earlier, Conrad Aiken had attempted to interest the London publisher J. M. Dent in issuing a British edition of *Harmonium*, but the publisher wanted a new book and Stevens did not then have it in him, so the matter was dropped.[44] It was not raised again until late in 1952 when a small press, the Fortune Press (who, by interesting coincidence, had preceded Dent as publishers of Dylan Thomas), apparently under agreement with Stevens' New York publisher, Alfred Knopf, issued a *Selected Poems*, edited by Dennis Williamson. Shortly thereafter, Fabers published their own version of a *Selected Poems*. Stevens discovered the existence of the Fortune Press printing only through receiving a copy of a review by Austin Clarke run by the *Irish Times*.[45] As was quickly established, the Knopf-Fortune Press agreement had lapsed and the London press consented to withdraw from circulation all copies except those sent out to reviewers. Stevens himself was soon eagerly seeking a copy of the book which, in the circumstances, became an instant collector's item.

The British reviewers – including such distinguished poets as William Empson, Donald Davie and the young Richard Murphy – welcomed the appearance of Stevens' book in Britain, with Davie, for example, saying: 'He is indeed a poet to be mentioned in the same breath as Eliot and Yeats and Pound' (No. 95); but once again Stevens' poetry was greeted with a mixture of respect and caution. His musical and verbal splendours were heralded, and Davie concluded that Stevens is 'a great poet', though not one altogether to his taste. Bernard Bergonzi (No. 97) speaks of 'a barren magnificence', and the barrenness he alludes to is a certain abstractness of texture imputed to Stevens' work by many reviewers of the *Selected Poems*. The verdict is put most neatly in a sentence of G. S. Fraser's: 'Apples grow on his trees to be looked at, not to be eaten' (No. 93).

The New York edition of Stevens' *Collected Poems* virtually coincided with the poet's seventy-fifth birthday, and the tone of the reviews is largely appropriate to such a venerable circumstance. E. E. Cummings *Poems 1923–1954*[46] appeared at approximately the same time and a number of reviewers, pairing the books, were respectful to both, tending to find in Cummings' work a greater measure of the concreteness so much sought after in the theory and practice of twentieth-century poetry. Several reviewers might well have taken a cue from Williams' positive reception of *The Auroras of Autumn*, for it now became quite a common assertion that the later poems were a progression from *Harmonium*, or that it was necessary to acquaint oneself with the whole canon to ascertain Stevens' full stature. This is a note struck by Morse (No. 99) and others.

To it, Delmore Schwartz adds the suggestion that 'Stevens converts aestheticism into contemplation in the full philosophical and virtually religious sense of the word. The surface of his poetry is very often verbal, visual and gay; beneath the surface, it is a deadly earnest scrutiny of attitudes towards existence, of "how to live, what to do"' (No. 101). A number of critics had begun to rebut the charge that Stevens is all surface coruscations by discovering a subliminal element, as it were, beneath the verbal glitter, or by finding in the poetry what Hayden Carruth calls 'meaning which transcends its verbal properties' (No. 104). In something of a variation on this theme, the British reviewer John Holloway speaks of 'the euphony of grave and lucid operations of the intellect' (No. 109). Some other British reviewers, notably Donald Davie (No. 108), were less favourably disposed than they had been a year or two earlier. In contrast, there is the complete conversion of the authoritative Randall Jarrell (No. 106), won over partly by the 'unimaginable new ways' of Stevens' late poems in 'The Rock', and most particularly by the managed and yet, paradoxically, liberated grandeurs of 'To an Old Philosopher in Rome'. (It would be a nice touch of irony were one able to establish that Stevens' title for the final section of the *Collected Poems* derived at least partly from Jarrell's remark, quoted above, about his being 'imprisoned in the rock of himself'.)

The initial American reviews of *Opus Posthumous* are

perhaps more notable for the list of reviewers' names than for any particular fresh insights about Stevens–Williams again, Kenneth Rexroth, Irving Howe, Karl Shapiro, Anthony Hecht – though Howe's nimble-paced overview (No. 113) has been perhaps undeservedly neglected, and Williams alights upon some lines of Stevens which may be applied to both poets, though to singularly contrasting point:

> Pass the whole of life hearing the clink of the
> Chisels of the stone-cutters cutting the stones.

A substantial article rather than a review, Howard Nemerov's 'The Poetry of Wallace Stevens', which appeared at this time,[47] is of consequence not only because of the subtlety and elegant independence of Nemerov's mind, but as a sensitive account of Stevens' career by a poet who may in some important respects be rated a disciple. Having mentioned Nemerov's, one may as well note Louis Martz's well-known 'classic' essay, 'Wallace Stevens: The World as Meditation', which appeared first in the summer 1958 *Yale Review*.

Stevens' British reputation was consolidated by the London publication of *Opus Posthumous* in 1959 and *The Necessary Angel*. Kermode, too, is a writer one is often tempted to quote, but there is space to succumb once only. Of both the prose and poetry, Kermode demonstrates how Stevens arrives by strange routes, and he says: 'These essays are constructed like meditative poems, circling beautifully around central images, proceeding with a grave gaiety to repetitive but ever-changing statements about the imagination....'[48] All this is a far cry from the pioneering essay of Julian Symons, but even further from those American critics who read *The Necessary Angel* as a gathering of the poet's rather turgid working notes.

Not that the British do not to some extent share this attitude. G. S. Fraser, for example, considered Stevens' critical writing 'very poor and often very pretentious', though he concedes the greatness of the poetry, saying that the best of it is 'a perfection emerging from a new known'.[49] Comparably, the anonymous *Times Literary Supplement* reviewer (No. 118) observes: 'Perhaps his thinking was basically a muddle; but his best poems rear a beautiful order on it'. There was also a certain amount of muddle among the reviewers, one or two of whom were philistine enough to express astonishment at the idea that an insurance man should not only write poetry but should do it as well as this. But there is still Kermode's distinguished voice to set against such gushings, reiterating his views briefly in the *Spectator* on New Year's Day 1960: 'it is inconceivable that the year [1959] has seen any other volume of poetry of comparable value'. Despite Kermode's advocacy, perhaps the poet Henry Reed (No. 120) took the truest measure of Stevens' British reception at that moment, in 1960, when he noted that, 'over here we are in a peculiar position as regards Stevens. Most of us don't, quite simply, know him well enough. It is not our fault entirely; but it is possible to feel, with some resentment, that when Stevens was finally published in England a few years ago, it was because the event could no longer be decently delayed'.

'Poet of a steadfast pattern', Williams once estimated Stevens, and the contrast between the two major Americans is instructive. Williams, the self-professed short-breathed poet, who published for a long time and relatively often in a variety of genres but had to wait through nearly thirty years of a career before really breaking into the 'big time'; and Stevens, for whom 'a book of poems is a damned serious affair', who hesitated long before publishing such a book, and as a consequence created the effect of having a small band of readers waiting eagerly for him to publish *something*.

One last dimension should be examined briefly to complete this appraisal of the development of Stevens' literary reputation during his lifetime. A decade after his death his daughter, Holly Stevens, edited his letters for publication, and these, of course, affect Stevens' reputation, and subsequent perceptions of him as a man and as a writer. 'Inevitably the man', Stanley Kunitz tells us, 'is more flawed than his art'. If he was 'not great-hearted' (and we are attending to Kunitz), 'not a magisterial force like Eliot and Pound ... or an American culture hero like Frost and Williams', Stevens was yet, personality flaws notwithstanding, 'a superior presence'.[50] The phrase is accurate, not only for the aloof individual with mandarin airs, but for the 'determining personality' of the poet. Accurate, yes, but while the letters give full measure of a plodding, pedestrian Stevens, there are also his verve and élan and the fact that he attracted a mixed bag of exotic correspondents, from Carl Van Vechten and Ronald Lane Latimer to Thomas McGreevy, Leonard Van Geyzel and Jose Rodriguez Feo. Once again it is Kermode, in 'Strange Contemporaries: Wallace Stevens and Hart Crane',[51] who rejoices in such gaudy vitality. When Kermode turns from Crane to Stevens, his own style is at once coloured by 'banyans and frangipani', and this is a fine testimonial to Stevens' power over the right reader.

NOTES

1 Holly Stevens, *Souvenirs and Prophecies: The Young Wallace Stevens* (New York: Knopf, 1977). Some poems from this period are included in Robert Buttel, *Wallace Stevens: The Making of Harmonium* (Princeton University Press, 1967).

2 *Poetry*, vol. V, no. 2, November 1914.

3 *An Anthology of Magazine Verse for 1915*, edited by William Stanley Braithwaite (New York: Lawrence S. Gomme).

4 *The New Era in American Poetry*, edited by Louis Untermeyer (New York: Henry Holt, 1919).

5 An important relevant study is Cyrena N. Pondrom, *The Road from Paris: French Influence on English Poetry 1900–1920* (Cambridge University Press, 1974). 'English' here includes Pound and Eliot. William Carlos Williams is twice mentioned in passing, but the book includes no reference to Stevens.

6 Joseph N. Riddle, Wallace Stevens' in *Fifteen Modern American Authors: A Survey of Research and Criticism*, edited by Jackson R. Bryer (Durham, North Carolina: Duke University Press, 1969), pp. 389–423, see p. 398. My introduction is indebted to some degree to Riddel's useful comments, though I have not everywhere agreed with him. See Untermeyer's reply to Aiken, *New Republic*, 10 May 1919, p. 59.

7 Maxwell Bodenheim, 'Modern Poetry', *Dial*, vol. LXVIII, January 1920, pp. 95–8.

8 Samuel French Morse, *Wallace Stevens: Poetry as Life* (New York: Pegasus, 1970).

9 Louis Untermeyer, *American Poetry Since 1900* (New York: Henry Holt, 1923).

10 René Taupin, *L'influence du symbolisme français sur la poésie américaine* (Paris: H. Champion, 1929). The phrase is quoted from an excerpt translated in *Wallace Stevens: A Critical Anthology*, edited by Irvin Ehrenpreis (Harmondsworth, Middlesex: Penguin Books, 1972).

11 *Letters of Wallace Stevens*, selected and edited by Holly Stevens (New York: Knopf, 1966), p. 241. (Hereafter cited as *Letters*.)

12 *Letters*, p. 231.

13 Horace Gregory, 'Highly Polished Poetry', *New York Herald Tribune Books*, 27 September 1931, p. 28.

14 *Letters*, p. 261.

15 *Letters*, p. 262.

16 *Letters*, p. 265.

17 *Fifty Poets: An Auto-Anthology*, edited by William Rose Benét (New York: Duffield & Green, 1933), p. 46.

18 *Letters*, p. 263.

19 *Letters*, p. 274.

20 *Letters*, pp. 288–9.

21 *Opus Posthumous*, p. 25.

22 Geoffrey Grigson, 'The Stuffed Goldfinch', *New Verse*, no. 19, February–March 1936, pp. 18–19.

23 *Letters*, p. 286. Burnshaw's review was later reprinted with a commentary in *Sewanee Review* (vol. LXIX, Summer 1961), wherein he explains that he was confused between his admiration for Stevens' work and his ideologically induced conviction that none the less Stevens was remiss in not directing his work towards responding to social conditions prevailing in the 1930s.

24 'Mr. Burnshaw and the Statue', *Opus Posthumous*, pp. 46–52.

25 Riddel, 'Wallace Stevens', p. 401.

26 *Letters*, p. 309.

27 Riddel, 'Wallace Stevens', p. 402.

28 *Letters*, p. 340.

29 Ben Belitt, 'Lion in the Lute', *Nation*, vol. 145, 6 November 1937, p. 509.

30 F. O. Matthiessen, 'Statement', *Harvard Advocate*, vol. 127, December 1940, p. 31.

31 Hi Simons, '"The Comedian as the Letter C": Its Sense and Significance', *Southern Review*, vol. V, Winter 1940, pp. 453–68.

32 Hi Simons, 'Wallace Stevens and Mallarmé', *Modern Philology*, vol. XLIII, May 1946, pp. 235–59.

33 *Letters*, pp. 278–9. Apparently Stevens corresponded on the possibility of a book with Dent's editor Richard Church, but nothing came of it.

34 *The Necessary Angel: Essays on Reality and Imagination* (New York: Knopf, 1951), p. 31.

35 *The Necessary Angel*, p. 41.

36 *Letters*, p. 446. Letter of 30 March 1943.

37 *Opus Posthumous*, p. 96.

38 *Letters*, p. 881.

39 *Letters*, p. 633.

40 *Collected Poems* (New York: Knopf, 1954), p. 350.

41 *Collected Poems*, p. 396.

42 Louise Bogan, *New Yorker*, 3 May 1947, p. 101.

43 J. V. Cunningham, 'The Poetry of Wallace Stevens', *Poetry*, vol. LXXV, December 1949, pp. 149–65. Reprinted in his *Tradition and Poetic Structure* (Denver: Alan Swallow, 1960).

44 *Selected Letters of Conrad Aiken*, edited by Joseph Killorin (New Haven, Connecticut: Yale University Press, 1978), p. 305.

45 Austin Clarke, *Irish Times*, 14 February 1953, p. 6.

46 E. E. Cummings, *Poems 1923–1954* (New York: Harcourt, Brace & World, 1954).

47 Howard Nemerov, 'The Poetry of Wallace Stevens', *Sewanee Review*, vol. LXV, Winter 1957, pp. 1–14.

48 Frank Kermode, *Wallace Stevens* (Edinburgh: Oliver & Boyd, 1960).

49 G. S. Fraser, 'Mind All Alone', *New Statesman*, 9 January 1960, pp. 43–4.

50 Stanley Kunitz, 'The Hartford Walker', *New Republic*, vol. 155, no. 20, pp. 23–6.

51 Frank Kermode, 'Strange Contemporaries: Wallace Stevens and Hart Crane', *Encounter*, vol. 28, no. 5, May 1967, pp. 65–70.

Note on the Text

Original notes are numbered a, b, c, etc. Notes added by the editor are numbered 1, 2, 3, etc.

EARLY REVIEWS

1. Shaemas O Sheel, from 'Chicago Poets and Poetry', *Minaret*

Vol. I, February 1916, 26–7

O Sheel's article is a general review of current numbers of *Poetry* magazine. Herbert Bruncken, editor of the *Minaret*, which was published in Washington, D.C., from 1911 to 1926, came to consider his magazine as a rival to *Poetry*. The first of the two stanzas quoted is the opening stanza from Stevens' 'Phases', a sequence of poems six of which comprise the initial work in *Opus Posthumous*, 'Poems from "Phases"'. The complete sequence has never been published.

In her comment on Stevens' *Harmonium* (see below, No. 15), Harriet Monroe explained how the War Number of *Poetry* (November 1914) had already been paged-up when 'Phases' arrived in the editorial offices (she describes the complete sequence offered as 'six or seven battle-sketches'). Room was at once made for four of these sketches.

Shaemas O Sheel (1886–1954) was an American poet and follower of the Irish renaissance. One of his poems gained renown, 'They Went Forth to Battle, but They Always Fell'. His selected poems, *Antigone and Selected Poems*, were published posthumously in 1960.

In spite of the fact that the subscribers to *Poetry* wished nothing but good neutral verse, Miss Monroe found it necessary to have a War Poem Number, and if anyone could suggest to me a magazine that has had worse poems through its whole existence, than this individual War Poem Number had, I would like to see the magazine. Moreover, we read enough about the war in the newspapers, why should we also have ranting poems thrust into our faces, which are untruthful, and nauseating to read. Here are two excellent examples –

> There's a little square in Paris,
> Waiting until we pass –
> They sit idly there.
> They sip the glass.

[The second example is four lines by Richard Aldington, which the reviewer characterizes as 'drivel'.]

2. Anonymous, from the *New York Times*

22 October 1917, 13

The occasion of this item was a brief report of the first tour of the Wisconsin Players in the eastern United States, and their appearance at the Neighborhood Playhouse in New York City for a two-week engagement, with 'a rather unfortunately selected program of one-act plays'.

... The most worthwhile piece on the first program is Zona Gale's 'Neighbors', which although hitherto unproduced in New York, has long been shown hereabouts by reason of the printed page.

'Neighbors' is a well-written and interesting analysis of the neighborly spirit, and is made thoroughly human by innumerable homely flashes. Its character drawing denotes keen observation, and even its story lacks all traces of dramatic exaggeration. It also has the advantage of the best acting of the evening, particularly good performances being given by Mrs. Sherry and Mary Wilder.

'On the Pier,' a not uninteresting but quite undramatic dialogue, is the work of Mrs. Sherry, the director. 'The Shadow,' by Howard Mumford Jones, is a play eminently suited to the library, but entirely too delicate a piece to be acted. The fourth piece, 'Carlos Among the Candles,' is a baffling monologue by Wallace Stevens, intended neither for the stage nor the library....

3. Ralph Block, from 'The Wisconsin Players Now at the Neighborhood Playhouse', New York Tribune

22 October 1917, 9

'Carlos Among the Candles,' by Wallace Stevens, is another indication of how fine a line may separate the false from the true. It is by itself a not uninteresting experiment in atmospheres, a game of hide and seek among the shadows of thought, a pursuit of elusive visions of unreality that the hand never closes on. In flavor it is not unlike a combination of Gertrude Stein's 'In a Department Store' and Henry James's story, 'The Altar of the Dead,' with a leaning in execution toward the less successful futurist of the two, Miss Stein. Carlos, who is a flunkey, enters a dark room and lights several candles, delivering himself in a passionately dreamy style of his ideas on the subject during the operation. He then blows out what candles have not of themselves given way to an electric fan in the wings, and retires by a window, probably, as he infers, to seek a moonbeam.

The process of this kind of entertainment, in analysis, appears to be to say something that has no meaning at all with all the bearing of significance, recalling what Alice said to – was it the Duchess? – about the sound and not the sense being most important. And yet there appears just enough method in the entire madness of the piece to make me believe that with real poetry behind it – such successfully mystic poetry, perhaps, as Emerson's 'Brahma' or Swinburne's 'Hertha' – it would yield an entire new crop of sensations for the miniature stage.

4. Conrad Aiken, on Stevens' 'delicate originality' of mind, from *Scepticisms: Notes on Contemporary Poetry*

New York, 1919, 161–2

Aiken (1889–1973), poet, critic, novelist and short-story writer, was a member of the Harvard class of 1911, which included T. S. Eliot, Walter Lippmann, Robert Benchley and Van Wyck Brooks. His numerous publications include *Collected Poems* (revised edition, 1970), *Collected Short Stories* (1960), *A Reviewer's ABC* (1958) and the biographical *Ushant: An Essay* (1962), *Collected Novels* (1964) and *Selected Letters* (1978).

These passages occur in Aiken's review of the second *Others: An Anthology of the New Verse* edited by Alfred Kreymborg (1917).

... it is a variegated band that Mr. Kreymborg has assembled, and if they have in common the one main tenet – that their poetic business is the expression of a sensation or mood as briefly and pungently (and oddly?) as possible, with or without the aids of rhyme, metre, syntax, or punctuation – they are by no means the slaves of a formula and present us with a variety that is amazing. There is much here, of course, that is merely trivial, and a measurable quantity of the proudly absurd and naively preposterous; but if there are no such outstandingly good things here as 'The Portrait of a Lady' by T. S. Eliot in the earlier issue, or Wallace Stevens's 'Peter Quince at the Clavier,' or John Rodker's 'Mario-nettes,' we can pass lightly over the studiously cerebral obscurantism of Marianne Moore, the tentacular quiverings of Mina Loy, the prattling iterations of Alfred Kreymborg, the delicate but amorphous self-consciousness of Jeanne d'Orge, Helen Hoyt, and Orrick Johns, and pause with admiration and delight before the 'Preludes' and 'Rhapsody of a Windy Night' by T. S. Eliot, and 'Thirteen Ways of Looking at a Blackbird' by Wallace Stevens. It is not that one is at all indifferent to the frequent charm and delicious originality (at least as regards sensibility) of the other poets, but that one finds in the two mentioned not only this delicate originality of mind but also a clearer sense of symmetry as regards both form and ideas: their poems are more apparent-ly, and more really, works of art.

5. Carl Sandburg, from a letter to Louis Untermeyer about *The New Era in American Poetry*

10 April 1919

Sandburg (1878–1967) is celebrated as the poet of Chicago and biographer of Lincoln. His works include *Chicago Poems* (1916), *Good Morning, America* (1928), *The*

People, Yes (1936) and *Complete Poems* (revised edition, 1970), plus his six volumes of Lincoln biography. There are several biographical and critical books on Sandburg, including one by Gay Wilson Allen (1972).

See headnote to No. 6. This letter is included in *The Letters of Carl Sandburg*, edited by Herbert Mitgang (New York, 1968), p. 153.

It was a book [*The New Era in American Poetry*] hard to keep in perspective. The only window you shut down and pass on in too much of a hurry is the *Others* bunch.[1] Wallace Stevens, for instance, holds for me repeated readings. The music of his lines and the dusk of implications in the phrases stays on and delivers its effect for me always in pieces like 'Thirteen Ways of Looking at a Blackbird' and one, about the elephant's ear shrivelled and the leaves ran like rats, is autumn in city corners immemorially....

NOTE

1 *Others* was edited by Alfred Kreymborg (1883–1966) and founded in the spring of 1915 by Kreymborg and Walter Arensberg, and was closely associated with the summer artists' colony at Grantwood, New Jersey. The '*Others* bunch' might be said to include the poets Mina Loy, Maxwell Bodenheim, William Carlos Williams, Alanson Hartpence and Orrick Johns, besides Kreymborg, Stevens and others. The art colony included also Marcel Duchamp and Man Ray. The final number of *Others*, July 1919, was edited by William Carlos Williams.

6. Conrad Aiken, on Stevens and the sociological-nationalistic view of poetry, *New Republic*

Vol. XIX, no. 236, 10 May 1919, 58–61

Part of a review of Louis Untermeyer's anthology *The New Era in American Poetry* (1919), and part of a running controversy between Untermeyer and Aiken which, incidentally, established the early critical view of Stevens as a hedonist and aestheticist. Replying in the same number of *New Republic*, Untermeyer castigates the 'craftsman, intent on style, polish, finesse' as being free to express merely his own 'disdain... inhibitions and disillusion'. Such freedom led to 'the mere verbal legerdemain of the Pound–Stevens–Arensberg–*Others*' variety.

... his [Untermeyer's] chief tenets are Americanism, lustihood, glorification of reality (facing of the world of fact) democracy (a word which few of his pages lack) and, of course, the postponed though not to be omitted, inevitable beauty. These tenets he works hard, particularly those of Americanism, lustihood and democracy. These are, indeed his touchstones. It is 'Americanism' he sees, above all, in Masters, Frost, Robinson, even Amy Lowell; it is 'democracy' he sees above all, in Giovannitti, Wood, Oppenheim, Sandburg, Brody, Lola Ridge; and it is chiefly for their manifestation of these qualities that, apparently, Mr. Untermeyer accords these poets the place of honor in his book, and, ipso facto, the place of honor in contemporary poetry. Poetry, according to Mr. Untermeyer 'is expressing itself once more in the terms of democracy. This democracy is two-fold: a democracy of the spirit and a democracy of speech. This is the unifying quality that connects practically all of the poets with whom I propose to deal; it intensifies what is their inherent Americanism; and it charges their varied art with a native significance. . . .' Art, our critic goes on to say is a community expression: away, therefore, with the pernicious doctrine of 'art for art's sake'; and down with the ivory tower. Art has a human function to perform. It has no right to cloister itself, to preoccupy itself solely with beauty.

Well, these ideas are appealing, they have their precise value. Let us grant in particular the rightness, and indeed the commonplace inevitability, of the fact that periodically a literature will renew itself by a descent into the Bethesda well of demotic speech. We may go even further, and say that from the sociological viewpoint nothing can be more interesting than the reflection of social changes and social hungers in literature. But, here, I think, we must pause. The implications become a trifle ominous. Are we to conclude from these premises that art is any the less art because it fails to satisfy a contemporary hunger for this or that social change? Are we to conclude that art is any the more richly art because it bears conspicuously and consciously the label 'Made in America'? Is Poe to be judged, as an artist, inferior to Whitman because he is less nationalistic or less preoccupied with social consciousness? Or, indeed, – since Mr. Untermeyer really raises the question, – is such an art as Poe's, which as well as any illustrates the virtues and defects of the theory of art for art's sake, a whit the less a form of community expression, a whit the less satisfying to the human hunger for articulation, than such an art as Mr. Untermeyer seems to favor?

These questions, it seems to me, can intelligently be answered only in the negative. It is at this point that the line of cleavage between the tendencies for which Mr. Untermeyer stands and those for which his reviewer stands become most sharply apparent. For Mr. Untermeyer's book answers all these questions, by implication, in the affirmative. I do not mean that he dispenses with the aesthetic approach altogether in his appraisal of contemporary poetry, his aesthetic approach I shall come to later. But I do mean that Mr. Untermeyer allows nationalistic and sociological considerations to play an equal part with the aesthetic. To put it curtly, he likes poetry with a message, – poetry which is, politically, from his viewpoint, on the right side. Surely he must perceive the shortsightedness and essential viciousness of this? Social ideas are local and temporary: they change like the fashions, the materials with which they deal are always in flux, and the odds are great that what is a burning issue today will be a familiar fact, and the occasion of a yawn, tomorrow. These are, from the standpoint of the artist, mere superficialities: if they are to be touched they must be touched lightly, tangentially grazed. It is not to the political odes of Wordsworth, Coleridge, Swinburne, that we most joyously turn in rereading those poets. And the social problems of Shelley's 'Revolt of Islam' merely excite our curiosity.

Here, then, lies the greatest fault of Mr. Untermeyer's book. This bias has harmfully deflected it from the very outset, it has cast into undue prominence the work of Oppenheim, Giovannitti, Charles Erskine Scott Wood, Alfred Brody; it has put a wrong emphasis on the work of Sandburg; and, per contra, it has thrown into a shadow by no means deserved the work of such poets as do not, in Mr. Untermeyer's opinion, fulfil their social contracts, – such poets as T. S. Eliot, John Gould Fletcher, Wallace Stevens, Maxwell Bodenheim, the Imagists, and the entire strain of poetry for which they inconspicuously stand, the strain which we indicate when we use the phrase 'art for art's sake.' The work of the latter poets is not, as concerns reputation, secure. I think there can be no question that all of them have given us poems which, judged as works of art, are clearly finer and more universal in appeal, than anything as yet given us by Oppenheim, Giovannitti, Wood, or Brody. The latter four are, in fact – with all due allowance made for their vitality, sincerity, and frequent skill – simply, viewed as artists, mediocre. Mere energy will not save them. It is indeed open to question whether they do not deserve the same indictment as thinkers; as deliverers of the 'message'. And to honor them as copiously as Mr. Untermeyer honors them is in a measure to derogate from the true value of those among whom they are placed – Frost, Masters, Amy Lowell, and Robinson.

But this sociological and nationalistic bias, while it is the prime factor in Mr. Untermeyer's error, is not the only one. It will not completely diagnose Mr. Untermeyer's case; it will not alone explain his too enthusiastic preferences, his too acrimonious antipathies. Let us revert for a moment to his love of the art that bears a message. This hunger carries with it in Mr. Untermeyer's mind homologous hungers in the spheres of metaphysics and aesthetics, hungers which reveal themselves as clearly in his poetry as in his criticism. His interests are, in short, – as was indicated earlier, – primitively naive; he is oratorically assertive, a trifle consciously robust; and quite aside, therefore, from questions of social ethics, his predilections in poetry are for the unflinchingly masculine, the explicitly affirmative (what Nietzsche termed the 'yea-saying'), the triumphantly and not too reflectively acceptant; the vigorous, in short, rather than the cerebral or oblique or disillusioned, the enthusiastic and downright or sanely sentimental rather than the interpretative or analytic or psychologically tenuous.

And here we come upon the matter of Mr. Untermeyer's aesthetic equipment and touch at once, flatly, upon his very serious limitations. Within these limitations Mr. Untermeyer has, if we recall his two first volumes of verse, grown remarkably; he has extended his sympathies further than one might have hoped. But, at the critical point, they fail. Beyond the delicately overtoned lyrics of de la Mare, unconventionally conventional in form, relatively simply in range or, on the other hand, beyond the matter-of-fact incisive satires of Spoon River, or the slightly too smoothly turned etchings of Robinson, they cannot reach. And, unfortunately for Mr. Untermeyer, it is precisely in these two directions that the fruit-work is being done. In the former directions it gives us the work of H. D., of Pound (at his best), of Fletcher, of Stevens, of Bodenheim; in the latter, that of Eliot, Kreymborg, Masters, (his later vein), and tentatively, that of various contributors to *Others*. What these two groups have in common is the fact that they are both after a kind of absolute poetry – a poetry which delivers no message, is imbued with no doctrine, a poetry which exists only for the sake of magic, – magic of beauty on the one hand, magic of reality on the other, but both struck at rather through a play of implication than through matter-of-fact statement. This sort of poetry is of course unmoral and unsociological. It is not idolatrous: the circumstances, the emotions, out of which it springs, are its instruments, merely, the musical strings on which it strikes, not the items in a conscious ritual. It is the be-all and end-all of such poetry that it should be a perfectly formed and felt work of art; and the greater the elaboration and subtlety consistent with such perfection the more inexhaustible will it be, the longer it will endure. Unhappily for us and for Mr. Untermeyer, this type of poetry merely excites his animosity. When it is in the Fletcher–Bodenheim–Stevens vein he grants its skilful use of word-color, but is distressed by its apparent emptiness; when it is in the Eliot–Kreymborg–Williams vein he is annoyed by its tenuousness, baffled by its elusive use of introspection; and he takes refuge in terming it decadent, or effeminate, or morbid. It is not sufficiently affirmative for Mr. Untermeyer; it does not obviously enough encourage him to believe in God, or in the divinity of man, or in the rightness of democracy, or in the beauty and immortality of life. Mr. Untermeyer suspects it of a kind of negativism. It is not frank with him, will not state its text with sufficient candor. Moreover one suspects in Mr. Untermeyer's reiterated denials of anything 'new' in such work, as well as in his use of such phrases as 'self-adulatory radicalism' the survival of some injury to a new hopelessly overborne belief that he is a radical himself. It is, in other words, precisely the finer note in contemporary poetry which Mr. Untermeyer most completely misses.

7. Harriet Monroe, from 'Mr. Yeats and the Poetic Drama', *Poetry*

Vol. XVI, no. 1, April 1920, 33–5

The address by William Butler Yeats (1865–1939) was given on 3 March 1920 at a banquet in his honour hosted by *Poetry* magazine.

Mr. Yeats, in his brief address, took the Poetic Drama for his subject, and told of the little theater and the small audience which he and other poets are conspiring for in Dublin; the aristocratic theater in which from a dozen to fifty of the elect shall see plays worthy of spirits highly attuned and keyed, and shall pass them on authoritatively to the next age; a theater modeled on the Noh drama of Japan, whose playwrights and players were always blissfully absorbed in their art and royally unconscious of the crowd.

Without venturing to question this aesthetic authority of the elect in our unimperial age, I was reminded of a dramatic exhibition which I had attended in New York two or three weeks before, one which fulfilled Mr. Yeats's conditions as closely as any little-theater enterprise is like to do in our time and country. The distinguished Irish poet, unfortunately, was not there, and it is only too probable that less important engagements kept him away during the entire week or two that the Provincetown Players were giving *Three Travellers Watch a Sunrise*; so that we are forever prevented from knowing whether the performance was in line with his desire. But there was the small audience (over fifty, perhaps, but under one hundred) of the presumably elect – for who but the elect would venture down past Washington Square through slushy snowdrifts too mountainous for taxis? There also was the small stage, almost as informal as a drawing room, upon which artists had thought out a not too elaborate setting. And there, in Wallace Stevens' play, was the Poetic Drama.

I had almost forgotten how beautiful this brief play is; even though I had read it twenty times, more or less, in manuscript and proof, when it took *Poetry's* play-contest prize and appeared in the July, 1916, issue of the magazine. But the 'three travellers' – were they from Provincetown or China? – appearing with their candle in the dark wood and vesting themselves in gorgeous robes for the ritual of the sunrise, took me back to those 'windless pavilions' of Mr. Stevens' magic country, and asserted with unimpeachable validity the high audacity of the poet's imagination.

The girl was not so adequate. It is her province to enforce the tragedy by bringing the three dreamers face to face with the grim realities of agony and death. With hardly a dozen lines to speak, she would need be a Duse to give them their due effect. As she seemed merely a high-school amateur, the elect audience had to imagine nobly during the tragic climax of the play; the more because the sunrise, instead of approaching slowly, with gradual revelation of the dead figure among the branches, appeared with the sudden flare of an electric light. However, for at least one auditor, the three travellers, uttering their beautiful lines, had woven a spell which no later inadequacy could destroy: the brief tragedy was complete and wonderful, as perfect as a Greek vase in its assertion of beauty....

8. Yvor Winters, from 'A Cool Master', *Poetry*

Vol. XIX, no. 5, February 1922, 287–8

Winters (1900–68) taught at Stanford University 1928–66, and established a solid, though controversial, reputation both as a critic and a poet. The main body of his criticism is included in *In Defence of Reason* (1947), *The Function of Criticism* (1962) and *Forms of Discovery* (1965).

But a more curious and interesting resemblance to a later poet is found in the 'Octaves' in the same volume:[1]

> To me the groaning of world-worshippers
> Rings like a lonely music played in hell
> By one with art enough to cleave the walls
> Of heaven with his cadence, but without
> The wisdom or the will to comprehend
> The strangeness of his own perversity,
> And all without the courage to deny
> The profit and the price of his defeat.

If the actual thought of this passage is not that of Wallace Stevens, nevertheless the quality of the thought, the manner of thinking, as well as the style, quite definitely is. To what extent Mr. Robinson may have influenced this greatest of living and of American poets, one cannot say, but in at least three of the 'Octaves', one phase of Mr. Stevens' later work – that of 'Le Monocle de Mon Oncle' and other recent and shorter poems – is certainly foreshadowed. Mr. Robinson's sound is inevitably the less rich, the less masterly....

NOTE

[1] Edwin Arlington Robinson, *Collected Poems* (New York: Macmillan, 1921).

HARMONIUM

New York, 1923

Published by Alfred A. Knopf in an edition of 1,500 copies.

9.   Mark Van Doren, 'Poets and Wits', *Nation*

Vol. 117, no. 340, 10 October 1923, 400, 402

Van Doren (1894–1972) was a poet, critic, novelist, short-story writer and editor. His *Collected Poems 1922–38* (1939) was awarded the Pulitzer Prize in 1940. His reputation otherwise rests on studies of Thoreau and Hawthorne, Dryden and Shakespeare.

The present review also deals with Alfred Kreymborg's *Less Lonely* and Robert Graves' *Whipperginny*.

Mr. Stevens' most famous poem, 'Peter Quince at the Clavier,' appeared in *Others* as long as seven years ago and he has continued ever since to dance like a tantalizing star through magazines and anthologies. But there was no volume until now. While some of his admirers called for one rather loudly, the rest were content that Mr. Stevens should exist in bright fragments, being afraid, perhaps that he might not glitter in the bulk. *Harmonium* will dissolve their doubt, for it places its author high among those wits of today who are also poets – T. S. Eliot, Ezra Pound, Maxwell Bodenheim, Alfred Kreymborg, William Carlos Williams, Aldous Huxley, Sacheverell Sitwell, and Robert Graves. His wit, of course, has nothing of the Augustan about it. It is not clear; it is not the expression of common sense. It is tentative, perverse, and superfine; and it will never be popular. What public will care for a poet who strains every nerve every moment to be unlike anyone else who ever wrote; who writes a remarkable spiritual biography no line of which is transparent and calls it 'The Comedian as the Letter C'; who writes not about a blackbird but about 'Thirteen Ways of Looking at a Blackbird'; who gives his pieces such titles as 'Le Monocle de Mon Oncle', 'Hibiscus on the Sleeping Shores', 'Homunculus et la Belle Etoile', 'The Emperor of Ice-Cream', 'Exposition of the Contents of a Cab'; and who offers this under 'Bantams in Pinewoods'?

[Quotes *Collected Poems* (hereafter cited as *CP*), p. 75.]

Mr. Stevens will never be much read. But some day there will be a monograph on him and his twentieth-century kin who ranged their restless faculties over all the deserts and hill-tops of the world to inaugurate a new era of what Dryden once called 'wit-writing' – an era which may be short and may be long. That monograph will pay particular tribute to the pure phrasing of Mr. Stevens, to his delicately enunciated melody, his economy, his clipped cleanliness of line, his gentle excellence. And it will not be wrong if it finds him more durable, even with all his obscurity, than much of the perfect sense and the perfect rhyme that passed for poetry in his day; if it represents his work as drifting permanently, like frozen chords, through certain memories – the overtone of our droll, creedless time. . . .

10. Matthew Josephson, on 'an extraordinary personality', *Broom*

Vol. 5, November 1923, 236–7

Josephson (1899–1978), American editor and biographer, was associated with a number of influential periodicals in the 1920s and 1930s, such as *Secession*, *Broom* and *transition*. His books include *Portrait of the Artist as an American* (1930) and *Life Among the Surrealists* (1962).

A singular breed of Sensitive Plants begins to flourish in the severe climate of America. Some, revolted by its moral and economic bars, may have fled to voice their bitter protest. Wallace Stevens remains. Oblivious to all elements, save the natural beauty which puzzles and humors and holds him, and for which he returns the music of his words.

One side of him is exotic: colors are richer, sounds are sharper in him than in other minds or in the real existence which the mass mind accepts. So that we have the poetry of sensuousness, a poetry which depends chiefly upon its exotic spirit to hold us, as in 'Banal Sojourn':

The sky is a blue gum streaked with rose.
    The trees are black.
The grackles crack their throats of bone in the smooth air.
Moisture and heat have swollen the garden
    into a slum of bloom.
Pardie! Summer is like a fat beast, sleepy in mildew, ...

Yet, the fallacy of this manner, even in its most admirable and sympathetic exponent, is that it must go on being more and more *strange*. The cultured sensuousness of Mr. Stevens in his next book would have to be more and more intimate and scandalous, *ad absurdum*. I stress this side of his production because it has influenced many of his younger contemporaries, and in them, at least, leads to pretense, and murkiness.

On the other hand there is a mathematical, a *metaphysical* quality in certain of these poems which is entertaining in the highest sense. Poems such as 'Thirteen Ways of Looking at a Blackbird', or 'The Cuban Doctor', or 'Anecdote of the Jar', 'The Worms at Heaven's Gate', will be spell-binding for hundreds of years. 'The Jar' is as finished and simple as any of the perfect Landor fragments:

[Quotes 'Anecdote of the Jar', *CP*, p. 76.]

The method of this is more impoverished, there is more under-emphasis than over-ripeness, and yet it has the geometrical interest of a piece of modern abstract painting. In the vein of 'The Jar' Mr. Stevens strikes absolutely fresh qualities in poetry, and with the authority of a superb virtuoso. Stevens, Williams (Wm. Carlos), Marianne Moore, Cummings, and one or two others alone have such cultured hands. One more perfect thing must be quoted ('The Worms at Heaven's Gate'):

> Out of the tomb, we bring Badroulbadour,
> Within our bellies, we her chariot.
> Here is an eye. And here are, one by one,
> The lashes of that eye and its white lid.
> Here is the cheek on which that lid declined,
> And, finger after finger, here, the hand,
> The genius of that cheek. Here are the lips,
> The bundle of the body and the feet.
>
> Out of the tomb, we bring Badroulbadour.

It is, of course, Miltonic blank verse. The marching rhythms are made with the severity and precision of Baudelaire and Rimbaud. Otherwise, there are two sensational feats: the nonsense-name, 'Badroulbadour'; the use of the word 'declined'.

This first book of Mr. Stevens contains the groups of poems which aroused such interest when published in magazines. They are in many manners, and as a book serve to isolate an extraordinary personality, a man who is in turn shy, child-like, sensuous, sophisticated, discursive, who blushes for his sentiments, who is possessed of boundless curiosity. It is to be hoped that this curiosity will cause him yet to break loose in those directions (mathematical, metaphysical) for which his personality is most singularly fitted.

11. Marjorie Allen Seiffert, from 'The Intellectual Tropics', *Poetry*

Vol. XXIII, no. 3, December 1923, 154–60

...*Harmonium* is Wallace Stevens first book, although he has been writing and publishing in magazines for the last nine years, so that the great majority of the poems the book contains are familiar, and many have been included in anthologies. For this reason, an unfamiliar title, 'The Comedian as the Letter C' awakened my curiosity; as I set sail with Crispin, the hero, Mr. Stevens' world soon lay all about me, and there was no other world.

One is swept at break-neck speed across the ocean, to Yucatan, past Havana, through polar moonlight (though one never does quite understand the moonlight) into the Carolina wilderness, where Crispin founds a colony and leaves one breathless with the line: 'So may the relation of each man be clipped' – a last line one might well resent, had last lines any significance in this poem. But they have not, for already one has looked back a dozen times, read and re-read passages, always at a headlong pace, catching up with oneself again, stumbling ahead breathless with eagerness, laughter, delight; and to come to the end means merely that one will turn back to this passage or that, which teased with a glimpse into something that demands to be more clearly comprehended before one is done with it! After all, there is a lot one never quite 'gets.' The topography is concealed by luxuriance, and one regretfully assumes that perhaps Mr. Stevens doesn't mean to be any more illuminating than life itself, which offers a glorious amount of experience, much of which teaches one nothing. Not that one demands to be educated by reading 'The Comedian,' only to be sure one hasn't missed anything.

The poem professes to show how life limits and frustrates Crispin, but it leaves one with the conviction that Crispin, in so far as he is identified with Wallace Stevens, has put his tongue in his cheek at life. Crispin, proceeding from theory to theory of how the poet shall express his environment, 'the quintessential fact,' 'the thing that makes him envious in phrase,' ends by expressing it in four blue-eyed daughters, 'leaving no room upon his cloudy knee, prophetic joint, for its diviner young!' A Crispin able to assimilate such events and put them into form is not the tool of his environment, but its master.

It is a matter of temperament whether life is material for tragedy or philosophy. The greatest poetry comes from that bitterer conflict in which the poet is unresigned. So in the two categories of poet as protagonist and poet as philosopher, Mr. Stevens seems to stand in the latter class. But upon closer analysis one perceives a black texture behind the elaborate and whimsical embroideries. This is immediately evident in 'Le Monocle de Mon Oncle,' wherein love is discussed from the standpoint of an elderly gentleman. All poets are intuitively middle-aged every four or five years or so, and as no indignant band of elderly persons arises to dispute them, one may assume that they speak with divine authority. Personally I feel that Mr. Stevens has as good a right to assume middle-age in the thirties as anybody, and his poem convinces me. The muted, sub-tragic note is audible through the varied and picturesque designs which make each of the twelve stanzas a complete unit, and bind them into the larger unity of the poem.

'Sunday Morning,' another long poem, discusses and dismisses personal immortality. Unlike the others it employs no device of phantasy to mask its substance, but is set forth in grave simplicity. For this reason it is not characteristic of the author as we know him, and is either a poem apart, or else inaugurates a style he has not elsewhere practised. It is incontestably beautiful, but taken out of the book could not be identified as his own, a thing that could hardly be said of many of his poems. . . .

Poems like this are easy of comprehension. They are like the sea, a terrain common to all. But when Mr. Stevens is most himself, most individual, most zestful, he is less direct. Sometimes there is an emotional substratum that quiets the too inquisitive spirit that demands to know 'what it is about'; sometimes the issue is left obscure, and the poet has contented himself with presenting a design, the meaning of which is not apparent. Perhaps such poems are constructed for design's sake alone. Of the former one might instance 'Tea at the Palaz of Hoon' and 'Fabliau of Florida'; of the latter 'Infanta Marina' and 'The Place of the Solitaires.' But by far the greater number of the poems have both the 'beauty of inflections' and the 'beauty of innuendoes'; they delicately convey, without plot or argument, a theme and its significance, yet seem to remain wholly simple. . . .

After this survey of Wallace Stevens' world one retires to one's own to think it over. It is a brilliant country, with tropic splendor beside which the real tropics seem faded and meagre, a world in which the accustomed realities are concealed under scenery of luxuriant and intricate design, but a world which has after all a rocky substratum of reality. Sometimes one wishes Mr. Stevens would write more poems in the manner of 'Ploughing on Sunday' or 'The Snow Man,' whose bare rigor is immensely effective. However, his tropics have no steamy sensuality about them, no sticky purple patches; rather they are curiously patterned like an East Indian painting. His emotion lurks behind design. We must peer through thickets to catch a glimpse of that shy wary bird as it flits into obscurity. Distinctly there is nothing homogeneous between *Harmonium* and our own back-yard except that bird, which roosts so trustingly on one's own clothes-pole that one can recognize the color of his tail even in a *tropic* landscape. . . .

12. John Gould Fletcher, from 'The Revival of Estheticism', *Freeman*

Vol. 8, 19 December 1923, 355–6.

Fletcher (1886–1950) was a poet and critic, associated with the Imagist movement. Publications include *Paul Gauguin: His Life and Art* (1921), the autobiographical *Life is My Song* (1937) and *Selected Poems* (1938), which was awarded a Pulitzer Prize.

'The Revival of Estheticism' includes consideration of volumes of poetry by Conrad Aiken, Alfred Kreymborg, Louis Grudin, Henry Bellaman and John Cournos.

On 27 December 1923, William Carlos Williams wrote to Marianne Moore about this review, particularly as it dealt with Stevens: 'Please read it and then please write me. Fletcher seems to be somewhat misanthropic toward that class of individuals, the younger American poets' (*The Selected Letters of William Carlos Williams*, p. 57).

...Mr. Wallace Stevens is an æsthete, but he is at all events an honest æsthete. The careful reader – and Mr. Stevens demands careful reading, if not many readings – can readily ascertain that Mr. Stevens is definitely out of tune with life and with his surroundings, and is seeking an escape into a sphere of finer harmony between instinct and intelligence. That he does seek for this speaks much for his integrity as an artist; what speaks even more clearly is the fact that of all the purely æsthetic artists of to-day, he wields the finest and most distinguished weapon of style. Any reader who will take the trouble to compare 'Le Monocle de Mon Oncle' or 'Sunday Morning' with Mr. T. S. Eliot's *Waste Land*, or the best work of the Sitwells, or even M. Paul Valéry's 'Jeune Parque,' will realize that Mr. Stevens need fear no comparisons with these internationally famous writers. He is head and shoulders above them all. It is true that he, like these others, is an obscure writer. But his obscurity comes from a wealth of meaning and allusion which are unavoidable; and his intention, when we finally do fathom it, is far clearer and more earnestly pursued than theirs. He holds that the artist can do nothing else but select out of life the elements to form a 'fictive' or fictitious reality. But this is not necessarily a higher reality; he is unable to take any moral category for granted. It is merely the artist's reality. And as such it becomes disintegrated against the banal, the ordinary, the commonplace, which is every-day reality. The result of this disintegration of the artist's personality is to be found in the poem which is entitled curiously, 'The Comedian as the Letter C'; and the brief attainment of his ideal is detailed in the exquisite 'To the One of Fictive Music.' Despite his gallant attempt to guard his secret preoccupation with something more important than externals from the knowledge of the crowd, by the deliberate use of misleading titles, I make bold to say that Mr. Stevens is the most accomplished and not one of the least interesting of modern American poets. But for the future he must face a clear choice of evils: he must either expand his range to take in more of human experience, or give up writing altogether. *Harmonium* is a sublimation which does not permit of a sequel....

13. Marianne Moore, 'Well Moused, Lion', *Dial*

Vol. LXXVI, January 1924, 84–91

Marianne Moore (1887–1972) graduated from Bryn Mawr College in 1909. In 1921, the poet H. D. (Hilda Doolittle) and the novelist Bryher (Winifred Ellerman) published, without Miss Moore's knowledge, her first volume, *Poems*. Her many later verse collections include *The Complete Poems of Marianne Moore* (New York, 1967). She also published *Predilections*, a volume of essays, and translated *The Fables of la Fontaine*. Winner of the Pulitzer Prize, the Bollingen Prize and the National Book Award, she edited the *Dial* from 1925 to 1929.

It is not too much to say that some writers are entirely without imagination – without that associative kind of imagination certainly, of which the final tests are said to be simplicity, harmony, and truth. In Mr. Stevens' work, however, imagination precludes banality and order prevails. In his book, he calls imagination 'the will of things,' 'the magnificent cause of being,' and demonstrates how imagination may evade 'the world without imagination'; effecting an escape which, in certain manifestations of 'bravura,' is uneasy rather than bold. One feels, however, an achieved remoteness as in Tu Muh's lyric criticism: 'Powerful is the painting ... and high is it hung on the spotless wall in the lofty hall of your mansion.' There is the love of magnificence and the effect of it in these sharp, solemn, rhapsodic elegant pieces of eloquence; one assents to the view taken by the author, of Crispin whose

mind was free
And more than free, elate, intent, profound.

The riot of gorgeousness in which Mr. Stevens' imagination
takes refuge recalls Balzac's reputed attitude to money, to
which he was indifferent unless he could have it 'in heaps or
by the ton.' It is 'a flourishing tropic he requires'; so wakeful
is he in his appetite for color and in perceiving what is needed
to meet the requirements of a new tone key, that Oscar
Wilde, Frank Alvah Parsons, Tappé, and John Murray
Anderson seem children asleep in comparison with him. One
is met in these poems by some such clash of pigment as
where in a showman's display of orchids or gladiolas, one
receives the effect of vials of picracarmine, magenta, gam-
boge, and violet mingled each at the highest point of
intensity:

> In Yucatan, the Maya sonneteers
> Of the Caribbean amphitheatre,
> In spite of hawk and falcon, green toucan
> And Jay, still to the night-bird made their plea,
> As if raspberry tanagers in palms,
> High up in orange air, were barbarous.

One is excited by the sense of proximity to Java Peacocks,
golden pheasants, South American macaw feather capes,
Chilcat blankets, hair seal needlework, Singhalese masks,
and Rousseau's paintings of banana leaves and alligators. We
have the hydrangeas and dogwood, the 'blue, gold, pink, and
green' of the temperate zone, the hibiscus, 'red as red,' of the
tropics.

> ... moonlight on the thick, cadaverous bloom
> That yuccas breed...

> ... with serpent-kin encoiled
> Among the purple tufts, the scarlet crowns,

and as in a shot-spun fabric, the infinitude of variation of the
colors of the ocean:

> ... the blue
> And the colored purple of the lazy sea,

the emerald, indigos, and mauves of disturbed water, the
azure and basalt of lakes; we have Venus 'the centre of
sea-green pomp' and America 'polar purple.' Mr. Stevens'

exact demand, moreover, projects itself from nature to human nature. It is the eye of no 'maidenly greenhorn' which has differentiated Crispin's daughters, which characterizes 'the ordinary women' as 'gaunt guitarists' and issues the junior-to-senior mandate in 'Floral Decorations for Bananas':

> Pile the bananas on planks.
> The women will be all shanks
> And bangles and slatted eyes.

He is a student of 'the flambeaued manner,'

> ...not indifferent to smart detail...

> ...hang of coat, degree
> Of buttons...

One resents the temper of certain of these poems. Mr. Stevens is never inadvertently crude; one is conscious, however, of a deliberate bearishness – a shadow of acrimonious, unprovoked contumely. Despite the sweet-Clementine-will-you-be-mine nonchalance of the 'Apostrophe to Vincentine,' one feels oneself to be in danger of unearthing the ogre and in 'Last Looks at the Lilacs,' a pride in unserviceableness is suggested which makes it a microcosm of cannibalism.

Occasionally the possession of one good is remedy for not possessing another, as when Mr. Stevens speaks of 'the young emerald, evening star,' 'tranquillizing ... the torments of confusion.' 'Sunday Morning' on the other hand – a poem so suggestive of a masterly equipoise – gives ultimately the effect of the mind disturbed by the intangible; of a mind oppressed by the properties of the world which it is expert in manipulating. And proportionately; aware as one is of the author's susceptibility to the fever of actuality, one notes the accurate gusto with which he discovers the Negro, that veritable 'medicine of cherries' to the badgered analyst. In their resilience and certitude, the 'Hymn From a Watermelon Pavilion' and the commemorating of a Negress who

> Took seven white dogs
> To ride in a cab,

are proud harmonies.

One's humor is based upon the most serious part of one's nature. 'Le Monocle de Mon Oncle'; 'A Nice Shady Home'; and 'Daughters with Curls': the capacity of self-mockery in these titles illustrates the author's disgust with mere vocativeness.

Instinct for words is well determined by the nature of the liberties taken with them, some writers giving the effect merely of presumptuous egotism – an unavoided outlandishness; others, not: Shakespeare arresting one continually with nutritious permutations as when he apostrophizes the lion in *A Midsummer Night's Dream* – 'Well Moused, Lion.' Mr. Stevens' 'Junipers Shagged with Ice' is properly courageous as are certain of his adjectives which have the force of verbs: 'the spick torrent,' 'tidal skies,' 'loquacious columns'; there is the immunity to fear, of the good artist, in 'the blather that the water made.' His precise diction and verve are grateful as contrasts to the current vulgarizations of 'gesture,' 'dimensions,' and 'intrigue.' He is able not only to express an idea with mere perspicuity; he is able to do it by implication, as in 'Thirteen Ways of Looking at a Blackbird' in which the glass coach evolved from icicles; the shadow, from birds; it becomes a kind of aristocratic cipher. 'The Emperor of Ice-Cream,' moreover, despite its not especially original theme of poverty enriched by death, is a triumph of explicit ambiguity. He gets a special effect with those adjectives which often weaken as in the lines:

> ... That all beasts should...
> be beautiful
> As large, ferocious tigers are

and in the phrase, 'the eye of the young alligator,' the adjective, as it is perhaps superfluous to point out, makes for activity. There is a certain bellicose sensitiveness in

> I do not know which to prefer...
> The blackbird whistling
> Or just after

and in the characterization of the snow man who

> ...nothing himself, beholds
> Nothing that is not there and the nothing that is.

In its nimbleness *con brio* with seriousness, moreover, 'Nomad Exquisite' is a piece of that ferocity for which one values Mr. Stevens most:

> As the immense dew of Florida
> Brings forth
> The big-finned palm
> And green vine angering for life.

Poetic virtuosities are allied – especially those of diction, imagery, and cadence. In no writer's work are metaphors less 'winter starved.' In 'Architecture' Mr. Stevens asks:

> How shall we hew the sun, ...
> How carve the violet moon
> To set in nicks?
>
> Pierce, too, with buttresses of coral air
> And purple timbers,
> Various argentines

and 'The Comedian as the Letter C,' as the account of the craftsman's un'simple jaunt,' is an expanded metaphor which becomes, as one contemplates it, hypnotically incandescent like the rose-tinged fringe of the night-blooming cereus. One applauds those analogies derived from an enthusiasm for the sea:

> She scuds the glitters,
> Noiselessly, like one more wave.
>
> The salt hung on his spirit like a frost,
> The dead brine melted in him like a dew.

In his positiveness, aplomb, and verbal security, he has the mind and the method of China; in such conversational effects as:

> Of what was it I was thinking?
> So the meaning escapes,

and certainly in dogged craftsmanship. Infinitely conscious in his processes, he says

> Speak even as if I did not hear your speaking
> But spoke for you perfectly in my thoughts.

One is not subject, in reading him, to the disillusionment experienced in reading novices and charlatans who achieve flashes of beauty and immediately contradict the pleasure afforded by offending in precisely those respects in which they have pleased – showing that they are deficient in conscious artistry.

Imagination implies energy and imagination of the finest type involves an energy which results in order 'as the motion of a snake's body goes through all parts at once, and its volition acts at the same instant in coils that go contrary ways.' There is the sense of the architectural diagram in the disjoined titles of poems with related themes. Refraining for fear of impairing its litheness of contour, from overelaborating felicities inherent in a subject, Mr. Stevens uses only such elements as the theme demands; for example, his delineation of the peacock in 'Domination of Black' is austerely restricted, splendor being achieved cumulatively in 'Bantams in Pine-Woods.' 'The Load of Sugar-Cane,' 'The Palace of the Babies,' and 'The Bird with the Coppery, Keen Claws.'

That 'there have been many most excellent poets that never versified, and now swarm many versifiers that need never answer to the name of poets,' needs no demonstration. The following lines, as poetry independent of rhyme, beg the question as to whether rhyme is indispensably contributory to poetic enjoyment:

> There is not nothing, no, no, never nothing,
> Like the clashed edges of two words that kill

and

> The clambering wings of birds of black revolved,
> Making harsh torment of the solitude.

It is of course evident that, subsidiary to beauty of thought, rhyme is powerful in so far as it never appears to be invented for its own sake. In this matter of apparent naturalness, Mr. Stevens is faultless – as in correctness of assonance:

> Chieftain Iffucan of Azcan in caftan
> Of tan with henna hackles, halt!

The better the artist, moreover, the more determined he will be to set down words in such a way as to admit of no interpretation of the accent but the one intended, his ultimate power appearing in a self-sufficing, willowy, firmly contrived cadence such as we have in 'Peter Quince at the Clavier' and in 'Cortège for Rosenbloom':

> That tread
> The wooden ascents
> Of the ascending of the dead.

One has the effect of poised uninterrupted harmony, a simple-appearing, complicated phase of symmetry of movements as in figure skating, tightrope dancing, in the kaleidoscopically centrifugal circular motion of certain medieval dances. It recalls the snake in *Far Away and Long Ago*, 'moving like quicksilver in a ropelike stream' or the conflict at sea when, after a storm, the wind shifts and waves are formed counter to those still running. These expertnesses of concept with their nicely luted edges and effect of flowing continuity of motion, are indeed.

> ... pomps
> Of speech which are like music so profound
> They seem an exaltation without sound.

One further notes accomplishment in the use of reiteration – that pitfall of half-poets:

> Death is absolute and without memorial,
> As in a season of autumn,
> When the wind stops,
>
> When the wind stops...

In brilliance gained by accelerated tempo in accordance with a fixed melodic sign, the precise patterns of many of these poems are interesting.

> It was snowing
> And it was going to snow

and the parallelism in 'Domination of Black' suggests the Hebrew idea of something added, although there is, one admits, more the suggestion of mannerism than in Hebrew poetry. Tea takes precedence of other experiments with which one is familiar, in emotional shorthand of this unwestern type, and in 'Earthy Anecdote' and the 'Invective Against Swans,' symmetry of design is brought to a high degree of perfection.

It is rude perhaps, after attributing conscious artistry and a severely intentional method of procedure to an artist, to cite work that he has been careful to omit from his collected work. One regrets, however, the omission by Mr. Stevens of 'The Indigo Glass in the Grass,' 'The Man Whose Pharynx Was Bad,' 'La Mort du Soldat Est Près des Choses Naturelles (5 Mars)' and 'Comme Dieu Dispense de Grâces':

> Here I keep thinking of the primitives –
> The sensitive and conscientious themes
> Of mountain pallors ebbing into air.

However, in this collection one has eloquence. 'The author's violence is for aggrandizement and not for stupor'; one consents, therefore, to the suggestion that when the book of moonlight is written, we leave room for Crispin. In the event of moonlight and a veil to be made gory, he would, one feels, be appropriate in this legitimately sensational act of a ferocious jungle animal.

14. Allen Tate, on Wallace Stevens as 'radical', *Nashville Tennessean*

10 February 1924

Tate (1899–1979), poet, critic, biographer, novelist, editor and teacher, was a member of the 'Fugitive' group of poets and edited the *Fugitive* from 1922 to 1925. He was Southern editor of *Hound and Horn* (1931–4) and editor of the *Sewanee Review*, from 1944 to1946. He was awarded the Bollingen Prize in 1956. Publications include one novel, *The Fathers* (1938), and *Essays of Four Decades* (1969). Best-known among books he edited are *I'll Take My Stand: The South and the Agrarian Tradition* (1930) and *The House of Fiction: An Anthology of the Short Story*, of which his wife Caroline Gorden was co-editor (1950). His *Collected Poems* were published in 1977 and *Memoirs and Opinions* in 1975.

Harmonium is here reviewed with *The Harp-Weaver and Other Poems* by Edna St Vincent Millay and *Bucolic Comedies* by Edith Sitwell. More than half of the review is given to Millay.

This review is taken from *The Poetry Reviews of Allen Tate 1924–1944*, edited by Ashley Brown and Frances Neel Cheney (Baton Rouge: Louisiana State University Press, 1983), pp. 10–11.

E. E. Cummings, Wallace Stevens, and William Carlos Williams are the foremost 'radicals' in America, and they probably rank in the order named; they are the American counterpart of *Wheels*.[1] But where Miss Sitwell often indulges in a bewildering 'fine excess' Mr. Stevens' exacting sense of verbal economy limits him to a few vivid and significant strokes, and his poem is done:

[Quotes 'The Curtains in the House of the Metaphysician', *CP*, p. 62.]

Or this:

> What syllable are you seeking,
> Vocallissimus,
> In the distance of sleep?
> Speak it.

Like the Elizabethans, these poets are after new meanings for old words – a new vocabulary for a completely individual expression. Mr. Stevens is an intellectualist, a tree of itself is meaningless to him:

But, after all, I know a tree that bears
A semblance to the thing I have in mind.

Wallace Stevens is an explorer of the exotic; his diction, in strangeness of effect, lags but little after Miss Sitwell. His better poems present a freshness of observation; the trite phrase is absent from his work.

NOTE

[1] Wheels was an experimental literary journal; Edith Sitwell was one of its editors.

15. Harriet Monroe, on 'a flavorously original poetic personality', *Poetry*

Vol. XXIII, no. 6, March 1924, 322–7

Harriet Monroe (1860–1936) made some reputation as a poet in the 1890s and wrote the 'Columbian Ode' for the Chicago Exposition of 1893. She published *The Passing Show*, a book of five verse-plays, in 1903, but became famous after founding *Poetry* magazine in 1912. *A Poet's Life*, her autobiography, was published in 1937. The article from which the following is excerpted is titled 'A Cavalier of Beauty'.

...Mr. Stevens is the most abstemious of poets. It is the unwritten poem in his mind which interests him – the old ones, once they are registered in some magazine, may go fluttering down the wind like dead leaves. For nearly a decade his admirers pleaded in vain for a book, and at last they feel lucky to get one at all, even though they scan it in vain for 'Three Travellers Watch a Sunrise,' 'Carlos Among the Candles,' and many a briefer poem which any other poet would be proud to claim. The future collector of Mr. Stevens' complete works will have to pay a fancy price for certain back numbers of *Poetry* and *Others*. Meantime, *Harmonium* contains most of our favorites, besides a few new poems of high importance.

One gets a stronger flavor of personality from a one-man show than from any mixed exhibition, and there was never a more flavorously original poetic personality than the author of this book. If one seeks sheer beauty of sound, phrase, rhythm, packed with prismatically colored ideas by a mind at once wise and whimsical, one should open one's eyes and ears, sharpen one's wits, widen one's sympathies to include rare and exquisite aspects of life, and then run for this volume of iridescent poems.

I should like to take my copy to some quiet-sea-flung space in Florida, where a number of the poems were written. The sky, perhaps, is cobalt, with mauve-white clouds; the sea is sapphire, flicking into diamonds under the wind; the sand is a line of purplish rose, and there are pink and yellow parasols on the beach. And here is a poet undaunted by all this splendor, a poet as sure of delight as nature herself, as serenely receptive of beauty. The bleak despairs of lesser men visit him not at all – his philosophy embraces the whole fantastic miracle of life, a miracle so wild and strange that man, confronting it, must feel the enormous humor of his lordly pose, and take refuge in

> The magnificent cause of being,
> The imagination, the one reality
> In this imagined world.

For the philosopher and the satirist temper the poet's rage in Wallace Stevens. Whether he ever writes his masterpiece or not – and that is always uncertain through the turmoil of conflicting claims which besets us all today – he is of the race of the great humorists, using the word in its most profound sense, the sense in which Cervantes, Shakespeare, Synge, Lincoln may be counted as great humorists. In such men agony sinks into depths dark, hidden and unconfessed. The hard black stone is there, but laughter washes over it, covers it up, conceals it. Tragedy is comedy with such men – they are aware of the laughter of the gods and the flaming splendor of man's fight against it. This poet is one of them; his book, however incomplete as yet, is haughty with their lineage.

Always, in his lightest play of whimsicalities as well as in his most splendid assertions of beauty, one feels this deeper note, this sense of ultimate vanities and ecstasies contending, in the human atom, against infinities that threaten it with doom. The play of whimsicalities may seem a mere banter of word-bubbles, as in 'Ordinary Women'; the assertions of beauty may be as magical in pomp of color and sound as 'Le Monocle de Mon Oncle,' which lifts to our thirsty lips

> This luscious and impeccable fruit of life –

or as 'The Paltry Nude,' moving forever

> Across the spick torrent, ceaselessly,
> Upon her irretrievable way –

but in either extreme of lovely or whimsical utterance one feels the larger rhythms, one measures the poet's sweep by spaces beyond our earthly inches.

Perhaps 'The Comedian as the Letter C' is the most complete assertion of cosmic humor which Mr. Stevens has as yet confessed to the world. It is at least the presentment, probably more or less autobiographical, of the predicament of man in general, or of highly sensitized man – let us say the artist – in particular, as he tries to live gloriously, and finds his soul caught in the meshes of life's allurements. Many poets have made a tragedy of this situation, shouting their agonies of rebellion and despair in more or less effective verse. Mr. Stevens is perhaps more keenly inspired in making of it a comedy searching and profound, a comedy whose azure laughter ripples almost inaudibly over hushed and sombre depths.

His little human unit – this 'Socrates of snails,' this 'wig of things,' this 'sovereign ghost,'

> This connoisseur of elemental fate,
> Aware of exquisite thought –

in short, this Crispin, who was 'washed away by magnitude,' is he not our modern exemplar of frustration, as Don Quixote was in his day?

> Against his pipping sounds a trumpet cried
> Celestial sneering boisterously.

And as he sails into the blue southern sea,

> How many poems he denied himself
> In his observant progress, lesser things
> Than the relentless contact he desired!

He is in search of 'a sinewy nakedness' – this Crispin poet-man;

> He gripped more closely the essential prose,
> As being, in a world so falsified,
> The one integrity for him.

But alas, he finds himself settling down:

> Crispin dwelt in the land, and dwelling there,
> Slid from his continent by slow recess
> To things within his actual eye, alert
> To the difficulty of rebellious thought
> When the sky is blue.

And so he falls into 'a nice shady home,' into bewildered marital allegiances, into parental loyalties to four daughters, bluet-eyed,

> Leaving no room upon his cloudy knee,
> Prophetic joint, for its diviner young.

Thus enmeshed, what is a puzzled prophet to do?

> Should he lay by the personal, and make
> Of his own fate an instance of all fate?
> What is one man among so many men?
> What are so many men in such a world?
> Can one man think one thing and think it long?
> Can one man be one thing and be it long?

So the poet in Crispin comes to a bad end:

So deep a sound fell down
It was as if the solitude concealed
And covered him and his congenial sleep.
So deep a sound fell down it grew to be
A long soothsaying silence down and down.

We must hope that the poem is not strictly autobiographical, that Mr. Stevens, unlike his baffled hero, will get his story
uttered – to such a degree at least, as may be within the reach
of poor mortality. For this poet, like a super-sensitized plate,
is aware of color-subtleties and sound-vibrations which most
of us do not detect, and of happiness in fine degrees which
most of us do not attain. He derives, so far as one may trace
the less obvious origins, from no one; but like Napoleon he
may say, *'Je suis ancêtre!'* for shoals of young poets derive
from him. Quite free of literary allegiances to period or
place, he distils into a pure essence the beauty of his own
world. And beauty's imperishable perfection among shifting
mortal shows is the incongruity at the heart of life which this
poet accepts with the kind of serene laughter that covers pain.

16. Edmund Wilson, on Stevens' lack of emotion, *New Republic*

Vol. XXXVII, no. 485, 19 March 1924, 102, 103

Wilson (1895–1972), critic, editor, novelist and poet,
was one of the ablest and most wide-ranging intellects of
his time. Among his many notable books are *Axel's
Castle*, a landmark study of the Symbolist movement
(1931), *The Wound and the Bow* (1931), *To the Finland
Station*, a study of the origins of the Russian revolution
(1940), *The Dead Sea Scrolls* (1955), *Memoirs of Hecate*

County (1946), and the anthologies *The Shock of Recognition* (1943) and *Patriotic Gore* (1962).

Two brief comments on Stevens are included in Wilson's book *The Twenties* (1975). When he read *Harmonium* towards the end of 1923 he thought Stevens 'a very distinguished poet in a fairly small way' (p. 154). This remark was actually made to Christian Gauss, the famous teacher of Wilson and Scott Fitzgerald, in a letter of 12 December 1923 (see Wilson's *Letters on Literature and Politics 1912–1972* (1977)). Early in 1924 he characterized *Harmonium* to John Peale Bishop as 'remarkably successful in a limited way' (p. 206).

Later, in a sharp exchange with Harrison Smith of the *Saturday Review of Literature*, part of the controversy generated by Ezra Pound's being awarded the first annual Bollingen Prize in 1949, Wilson noted, 'I do not remember anything in the work of Pound at that period so difficult as many of the poems in this book'. The book he refers to is *Harmonium* (see *Letters*, pp. 483–4).

In 1969, years after Stevens' death, Wilson told a correspondent that he had never met Stevens, then recounted an incident on one of Stevens' solitary trips to Florida, this time involving John Dos Passos. 'The idea of the Hartford insurance man who has never been abroad,' continues Wilson, 'but fancies himself as a wistful Pierrot inhabiting the *fin de siècle* I have always found somewhat repellant. His early book *Harmonium* has some nice – purely verbal – writing, but his more pretentious stuff bores me....'

Also under review here is E.E. Cummings' *Tulips and Chimneys*.

Mr. Wallace Stevens is the master of a style: that is the most remarkable thing about him. His gift for combining words is fantastic but sure: even when you do not know what he is saying, you know that he is saying it well. He derives plainly from several French sources of the last fifty years but he never – except for a fleeting phrase or two – really sounds like any of them. You could not mistake even a title by Wallace Stevens for a title by anyone else: 'Invective Against Swans,' 'Hibiscus on the Sleeping Shores,' 'A High-Toned Old Christian Woman,' 'The Emperor of Ice-Cream,' 'Exposition of the Contents of a Cab,' 'The Bird with the Coppery Keen Claws,' 'Two Figures in Dense Violet Light,' 'Hymn from a Watermelon Pavilion,' and 'Frogs Eat Butterflies. Snakes Eat Frogs. Hogs Eat Snakes. Men Eat Hogs.'

These titles also represent Mr. Stevens's curious ironic imagination at its very best. The poems themselves – ingenious, charming and sometimes beautiful as they are – do not always quite satisfy the expectation aroused by the titles. When you read a few poems of Mr. Stevens, you get the impression from the richness of his verbal imagination that he is a poet of rich personality, but when you come to read the whole volume through you are struck by a sort of aridity. Mr. Stevens, who is so observant and has so distinguished a fancy, seems to have emotion neither in abundance nor in intensity. He is ironic a little in Mr. Eliot's manner; but he is not poignantly, not tragically ironic. Emotion seems to emerge only furtively in the cryptic images of his poetry, as if it had been driven, as he seems to hint, into the remotest crannies of sleep or disposed of by being dexterously turned into exquisite amusing words. Nothing could be more perfect in its tone and nothing by itself could be more satisfactory than such a thing as 'Last Looks at the Lilacs.' But when we have gone all through Mr. Stevens, we find ourselves putting to him the same question which he, in the last poem of his book, puts 'To the Roaring Wind':

> What syllable are you seeking,
> Vocallissimus,
> In the distance of sleep?
> Speak it.

... Mr. Cummings has an advantage over Mr. Stevens. Whatever Cummings is he is not chilled; he is not impervious to life....

17. Llewelyn Powys, 'The Thirteenth Way', *Dial*

Vol. LXXVII, July 1924, 45–50

Llewelyn Powys (1884–1939), an English essayist and writer of fiction, was a journalist in New York City, 1920–5.

Just as in the 'nineties, golden quill in hand, Aubrey Beardsley, seated under a crucifix, traced with degenerate wax-white finger pictures that revealed a new world, a world exact, precise, and convincing, squeezed out, so to speak, between the attenuated crevices of a hypersensitive imagination, so in his poetry Mr. Wallace Stevens chips apertures in the commonplace and deftly constructs on the other side of the ramparts of the world, tier upon tier, pinnacle upon pinnacle, his own supersophisticated superterrestrial township of the mind.

And it may well be that his eccentric verse does actually reveal more of the insecure fluctuating secrets of the universe than are to be found in other more sedate, more decorous artistic creations. Wavering, uncertain, bereft of ancient consolations, the human race comes more and more to realize that it has won to consciousness in a world in which all is relative and undulating. In such a world it is indeed possible that intimations of some incalculable absolute are more nearly to be come at under the influence of cloud-shadows floating beneath a violet moon than under that of the splashes of actual sunshine lying so confidently on grass, and brick, and stone, and metal.

From king to beggar we are aware of our manifold delusions, aware that nothing is as false as the face value of things. We have, alas! grown only too cognizant of the essential mendacity of the physical aspects of a universe that has no bottom. And this being so, it is perhaps in suggestions, in mere phantasms, that we come nearest to the evocations of the fourth-dimensional consciousness which may well be farthest removed from illusion. If the surface of the visible world then is nothing, who can tell but that the shadows of the surface of the visible world may be everything? And no poet, not Baudelaire, not Edgar Allan Poe even, has revealed with a surer touch, a surer ambiguity, the very shades and tinctures of this indefinable borderland than has this ultramodern supersubtle lawyer from the confines of Hartford, Connecticut.

It is impossible for us to read Mr. Stevens' poetry without feeling that we are being initiated into the quintessential tapering expression of a unique personality – a personality as original and authentic as it is fastidious and calculating. He stands quite alone amongst the poets of the more modern schools in that each unexpected verbal manipulation conceals some obscure harmony of sense and sound which not only provokes intellectual appreciation, but in the strangest possible way troubles the imagination. Listening to his poetry is like listening to the humming cadences of an inspired daddy longlegs akimbo in sunset light against the colored panes of a sanct window above a cathedral altar.

Mr. Wallace Stevens' poetry is beyond good and evil, beyond hope and despair, beyond thought of any kind, one might almost say.

> The soul, O ganders, flies beyond the parks
> And far beyond the discords of the wind.

And yet he is not so far removed from the palpable foundations of existence as to be altogether oblivious to the passing of the seasons. Like other poets before him, his spirit feels the impact of the spring and finds for its emotions unabashed punctilious expression.

> Timeless mother,
> How is it that your aspic nipples
> For once vent honey?

Very curious, very corrupt, very artificial are the seascape vignettes, the landscape vignettes of his demi-world, arti-

ficial and yet pointed and penetrating in their decorative
integrity.

> In the sea, Biscayne, there prinks
> The young emerald, evening star. . . .

> By this light the salty fishes
> Arch in the sea like tree-branches,
> Going in many directions
> Up and down.

> Her terrace was the sand
> And the palms and the twilight. . . .

> And thus she roamed
> In the roamings of her fan,

> Partaking of the sea,
> And of the evening,
> As they flowed around
> And uttered their subsiding sound.

Indeed, as in the last quotation, one continually comes
upon passages that seem to suggest a curious sensuality such
as one might fancifully associate with certain of the stranger
apparitions seen in the circus ring, a bizarre niggling
sensuality in accord with some dainty physical disability: the
sensuality of a crotchety detached mind which itself is
removed from the object of its adoration by convoluted
covert laws of super-refined cerebrations.

> To what good, in the alleys of the lilacs,
> O caliper, do you scratch your buttocks
> And tell the divine ingénue, your companion,
> That . . .

> Poor Buffo! Look at the lavender
> And look your last and look still steadily,
> And say how it comes that you see
> Nothing but trash and that you no longer feel
> Her body quivering in the Floréal

Toward the cool night and its fantastic star,
Prime paramour and belted paragon,
Well-booted, rugged, arrogantly male,
Patron and imager of the gold Don John,
Who will embrace her before summer comes.

It may be, however, that what I wish to convey will be still better illustrated by a quotation from that enchanting poem entitled 'Cy Est Pourtraicte, Madame Ste Ursule, et Les Unze Mille Vierges,' in which God himself is portrayed as being subject to the most unexpected emotion in realizing, with delicious perverse satisfaction, that the young girl's sacrifice of 'radishes and flowers' in no way interests him.

The good Lord in His garden sought
New leaf and shadowy tinct,
And they were all His thought.
He heard her low accord,
Half prayer and half ditty,
And He felt a subtle quiver,
That was not heavenly love,
Or pity.

Or does one approach more closely to a clear understanding of Wallace Stevens' hermetic art and finicky preoccupations in contemplating the glazed halls and nocturnal palaces that his eclectic fantasy has set dangling for us in mid-space? There is something terrible about these suspended edifices. They are made of the same stuff, of the same unreal reality, obscure and yet objective, that might disturb the painted dreams of a praying mantis asleep in all its scaly emerald beauty on a linen-laid tropical table.

Then from their poverty they rose,
From dry catarrhs, and to guitars
They flitted
Through the palace walls.

They flung monotony behind,
Turned from their want, and, nonchalant,
They crowded
The nocturnal halls....

> How explicit the coiffures became,
> The diamond point, the sapphire point,
> The sequins
> Of the civil fans!

The construction of such dagobas is no easy matter.

> How shall we hew the sun,
> Split it and make blocks,
> To build a ruddy palace?
> How carve the violet moon
> To set in nicks?
> Let us fix portals, east and west,
> Abhorring green-blue north and blue-green south.

And none knows better than the poet himself that it is no wise thing to let one's glance wander from these charmed interiors.

> Out of the window
> I saw how the planets gathered
> Like the leaves themselves
> turning in the wind.
> I saw how the night came,
> Came striding like the color of the heavy hemlocks.
> I felt afraid.
> And I remembered the cry of the peacocks.

Surely this 'Socrates of snails, musician of pears ... lutanist of fleas' can make us aware of the ghastly lot of our kind with a most exquisite and convincing dexterity.

> If her horny feet protrude, they come
> To show how cold she is and dumb.

Clearly enough we are made to feel the ultimate fate of that company who, 'gaudy as tulips,' mount the stairways of those 'wickless halls.' The worms speak at Heaven's gate:

> Out of the tomb, we bring Badroulbadour,
> Within our bellies, we her chariot.
> Here is an eye. And here are, one by one,
> The lashes of that eye and its white lid.

But possibly the most perfect example of Mr. Stevens' genius is to be found in the poem called 'The Cortège of Rosenbloom' (*sic*). It defies completely all rational explanations, and yet at the same time tingles with vague imaginative evocations. What strange subterfugitive symphonies of infinitesimal tomtoms titillate the listener's ears as the cadaver of the wry, wizened one 'of the color of horn' is carried to his burial place up in the sky! What sly bemused tambourine cacophony beats upon the eardrum with the reiterated 'tread, tread' of the mourners.

> It is turbans they wear
> And books of fur.

One of Mr. Stevens' most impertinent and precocious productions is entitled 'Thirteen Ways of Looking at a Blackbird.' The sixth of the thirteen ways is described as follows:

> Icicles filled the long window
> With barbaric glass.
> The shadow of the blackbird
> Crossed it, to and fro.
> The mood
> Traced in the shadow
> An indecipherable cause,

the eleventh way after this manner:

> He rode over Connecticut
> In a glass coach.
> Once, a fear pierced him,
> In that he mistook
> The shadow of his equipage
> For blackbirds.

May we not be perhaps permitted to regard Mr. Stevens' own poetry as the thirteenth way of looking upon life – the thirteenth ways of Mr. Wallace Stevens, this 'tiptoe cozener':

> This connoisseur of elemental Fate
> Aware of exquisite thought.

18. Louis Untermeyer, on 'a reticence which results in determined obscurity', *Yale Review*

Vol. 14, no. 1, October 1924, 159–60

Untermeyer (1885–1977), a man of letters, is best remembered as an anthologist; he was at one time an influential arbiter of taste in American poetry, from *The New Era in American Poetry* (1919) to the revised shorter edition of *Modern American and British Poetry* (1955). *The Letters of Robert Frost to Louis Untermeyer* was published in 1963.

'Five American Poets', from which this review of Stevens is taken, also includes consideration of books by Robert Frost, Louise Bogan, Donald Davidson and Edna St Vincent Millay.

...The really reticent poet of this quintet is Wallace Stevens. His is a reticence which results in determined obscurity, an obscurity of intention as well as an uncertainty of communication. There are, in fact, many pages in *Harmonium* which lead one to doubt whether its author even cares to communicate in a tongue familiar to the reader; he is preoccupied with language as color or contrasting sound-values, scarcely as a medium for registering degrees of emotion. Moreover, what Stevens spreads before us is less like a canvas and more like a color-palette. The book abounds in arrangements like:

> Pierce, too, with buttresses of coral air
> And purple timbers,
> Various argentines,
> Embossings of the sky.

Or, more brilliantly:

> In Yucatan, the Maya sonneteers,
> In spite of hawk and falcon, green toucan
> And jay, still to the night-bird made their plea,
> As if raspberry tanagers in palms,
> High up in orange air, were barbarous.

Nor are these exotically splashed lines without a certain sonority. Although Stevens displays an almost childish love of alliteration and assonance (one can only smile indulgently at 'Chieftan Iffucan of Azcan in caftan' or 'Gloomy grammarians in golden gowns') he strikes out splendid phrases. That autobiographical confession of withdrawal ('The Comedian as the Letter C') is alert with such witty precisions as 'Crispin, the lutanist of fleas,' 'this auditor of insects,' 'the florist asking aid from cabbages... the blind man as astronomer.' Both 'Sunday Morning' and 'Peter Quince at the Clavier' attain a verbal elegance that far surpasses Stevens's more habitual dexterities. But for the most part, this conscious aesthete 'at war with reality' achieves little beyond an amusing preciosity; he luxuriates in an ingeniously distorted world. Even his titles – which deliberately add to the reader's confusion by having little or no connection with most of the poems – are typical: 'The Emperor of Ice Cream,' 'The Paltry Nude Starts on a Spring Voyage,' 'Frogs Eat Butterflies. Snakes Eat Frogs. Hogs Eat Snakes. Men Eat Hogs.' For all its word-painting, there is little of the human voice in these glittering lines, and so, lacking the spell of any emotion, *Harmonium* loses both itself and its audience. It has much for the eye, something for the ear, but nothing for that central hunger which is at the heart of all the senses.

19. Paul Rosenfeld, on 'Another Pierrot', from *Men Seen – Twenty-Four Modern Authors*

1925, 151–62

Rosenfeld (1890–1946) was a literary, art and music critic, whose best-known critical work, *Port of New York* (1924), was reissued by the University of Illinois Press (1961) with an introduction by Sherman Paul.

Men Seen was published in New York by the Dial Press in 1925. Rosenfeld also wrote a novel, *The Boy in the Sun* (1928).

The playing of a Chinese orchestra. On a gong a bonze creates a copper din. The most amazing cacophony amid dissolving labials and silkiest sibilants. Quirks, booms, whistles, quavers. Lord, what instruments has he there? Small muffled drums? Plucked wires? The falsetto of an ecstatic eunuch? Upon deliberate examination it appears Stevens' matter is the perfectly grammatical arrangement of an English vocabulary not too abstract, Elizabethan, legal, with accidentals of alien terms and purely imitative sounds. But so novel and fantastic is the tintinnabulation of unusual words, and words unusually rhymed and arranged, that you nearly overlook the significations, and heard outlandish sharp and melting musics. While the motley collection prances past, a horn winds its golden cantilene; funeral tam-tams pulse; a violin modulates sharply through quarter-tones and metal particles chunk and chink. Irregular and occasional interior rhymes furnish curious accords. And mixed with the instrumental tones, the fowl persuasion utters its proper squawky staccato: clucking of strutting bantams –

Chieftain Iffucan of Azcan in caftan
Of tan with henna hackles, halt!

parleyings of cockatoos in tropic woods –

He is not paradise of parakeets
Of his gold ether, gold alguazil.

Together with new auditory sensations, the poems of
Wallace Stevens release new intensities of visual ones. Music
remains the prime element of this diverting art; with Alfred
Kreymborg the author represents the musical imagist;
nevertheless he lets us perceive sea water

dissolved in shifting diaphanes
Of blue and green,

as well as hear it swish alongside the boat; and brings with
the whisper of the surf upon Florida beaches the nuances of
balmy summer twilights. And the visual imagery alternates
extremely refined with biting forceful impressions no less
suavely and deliciously than does the auditory. Stevens is
precise among the shyest, most elusive of movements and
shadings. He sees distinctly by way of delicacy the undulations of the pigeon sinking downward, the darkening of a
calm among water-lights, the variations of the deep-blue
tones in dusky landscapes. Quite as regularly as the colors
themselves, it is their shades of difference that are registered
by him:

green sides
And gold sides of green sides;

raspberry tanagers in palms
High up in orange air;

sea-shades and sky-shades
Like umbrellas in Java;

Yet this fastidious, aristocratic nature possesses a blunt
power of utterance, a concentrated violence, that is almost
naturalistic. Stevens recognizes the cruel, the combative
principles of life as well as the soft and yielding; sees hanging
by the side of the 'golden gourds' he loves to contemplate,
some 'warty squashes, streaked and rayed'; knows that

73

together with purple tufts and scarlet crowns the tropics hold 'the green vine angering for life.' We discover him momentarily piling gristling images, the fine roughnesses of color and acrid turns of language upon each other, hacking with lines of poetry and banging harsh rhyme upon rhyme. 'Last Looks at the Lilacs' and 'Floral Decorations for Bananas,' for all their levity of manner, approach the pitch of crude and ferocious language.

But sensation alone is liberated to new intensities by Stevens' forms. Emotion, on the contrary, is curiously constrained by them within a small range of experience and small volumes of expression. The title *Harmonium*, given by the author to his unique collection, makes to declare this littleness the effect entirely of deliberate simplification, and the conscious accommodation of matter to the range of an intimate instrument. But *Harmonium* seems to us something of a misnomer. Stevens appears to us not so much with the aspect of the austere artist as with that of the artist mysteriously, disconcertingly faithful to the technique of an instrument long transcended by the requirements of his nature and incapable of drawing out of himself in all their power his latent emotions. He resembles one born, say, for the grand piano who, while lovingly touching the keys as only the born pianist can, nevertheless persists in using certain processes appropriate to the reed organ, and consequently produces a strange and hybrid music, half Stravinsky and half hymn tune. That chamber orchestra of his, with its range of novel and delightful sounds – he has a genuine feeling for it. He loves its odd and piercing timbres, and toys bewitchingly with them. And still, we get no indication of its real limits. We are never given to know quite the fullness of its dynamics; it is too exclusively engaged in *chinoiseries*. Stevens' rhythms are chiefly secondary rhythms. Scarcely ever is his attack a direct and simple one. Generally, it is oblique, patronizing, and twisted with self-intended mockery. The measure is sometimes languid, sometimes mincing, almost invariably buffoon-like. It trips, pirouettes, executes an hundred little foppish turns and graces. It rocks complacently like a preening waterfowl upon its perch; waltzes in grotesque fury; keens like a comic rabbi; begins a movement and lets it end in air. Besides, the humor is consistently personal in reference. The poet is perceived leaning in evident boredom against the corner of a mantelpiece, or adjusting his monocle with a look of martyrdom.

Another Pierrot. The white clown will not from the pages (*sic*). For as defined by Laforgue and his following he stands the spiritual type for all correct young men in mourning, like Wallace Stevens, for an 'I-the-Magnificent.' You recalled it was too evident Destiny intended that Lord Pierrot play a princely tragic role. She gave him noble melancholy, contempt for the vulgar, proud port and gesture; poured into his mold the very stuff of Hamlets. Unfortunately, Pierrot glanced down along his body; and as he did so, it seemed to him that he was clad in loose flopping ridiculous raiment. And the sentiment of the preposterousness of his person follows the white clown more faithfully than a shadow, and lays fingers of ice on every living moment. Uncomfortably self-aware, the pitiable gentleman can never quite spend himself in living, and remains emotionally naïve, O Horrors! as a romantic poet. To be sure, little in his mask betrays him. Pierrot is sophisticated, worldly lettered, read in philosophical authors Greek and Germanic. He is excessively correct, partly from natural elegance and partly in protest against romantic dishevelment; and functions suavely as reader to an empress, teller of a London bank, or lawyer in Hartford, Connecticut. Nevertheless, his unprojected energies and nobilities and grandiosities are perpetually assuming shapes of self-pity, yearning for enveloping love, and woman-worship; and although Pierrot is entirely too aware to mistake them for cosmic pains or enchantments of the heart, his sentimentalities threaten shamelessly to overcome him, and add immeasurably to his embarrassment. Hence his ideal self, the cruelly murdered 'I-the-Magnificent,' incapable of revealing itself in all its princeliness, gains satisfaction in the shape of revenge. It takes the exaltations of the subject emotional self, and very archly turns them into parody. Of melancholy soliloquy and philosophical dudgeon it makes a silvery music signifying nothing. Amid the tinkling ice of exquisite perceptions it lightly ridicules the objects of sentimental effusion, diverts the emotional current toward slightly grotesque ones, or comes

as belle design
Of foppish line;

thus simultaneously ceding to the pressure of inferior emotion and attesting amid extravagant waltzes and verbal fireworks its own ineffable superiorities.

Nor is Wallace Stevens the sole distinguished American poet of distinct Laforguian cut. Lord Pierrot is called T. S. Eliot, too, and sports other and smaller names as well. The series is a perfectly natural one. American life has hitherto tended to excite the painful tension between the two portions of the self, so determining a factor in the Laforguian expression; the curiously Yankee flavor of the parodistic manner of the 'Watteau of the café-concerts,' and of his ironic usage of journalistic and demotic idiom, has been remarked by not a few critics. Certainly, each of the new western additions to the company, poorer in general virtuosity than their great archetype although they are, have enriched the tradition with a perfectly individual color, and enlarged its scope. Stevens, for example, is full of a jazzy American sensuousness; and the polyglot American towns have made him peculiarly sensitive to the unusual and remote sounds of the English language. Nevertheless, the expression which he brings amid flowers, frost and 'good fat guzzly fruit,' remains to a degree characteristic of the school. His music is a music signaled as vain, an exaltation, not so much 'without sound' as without object, a bland, curiously philosophical movement of the soul without signification. What he has to say appears too useless for him to say it out. The words, deliciously Elizabethan and comically abstract, remain 'musical' merely, morsels rolled upon an epicure's palate. And world-weariness becomes an 'Invective Against Swans,' woman-worship a burlesque hymn to 'Heavenly Vincentine,' and exaltation takes idly to tracing the processional of clouds across the sky. The senses dance, but they achieve only a sort of titillation, a vague naughtiness; intelligence sits coldly in the center of the ring and directs their gyrations.

The disillusionments troop across: the story of the wildcat which always bars the center of the road and falls asleep only in death; Florida nights which yield nothing more than a caress of fingertips; love turned stale at forty; vain dreams erected 'upon the basis of the common drudge.' The lengthy narrative poem 'The Comedian as the Letter C' contains the history of a poetic career, the feeling of the war, the hope of a national expression, the tragedy of environment; but it secretes them behind a shimmer of language and archness piled upon archness; and takes for its protagonist – Crispin.

In spite of its perfect things, 'Nuances of a Theme by Williams' and the others, *Harmonium* does not, therefore, entirely represent the day. Little reveals the movement which has occurred in the American mind of late more simply than the fact that we should wilingly feel its qualities of evasiveness, of archness and comic pudicity as slightly timed. The characteristic note of 1890 was not outworn for us ten years ago; and yet, today, even though nothing in the basic character of life appears transformed, and Plymouth Rock in the bosom of all has not offered to melt, or freemen's arms grown lighter, we have transcended it. We are somewhat less self-aware; are irritated by what tends to recall us to the old bad consciousness. And it is precisely embarrassment, shyness, and holy shame which do the wicked work; we find the attitude of the Venus de' Medici suggestive. An impulse in us bids authors be more simple and direct, and give completely what they feel; above all to advance from behind the curtain of language. Tragical disabilities are the very ordinary stuff of life, and what today requires most is impersonality, perspective, objectivity. No need subtracting from James Joyce. – And yet, *Harmonium* remains one of the jewel boxes of contemporary verse. If certain of its elements appear a trifle outworn, others very definitely thrust the art of poetry toward unknown boundaries. As a musician, Stevens is revealed an almost impeccable craftsman. Not only is his idiom new and delicious; his surface is almost invariably complete. Experimental rhymes have an inevitability under his hands, and his rhythms do no break. He produces his material as conceived by him with exquisite tact, giving the just amount, and not re-covering traversed ground. The terminations and cadences of his pieces are usually quite unpredictable; only very rarely, as in 'Six Significant Landscapes,' do the final surprising extensions of the idea grow mechanical. We have a number of artists working in the medium of poetry; Pound, Eliot and others have produced work both delicate and hard. Yet the arrival of a volume of verse on each of its one hundred and twenty-odd pages very patently the pretty booklet *arida modo pumice expolitum* is an event not hitherto seen by our generation. And for the moment Wallace Stevens remains eminently the artist in his field.

20. Gorham B. Munson, 'The Dandyism of Wallace Stevens', *Dial*

Vol. LXXIX, November 1925, 413–7

Munson (1896–1969), a social and literary critic, taught for many years at the New School for Social Research in New York. In the 1920s he edited first the periodical *Secession* and then *Psychology*. From 1933 to 1936 he edited *New Democracy* and was an exponent of Social Credit theories. His books include studies of Robert Frost and Waldo Frank.

This essay was later included in Munson's influential *Destinations: A Canvass of American Literature Since 1900* (1928).

The impeccability of the dandy resolves itself into two elements: correctness and elegance. Both elements transcend merely good taste, for correctness implies a knowledge of the rules governing the modes of expression, feeling, thinking, conduct; and elegance is, of course, good taste that has been polished.

Until the advent of Wallace Stevens, American literature has lacked a dandy. Of swaggering macaronis there have been aplenty, but the grace and ceremony, the appropriate nimbleness of the dandy, have been lacking. Certainly, as a craftsman, he has absorbed the teachings of the academy; at any rate he can trust himself to the musical risks of poetry – making use of alliteration, assonance, free rhymes, irregular stanzaic forms, and *vers libre* – and can be counted on to overcome them. The effective use of exclamation in poetry is exceedingly difficult, because the accent must be carefully prepared for and must coincide with a real rise in the material. He has many times run the risk of overexclamation, always winning, and perhaps most handsomely in 'Bantams in Pine-Woods':

[Quotes 'Bantams in Pine-Woods', *CP*, p. 75.]

Elegance he attains in his fastidious vocabulary – in the surprising aplomb and blandness of his images. He will say 'harmonium' instead of 'small organ,' 'lacustrine' instead of 'lakeside,' 'sequin' instead of 'spangle'; he will speak of 'hibiscus,' 'panache,' 'fabliau,' and 'poor buffo.' The whole tendency of his vocabulary is, in fact, toward the lightness and coolness and transparency of French. As for his images, they are frequently surprising in themselves, yet they always produce the effect of naturalness – an effect which is cool, bland, transparent, natural, and gracefully mobile.

In the dandy of letters, impeccability is primarily achieved by adding elegance to correctness. Yet life is disturbing and horrifying as well as interesting and delightful: one is inevitably tossed by the 'torments of confusion'; and the dandy, if he would maintain his urbane demeanor, must adopt protective measures. The safeguards employed by Mr. Stevens against 'the torments of confusion' are three: wit, speculation, and reticence. As an antidote to love-sick quandary, to the fear of decrepitude, to the disturbing vastness of the ocean, there is wit – that self-mockery which we have in 'Le Monocle de Mon Oncle,' and 'The Comedian as the Letter C.' Doubt of reality must be admitted as a purely speculative doubt, 'as a calm darkens among water-lights.' Let speculative doubt play gently across the surface of a steadfast materialism. And finally, let us be reticent, for reticence is becoming in its implication that one is aware of enigmatic miseries, and yet too proud to wear one's heart upon one's sleeve.

Mr. Stevens possesses an imagination that is ordered. 'Imagination,' he says, 'is the will of things.' It is 'the magnificent cause of being . . . the one reality in this imagined world.' By its aid, at least, one may invent a literary cosmos, moving according to calculations, subject to its own laws and hierarchies, consistent with itself, a minute but sustained harmony floating above the chaos of life. It is whole and understandable and therefore a refuge in a life that is fragmentary and perplexing. It, in being form, is a polite answer to the hugeness which we cannot form.

Upon what, may we ask, is this imaginative order of Wallace Stevens based? It is not humanism, for the humanist searches for unifying standards of general human experience. Needless to say, it is not religion, for the religious man strives for a knowledge of the absolute. It is discipline – the discipline of one who is a connoisseur of the senses and the emotions. Mr. Stevens' imagination comes to rest on them; it is at their service, it veils them in splendor. The integration achieved is one of feeling; in the final analysis, it is a temperate romanticism.

Wallace Stevens has a quality, however, which is rarely associated with romanticism, a quality that his illustrious predecessor, Baudelaire, lacked to complete his dandyism. Baudelaire's dandyism might be called a metallic shell secreted by a restless man against a despised shifting social order. It cannot be called a placid dandyism, whereas tranquillity enfolds Mr. Stevens. This same lack of tranquillity impairs the dandyism of T. S. Eliot in those respects in which he is a dandy – turning his promenade through the alleged barrenness of modern life into bitter melancholy. Mr. Stevens, however, appears to sit comfortably in the age, to enjoy a sense of security, to be conscious of no need of fighting the times. The world is a gay and bright phenomenon, and he gives the impression of feasting on it without misgiving. Here in 'Gubbinal' is his answer to those who repine because the world is blasted and its people are miserable:

> That strange flower, the sun,
> Is just what you say.
> Have it your way.
>
> The world is ugly,
> And the people are sad.
>
> That tuft of jungle feathers,
> That animal eye,
> Is just what you say.
>
> That savage of fire,
> That seed,
> Have it your way.
>
> The world is ugly,
> And the people are sad.

Because of this tranquillity, this well-fed and well-booted dandyism of contentment, Mr. Stevens has been called Chinese. Undeniably, he has been influenced by Chinese verse, as he has been by French verse, but one must not force the comparison. For Chinese poetry as a whole rests upon great humanistic and religious traditions: its quiet strength and peace are often simply by-products of a profound understanding; its epicureanism is less an end, more a function, than the tranquillity – may I say – the decidedly American tranquillity of Wallace Stevens.

The American nation drives passionately toward comfort. The aim of the frenzied practical life in which it engages is to attain material ease, and the symbols of its paradise are significant. They are wide, accurately barbered lawns, white yachts with bright awnings, the silvered motorcar, the small regiment of obsequious servants. Naturally, in paradise one would not wish to be annoyed by a suspicion that all was a brilliant fake, a magnificent evanescent dream, but rather, to refine upon one's luxurious means of existence. This is where in America the artistic intelligence may enter and play, elaborating, coloring, bedecking, adding splendor to the circumstances of one's comfort. Is there not fundamentally a kinship between the sensory discriminations and comfortable tranquillity of Wallace Stevens' poetry and the America that owns baronial estates?

Growing more reckless, we might say that if Dr. Jung is correct in asserting that in American psychology there is a unique alliance of wildness and restraint, then Wallace Stevens would seem in another respect to be at one with his country. I do not discover in him the ferocity that some critics have remarked upon, but there is at least a flair for bright savagery, for 'that tuft of jungle feathers, that animal eye, that savage of fire.' In the case of certain romanticists, such symbols would betray insatiable longing, the desire for a nature that never existed. In his case, they are purely spectacular. The Old World Romantic, restless amid the stratifications of his culture, yearns for the untamed: the New World Romantic assumes the easy posture of an audience.

American readers may well rejoice in this artist who is so gifted in depicting sea-surfaces full of clouds. No American poet excels him in the sensory delights that a spick-and-span craft can stimulate: none is more skillful in arranging his music, his figures, and his design. None else, monocled and gloved, can cut so faultless a figure standing in his box at the circus of life.

There are masters of art and art-masters. Seldom has an artist been more canny and more definite in distinguishing between major and minor than Wallace Stevens. No one has more carefully observed to the letter the restrictions of the art-master, or more perfectly exemplified to us the virtue of impeccable form.

21. Allen Tate, on Stevens' underlying Puritanism, from 'American Poetry Since 1920', *Bookman*

Vol. LXVIII, January 1929, 506–7

In 'American Poetry Since 1920', Allen Tate emphasizes what he perceived as the eclecticism and provincialism (a term used approvingly) of American poetry. 'A certain quality of excellence, it must be said, is the sole connection between a great number of very different poets.' This is the context in which he links Stevens with Marianne Moore.

... Marianne Moore and Wallace Stevens, different as they are from each other, have in common certain elements of style: precision of statement, decorative imagery, and a sense of the allusive value of nonsense phrases. The intention of Miss Moore's *Observations* (1924) is slight, but its technical perfection has not been surpassed by a contemporary writer. She is a Victorian in whom Victorian convictions are lacking, but in whom the habits of feeling which correspond to those convictions remain; she is, in fact, deficient in compulsions of any sort – that is to say, in 'ideas'; and her verse proceeds from a perceptive mechanism which seems to run on its own momentum. Stevens is quite differently motivated. *Harmonium* (1922) contains an impulse more serious than Miss Moore's. His dandyism, which has been ably described by Mr. Gorham B. Munson, is the perfect surface beneath which plays an intense Puritanism. He is undoubtedly the most finished poet of the age, and he is the only American poet who has been intelligently affected by the Parnassians and the Symbolists....

22. Alfred Kreymborg, on Stevens as one of the 'Originals and Eccentrics', from *Our Singing Strength*

1929, 500–4

Besides editing the *Globe* and *Others,* Kreymborg (1883–1966) was a member of the Grantwood, N.J., arts colony in which Stevens also participated. Kreymborg also published *Troubadour: An Autobiography* (1925).

... If he has written poetry for its own sake, it is not because, like Bodenheim, he hates life and embraces an escapist philosophy. No one enjoys life more and makes a richer festival of his pleasure. Unlike the eccentric Max and like Marianne Moore, the Hartford lawyer is contemptuous of wordly popularity. For a number of years, his poems appeared in *Rogue, Poetry, Others, The Little Review,* etc., but not until 1923 did his volume, *Harmonium,* emerge. For years his friends had begged him to publish a book, and Stevens, bored with being the sole poet who had refused to publish a book, permitted Carl Van Vechten to cajole Alfred Knopf into printing *Harmonium.* Comparatively few copies were sold; the rest were remaindered. The volume contains the whole of Stevens' life-work with the exception of the exquisite plays: 'Three Travellers Watch a Sunrise' and 'Carlos Among the Candles.' Formerly, it was impossible to get him to publish a book; now it is impossible to get him to publish a poem. Write him, wire him or visit him, one always receives the same answer: he has written nothing for years. One reverts to the reading of duller poets and waits in vain for the fist of the Connecticut giant to scratch off another perfect etching. But even the perfect letters, as minute and undecipherable as those of Robinson, have ceased coming to town. Continued self-deprecation has finally removed the man from the scene in which he had always refused to participate. He wrote purely for the pleasure of writing, as he has lived for the pleasure of living....

Stevens is more than a dandy, a designer, an esthete. Each of these persons is a phase of a central person, each a mask in a masquerade at the heart of which philosophy and tragi-comedy view the world with serenity. If the earth is a tawdry sphere, America a tawdry land, the relation of human to human the most tawdry of all, Stevens refuses to despair. Nor does he satirize the situation. He may seem superior to his surroundings; one may suspect him even of snobbery. But he is neither a misanthrope nor a snob, but one of the wisest and subtlest of natives: an American reared on French Symbolism, on the philosophic poetry of the aristocratic Jules Laforgue. Not to mention an older race: the aristocratic Elizabethans. Again we are in the presence of an enigma. Here is a cultivated man in the midst of the American mob, shrugging his shoulders at Mammon and indifferent to fame; a man of affairs lolling in railroad coaches en route to Florida, eating and drinking like a sybarite – and jotting down a note or two. But what notes these are. They are among the perfect things in any literature: perfect in sensation, color and sound, versification, whether in old or new forms; perfect in language, the relation of phrase to phrase, vowel to vowel, consonant to consonant. Emotion has achieved its thought, thought its system, system its poetry: a poetry now clear, now vague, as clear and vague as life. Behind the veils, there is always a meaning, though the poet employs supersubtlety for veiling the meaning as well. No one hates the obvious more. No one knows better than he that all these things have been felt and thought and known before. One can only improvise on material used over and over again, and improvise for oneself alone. Here is no question of pleasing anybody. Here is no question of pleasing even the ego....

To the yearning national question, where is our next major poet to come from, I always feel like responding: Out of Wallace Stevens, if Stevens would let him come. But the exasperating fellow sticks to his laws and lawyers. It is not that the banality of existence is too much for him. He has done magic things with banalities, tuned them to huge enjoyments. If this man wrote a poem about Main Street, that universal locale, without losing its identity, would become transformed into the only Nirvana worth sighing for. It is what he does to things that makes them memorable. Simply by being himself, and viewing things through his temperament, gorgeous poems evolve. He may be fantastic and grotesque on the surface, a lover of nonsense and alliterative games; but a deep imagination directs his observation. And what an ear he has for orchestral language. If one cannot understand his poems, there is always the orchestration, as in 'Sunday Morning,' 'The Comedian as the Letter C,' 'To The One of Fictive Music,' and many others. 'Sunday Morning,' though obscure, is a great poem....

I wish there were space to quote a number of the shorter poems, each so different in mood and language: the poem in which 'rationalists, wearing square hats ... in square rooms' are advised to wear sombreros; the exquisite Chinese bits about the blackbird; the haunting lyrics on death, on nonentity. I wish there were room to quote the whole of 'Peter Quince' (the only fairly well-known poem), with its subtle change of movements; or the delicious doggerel concerning Vincentine; or the metaphysical poems written by an ironist aware of the nonsense inherent in any one system of thought. Or the 'Nomad Exquisite,' the only frank self-portrait; or the many downright comedies; or the poem on Fictive Music – another poem in the grand manner. The wish is genuinely poignant in view of the fact that *Harmonium* is out of print and inaccessible to the average reader. Nor will the author make the slightest effort to revive and reprint it....

HARMONIUM

New York, 1931

Second edition, with additional poems, published by Knopf in a run of 1,500 copies.

---

23. Conrad Aiken, on Stevens as humorist, from a letter to R.P. Blackmur

14 February 1931, *Selected Letters of Conrad Aiken*, 170

Aiken's letters, selected and edited by Joseph Killorin, were published by Yale University Press in 1978.

This letter was written while Blackmur was preparing for his authoritative early overview of Stevens, 'Examples of Wallace Stevens' (see No. 28).

... As for Stevens – I don't know what to suggest. You can link him up, of course, with the Rimbaud-symbolist business – even with Valéry, and 'pure' poetry – in the latter connection I once, in a drunken moment, called him the playboy of the western *word*, which again suggests a corner to be discussed: the mere delight in verbal legerdemain etc. for its own sake. But again, and I think this is important, and I haven't ever seen it suggested in any discussion of Stevens, he's perhaps the most remarkable *humorist* in poetry: I mean, he carries humor farther into terms of poetry than has perhaps ever been done. This is something to shout about. Even his titles are like those changeable signs one used to see: they are funny and/or beautiful. Then, finally, there is of course the extremely keen critical awareness knocking about everywhere under all this brilliant and delicious meringue of surface. Crispin is fuller of things than *The Waste Land*, and then some! Hamlet married and put to bed and the father of daughters and a good indigenous tiller of soils and all with a laconic bright precarious la-la for the lost world. (This among other things?) Ideas all over the place: but presented with such fastidious and indifferent nonchalance, such absurd inflations or deflations, with rings in their noses and cockatoos on their wrists. An aesthetic, and a pretty complete one, presented polychromatically piecemeal: now in terms of music now in colour. And of course, often enough if not too often the colour-buffoonery for its own sake, with (at least as far as I can see) no hidden complexities of moral anagram. – But I'm rambling, I'm rambling. All I can add to this I've said to you before – that I think him as sure of a permanent place of importance as Eliot, if not surer. Eliot will go *down*, somewhat, (keeping however a marked historical importance, in addition to his pure merit) and Stevens will, I feel sure, come up. – Incidentally, you ought to look up his three or four verse or prose-verse plays, in *Poetry*, etc., if you don't already know them. 'Carlos Among the Candles', 'Three Travellers at Sunrise', and one or two more....

24. Percy Hutchison, 'Pure Poetry and Mr. Wallace Stevens', *New York Times Book Review*

9 August 1931, 4

More than one critic, and not a few poets, have toyed with the idea of what has been termed 'pure poetry,' which is to say, a poetry which should depend for its effectiveness on its rhythms and the tonal values of the words employed with as complete a dissociation from ideational content as may be humanly possible. Those who have argued for such 'pure poetry' have frequently, if not always, been obsessed with some hazy notion of an analogy between music and poetry. As a shining example of this school take Sidney Lanier, who was a skilled musician as well as a notable poet. Lanier advanced the theory that every vowel has its color value. This was not an association of ideas; the letter 'e' was not red because, it is in the word red, or green because it is in the word green, but the hearer, experiencing the word should, on Lanier's theory, experience, simultaneously with the sound, a distinct sensation of color. In the second decade of this century – the movement began in the first decade – numerous poetic schools drove theory hard. Perhaps none strove especially to carry out Lanier's color hypothesis, but there were the Imagists, and there was Vorticism and Cubism, and many more 'isms' besides. For the most part, these schools have died the death which could have been prophesied for them. Poetry is founded in ideas; to be effective and lasting, poetry must be based on life, it must touch and vitalize emotion. For proof, one has but to turn to the poetry that has endured. In poetry, doctrinaire composition has no permanent place.

Hence, unpleasant as it is to record such a conclusion, the very remarkable work of Wallace Stevens cannot endure. The verses which go to make up the volume *Harmonium* are as close to 'pure poetry' as one could expect to come. And so far as rhythms and vowels and consonants may be substituted for musical notes, the volume is an achievement. But the achievement is not poetry, it is a tour de force, a 'stunt' in the fantastic and the bizarre. From one end of the book to the other there is not an idea that can vitally affect the mind, there is not a word that can arouse emotion. The volume is a glittering edifice of icicles. Brilliant as the moon, the book is equally dead. Only when Stevens goes over to the Chinese does he score, and then not completely, for with all the virtuosity that his verse displays he fails quite to attain the lacqueur [*sic*] finish of his Oriental masters. The following,

'Hibiscus on the Sleeping Shores,' is the piece that comes nearest to the Chinese, and this is marred by the intrusion in the last line of the critical adjective 'stupid.'

[Quotes *CP*, p. 22.]

For the full tonal and rhythmic effect of this it must be read aloud, chanted, as Tennyson and Swinburne chanted their verses. Then, within its limits, its very narrow limits, 'Hibiscus' will be found to be a musical attainment not before guessed at. But it is not poetry in the larger meaning of the term. And it is not actually music that one has here, but an imitation of music. And if there is a mood conveyed, the mood could have been equally as well conveyed by other lines equally languid of rhythm. No doubt the theorists in poetry have enriched their craft, but at a disservice to themselves. Wallace Stevens is a martyr to a lost cause.

25. Eda Lou Walton, 'Beyond the Wasteland', *Nation*

Vol. CXXXII, 9 September 1931, 263–4

Walton (1896–1962), literary critic, anthologist, poet and friend of Hart Crane, taught at New York University from 1924 to 1960. Her publications include *So Many Daughters* (poems, 1952).

Mr. Eliot merely defined the territory of the Wasteland and of its emotional ennui in a few stark details. Then he escaped from it into scholarship, into religion, leaving other poets to explore. Ivor Winters pushed its boundaries still further into hopelessness by pointing out that the passion of scholarship was in itself sterile, that man crumbled not only within his environment, but within the brain itself. Archibald MacLeish returned in desperation to the desert, naming it, whatever else it might be, the necessary 'New Found Land,' and better than exile from home. But none of these poets faced the problem which was Wallace Stevens's: here was a poet of the senses, a poet desirous of moonlight as any Keats, a poet aware of and sensitive to every subtle sensuous delight – what was he to do in death valley? Stevens's answer to this question is the very extreme of the Wasteland theory. His is the final word.

In the deliberate deflation of the emotions he has exceeded any of these others, for he has chosen to explore every mood, with full realization of its several anti-moods; he has chosen to build up the vision, only to prick it. He points out that the disassociation of the emotions lies not between one point in time or space and another point in time or space, but within the very inception of the emotion itself. No feeling is more than acknowledged before it splays out into a dozen different and antithetical feelings. No intensity mounts to its climax without the insidious question at its center.

Stevens will allow himself no protection: he will not cry out in bitterness, he will not deny one detail of multiform beauty, he will not play the 'flat historic scale of memory,' nor take momentary delight in 'doleful heroics.' He knows that love is a book too mad to read 'before one merely reads to pass the time' and yet he reads it aloud. All is fantasy: the book of moonlight never has been written, and the protagonist, Crispin, is merely a fagot in the lunar fire whose heat comes only from the fables he, himself, scrawls. Stevens persists in being a poet of moonlight who in the end pricks the bubble of the moon itself.

For all these reasons, Wallace Stevens has been called a 'Dandy.' The word is unfortunate in its implications of superficiality, posturing, and super-refinement. Stevens's highly mannered, technically superb verse is so written because it best expresses his particular creative imagination: to this mind no simple statement is possible, every word has innumerable associations. This poet is sincere in being insincere, since to be sincere would for him be ridiculous. His sincerity lies in his attitude. Moreover if Stevens is over-refined, it is only because we still measure refinement by the normal bluntness preserving the ordinary man for his mechanical world – not by the truer instrument of the sensitive imagination. Refinement is all we have today of exuberance and vitality. It is no mere pose when for Stevens God is where,

> Above the forest of the parakeets,
> A Parakeet of parakeets prevails
> A pip of life amid a mort of tails,

no more pose that woman worship, is for this poet merely an emanation from sensuous delight in 'heavenly Vincentine.'

Stevens having been driven by the afflatus of other poets into wandering away from such counterfeit, tells us that poetry is the 'supreme fiction,' that

> He gripped more closely the essential prose
> As being, in a world so falsified,
> The one integrity for him, the one
> Discovery still possible to make,
> To which all poems were incident, unless
> That prose should wear a poem's guise at last.

This is a new edition of *Harmonium*. It is interesting to note that since 1923 the poet has repudiated only two poems, the 'Silver Plough Boy,' a meaningless pretty imagistic verse, and 'Architecture,' a poem in which the manner exceeded in difficulty the subject. He has included fourteen new poems amplifying the theme of the Crispin poems, grown slightly more autumnal:

> One might in turn become less diffident,
> Out of such mildew plucking mould
> And spouting new orations of the cold.
> One might, One might. But time will not relent.

26. Morton Dauwen Zabel, on Stevens' sincerity and exactitude, from 'The Harmonium of Wallace Stevens', *Poetry*

Vol. 39, no. 3, December 1931, 46–51

Zabel (1901–64) is best known for his anthology of criticism, *Literary Opinion in America* (1951). He contributed an essay to the Stevens number of the *Harvard Advocate* (December 1940).

The passage quoted here is from the concluding paragraph of the essay, as revised for *The Achievement of Wallace Stevens*, edited by Ashley Brown and Robert S. Haller (Philadelphia, 1962).

... The poetic means whereby Mr. Stevens has sublimated this individualism has made his style in every detail the component of his convictions as they emerge from experience. This hairline correspondence is at once the clue to the sensuous logic of his style, and to the realism which saves his imagery from imaginative extravagance, his wit from verbal exercise, and his morality from the illusory intellectual casuistry which has betrayed most of his colleagues. As the most perverse of his conceits holds to its roots in sincerity, so the most circuitous of his deductions refers directly to the actual conflict or moral challenge that initially demanded its unraveling. Mr. Stevens' method – on a different scale of emotional adjustment and sympathies – is almost exactly like Miss Moore's, although he has sought a fundamentally simpler resolution of the disparity between perception and intellectual habit than Miss Moore has in poems like 'A Grave,' 'A Fish,' and 'Marriage.' His book's resources of exactitude in imagery and rhythm, its supple variety of measure, and its creative virtuosity are at length referable to a set of pure principles which make his work a unity as well as a model of severe intention. Imputed derivations from the methods of France, China, and Skeltonic English still leave intact a personality which shares its brilliance with only a few contemporaries. It is a personality whose lucid fitness of phrase and imagery clarifies today – as it did in an earlier more excited decade – the discord and prolixity of literary experience....

27. Raymond Larsson, from 'The Beau as Poet', *Commonweal*

Vol. 15, 6 April 1932, 604

... A very Proust of poets, in such pieces as the more recent 'Sea Surface Full of Clouds,' Stevens is to be discovered examining, arranging, retreating from, comparing, rearranging, retouching, recomparing things – fastidious, elegant, the 'beau with a muff,' finding in the world of things something akin to security, one fancies.

His world is the *beau monde,* his character the dandy's, with a distinct, a personal and yet a typical taste for the exotic. The exoticism of New England (his milieu, one understands, is Connecticut) had more to do with transported teas and crockery than with the Orient, its lights and waters and its trees, or with the jungle and 'the tuft of jungle feathers.' His jungle is a garden. It exists in his imagination sensuously to be perceived: the flower, the leaf, the plumage of its birds. His jungle does not excite in him the primitiveness of Vachel Lindsay, with his drums. Stevens is nothing if he is not civilized, cosmopolitan. His surfaces are polished not for brightness but for sensuousness of effect.

Mr. Stevens is a minor poet. Yet it is not to be inferred that his poems are easily to be dismissed – quite the contrary. Although the present collection is, for the most part, merely a reprinting of an earlier book (only three pieces of which have been eliminated, while fourteen new ones have been added), one is surprised to find how well wear certain of these poems. They have a definite, precise character, a decorative elegance and they will be, one imagines, rather than remote curiosities of the period, one of the distinct values of contemporary poetry, while the bulk of what came of Imagism, one imagines, will have value merely for the scholar, the pedant, the historian.

28. R.P. Blackmur, 'Examples of Wallace Stevens', *Hound and Horn*

Vol. 5, Winter 1932, 223–55

An influential critic and theorist of the New Criticism, Blackmur (1904–65) did much to determine the proper relationship between literary criticism and scholarship. 'Examples of Wallace Stevens' has been widely reprinted, and is included in Blackmur's own volumes *The Double Agent* (1935), *Language as Gesture* (1954) and *Form and Value in Modern Poetry* (1957). It is included here as indispensable to an account of the development of Stevens' reputation.

Blackmur's other books include *The Lion and the Honeycomb* (1955) and *The New Criticism in the United States* (1959).

In recent years Denis Donoghue has edited Blackmur's *Poems* (1977) and *Henry Adams* (1981), the book which was Blackmur's preoccupation for many years.

Blackmur's personality, and his friendship with John Berryman, are interestingly portrayed in Eileen Simpson's *Poets in Their Youth* (New York, 1981).

The most striking if not the most important thing about Mr. Stevens' verse is its vocabulary – the collection of words, many of them uncommon in English poetry, which on a superficial reading seems characteristic of the poems. An air of preciousness bathes the mind of the casual reader when he finds such words as fubbed, girandoles, curlicues, catarrhs, gobbet, diaphanes, clopping, minuscule, pipping, pannicles, carked, ructive, rapey, cantilene, buffo, fiscs, phylactery, princox, and funest. And such phrases as 'thrum with a proud douceur,' or 'A pool of pink, clippered with lilies scudding the bright chromes,' hastily read, merely increase the feeling of preciousness. Hence Mr. Stevens has a bad reputation among those who dislike the finicky, and a high one, unfortunately, among those who value the ornamental sounds of words but who see no purpose in developing sound from sense.

Both classes of reader are wrong. Not a word listed above is used preciously; not one was chosen as an elegant substitute for a plain term; each, in its context, was a word definitely meant. The important thing about Mr. Stevens' vocabulary is not the apparent oddity of certain words, but the uses to which he puts those words with others. It is the way that Mr. Stevens combines kinds of words, unusual in a single context, to reveal the substance he had in mind, which is of real interest to the reader.

Good poets gain their excellence by writing an existing language *as if* it were their own invention; and as a rule success in the effect of originality is best secured by fidelity, in an extreme sense, to the individual words as they appear in the dictionary. If a poet knows precisely what his words represent, what he writes is much more likely to seem new and strange – and even difficult to understand – than if he uses his words ignorantly and at random. That is because when each word has definite character the combinations cannot avoid uniqueness. Even if a text is wholly quotation, the condition of quotation itself qualifies the text and makes it so far unique. Thus a quotation made from Marvell by Eliot has a force slightly different from what it had when Marvell wrote it. Though the combination of words is unique it is read, if the reader knows his words either by usage or dictionary, with a shock like that of recognition. The recognition is not limited, however, to what was already known in the words; there is a perception of something previously unknown, something new which is a result of the combination of the words, something which is literally an access of knowledge. Upon the poet's skill in combining words as much as upon his private feelings, depends the importance or the value of the knowledge.

In some notes on the language of E. E. Cummings I tried to show how that poet, by relying on his private feelings and using words as if their meanings were spontaneous with use, succeeded mainly in turning his words into empty shells. With very likely no better inspiration in the life around him, Mr. Stevens, by combining the insides of those words he found fit to his feelings, has turned his words into knowledge. Both Mr. Stevens and Cummings issue in ambiguity – as any good poet does; but the ambiguity of Cummings is that of the absence of known content, the ambiguity of a phantom which no words could give being; while Mr. Stevens' ambiguity is that of a substance so dense with being, that it resists paraphrase and can be truly perceived only in the form of words in which it was given. It is the difference between poetry which depends on the poet and poetry which depends on itself. Reading Cummings you either guess or supply the substance yourself. Reading Mr. Stevens you have only to know the meanings of the words and to submit to the conditions of the poem. There is a precision in such ambiguity all the more precise because it clings so closely to the stuff of the poem that separated it means nothing.

Take what would seem to be the least common word in the whole of *Harmonium*[a] – funest (page 74, line 6). The word means sad or calamitous or mournful and is derived from a French word meaning fatal, melancholy, baneful, and has to do with death and funerals. It comes ultimately from the Latin *funus* for funeral. Small dictionaries do not stock it. The poem in which it appears is called 'Of the Manner of Addressing Clouds,' which begins as follow:

> Gloomy grammarians in golden gowns,
> Meekly you keep the mortal rendezvous,
> Eliciting the still sustaining pomps
> Of speech which are like music so profound
> They seem an exaltation without sound.
> Funest philosophers and ponderers,
> Their evocations are the speech of clouds.
> So speech of your processionals returns
> In the casual evocations of your tread
> Across the stale, mysterious seasons....

The sentence in which funest occurs is almost a parenthesis. It *seems* the statement of something thought of by the way, suggested by the clouds, which had better be said at once before it is forgotten. In such a casual, disarming way, resembling the way of understatement, Mr. Stevens often introduces the most important elements in his poems. The oddity of the word having led us to look it up we find that, once used, funest is better than any of its synonyms. It is the essence of the funeral in its sadness, not its sadness alone, that makes its the right word: the clouds are going to their death, as not only philosophers but less indoctrinated ponderers know; so what they say, what they evoke, in pondering, has that much in common with the clouds. Suddenly we realize that the effect of funest philosophers is due to the larger context of the lines preceding, and at the same time we become aware that the statement about their evocations is central to the poem and illuminates it. The word pomps, above, means ceremony and comes from a Greek word meaning procession, often, by association, a funeral, as in the phrase funeral pomps. So the pomps of the clouds suggests the funeral in funest.

The whole thing increases in ambiguity the more it is analyzed but if the poem is read over after analysis, it will be seen that *in the poem* the language is perfectly precise. In its own words it is clear, and becomes vague in analysis only because the analysis is not the poem. We use analysis properly in order to discard it and return that much better equipped to the poem.

The use of such a word as funest suggests more abstract considerations, apart from the present instance. The question is whether or not and how much the poet is stretching his words when they are made to carry as much weight as funest carries above. Any use of a word stretches it slighly, because any use selects from among many meanings the right one, and then modifies that in the context. Beyond this necessary stretching, words cannot perhaps be stretched without coming to nullity – as the popular stretching of awful, grand, swell, has more or less nullified the original senses of those words. If Mr. Stevens stretches his words slightly, as a live poet should and must, it is in such a way as to make them seem more precisely themselves than ever. The context is so delicately illuminated, or adumbrated, that the word must be looked up, or at least thought carefully about, before the precision can be seen. This is the precision of the expert pun, and every word, to a degree, carries with it in any given sense the puns of all its senses.

But it may be a rule that only the common words of a language, words with several, even groups of meanings, can be stretched the small amount that is possible. The reader must have room for his research; and the more complex words are usually plays upon common words, and limited in their play. In the instance above the word funest is not so much itself stretched by its association with philosophers as the word philosophers – a common word with many senses – stretches funest. That is, because Mr. Stevens has used the word funest, it cannot easily be detached and used by others. The point is subtle. The meaning so doubles upon itself that it can be understood only in context. It is the context that is stretched by the insertion of the word funest; and it is that stretch, by its ambiguity, that adds to our knowledge.

A use of words almost directly contrary to that just discussed may be seen in a very different sort of poem – 'The Ordinary Women' (page 13). I quote the first stanza to give the tone:

Then from their poverty they rose.
From dry catarrhs, and to guitars
They flitted
Through the palace walls.

Then skipping a stanza, we have this, for atmosphere:

The lacquered loges huddled there
Mumbled zay-zay and a-zay, a-zay.
The moonlight
Fubbed the girandoles.

The loges huddled probably because it was dark or because they didn't like the ordinary women, and mumbled perhaps because of the moonlight, perhaps because of the catarrhs, or even to keep key to the guitars. Moonlight, for Mr. Stevens, is mental, fictive, related to the imagination and meaning of things; naturally it fubbed the girandoles (which is equivalent to cheated the chandeliers, was stronger than the artificial light, if any) ... Perhaps and probably but no doubt something else. I am at loss, and quite happy there, to know anything literally about this poem. Internally, inside its own words, I know it quite well by simple perusal. The charm of the rhymes is enough to carry it over any stile. The strange phrase, 'Fubbed the girandoles,' has another charm, like that of the rhyme, and as inexplicable: the approach of language, through the magic of elegance, to nonsense. That the phrase is not nonsense, that on inspection it retrieves itself to sense, is its inner virtue. Somewhere between the realms of ornamental sound and representative statement, the words pause and balance, dissolve and resolve. This is the mood of Euphues, and presents a poem with fine parts controlled internally by little surds of feeling that save both the poem and its parts from preciousness. The ambiguity of this sort of writing consists in the double importance of both sound and sense where neither has direct connection with the other but where neither can stand alone. It is as if Mr. Stevens wrote two poems at once with the real poem somewhere between, unwritten but vivid.

A poem which exemplifies not the approach merely but actual entrance into nonsense is 'Disillusionment of Ten

O'Clock' (page 88). This poem begins by saying that houses are haunted by white nightgowns, not nightgowns of various other colors, and ends with these lines:

> People are not going
> To dream of baboons and periwinkles.
> Only, here and there, an old sailor,
> Drunk and asleep in his boots,
> Catches tigers
> In red weather.

The language is simple and declarative. There is no doubt about the words or the separate statements. Every part of the poem makes literal sense. Yet the combination makes a nonsense, and a nonsense much more convincing than the separate sensible statements. The statement about catching tigers in red weather coming after the white nightgowns and baboons and periwinkles, has a persuasive force out of all relation to the sense of the words. Literally, there is nothing alarming in the statement, and nothing ambiguous, but by so putting the statement that it appears as nonsense, infinite possibilities are made terrifying and plain. The shock and virtue of nonsense is this: it compels us to scrutinize the words in such a way that we see enormous ambiguity in the substance of every phrase, every image, every word. The simpler the words are the more impressive and certain is the ambiguity. Half our sleeping knowledge is in nonsense; and when put in a poem it wakes.

The edge between sense and nonsense is shadow thin, and in all our deepest convictions we hover in the shadow, uncertain whether we know that our words mean, nevertheless bound by the conviction to say them. I quote the second half of 'The Death of a Soldier' (page 129):

> Death is absolute and without memorial,
> As in a season of autumn,
> When the wind stops,
> When the wind stops and, over the heavens,
> The clouds go, nevertheless,
> In their direction.

To gloss such a poem is almost impertinent, but I wish to

observe that in the passage just quoted, which is the important half of the poem, there is an abstract statement, 'Death is absolute and without memorial', followed by the notation of a natural phenomenon. The connection between the two is not a matter of course; it is syntactical, poetic, human. The point is, by combining the two, Mr. Stevens has given his abstract statement a concrete, sensual force; he has turned a conviction, an idea, into a feeling which did not exist, even in his own mind, until he had put it down in words. The feeling is not exactly in the words, it is because of them. As in the body sensations are definite but momentary, while feelings are ambiguous (with reference to sensations) but lasting; so in this poem the words are definite but instant, while the feelings they raise are ambiguous (with reference to the words) and have importance. Used in this way, words, like sensations, are blind facts which put together produce a feeling no part of which was in the data. We cannot say, abstractly, in words, any better what we know, yet the knowledge has become positive and the conviction behind it indestructible, because it has been put into words. That is one business of poetry, to use words to give quality and feeling to the precious abstract notions, and so doing to put them beyond words and beyond the sense of words.

A similar result from a different mode of the use of words may be noticed in such a poem as 'The Emperor of Ice-Cream' (page 85):

Call the roller of big cigars,
The muscular one, and bid him whip
In kitchen cups concupiscent curds.
Let the wenches dawdle in such dress
As they are used to wear, and let the boys
Bring flowers in last month's newspapers.
Let be be finale of seem.
The only emperor is the emperor of ice-cream.

Take from the dresser of deal,
Lacking the three glass knobs, that sheet
On which she embroidered fantails once
And spread it so as to cover her face.
If her horny feet protrude, they come

To show how cold she is, and dumb.
Let the lamp affix its beam.
The only emperor is the emperor of ice-cream.

The poem might be called 'Directions for a Funeral, with Two Epitaphs.' We have a corpse laid out in the bedroom and we have people in the kitchen. The corpse is dead; then let the boys bring flowers in last month's (who would use today's?) newspapers. The corpse is dead; but let the wenches wear their everyday clothes – or is it the clothes they are used to wear at funerals? The conjunction of a muscular man whipping desirable desserts in the kitchen and the corpse protruding horny feet, gains its effect because of its oddity – not of fact, but of expression: the light frivolous words and rapid meters. Once made the conjunction is irretrievable and in its own measure exact. Two ideas or images about death – the living and the dead – have been associated, and are now permanently fused. If the mind is a rag-bag, pull out two rags and sew them together. If the materials were contradictory, the very contradiction, made permanent, becomes a kind of unison. By associating ambiguities found in nature in a poem we reach a clarity, a kind of transfiguration even, whereby we learn *what* the ambiguity was.

The point is, that the oddity of association would not have its effect without the couplets which conclude each stanza with the pungency of good epitaphs. Without the couplets the association would sink from wit to low humor or simple description. What, then, do the couplets mean? Either, or both, of two things. In the more obvious sense, 'Let be be finale of seem,' in the first stanza, means, take whatever seems to be, as really being; and in the second stanza, 'Let the lamp affix its beam,' means let it be plain that this woman is dead, that these things, impossibly ambiguous as they may be, are as they are. In this case, 'The only emperor is the emperor of ice-cream,' implies in both stanzas that the only power worth heeding is the power of the moment, of what is passing, of the flux.[b]

The less obvious sense of the couplets is more difficult to set down because, in all its difference, it rises out of the first sense, and while contradicting and supplanting, yet guarantees it. The connotation is, perhaps, that ice-cream and what it represents is the only power *heeded,* not the only power there is to heed. The irony recoils on itself: what seems *shall* finally be; the lamp *shall* affix its beam. The only emperor is the emperor of ice-cream. The king is dead; long live the king.

The virtue of the poem is that it discusses and settles these matters without mentioning them. The wit of the couplets does the work.

Allied to the method of this poem is the method of much of 'Le Monocle de Mon Oncle.' The light word is used with a more serious effect than the familiar, heavy words commonly chosen in poems about the nature of love. I take these lines from the first stanza (page 16):

> The sea of spuming thought foists up again
> The radiant bubble that she was. And then
> A deep up-pouring from some saltier well
> Within me, bursts its watery syllable.

The words foist and bubble are in origin and have remained in usage both light. One comes from a word meaning to palm false dice, and the other is derived by imitation from a gesture of the mouth. Whether the history of the words was present in Mr. Stevens' mind when he chose them is immaterial; the pristine flavor is still active by tradition and is what gives the rare taste to the lines quoted. By employing them in connection with a sea of spuming thought and the notion of radiance whatever vulgarity was in the two words is purged. They gain force while they lend their own lightness to the context; and I think it is the lightness of these words that permits and conditions the second sentence in the quotation, by making the contrast between the foisted bubble and the bursting syllable possible.

Stanza IV of the same poem (pages 17 – 18) has a serious trope in which apples and skulls, love and death, are closely associated in subtle and vivid language. An apple, Mr. Stevens says, is as good as any skull to read because, like the skull, it finally rots away in the ground. The stanza ends with these lines:

> But it excels in this, that as the fruit
> Of love, it is a book too mad to read
> Before one merely reads to pass the time.

The light elegance and conversational tone give the stanza the cumulative force of understatement, and make it seem to carry a susurrus of irony between the lines. The word excels has a good deal to do with the success of the passage; superficially a syntactical word as much as anything else, actually, by its literal sense it saves the lines from possible triviality.

We have been considering poems where the light tone increases the gravity of the substance, and where an atmosphere of wit and elegance assures poignancy of meaning. It is only a step or so further to that use of language where tone and atmosphere are very nearly equivalent to substance and meaning themselves. 'Sea Surface Full of Clouds' (page 132) has many lines and several images in its five sections which contribute by their own force to the sense of the poem, but it would be very difficult to attach special importance to any one of them. The burden of the poem is the color and tone of the whole. It is as near a tone-poem, in the musical sense, as language can come. The sense of single lines cannot profitably be abstracted from the context, and literal analysis does nothing but hinder understanding. We may say, if we like, that Mr. Stevens found himself in ecstasy – that he stood aside from himself emotionally – before the spectacle of endlessly varied appearances of California seas of Tehuantepec; and that he has tried to equal the complexity of what he saw in the technical intricacy of his poem. But that is all we can say. Neither the material of the poem nor what we get out of it is by nature susceptible of direct treatment in words. It might at first seem more a painter's subject than a poet's, because its interest is more obviously visual and formal than mental. Such an assumption would lead to apt criticism if Mr. Stevens had tried, in his words, to present a series of seascapes with a visual atmosphere to each picture. His intention was quite different and germane to poetry; he wanted to present the tone, in the mind, of five different aspects of the sea. The strictly visual form is in the background, merely indicated by the words; it is what the visual form gave off after it had been felt in the mind that concerned him. Only by the precise interweaving of association and suggestion, by the development of a delicate verbal pattern, could he secure the overtones that possessed him. A looser form would have captured nothing.

The choice of certain elements in the poem may seem arbitrary, but it is an arbitrariness without reference to their rightness and wrongness. That is, any choice would have been equally arbitrary, and, esthetically, equally right. In the second stanza of each section, for example, one is reminded of different kinds of chocolate and different shades of green, thus: rosy chocolate and paradisal green; chop-house chocolate and sham-like green; porcelain chocolate and uncertain green; musky chocolate and too-fluent green; Chinese chocolate and motley green. And each section gives us umbrellas variously gilt, sham, pied, frail, and large. The ocean is successively a machine which is perplexed, tense, tranced, dry, and obese. The ocean produces sea-blooms from the clouds, mortal massives of the blooms of water, silver petals of white blooms, figures of the clouds like blooms, and, finally, a wind of green blooms. These items, and many more, repeated and modified, at once impervious to and merging each in the other, make up the words of the poem. Directly they do nothing but rouse the small sensations and smaller feelings of atmosphere and tone. The poem itself, what it means, is somewhere in the background; we know it through the tone. The motley hue we see is crisped to 'clearing opalescence.'

> Then the sea
> And heaven rolled as one and from the two
> Came fresh transfigurings of freshest blue.

Here we have words used as a tone of feeling to secure the discursive evanescence of appearances; words bringing the senses into the mind which they created; the establishment of interior experience by the construction of its tone in words. In 'Tattoo' (page 108), we have the opposite effect, where the mind is intensified in a simple visual image. The tone existed beforehand, so to speak, in the nature of the subject.

The light is like a spider.
It crawls over the water.
It crawls over the edges of the snow.
It crawls under your eyelids
And spreads its webs there
Its two webs.

The webs of your eyes
Are fastened
To the flesh and bones of you
As to rafters or grass.

There are filaments of your eyes
On the surface of the water
And in the edges of the snow.

The problem of language here hardly existed: the words make the simplest of statements, and the poet had only to avoid dramatizing what was already drama in itself, the sensation of the eyes in contact with what they looked at. By attempting *not* to set up a tone the tone of truth is secured for statements literally false. Fairly tales and Mother Goose use the same language. Because there is no point where the statements stop being true, they leap the gap unnoticed between literal truth and imaginative truth. It is worth observing that the strong sensual quality of the poem is defined without the use of a single sensual word; and it is that ambiguity between the words and their subject which makes the poem valuable.

There is nothing which has been said so far about Mr. Stevens' uses of language which might not have been said, with different examples, of any good poet equally varied and equally erudite[c] – by which I mean intensely careful of effects. We have been dealing with words primarily, and words are not limited either to an author or a subject. Hence they form unique data and are to be understood and commented on by themselves. You can hardly more compare two poets' use of a word than you can compare, profitably, trees to cyclones. Synonyms are accidental, superficial, and never genuine. Comparison begins to be possible at the level of more complicated tropes than may occur in single words.

Let us compare then, for the sake of distinguishing the kinds of import, certain tropes taken from Ezra Pound, T.S. Eliot, and Mr. Stevens.

From Mr. Pound – the first and third from the *Cantos* and the second from *Hugh Selwyn Mauberley:*

In the gloom, the gold gathers the light against it.

Tawn foreshores
Washed in the cobalt of oblivion.

A catalogue, his jewels of conversation.

From T.S. Eliot – one from 'Prufrock,' one from *The Waste Land,* and one from *Ash Wednesday:*

I should have been a pair of ragged claws
Scuttling across the floors of silent seas.

The awful daring of a moment's surrender
Which an age of prudence can never retract.

Struggling with the devil of the stairs who wears
The deceitful face of hope and of despair.

The unequaled versatility of Ezra Pound (Eliot in a dedication addresses him as *Il miglior fabbro*) prevents assurance that the three lines quoted from him are typical of all his work. At least they are characteristic of his later verse, and the kind of feeling they exhibit may be taken as Pound's own. Something like their effect may be expected in reading a good deal of his work.

The first thing to be noticed is that the first two tropes are visual images – not physical observation, but something to be seen in the mind's eye; and that as the images are so seen their meaning is exhausted. The third trope while not directly visual acts as if it were. What differentiates all three from physical observation is in each case the non-visual associations of a single word – *gathers*, which in the active voice has an air of intention; *oblivion*, which has the purely mental, sense of forgetfulness; and, less obviously, *conversation*, in the third trope, which while it helps *jewels* to give the line a visual quality it does not literally possess, also acts to condense in the line a great many non-visual associations.

The lines quoted from T.S. Eliot are none of them in intention visual; they deal with a totally different realm of experience – the realm in which the mind dramatizes, at a given moment, its feelings toward a whole aspect of life. The emotion with which these lines charge the reader's mind is a quality of emotion which has so surmounted the senses as to require no longer the support of direct contact with them. Abstract words have reached the intensity of thought and feeling where the senses have been condensed into abstraction. The first distich is an impossible statement which in its context is terrifying. The language has sensual elements but as such they mean nothing: it is the act of abstract dramatization which counts. In the second and third distichs words such as *surrender* and *prudence, hope* and *despair*, assume, by their dramatization, a definite sensual force.

Both Eliot and Pound condense; their best verse is weighted – Pound's with sensual experience primarily, and Eliot's with beliefs. Where the mind's life is concerned the senses produce images, and beliefs produce dramatic cries. The condensation is important.

Mr. Stevens' tropes, in his best work and where he is most characteristic, are neither visual like Pound nor dramatic like Eliot. The scope and reach of his verse are no less but are different. His visual images never condense the matter of his poems; they either accent or elaborate it. His dramatic statements, likewise, tend rather to give another, perhaps more final, form to what has already been put in different language.

The best evidence of these differences is the fact that it is almost impossible to quote anything short of a stanza from Mr. Stevens without essential injustice to the meaning. His kind of condensation, too, is very different in character and degree from Eliot and Pound. Little details are left in the verse to show what it is he has condensed. And occasionally, in order to make the details fit into the poem, what has once been condensed is again elaborated. It is this habit of slight re-elaboration which gives the firm textural quality to the verse.

Another way of contrasting Mr. Stevens' kind of condensation with those of Eliot and Pound will emerge if we remember Mr. Stevens' *intentional* ambiguity. Any observation, as between the observer and what is observed, is the notation of an ambiguity. To Mr. Stevens the sky, 'the basal slate,' 'the universal hue,' which surrounds us and is always upon us is the great ambiguity. Mr. Stevens associates two or more such observations so as to accent their ambiguities. But what is ambiguous in the association is not the same as in the things associated; it is something new, and it has the air of something condensed. This is the quality that makes his poems grow, rise in the mind like a tide. The poems cannot be exhausted, because the words that make them, intentionally ambiguous at their crucial points, are themselves inexhaustible. Eliot obtains many of his effects by the sharpness of surprise, Pound his by visual definition; they tend to exhaust their words in the individual use, and they are successful because they know when to stop, they know when sharpness and definition lay most hold on their subjects, they know the maximal limit of their kinds of condensation. Mr. Stevens is just as precise in his kind; he brings ambiguity to the point of sharpness, of reality, without destroying, but rather preserving, clarified, the ambiguity. It is a difference in subject matter, and a difference in accent. Mr. Stevens makes you aware of how much is *already* condensed in any word.

The first stanza of 'Sunday Morning' may be quoted (page 89). It should be remembered that the title is an integral part of the poem, directly affecting the meaning of many lines and generally controlling the atmosphere of the whole.

> Complacencies of the peignoir, and late
> Coffee and oranges in a sunny chair,
> And the green freedom of a cockatoo
> Upon a rug mingle to dissipate
> The holy hush of ancient sacrifice.
> She dreams a little, and she feels the dark
> Encroachment of that old catastrophe,
> As a calm darkens among water-lights.
> The pungent oranges and bright, green wings
> Seem things in some procession of the dead,
> Winding across wide water, without sound.
> The day is like wide water, without sound,

Stilled for the passing of her dreaming feet
Over the seas, to silent Palestine,
Dominion of the blood and sepulchre.

A great deal of ground is covered in these fifteen lines, and
the more the slow ease and conversational elegance of the
verse are observed, the more wonder it seems that so much
could have been indicated without strain. Visually, we have a
women enjoying her Sunday morning breakfast in a sunny
room with a green rug. The image is secured, however, not
as in Pound's image about the gold gathering the light against
it, in directly visual terms, but by the almost casual
combination of visual images with such phrases as '*complacencies* of the peignoir,' and 'the green *freedom* of the
cockatoo,' where the italicized words are abstract in essence
but rendered concrete in combination. More important, the
purpose of the images is to show how they dissipate the 'holy
hush of ancient sacrifice,' how the natural comfort of the
body is aware but mostly unheeding that Sunday is the
Lord's day and that it commemorates the crucifixion.

From her half-awareness she feels the more keenly the 'old
catastrophe' merging in the surroundings, subtly, but deeply, changing them as a 'calm darkness among water-lights'
The feeling is dark in her mind, darkens, changing the whole
day. The oranges and the rug and the day all have the quality
of 'wide water, without sound', and all her thoughts, so
loaded, turn on the crucifixion.

The transit of the body's feeling from attitude to attitude is
managed in the medium of three water images. These images
do not replace the 'complacencies of the peignoir,' nor
change them; they act as a kind of junction between them and
the Christian feeling traditionally proper to the day. By the
time the stanza is over the water images have embodied both
feelings. In their own way they make a condensation by
appearing in company with and showing what was already
condensed.

If this stanza is compared with the tropes quoted from
Pound, the principal difference will perhaps seem that while
Pound's lines define their own meaning and may stand alone,
Mr. Stevens' various images are separately incomplete and,

on the other hand, taken together, have a kind of completeness to which Pound's lines may not pretend: everything to
which they refer is present. Pound's images exist without
syntax, Mr. Stevens' depend on it. Pound's images are
formally simple, Mr. Stevens' complex. The one contains a
mystery, and the other, comparatively, expounds a mystery.

While it would be possible to find analogues to Eliot's
tropes in the stanzas of 'Sunday Morning,' it will be more
profitable to examine something more germane in spirit.
Search is difficult and choice uncertain, for Mr. Stevens is not
a dramatic poet. Instead of dramatizing his feelings, he takes
as fatal the drama that he sees and puts it down either in its
least dramatic, most meditative form, or makes of it a simple
statement. Let us then frankly take as pure a meditation as
may be found, 'The Snow Man' (page 12), where, again, the
title is integrally part of the poem:

> One must have a mind of winter
> To regard the frost and the boughs
> Of the pine-trees crusted with snow;
>
> And have been cold a long time
> To behold the junipers shagged with ice,
> The spruces rough in the distant glitter
>
> Of the January sun; and not to think
> Of any misery in the sound of the wind,
> In the sound of a few leaves,
>
> Which is the sound of the land
> Full of the same wind
> That is blowing in the same bare place
>
> for the listener, who listens in the snow,
> And, nothing himself, beholds
> Nothing that is not there and the nothing that is.

The last three lines are as near as Mr. Stevens comes to the
peculiar dramatic emotion which characterizes the three
tropes quoted from Eliot. Again, as in the passage compared
to Pound's images, the effect of the last three lines depends
entirely on what preceded them. The emotion is built up
from chosen fragments and is then stated in its simplest form.

The statement has the force of emotional language but it remains a statement – a modest declaration of circumstance. The abstract word *nothing*, three times repeated, is not in effect abstract at all; it is synonymous with the data about the winter landscape which went before. The part which is not synonymous is the emotion: the overtone of the word, and the burden of the poem. Eliot's lines,

> The awful daring of a moment's surrender
> Which an age of prudence can never retract,

like Pound's lines, for different reasons, stand apart and on their own feet. The two poets work in contrary modes. Eliot places a number of things side by side. The relation is seldom syntactical or logical, but is usually internal and sometimes, so far as the reader is concerned, fatal and accidental. He works in violent contrasts and produces as much by prestidigitation as possible. There was no reason in the rest of 'Prufrock' why the lines about the pair of ragged claws should have appeared where they did and no reason, perhaps, why they should have appeared at all; but once they appeared they became for the reader irretrievable, complete in themselves, and completing the structure of the poem.

That is the method of a dramatic poet, who molds wholes out of parts themselves autonomous. Mr. Stevens, not a dramatic poet, seizes his wholes only in imagination; in his poems the parts are already connected. Eliot usually moves from point to point or between two termini. Mr. Stevens as a rule ends where he began; only when he is through, his beginning has become a chosen end. The differences may be exaggerated but in their essence is a true contrast.

If a digression may be permitted, I think it may be shown that the different types of obscurity found in the three poets are only different aspects of their modes of writing. In Pound's verse, aside from words in languages the reader does not know, most of the hard knots are tied round combinations of classical and historical references. A passage in one of the Cantos, for example, works up at the same time the adventures of a Provencal poet and the events in one of Ovid's *Metamorphoses*. If the reader is acquainted with the details of both stories, he can appreciate the criticism in

Pound's combination. Otherwise he will remain confused: he will be impervious to the plain facts of the verse.

Eliot's poems furnish examples of a different kind of reference to and use of history and past literature. The reader must be familiar with the ideas and the beliefs and systems of feeling to which Eliot alludes or from which he borrows, rather than to the facts alone. Eliot does not restrict himself to criticism; he digests what he takes; but the reader must know what it is that has been digested before he can appreciate the result. The Holy Grail material in *The Waste Land* is an instance: like Tiresias, this material is a dramatic element in the poem.

Mr. Stevens' difficulties to the normal reader present themselves in the shape of seemingly impenetrable words or phrases which no wedge of knowledge brought from outside the body of Mr. Stevens' own poetry can help much to split. The wedge, if any, is in the words themselves, either in the instance alone or in relation to analogous instances in the same or other poems in the book. Two examples should suffice.

In 'Sunday Morning,' there is in the seventh stanza (page 93) a reference to the sun, to which men shall chant their devotion –

> Not as a god, but as a god might be,
> Naked among them, like a savage source.
> Their chant shall be a chant of paradise,
> Out of their blood, returning to the sky;...

Depending upon the reader this will or will not be obscure. But in any case, the full weight of the lines is not felt until the conviction of the poet that the sun is origin and ending for all life is shared by the reader. That is why the god might be naked among them. It takes only reading of the stanza, the poem, and other poems where the fertility of the sun is celebrated, to make the notion sure. The only bit of outside information that might help is the fact that in an earlier version this stanza concluded the poem. – In short, generally, you need only the dictionary and familiarity with the poem in question to clear up a good part of Mr. Stevens' obscurities.

The second example is taken from 'The Man Whose Pharynx was Bad' (age 128):

> Perhaps, if winter once could penetrate
> Through all its purples to the final slate.

Here, to obtain the full meaning, we have only to consult the sixth stanza of 'Le Monocle de Mon Oncle' (page 18):

> If men at forty will be painting lakes
> The ephemeral blues must merge for them in one,
> The basic slate, the universal hue.
> There is a substance in us that prevails.

Mr. Stevens has a notion often intimated that the sky is the only permanent background for thought and knowledge; he would see things against the sky as a Christian would see them against the cross. The blue of the sky is the prevailing substance of the sky, and to Mr. Stevens it seems only necessary to look at the sky to share and be shared in its blueness.

If I have selected fairly types of obscurity from these poets, it should be clear that whereas the obscurities of Eliot and Pound are intrinsic difficulties of the poems, to which the reader must come well armed with specific sorts of external knowledge and belief, the obscurities of Mr. Stevens clarify themselves to the intelligence alone. Mode and value are different – not more or less valuable, but different. And all result from the concentrated language which is the medium of poetry. The three poets load their words with the maximum content; naturally, the poems remain obscure until the reader takes out what the poet puts in. What still remains will be the essential impenetrability of words, the bottomlessness of knowledge. To these the reader, like the poet, must submit.

Returning, this time without reference to Pound and Eliot, among the varieties of Mr. Stevens' tropes we find some worth notice which comparison will not help. 'Le Monocle de Mon Oncle,' the ninth stanza (page 20), has nothing logically to do with the poem; it neither develops the subject nor limits it, but is rather a rhetorical interlude set in the poem's midst. Yet it is necessary to the poem, because its

rhetoric, boldly announced as such, expresses the feeling of
the poet toward his poem, and that feeling, once expressed,
becomes incorporated in the poem.

> In verses wild with motion, full of din,
> Loudened by cries, by clashes, quick and sure
> As the deadly thought of men accomplishing
> Their curious fates in war, come, celebrate
> The faith of forty, ward of Cupido.
> Most venerable heart, the lustiest conceit
> Is not too lusty for your broadening.
> I quiz all sounds, all thoughts, all everything
> For the music and manner of the paladins
> To make oblation fit. Where shall I find
> Bravura adequate to this great hymn?

It is one of the advantages of a non-dramatic, meditative
style, that pure rhetoric may be introduced into a poem
without injuring its substance. The structure of the poem is,
so to speak, a structure of loose ends, spliced only verbally,
joined only by the sequence in which they appear. What might
be fustian ornament in a dramatic poem, in a meditative
poem casts a feeling far from fustian over the whole, and the
slighter the relation of the rhetorical interlude to the
substance of the whole, the more genuine is the feeling cast.
The rhetoric does the same thing that the action does in a
dramatic poem, or the events in a narrative poem; it produces
an apparent medium in which the real substance may be
borne.

Such rhetoric is not reserved to set interludes; it often
occurs in lines not essentially rhetorical at all. Sometimes it
gives life to a serious passage and cannot be separated
without fatal injury to the poem. Then it is the trick without
which the poem would fall flat entirely. Two poems occur
where the rhetoric is the vital trope – 'A High-Toned Old
Christian Woman' (page 79), and 'Bantams in Pine-Woods'
(page 101), which I quote entire:

> Chieftain Iffucan of Azcan in caftan
> Of tan with henna hackles, halt!

Damned universal cock, as if the sun
Was blackamoor to bear your blazing tail.

Fat! Fat! Fat! I am the personal.
Your world is you. I am my world.

You ten-foot poet among inchlings. Fat!
Begone! An inchling bristles in these pines,

Bristles, and points their Appalachian tangs,
And fears not portly Azcan nor his hoos.

The first and last distichs are gauds of rhetoric; nevertheless
they give not only the tone but the substance to the poem. If
the reader is deceived by the rhetoric and believes the poem is
no more than a verbal plaything, he ought not to read poetry
except as a plaything. With a different object, Mr. Stevens'
rhetoric is as ferociously comic as the rhetoric in Marlowe's
Jew of Malta, and as serious. The ability to handle rhetoric so
as to reach the same sort of intense condensation that is
secured in bare, non-rhetorical language is very rare, and
since what rhetoric can condense is very valuable it ought to
receive the same degree of attention as any other use of
language. Mr Stevens' successful attempts in this direction
are what make him technically most interesting. Simple
language, dealing obviously with surds, draws emotion out
of feelings; rhytorical language, dealing rather, or apparently, with inflections, employed with the same seriousness,
creates a surface *equivalent* to an emotion by it approximately
complete escape from the purely communicative function of
language.[d]

We have seen in a number of examples that Mr. Stevens
uses language in several different ways, either separately or in
combination; and I have tried to imply that his success is
due largely to his double adherence to words and experience
as existing apart from his private sensibility. His great labor
has been to allow the reality of what he felt personally to pass
into the superior impersonal reality of words. Such a
transformation amounts to an access of knowledge, as it
raises to a condition where it may be rehearsed and
understood in permanent form that body of emotional and

sensational experience which in its natural condition makes life a torment and confusion.

With the technical data partly in hand, it ought now to be possible to fill out the picture, touch upon the knowledge itself, in Mr. Stevens' longest and most important poem, 'The Comedian as the Letter C.' Everywhere characteristic of Mr. Stevens' style and interests, it has the merit of difficulty – difficulty which when solved rewards the reader beyond his hopes of clarity.

Generally speaking the poem deals with the sensations and images, notions and emotions, ideas and meditations, sensual adventures and introspective journeyings of a protagonist called Crispin. More precisely, the poem expounds the shifting of a man's mind between sensual experience and its imaginative interpretation, the struggle, in that mind, of the imagination for sole supremacy and the final slump or ascent where the mind contents itself with interpreting plain and common things. In short, we have a meditation, with instances, of man's struggle with nature. The first line makes the theme explicit: 'Nota: man is the intelligence of his soil, the sovereign ghost.' Later, the theme is continued in reverse form: 'His soil is man's intelligence.' Later still, the soil is qualified as suzerain, which means sovereign over a semi-independent or internally autonomous state; and finally, at the end of the poem, the sovereignty is still further reduced when it turns out that the imagination can make nothing better of the world (here called a turnip), than the same insoluble lump it was in the beginning.

The poem is in six parts of about four pages each. A summary may replace pertinent discussion and at the same time preclude extraneous discussion. In Part I, called The World without Imagination, Crispin, who previously had cultivated a small garden with his intelligence, finds himself at sea, 'a skinny sailor peering in the sea-glass.' At first at loss and 'washed away by magnitude,' Crispin, 'merest minuscule in the gales,' at last finds the sea a vocable thing,

> But with a speech belched out of hoary darks
> Noway resembling his, a visible thing,
> And excepting negligible Triton, free

From the unavoidable shadow of himself
That elsewhere lay around him.

The sea 'was no help before reality,' only 'one vast subjugating final tone,' before which Crispin was made new. Concomitantly, with and because of his vision of the sea, 'The drenching of stale lives no more fell down.'

Part II is called Concerning the Thunder-Storms of Yucatan, and there, in Yucatan, Crispin, a man made vivid by the sea, found his apprehensions enlarged and felt the need to fill his senses. He sees and hears all there is before him, and writes fables for himself

> Of an aesthetic tough, diverse, untamed,
> Incredible to prudes, the mint of dirt,
> Green barbarism turning paradigm.

The sea had liberated his senses, and he discovers an earth like 'A jostling festival of seeds grown fat, too juicily opulent,' and a 'new reality in parrot-squawks.' His education is interrupted when a wind 'more terrible than the revenge of music on bassoons,' brings on a tropical thunder-storm. Crispin, 'this connoisseur of elemental fate,' identifies himself with the storm, finding himself free, which he was before, and 'more than free, elate, intent, profound and studious' of a new self:

> the thunder, lapsing in its clap,
> Let down gigantic quavers of its voice,
> For Crispin to vociferate again.

With such freedom taken from the sea and such power found in the storm, Crispin is ready for the world of the imagination. Naturally, then, the third part of the poem, called Approaching Carolina, is a chapter in the book of moonlight, and Crispin 'a faggot in the lunar fire.' Moonlight is imagination, a reflection or interpretation of the sun, which is the source of life. It is also, curiously, this moonlight, North America, and specifically one of the Carolinas. And the Carolinas, to Crispin, seemed north; even the spring seemed arctic. He meditates on the poems he has denied himself because they gave less than 'The relentless contact he desired.' Perhaps the moon would establish the necessary liaison between himself and his environment. But perhaps not. It seemed

> Illusive, faint, more mist than moon, perverse,
> Wrong as a divagation to Peking....
> Moonlight was an evasion, or, if not,
> A minor meeting, facile, delicate.

So he considers, and teeters back and forth, between the sun and moon. For the moment he decides against the moon and imagination in favor of the sun and his senses. The senses, instanced by the smell of things at the river wharf where his vessel docks, 'round his rude aesthetic out' and teach him 'how much of what he saw he never saw at all.'

> He gripped more closely the essential prose
> As being, in a world so falsified,
> The one integrity for him, the one
> Discovery still possible to make,
> To which all poems were incident, unless
> That prose should wear a poem's guise at last.

In short, Crispin conceives that if the experience of the senses is but well enough known, the knowledge takes the form of imagination after all. So we find as the first line of the fourth part, called The Idea of a Colony, 'Nota: his soil is man's intelligence,' which reverses the original statement that man is the intelligence of his soil. With the new distinction illuminating his mind, Crispin plans a colony, and asks himself whether the purpose of his pilgrimage is not

> to drive away
> The shadow of his fellows from the skies,
> And, from their stale intelligence released,
> To make a new intelligence prevail?

The rest of the fourth part is a long series of a synonymous tropes stating instances of the new intelligence. In a torment of fastidious thought, Crispin writes a prolegomena for his colony. Everything should be understood for what it is and should follow the urge of its given character. The spirit of things should remain spirit and play as it will.

> The man in Georgia waking among pines
> Should be pine-spokesman. The responsive man,
> Planting his pristine cores in Florida,
> Should prick thereof, not on the psaltery,
> But on the banjo's categorical gut.

And as for Crispin's attitude toward nature, 'the melon should have apposite ritual' and the peach its incantation. These 'commingled souvenirs and prophecies' – all images of freedom and the satisfaction of instinct – compose Crispin's idea of a colony. He banishes the masquerade of thought and expunges dreams; the ideal takes no form from these. Crispin will be content to 'let the rabbit run, the cock declaim.'

In Part V, which is A Nice Shady Home, Crispin dwells in the land, contented and a hermit, continuing his observations with diminished curiosity. His discovery that his colony has fallen short of his plan and that he is content to have it fall short, content to build a cabin,

> who once planned
> Loquacious columns by the ructive sea,

leads him to ask whether he should not become a philosopher instead of a colonizer.

> Should he lay by the personal and make
> Of his own fate an instance of all fate?

The question is rhetorical, but before it can answer itself, Crispin, sapped by the quotidian, sapped by the sun, has no energy for questions, and is content to realize, that for all the sun takes

> it gives a humped return
> Exchequering from piebald fiscs unkeyed.

Part VI, called And Daughters with Curls, explains the implications of the last quoted lines. The sun, and all the new intelligence which is enriched, mulcted the man Crispin, and in return gave him four daughters, four questioners and four sure answerers. He has been brought back to social nature, has gone to seed. The connoisseur of elemental fate has become himself an instance of all fate. He does not know whether the return was 'Anabasis or slump, ascent or chute.'

His cabin – that is the existing symbol of his colony – seems now a phylactery, a sacred relic or amulet he might wear in memorial to his idea, in which his daughters shall grow up, bidders and biders for the ecstasies of the world, to repeat his pilgrimage, and come, no doubt, in their own cabins, to the same end.

Then Crispin invents his doctrine and clothes it in the fable about the turnip:

> The world, a turnip once so readily plucked,
> Sacked up and carried overseas, daubed out
> Of its ancient purple, pruned to the fertile main,
> And sown again by the stiffest realist,
> Came reproduced in purple, family font,
> The same insoluble lump. The fatalist
> Stepped in and dropped the chuckling down his craw,
> Without grace or grumble.

But suppose the anecdote was false, and Crispin a profitless philosopher,

> Glozing his life with after-shining flicks,
> Illuminating, from a fancy gorged
> By apparition, plain and common things,
> Sequestering the fluster from the year,
> Making gulped potions from obstreperous drops,
> And so distorting, proving what he proves
> Is nothing, what can all this matter since
> The relation comes, benignly, to its end.

> So may the relation of each man be clipped.

The legend or subject of the poem and the mythology it develops are hardly new nor are the instances, intellectually considered, very striking. But both the clear depth of conception and the extraordinary luxuriance of rhetoric and image in which it is expressed, should be at least suggested in the summary here furnished. Mr. Stevens had a poem with an abstract subject – man as an instance of fate, and a concrete experience – the sensual confusion in which the man is waylaid; and to combine them he had to devise a form suitable to his own peculiar talent. The simple statement – of which he is a master – could not be prolonged to meet the dimensions of his subject. To the dramatic style his talents were unsuitable, and if by chance he used it, it would prevent both the meditative mood and the accent of intellectual with which he needed to make the subject his own. The form he used is as much his own and as adequate, as the form of *Paradise Lost* is Milton's or the form of *The Waste Land* is Eliot's. And as Milton's form filled the sensibility of one aspect of his age, Mr. Stevens' form fits part of the sensibility – a part which Eliot or Pound or Yeats do little to touch – of our own age.

I do not know a name for the form. It is largely the form of rhetoric, language used for its own sake, persuasively to the extreme. But it has, for rhetoric, an extraordinary content of concrete experience. Mr. Stevens is a genuine poet in that he attempts constantly to transform what is felt with the senses and what is thought in the mind – if we can still distinguish the two – into that realm of being, which we call poetry, where what is thought is felt and what is felt has the strict point of thought. And I call his mode of achieving that transformation rhetorical because it is not lyric or dramatic or epic, because it does not transcend its substance, but is a reflection upon a hard surface, a shining mirror of rhetoric.

In its nature depending so much on tone and atmosphere, accenting precise management of ambiguities, and dealing with the subtler inflections of simple feelings, the elements of the form cannot be tracked down and put in order. Perhaps the title of the whole poem, 'The Comedian as the Letter C,' is as good an example as any where several of the elements can be found together. The letter C is, of course, Crispin, and he is called a letter because he is small (he is referred to as 'merest minuscule,' which means small letter, in the first part of the poem) and because, though small, like a letter he stands for something – his colony, cabin, and children – as a comedian. He is a comedian because he deals finally with the quotidian (the old distinction of comedy and tragedy was between everyday and heroic subject matter), gorged with apparition, illuminating plain and common things. But what he deals with is not comic; the comedy, in that sense, is restricted to his perception and does not touch the things perceived or himself. The comedy is the accent, the play of the words. He is at various times a realist, a clown, a philosopher, a colonizer, a father, a faggot in the lunar fire, and so on. In sum, and any sum is hypothetical, he may be a comedian in both senses, but separately never. He is the hypothesis of comedy. He is a piece of rhetoric – a persona in words – exemplifying all these characters, and summing, or masking, in his persuasive style, the essential prose he read. He is the poem's guise that the prose wears at last.

Such is the title of the poem, and such is the poem itself. Mr. Stevens has created a surface, a texture, a rhetoric in which his feelings and thoughts are preserved in what amounts to a new sensibility. The contrast between his subjects – the apprehension of all the sensual aspects of nature as instances of fate, – and the form in which the subjects are expressed is what makes his poetry valuable. Nature becomes nothing but words and to a poet words are everything.

NOTES

a The references are to the new edition of *Harmonium*, New York: Alfred A. Knopf, 1931. This differs from the first edition in that three poems have been cut out and fourteen added.

b Mr. Stevens wrote me that his daughter put a superlative value on icecream. Up daughters!

c See *Words and Idioms*, by Logan Pearsall Smith, Boston: Houghton Mifflin, 1926, page 121. 'One of the great defects of our critical vocabulary is the lack of a neutral, non-derogatory name for these great artificers, these artists who derive their inspiration more from the formal than the emotional aspects of their art, and who are more interested in the masterly control of their material, than in the expression of their own feelings, or the prophetic aspects of their calling.' Mr. Smith then suggests the use of the words erudite and erudition and gives as reason their derivation 'from *erudire* (*E* 'out of', and *rudis,* 'rude', 'rough' or 'raw'), a verb meaning in classical Latin to bring out of the rough, to form by means of art, to polish, to instruct.' Mr. Stevens is such an *erudite*; though he is often more, when he deals with emotional matters as if they were matters for *erudition*.

d There is a point at which rhetorical language resumes its

communicative function. In the second of 'Six Significant Landscapes' (page 98), we have this image:

> A pool shines
> Like a bracelet
> Shaken at a dance,

which is a result of the startling associations induced by an
ornamental, social, rhetorical style in dealing with nature. The
image perhaps needs its context to assure its quality.

IDEAS OF ORDER

New York, Alcestis Press, 1935
New York, Knopf, 1936

The director of the Alcestis Press, Ronald Lane Latimer, published a limited edition of 135 copies. Stevens wrote to Latimer on 10 August 1935 to say he had just received copies. 'Too bad that I can't read it. Of course if I were to read any of these things again I should jump out of my skin' (*Letters*, p. 283). Within three days Stevens had decided to send the book to Knopf and offer it for trade publication. Knopf published an edition of 1,000 copies in 1936.

---

29. Howard Baker, Stevens as an explorer of consciousness, from 'Wallace Stevens and Other Poets', *Southern Review*

Vol. I, Autumn 1935, 373–89

Howard Baker (b. 1905) is a poet, playwright, novelist and professional olive and citrus grower, whose chief literary work is *Ode to the Sea and Other Poems* (1966).

The other poets reviewed are T. Sturge Moore, John Gould Fletcher, Herbert Read, Witter Bynner and Theodore Morrison, together with Yeats' *The King of the Great Clock Tower*.

... Clashes in points of view are the subjects of many of Stevens' poems. His ability to see things from several sides induces at once his intellectual breadth and impersonal interest in his subject matter. He subject of poems, the perception of order, of pattern, in external nature. It is significan he can see lines 'straight and swift bet Similarly a wild and disorderly landscape is transform order by the presence of a symmetrical vase:

[Quotes 'Anecdote of the Jar', *CP,* p. 76.]

The jar acts in the imagination like one of the poles of the earth, the imaginary order of the lines of latitude and longitude projecting around the pole. The jar itself – simple and symmetrical, a product of the human consciousness and not of nature – is a very fitting symbol for man's dominion over nature. The appearance of the wilderness is deftly suggested; in contrast with it the jar is striking, but, after some familiarity with the poem, it is striking chiefly because it is so precisely an opposite to the wilderness. The spare precision of Stevens produces his initially surprising surfaces; and fortunately, since he surfaces of poems are of only momentary interest, his precision also produces that which is of lasting value in his work: the unmistakable justice of his observations and his combinations of ideas.

The range of his ideas, however, can be got at best in any of his long poems – 'Sunday Morning', 'Le Monocle de Mon Oncle', or 'The Comedian as the Letter C.' These are three examples of the finest of modern poems; but we shall be forced to confine our remarks only to the last, which is in many respects the most imposing of the three. 'The Comedian as the Letter C' recounts the spiritual adventures of a poet named Crispin. Crispin is small in comparison with the regions through which he adventures, a 'merest minuscule in the gales,' and is therefore referred to merely by the letter which begins his name; he is a comedian in that he is concerned with 'daily' things, just as comedies are, in the classical definition, concerned with daily matters. He is named after the stock valet of Italian and French comedy, he is a valet to experience, and thus he is also a varlet, a knave, etc. His adventures lead him – to resort to rough terms – through a restricted, personal Idealism into sensory realism

, thence into a decline into the purely practical. The objective of his adventures is to discover means by which the human faculties can take hold of the world and reduce it to order ....

The drift of this poem is unmistakable. It is not philosophical, though it does have philosophical implications. It is somewhat inconclusive, for it is content to show several attitudes towards experience rather than to choose from them: it seems to be not particularly significant that Crispin ends up a realist. But on the other hand the poem is first and last an exploration of psychological depths. The stuff out of which it is made is the stuff of basic psychological forces, ancient and powerful images, archetypes of experience. Reduced to lowest terms, it is a poem built out of the symbols in which the new psychology is interested – the sun and moon, the sea, the voyages, the primitive, the obscure pursuit which ends in marriage.

The psychological character of this and of other poems of Stevens is obvious when we put his work beside that of other writers who are following similar bents. Here is, for instance, a passage from Thomas Mann's *Joseph and his Brothers:*

'Much is in doubt,' answered Joseph ... 'For instance, is it the night that conceals the day, or the day the night? For it would be important to distinguish this, and often in the field and hut have I considered it, hoping, if I could decide, to draw from the decision conclusions as to the virtue of the blessing of the sun and of the moon ... Oil and wine are sacred to the sun, and well for him whose brow drippeth with oil and his eyes are drunken with the shining of red wine! For his words will be a brightness and a laughing and a consolation to the peoples ... But the sweet fruit of the fig is sacred to the moon, and well for him whom the little mother nourisheth out of the night with its flesh. For he will grow as though beside a stream, and his soul have roates whence the streams arise, and his word be made flesh and living as a body of earth, and with him shall be the spirit of prophecy ...'

With this, compare 'The Comedian as the Letter C':

The book of moonlight is not written yet
Nor half begun, but, when it is, leave room

For Crispin, faggot in the lunar fire,
Who, in the hubbub of his pilgrimage
Through sweating changes, never could forget
That wakefulness or meditating sleep,
In which the sulky strophes willingly
Bore up, in time, the somnolent, deep songs...

Perhaps the Arctic moonlight really gave
The liaison, the blissful liaison,
Between himself and his environment,
Which was, and is, chief motive, first delight,
For him, and not for him alone...

Thus he conceived his voyaging to be
An up and down between two elements,
A fluctuating between sun and moon...

For Stevens, as for Mann, the moon is the interpreter of things, is mental, poetic, imaginative, feminine; and the sun is the origin and destination of life, physical, masculine, 'the essential prose.' This information is necessary for a full understanding of many of the poems in both of Stevens' books....

Just as the sun and moon are consistent symbols, so are the others. The sea, like the sun, is a source of life, but a more immediate one than the sun; and it, since it is subject to time, becomes an image of fundamental destiny – that is to say, of all things ruled by time and therefore by fate, it is the closest to being eternal and absolute and freed from fate. The various voyages and pilgrimages stand for spiritual changes. The primitive and tropical scene is explored because of its richness in broadly significant, dream-like images. Each of these images is a problem in itself, but often an image like

an old sailor,
Drunk and asleep in his boots,
Catches tigers
In red weather.

seems to be a product of the obscurer depths of consciousness, interesting in itself but non-significant.

Certainly it is not a coincidence that the sun and moon

have the same significance in both 'The Comedian as the Letter C' and in *Joseph and His Brothers*. Nor is it a coincidence that scientists, as well as Stevens, regard the sea as a source of life; nor that many men in all ages have meditated on the patterns of the stars. Notions of this kind are as old as speculation about the world. They are at present a peculiar property of the psychologists, but they belong as well to every century – to religion and literature as well as to science . . . .

To avoid ambiguity we must attempt now to state how closely we may presume the poetry of Wallace Stevens to be related to modern psychology. Certainly it is unimportant whether we think that Stevens was or was not under the direct influence of psychoanalysis. But it does seem that, as often happens, the direction of his interests has paralleled that of other important men of his time and particularly, it happens, the psychologists; just as, in a similar fashion, the interests of Proust and Einstein, for instance, seem to have paralleled each other. The times that produced psychoanalysis probably gave an emphasis to Stevens' psychical symbols, and perhaps encouraged the use of some extent of 'free association' of ideas rather than strict logic in the writing of verse. But the symbols to which psychology has been attentive are the traditional materials of poetry, and no poetry is strictly logical. So we cannot hold that Stevens' poetry is 'explained' by an enumeration of its psychological elements. Psychology, it must be clear, is in these pages simply one convenient instrument for criticism out of the many which would be possible. These poems could be studied and interpreted along any of the various lines that, before the day of modern psychology, the Greek myths, for instance, were studied and interpreted.

And I think that with psychology as an instrument we can go one step further towards describing the essential nature of Stevens' work. We observe that C.G. Jung and Wallace Stevens are contemporaries and that each is interested in his fashion in abiding images such as the sun and moon and the sea. It would be valuable to know how far the paths of their work run side by side and whether they have similar goals in view. Though it is rash even to try, without exhaustive study, to summarize achievements of this kind, still some notes may be offered tentatively.

When the human being, according to Jung, explores his consciousness in its several levels, he becomes acquainted with the sovereign images, the archetypes of racial experience, which we have been considering. These images, he begins to realize, have an influence upon his character and actions. Therefore his ego is not so important as he had thought it, and the demands of his personal desires become less strong. Continuing in his explorations, he gradually comes into harmony with these psychical images. And then he perceives that he is viewing the world not from the purely egoistic point of view but from a new and more or less impersonal angle, from a spiritual platform which is built both of his personal and of racial and human values. The non-personal quality in this new center of consciousness is of greatest importance. For it, Jung seems to say, has the ability to mature, to empower, and to humble men as they must be empowered and humbled, and as they may be by an active social ideal or by an active religion.

The kind of poetry which we have at hand is also an exploration of consciousness. It also aims at an understanding of the archetypes of experience and doubtless does beget a harmonious relationship between the individual and such experience. Moonlight, which Stevens makes synonymous with poetry, is 'the liaison, the blissful liaision' between oneself and what Stevens calls one's environment; and this is to say that poetry is a liaison between the individual and his most complex experience. This liaison, moreover, as Stevens says of Crispin,

> was, and is, chief motive, first delight,
> For him, and not for him alone...

The liaison effectuates a non-personal attitude: one sees Stevens, in the phrase 'not for him alone,' gliding over from the egoistic to the impersonal. We can add to our earlier remarks on the impersonal quality of Stevens' poetry that it results simply from the fact that the poet's own wishes and needs have been transformed into a sympathy with the larger figures of his poetry; it is a classical kind of detachment in which there is no lessening of human feeling, the 'I' is simply enlarged.

We cannot be content merely to say that Stevens and Jung follow similar paths to similar goals. Such a statement would be both too general and too shaky in details. In Jung, for instance, we wonder how the individual can find in himself memories of racial experience, and how ideas can be inherited; we wonder at the source of the inspiration in a meditative poetry like Stevens'. On the other hand we observe that the impersonal and timeless objective is by no means confined to the poetry of Stevens or the thinking of Jung. Consequently it may be necessary to postulate, for the moment at least, an unchanging spiritual world which is independent of the time process, and with which the human being may come in touch and yet at the same time retain his individuality. Such a world might be said to draw or to pull the individual spirit towards it, and to draw thinking as a whole in the direction of absolutes. This hypothesis would account, for instance, for the fact that love appears as the motive power of the universe, not only in modern psychology, but in Hesiod and Thomas Aquinas and Dante. It would indicate the common ground between Jung's psychology and religion, and between poetry and religion. Certainly it is upon very general and difficult and important grounds that Stevens and Jung are alike. (In this paragraph I have followed the metaphors which V.A. Demant uses in his excellent essay 'Dialectics and Prophecy', in the Criterion, July, 1935.)

Since Stevens' poetry aims very clearly at an exploration of consciousness, one sees immediately why it has been found difficult by many readers. They have found it difficult because they expected it to do things that it had no intention of doing. But once readers are somewhat acquainted with the outlands of consciousness, the poetry will be clear. Once the modes of thought of the times which produced *Harmonium* are understood, as they will inevitably be understood, then the poetry will be understood.

We are concerned in Stevens' work with a mental poetry. It is not a poetry of 'wit' – not a poetry of intellectual invention like that of the seventeenth and eighteenth centuries; it is not, that is to say, a poetry which, although it, as Dr.

Johnson said, surprises and delights by producing something unexpected, aims in the large at clarity and logical progression. Stevens' poetry does not progress; instead it gradually hems in the illusive stuff of the poem. It aims not to expound familiar experience so much as to grasp fundamental experience in all its complexity. It uses a rhetoric of appositives, it encircles and closes in upon its subject matter. It seems to be more like the rhetoric of Donne's sermons than anything else:

[Quotes a passage from a John Donne sermon.]

In commenting on this passage, James M. Cline has said that 'there is no advance in thought, only a refinement of it, a deepening and a gathering intensity of realization; until finally the great period crashes to a close, still reiterating, still sustaining an incremental movement of passion and of mind.'[1]

And Stevens likewise. Stevens' poems are incremental movements of passionate, mental rhetoric. They are 'unintelligible' in the way that the passage from Donne, if readers were unfamiliar with the notion of damnation, would be unintelligible, and for the same kind of reason. We may illustrate this incremental rhetoric, this closing in upon the stuff of the poem, and at the same time draw together our remarks on *Harmonium* by quoting one more poem, a poem about clouds:

[Quotes 'Of the Manner of Addressing Clouds', *CP*, p. 55.]

Such is persistently the world as Stevens visualizes it – a small region filled with transitory but significant forms under the eternal sun. We are like clouds, we 'ponderers'; we too are going to our deaths, and during our passage our best efforts are bent to brilliant words. In this poem, as very often in Stevens' work, the rhetoric itself fertilizers the thinking: the thought simply leaps from 'gloomy grammarians' to 'funest philosophers', from clouds to men, from the transitoriness of the speaking voice to the transitoriness of thought. This conviction that, between the silent eternals, the transitory graces are our best possession, is the motivation of Stevens' rhetoric.

The thirty-three poems in *Ideas of Order* turn upon the same symbols that figure in *Harmonium*. The sun, for instance, appears as the eternal source of things in at least half of the new poems. And the world is still filled with 'forms' that require poetic meditation. But the attitude to these symbols has changed. The sun is farther off, or is remembered from another season. The 'forms' are complicated because contemporary men and their problems appear among them. The new work bespeaks a need for a practical philosophy and an active social doctrine. And since a number of these poems are expressions of a *desire* for order rather than of order, Stevens' admirable concern with contemporary problems seems unfortunately to have interfered to some extent with the writing of this collection.

In the first place there are notes of regret about the difficulties of the present:

> My old boat goes round on a crutch
> And doesn't get under way.
> It's the time of the year
> And the time of the day.
>
> ('Sailing after Lunch')

The tone of regret carries over into several poems on the seasons, so that Stevens could be accused of falling into one of Crispin's early faults – of writing about vanishing autumn 'by way of decorous melancholy.' A certain unfortunate nostalgia, in other words, has crept in to replace the fine, firm impersonality of *Harmonium*.

Despair, in some other instances, is associated with specific problems. Here the scene is the Alps:

> Panoramas are not what they used to be.
> Claude has been dead a long time
> And apostrophes are forbidden on the funicular.
> Marx has ruined Nature,
> For the moment.
>
> ('Botanist on Alp – No. 1')

The whole poem from which these lines are taken seems to be relaxed both in writing and in thinking. Claude does not take on the symbolic weight that such personages in Stevens' work usually have: the poem seems to slip into private references. But it does, farther along, set up momentarily a vision of lost order, of the world 'resting on pillars,' with which it opposes the emotion of despair. This tendency to disorganization is perhaps most painful in the long piece 'Like Decorations in a Nigger Cemetery', which, doubtless because of the questionable device for holding it together seems to be completely fragmentary.

But the greater number of the new poems are manly and staunch, and seem to overcome the new difficulties. The 'Dance of the Macabre Mice' is a crisp statement of the dignity of government and its inability to change as the necessities of the people change. 'Lions in Sweden' is one of the best examples of Stevens' new work. The lion is here an image or concretion of civil order; as such it has the moral qualities of faithfulness, justice, patience, and fortitude; and it has come to be a decoration for savings banks. It has also been an image for the delight of the soul. The poet, finding it now an inadequate image, discards it with the indication that better images must be hunted out. What these may be seems to remain, in this book, a little in doubt.

In general however, the new ideas of order are not greatly different from those in *Harmonium*. one of the best poems, 'Botanist on Alp – No. 2,' puts into brilliant language the favorite theme of the balance between transitory graces and tug of the eternal. The excellent sense of the power of music reappears in 'The Idea of Order at Key West'; this poem ends with the following lines:

> The lights in the fishing boats at anchor there,
> As the night descended, tilting in the air,
> Mastered the night and portioned out the sea,
> Fixing emblazoned zones and fiery poles,
> Arranging, deepening, enchanting night.
>
> Oh! Blessed rage for order, pale Ramon,
> The maker's rage to order words of the sea,
> Words of the fragrant portals, dimly-starred,
> And of ourselves and of our origins,
> In ghostlier demarcations, keener sounds.

This obviously is dipped from the clear spring from which *Harmonium* came.

It might well be maintained that some of the new poems have suffered not so much from a revision of ideas as from a relaxing of technique. If we put some potentially excellent lines beside those we just quoted, I think that the looseness in metrics will be noticeable first of all:

In the far South the sun of autumn is passing
Like Walt Whitman walking along a ruddy shore.
He is singing and chanting the things that are part of him,
The worlds that were and will be, death and day.
Nothing is final, he chants. No man shall see the end.
His beard is of fire and his staff is a leaping flame.
('Like Decorations in a Nigger Cemetery')

Though Whitman may not grace these lines, his name would be more welcome than his meter. And this is unfortunate, for Stevens has seized here upon that sovereign image, the sun, with a vigor that few other poets could command. But it is a fact worth insisting upon that the best work in *Harmonium* is in very strict meter and that in a different form it would be worth not at all what it is. Since, moreover, the new poems tend to be intellectual and logical, rather than passionately mental and incremental as are those in *Harmonium*, the need for rigorous form is undoubtedly just that much the greater.

One of the things that should be said about the new work is that at its best it does not deny *Harmonium*. Although it labors a little inconclusively with the social and economic problems of these disturbed years, its solutions are generally an interesting application of the earlier and larger notions to the specific difficulty. Such application is valuable and necessary. But the earlier notions – the perception of elemental structure in the universe, the balance between the individual and the impersonal – are more valuable than any applications.

NOTE

1 'Poetry of the Mind', *Essays in Criticism* (University of California Press, 1934).

30. Stanley Burnshaw, from 'Turmoil in the Middle Ground', *New Masses*

Vol. 17, 1 October 1935, 41–2

Burnshaw (b. 1906), poet, critic, editor and publisher, is best-known for *The Seamless Web* (1970) and the anthology *The Poem Itself* (1960).

The Alcestis Press edition is reviewed with Haniel Long's *Pittsburgh Memoranda* (notice of which is omitted here). Stevens responded to this review with his poem 'Mr. Burnshaw and the Statue', first published in Alfred Kreymborg's *The New Caravan*, and included in *Owl's Clover* (see below) and eventually in *Opus Posthumous*. Commenting on the poem to Ronald Lane Latimer, he said 'Mr. Burnshaw applied the point of view of the practical Communist to *Ideas of Order*; in "Mr. Burnshaw and the Statue" I have tried to reverse the process' (*Letters*, p. 289). Several weeks earlier, on 9 October 1935, he had written to Latimer: 'The review in [*New*] *Masses* was a most interesting review; because it placed me in a new setting. I hope I am headed left, but there are lefts and lefts, and certainly I am not headed for the ghastly left of *Masses*' (*Letters*, 286). Burnshaw provides background for his writing the review in 'Wallace Stevens and the Statue', *Sewanee Review*, vol. 69, 1961, pp. 355–66.

Among the handful of clichés which have crept into left-wing criticism is the notion that contemporary poets – except those on the left and extreme right – have all tramped off to some escapist limbo where they are joyously gathering moonshine. That such an idiot's paradise has existed no one can deny; but today the significant middle-ground poets are laboring elsewhere. And the significant trend is being marked by such writers as Wallace Stevens and Haniel Long: poets whose artistic statures have long been recognized, whose latest books (issued in middle age) form a considered record of agitated attitudes toward the present social order. Like all impressive phenomena of the middle ground, *Pittsburgh Memoranda* and *Ideas of Order* show troubled, searching minds.

As a matter of record Haniel Long has been struggling for a 'solution' ever since his singular stories and poems appeared in the liberal magazines a dozen years ago....

Confused as it is, *Pittsburgh Memoranda* is a marvel of order alongside Wallace Stevens' volume; and yet to many readers it is something of a miracle that Stevens has at all bothered to give us his *Ideas of Order*. When *Harmonium* appeared a dozen years ago Stevens was at once set down as an incomparable verbal musician. But nobody stopped to ask if he had any ideas. It was tacitly assumed that one read him for pure poetic sensation; if he had 'a message' it was carefully buried and would take no end of labor to exhume. Yet he often comes out with flat judgments and certain ideas weave through the book consistently:

> The magnificent cause of being,
> The imagination, the one reality
> In this imagined world

underlies a number of poems. Realists have been bitter at the inanity of Pope's 'Whatever is is right,' but Stevens plunges ahead to the final insolence: 'For realists, what is is what should be.' And yet it is hard to know if such a line is not Stevens posing in self-mockery. One can rarely speak surely of Stevens' ideas.

But certain general convictions he admits in such a poem as 'To One of Fictive Music.' Bound up with the sovereignty of the imagination is his belief in an interfusion of music among the elements and man. And 'Music is feeling ... not sound.' This trinity of principles makes the business of living to him a matter of searching out the specific harmonies.

Harmonium, then, is mainly sense poetry, but not as Keats's is sense poetry, because this serener poet is not driven to

suffuse sensuous imagery with powerful subjective emotions. This is 'scientific,' objectified sensuousness separated
from its kernel of fire and allowed to settle, cool off, and
harden in the poet's mind until it emerges a strange amazing
crystal. Reading this poetry becomes a venture in crystal-
lography. It is remembered for its curious humor, its
brightness, its words and phrases that one rolls on the
tongue. It is the kind of verse that people concerned with the
murderous world collapse can hardly swallow today except
in tiny doses.

And it is verse that Stevens can no longer write. His
harmonious cosmos is suddenly screeching with confusion.
Ideas of Order is the record of a man who, having lost his
footing, now scrambles to stand up and keep his balance. The
opening poem observes

> ... This heavy historical sail
> Through the mustiest blue of the lake
> In a wholly vertiginous boat
> Is wholly the vapidest fake....

And the rest follows with all the ironical logic of such a
premise. The 'sudden mobs of men' may have the answer;

> But what are radiant reason and radiant will
> To warblings early in the hilarious trees....

Sceptical of man's desire in general, there is still much to be
said for the ordering power of the imagination. But there
remains a yearning – and escape is itself an irony. 'Marx has
ruined Nature, for the moment,' he observes in self-
mockery; but he can speculate on the wisdom of turning
inward, and a moment later look upon collective mankind as
the guilty bungler of harmonious life, in 'a peanut parody for
a peanut people.' What answer is there in the cosmic
law – 'everything falls back to coldness'? With apparent
earnestness he goes a step beyond his former nature-man
interfusing harmony:

> Only we two are one, not you and night,
> Nor night and I, but you and I, alone,
> So much alone, so deeply by ourselves,

So far beyond the casual solitudes,
That night is only the background of our selves...

And in a long poem he pours out in strange confusion his
ideas of order, among them:

If ever the search for a tranquil belief should end,
The future might stop emerging out of the past,
Out of what is full of us; yet the search
And the future emerging out of us seem to be one.

Paraphrase, always a treacherous tool, is especially dangerous when used on so *raffiné* a poet as Stevens. Does he talk of
himself when he explains that 'the purple bird must have
notes for his comfort that he may repeat through the gross
tedium of being rare'? Does he make political reference in
declaring 'the union of the weakest develops strength, not
wisdom'?

Asking questions may not be a reviewer's function, but
uncertainties are unavoidable when reading such poets as the
two under review; for the texture of their thought is made of
speculations, questionings, contradictions. Acutely conscious members of a class menaced by the clashes between
capital and labor, these writers are in the throes of struggle
for philosophical adjustment. And their words have intense
value and meaning to the sectors within the class whose
confusions they articulate. Their books have deep importance for us as well.

Of course, objectively, neither poet is weakening the class
in power – as yet they are potential allies as well as potential
enemies – but one of them looks for a new set of values and
the other earnestly propagates (however vaguely) some form
of collectivism. Will Long emancipate himself from his
paralyzing faith in inner perfection? Will Stevens sweep his
contradictory notions into a valid Idea of Order? The
answers depend not only on the personal predispositions of
these poets but on their full realization of the alternatives
facing them as artists.

31. Harriet Monroe, on Stevens' 'serene acceptance', from 'He Plays the Present', *Poetry*

Vol. 47, no. 3, December 1935, 153–7

The last two paragraphs of the review are cited.

... This latest book may give tremors of trepidation to some of Stevens' loyal admirers – fears that his delight in all the beauty and oddity may be shaken by the clamor and confusion of the modern scene. 'Too many waltzes have ended,' he laments in 'Sad Strains of a Gay Waltz':

[Quotes the poem, *CP*, p. 121.]

We do not need this poem to show us that Mr. Stevens is always aware of his world, but even this poem can not convince us that he will ever lose his delight in it. His mind delves deeper and rides higher than that of the 'harmonious skeptic' who is to write the 'epic of disbelief.' His epic will always be one of serene acceptance; it will present values that are immediate and yet timeless. Even a revolution, even communism or fascism, will never disturb the firm foundations of his philosophy, or blind him to the delicate perfections of beauty in a miracle-breeding world.

32. Babette Deutsch, 'The Gaudiness of Poetry', *New York Herald Tribune Books*

15 December 1935, 18

A poet, novelist, critic, translator and reviewer, Babette Deutsch (1895–1982) is best known for *Poetry in Our Time* (1952; 1967). Her *Collected Poems* were published in New York in 1969.

Wallace Steven's favorite among his own poems is 'The Emperor of Ice-Cream,' because it has what he calls 'the essential gaudiness of poetry.' Yet he praises his friend William Carlos Williams for the anti-poetic attitude of a Diogenes. In this new volume of verse, Stevens is both gaudy and, to a lesser degree, anti-poetic. Consider his 'Dance of the Macabre Mice,' which suggests a surrealist painting, and begins;

> In the land of turkeys in turkey weather.
> At the base of the statue, we go round and round.
> What a beautiful history, beautiful surprise!
> Monsieur is on horseback. The horse is covered with
> mice.

As the poem progresses the symbolism becomes clear, and the ornament, shall we say, functional:

> This dance has no name. It is a hungry dance.
> We dance it out to the tip of Monsieur's sword,
> Reading the lordly language of the inscription,
> Which is like zithers and tambourines combined:

> The Founder of the State. Whoever founded
> A State that was free, in the dead of winter, from mice?

What a beautiful tableau tinted and towering.
The arm of bronze outstretched against all evil!

The, bizarre picture transforms itself into a sardonic
commentary on civilization.

But though Stevens punctuates his observations with
thought, though he gives sensation and sentiment a coloring
of reflection, for the most part he is content to chronicle a
mood, to embroider musically upon his responses to sunrise
and twilight, the orchestra and the ocean, birds, fruits,
landscapes. His poems are not so much 'ideas of order' as
order itself, – the pattern that the artist imposes upon nature.
He is assisted by the fact that he sees nature in a state that is
only semi-savage. He is assisted further by a nice ear and by a
keen delight in color, preferably barbaric. There are moments when the present intrudes, as in 'Sad Strains of a Gay
Waltz':

> There are these sudden mobs of men,
> These sudden clouds of faces and arms,
> An immense suppression, freed.
> These voices crying without knowing for what.
> Except to be happy, without knowing how.
> Imposing forms they cannot describe.
> Requiring order beyond their speech.

Or again, in 'Mozart, 1935,' which recalls, with a
difference, MacLeish's 'Men of My Century Have Loved,
Mozart':

> Poet, be seated at the piano.
> Play, the present, its hoo-hoo-hoo,
> Its shoo-shoo-shoo, its ric-a-nic,
> Its envious cachinnation.
> If they throw stones upon the roof
> While you practice arpeggios,
> It is because they carry down the stairs,
> A body in rags.
> Be seated at the piano.

Yet Stevens is not concerned with the present. He is too
much engrossed with what is present peculiarly to himself.

If one comes to these verses with a raw sense of the times in which we live – and more generally die – their delicate aloofness may offend. To surrender to them, however, is to be admitted, to a world no more private than age and death, no more reprehensible than those moments of heightened being which poetry rescues from the black bag of age and death. For

> Poetry is a finikin thing of air
> That lives uncertainly and not for long
> Yet radiantly beyond much lustier blurs.

Stevens's work is not quite as finikin here as heretofore. He is, as ever, interested in Havana and its particular and rather trifling ornaments. But occasionally he draws a deep breath and fetches forth a more generous canvas, as for this resplendent image:

> In the far South the sun of autumn is passing
> Like Walt Whitman walking along a ruddy shore.
> He is singing and chanting the things that are part of
> him.
> The worlds that were and will be, death and day.
> Nothing is final, he chants. No man shall see the end.
> His beard is of fire and his staff is a leaping flame.

Sometimes he denies his impulse to be gaudy and accepts a simple adequate metaphor, as when he speaks of 'The ever-hooded, tragic-gestured sea.' 'The Brave Man,' the declamation of a sun worshiper, might be – except for the line describing the stars' 'Pale helms and spiky spurs' – a translation of an Indian chant. There is a new sombreness, a new gravity, about the collection as a whole, so that if he is preoccupied with the Emperor of Ice-Cream, who is death, the poet sees him in a more dignified if no less disturbing guise.

The book is carefully made and printed in hand-set type. The poems are finely spaced on the page, and the ivory paper binding is beautifully simple. But the decorative type calls attention to itself and gives the volume an air of affectation not unusual to limited editions. In any case, the poems, while

written for a small fastidious public, should enjoy a larger
audience than this edition can demand.

33. Marianne Moore, on Stevens' 'unembarrassing souvenirs', *Criterion*

Vol. XV, January 1936, 307–9

Poetry is an unintelligible unmistakable vernacular like the
language of the animals – a system of communication whereby a fox with a turkey too heavy for it to carry, reappears
shortly with another fox to share the booty, and Wallace
Stevens is a practised hand at this kind of open cypher. With
compactness beyond compare and the *forte agitato* competence of the concert room, he shows one how not to call joy
satisfaction, and how one may be the epic one indites and yet
be anonymous; how one may have 'mighty Fortitudo, frantic
bass' while maintaining one's native rareness in peace. Art is
here shown to be a thing of proprieties, of mounting 'the
thickest man on thickest stallion-back'; yet a congruence of
opposites as in the titles, 'Sad Strains of a Gay Waltz', and 'A
Fish-scale Sunrise'. Meditation for the fatalist is a surrender
to 'the morphology of regret' – a drowning in one's welter of
woes, dangers, risks, obstacles to inclination. Poetry viewed
morphologically is 'finikin thing of air', 'a few words tuned
and tuned and tuned and tuned'; and 'the function of the poet'
is 'sound to stuff the ear'; or – rather – it is 'particles of order,
a single majesty'; it is 'our unfinished spirits realized more
sharply in more furious selves'. Art is both 'rage for order'
and 'rage against chaos'. It is a classifying, a botanizing, a
voracity of contemplation. 'The actual is a deft beneficence.'

These thirty-three poems, composed since the enlarged

edition of *Harmonium* appeared, present various conclusions
about art as order. They are a series of guarded definitions
but also the unembarrassing souvenirs of a man and

> ...the time when he stood alone,
> When to be and delight to be seemed to be one.

In the untrite transitions, the as if sentimental unsen-
timentality, the meditativeness not for appraisal, with hints
taken from the birds, as in Brahms, they recall Brahms; his
dexterousness, but also his self-relish and technique of evasion as in the incident of the lion-huntress who was inquiring
for the celebrated Herr Brahms: 'You will find him yonder,
on the other side of the hill, this is his brother.'

Wallace Stevens can be as serious as the starving-times of
the first settlers, and he can be Daumier caricaturing the
photographer, making a time exposure watch in hand, above
the title, 'Patience is an Attribute of the Donkey.' The pieces
are marvels of finish, and they are a dashing to oblivion of
that sort of impropriety wherein 'the chronicle of affected
homage foxed so many books'. They are 'moodiest no-
things'; 'the trees are wooden, the grass is thin'; and they
are

> ...Evening, when the measure skips a beat
> And then another, one by one, and all
> To a seething minor swiftly modulate.

Mr. Stevens alludes to 'the eccentric' as 'the base of design',
'the revealing aberration'; and employs noticeably in such a
poem as 'Sailing After Lunch', the principle of dispersal
common to music; that is to say, a building up of the theme
piecemeal in such a way that there is no possibility of
disappointment at the end. But ease accompanies the
transpositions and pauses; it is indeed a self-weighted
momentum as when he says of the eagle,

> Describe with deepened voice
> And noble imagery
> His slowly-falling round
> Down to the fishy sea.

An air of 'merely circulating' disguises material of the
dizziest: swans, winter stars; that 'body wholly body', the

sea; 'roses, noble in autumn, yet nobler than autumn'; 'the mythy goober khan'; 'peanut people'; 'roughed fruits'; 'the vermillion pear'; 'a casino in a wood'; 'this tufted rock'; 'the heroic height'; 'tableau tinted and towering'; the fairy-tale we wished might exist; in short, everything ghostly yet undeniable.

Serenity in sophistication is a triumph, like the behaviour of birds. The poet in fact is the migration mechanism of sensibility, and a medicine for the soul. That exact portrayal is intoxicating, that realism need not restrict itself to grossness, that music is 'an accord of repetitions' is evident to one who examines *Ideas of Order*; and the altitude of performance makes the wild boars of philistinism who rush about interfering with experts, negligible. In America where the dearth of rareness is conspicuous, those who recognize it feel compelled to acknowledgement; yet such a thing as a book notice seems at best an advertisement of one's inability to avoid bluntness.

34. F. O. Matthiessen, from 'Society and Solitude in Poetry', *Yale Review*

Vol. XXV, no. 3, March 1936, 603–7

One of the finest scholar-critics of his generation, Matthiessen (1902–50) spent most of his teaching career at Harvard. His most notable work includes *The Achievement of T. S. Eliot: An Essay on the Nature of Poetry* (1935), *Henry James: The Major Phase* (1944) and *The James Family* (1947), though perhaps his masterpiece is *American Renaissance: Art and Expression in the Age of Emerson and Whitman* (1941). Matthiessen's suicide on 1 April 1950 was apparently caused by the tensions of the Cold War.

The other poems reviewed are by Robinson, Rukeyser, Jeffers and Stanley Burnshaw. Given the 'ideological' clash between Stevens and Burnshaw, it is perhaps worth noting Matthiessen's comment on Burnshaw's book of poems, *The Iron Land*: 'Mr. Burnshaw's mill town, though observed sharply, is not portrayed with the detail that would take it out of the realm of political theory and make its anguish seem as real as it is.'

... But of the poets at hand the one whose lines yield both the sense of strong individual life and a mature apprehension of actual society is Wallace Stevens in his *Ideas of Order*. In building around such ideas, the best of these poems mark an advance over his previous volume, *Harmonium*. They seem more robustly integrated; there is no longer the *dandyisme* of 'Le Monocle de Mon Oncle,' or the slightly affected traces as in the elaborate language of 'The Comedian as the Letter C.' But there has been no waning in the lusty joy of his senses, or in the acute perception that discovered 'Thirteen Ways of Looking at a Blackbird,' or in what has always been his outstanding gift, the subtle resilient modulations of his rhythm. As a result his poems do not make statements about life; they create for the reader an illusion of sharing in a complete experience. When Mr. Stevens comments on the present state of the world, you are not given Mr. Jeffers's melodramatic vision of all mankind plunging down the hill to a darkened sea, or the romantic utopian dawn of the current revolutionists. Instead, 'Sad Strains of a Gay Waltz' notes the emptiness that has crept into conventional forms of thought and feeling, and the stirring of the immense suppressed energies that are rising beyond those forms, and comes to this conclusion:

> Too many waltzes have ended. Yet the shapes
> For which the voices cry, these, too, may be
> Modes of desire, modes of revealing desire.
>
> Too many waltzes – The epic of disbelief
> Blares oftener and soon, will soon be constant.
> Some harmonious skeptic soon in a skeptical music

Will unite these figures of men and their shapes
Will glisten again with motion, the music
Will be motion and full of shadows.

Beneath the haunting expert cadence of these lines Mr.
Stevens is passionately concerned with human proportion.
He does not rush to any easy extreme; he envisages life not
merely as change but as continuity. Both 'grief' and
'grievance' unite to cause the shudder that is produced by
'Dance of the Macabre Mice' when the silhouette of the
statue of the Founder of the State is suddenly seen in the dead
of winter to be swarming with black forms. Likewise, in
'Re-statement of Romance,' in 'How to Live. What to Do,'
or in the complex 'Idea of Order at Key West,' which has
music for its subject as well as for its effect, Mr. Stevens has
brought his talents to an expression that is at once precise and
opulent. One is tempted to say that this is the nearest
approach to major poetry being made in this country to-day.
At the very least, it is the one fully ripened book of poems to
have originated here within the past year, the only one that
would lend great distinction to a Pulitzer prize.

35. John Holmes, 'But this time some meaning has crept in', from 'Five American Poets', *Virginia Quarterly Review*

Vol. 12, no. 2, April 1936, 294

Three of the other four books reviewed were published
by the Alcestis Press. These are Allen Tate, *The
Mediterranean and Other Poems*, Robert Penn Warren,

Thirty-Six Poems, and John Peale Bishop, *Minute Particulars*. The remaining book is Edwin Arlington Robinson's *King Jasper*.

... What Louis Untermeyer calls the ambiguous world of Wallace Stevens' poetry is further enlarged in a new book called *Ideas of Order*. Mr. Stevens is well known for the rarity with which he publishes collections, his last but one having come in 1923, after ten years of publication in magazines. His name is also well known for the curious fascination his poetry exerts without ever seeming to mean anything at all more than a mood, an exotic and shifting dream. It is poetry that, as Llewelyn Powys says, 'is beyond good and evil, beyond hope and despair, beyond thought of any kind, one might almost say.' Mr. Stevens is, in short, one of the most successful non-communicating poets of his day. But it is only ideas that he does not communicate, ideas, morals, epigrams of a sententious kind. Through the most fantastically logical world of imagery which these generations know, he does communicate feeling. That feeling is specific and pleasing. Anything that Mr. Stevens does is pleasing, is in fact a matter for sincere amazement and admiration. Meaning it has never had, in the ordinary superficial sense, because it has so little to do with the world of actuality. But this time some meaning has crept in. If Mr. Stevens' poetry is of his own mood, then recent moods of the real world have affected him, and they show in this book. Among the wilful and delightfully patterned movements of his new poems there moves an unaccustomed form of meaning. The reader feels this most in the piece called, though only God and Mr. Stevens know why, 'Like Decorations in a Nigger Cemetery.' It is a series of fifty of his most pungent statements, brief, various, and brilliant....

36. Theodore Roethke, on 'a rich and special sensibility', *New Republic*

15 July 1936, 305

Roethke (1907–63) was a 'confessional' poet whose work was strongly influential in the 1960s. His best-known single volume is *The Lost Son* (1948). *Collected Poems* was published in 1966, and in the same year *On the Poet and His Craft: Selected Prose*, and in 1968 *Selected Letters*.

This book is further proof of Wallace Stevens' poetic vitality. Most of the characteristics of his earlier work are here: the wit that frequently turns upon itself, the special and sometimes precious vocabulary, the ambiguity astutely employed, the grave irony, the sad resignation. However, the colors are less exotic, the associations less strange than in *Harmonium*. The times and a ripened maturity have begun to stiffen Mr. Stevens' rhetoric. Some of the poems seem merely the record of experience taken from the surface of the mind, the thing instantly perceived and set down. But 'Sad Strains of a Gay Waltz,' 'Dance of the Macabre Mice,' 'The Sun This March' and at least a dozen others are important and complete in design. It is a pity that such a rich and special sensibility should be content with the order of words and music, and not project itself more vigorously upon the present-day world.

37. R. P. Blackmur, Stevens' double language, from 'The Composition in Nine Poets', *Southern Review*

Vol. 2, Winter 1937, 574–5

Passing mention is made of *Owl's Clover*, and some parallels are drawn between Stevens' poetry and Conrad Aiken's. The other poets reviewed are A. E. Housman, Sandburg, Masters, Witter Bynner, Arthur Guiterman, Frederic Prokosch and the translation of Euripides' *Alcestis* by Dudley Fitts and Robert Fitzgerald.

... Ideas are principles, notions, clues, guesses, abstractions of hope, deposits of insight; but they are also things seen, both casually and deliberately envisaged. It is the function of poetry – or of Mr. Stevens' poetry – to experience ideas of the first kind with the eyes of the second kind, and to make of the experience of both a harmony and an order: a harmonium. Thus Mr. Stevens' values inhabit his words; and if he can make his words grow together he will be composing on his harmonium. The machinery of composition – the ways he uses words – is double; he fuses two separable vocabularies. There is a vocabulary of concepts or symbols – the nubs and cores and condensations of meaning – which is almost altogether dissimulated, by great craft, in the simplest and most familiar general terms of the language, in terms of the sun, moon, sky, clouds, in terms of sea and landscape, in the almost natural terms that cats and dogs can understand. And there is, forced into this, a vocabulary of difficult, striking, or puzzling words ... – words that have to be looked up in the dictionary, and, looked up, always turn out to be the very instruments that make the general terms precise, predominant, and imaginatively actual. It is, then, with Mr.

Stevens, the reality in the words themselves that is composed by the skill and precision with which the specific is made to work upon the general....

38. William Rose Benét, on 'a virtuoso and voluptuary of language', from 'Three Poets and a Few Opinions', *North American Review*

Vol. 243, Spring–Summer 1937, 195–7

Elder brother of Stephen Vincent Benét and husband of Elinor Wylie, William Rose Benét (1886–1950) won the Pulitzer Prize in 1942. His many volumes of poetry include a verse autobiography, *The Dust Which is God* (1941).

The other two poets noticed are Robert Francis and Thomas Caldecot Chubb.

... He has always been an elusive poet, but his work has a particular flavor and savor of its own. In most cases a taste for it must be acquired, but once acquired a new book by Wallace Stevens can be deeply relished. What he supplies is original design, pure color, and pure music. He comes near fulfilling what George Moore, some time ago, tried rather cloudily to describe as 'pure poetry.' Mr. Stevens can always create a highly original atmosphere around a subject. One does not go to him for direct discourse, but for meanings like Chinese boxes concealed one inside the other, for improvisations with language that are akin to musical improvisations and also to modern painting. Mr. Stevens avoids the obvious with incessant alertness. He is a virtuoso and voluptuary of language.

Some of us can delight in the way a thing is said without worrying too haggardly as to *what* is said. Such people can enjoy, for instance, the following opening of Mr. Steven's 'Academic Discourse at Havana.' Others find such writing either intensely irritating or simply bewildering:

> Canaries in the morning, orchestras
> In the afternoon, balloons at night, That is
> A difference, at least, from nightingales,
> Jehovah and the great sea-worm. The air
> Is not so elemental nor the earth
> So near.
> But the sustenance of the wilderness
> Does not sustain us in the metropoles.

Later on in the same poem Mr. Stevens asks:

> Is the function of the poet here more sound,
> Subtler than the ornatest prophecy,
> To stuff the ear?

If the reader is inclined to shout 'Yes!' he is far too hasty; for the poem thoroughly read, and it runs to four pages, is found to build up just the sort of original atmosphere to which I have referred above, until we are in that particular place and no other and can appreciate all it suggests. Most of the thirty-six poems here present are not nearly so long, though one of the best, 'The Idea of Order at Key West,' which is almost pure music, is longish. The poet's attitude toward the epoch in which he finds himself comes out most clearly in 'Mozart, 1935.'

> If they throw stones upon the roof
> While you practice arpeggios,
> It is because they carry down the stairs
> A body in rags.
> Be seated at the piano.

This poem ends with a statement which happens to appeal particularly to me, because I am of Mr. Stevens's time, and it seems to me a natural feeling under the circumstances.

We may return to Mozart.
He was young, and we, we are old.
The snow is falling
And the streets are full of cries.
Be seated, thou.

You will perceive that this man is an esthete (new style) but he has also a quality that pleases me. It is often quite difficult to tell whether he is serious or not. As for beauty, he has seen the most bizarre beauty everywhere. He has a whole pavilion all to himself in modern poetry....

OWL'S CLOVER

New York, 1936

Published by the Alcestis Press in an edition of 105 copies.

39. Ruth Lechlitner, 'Imagination as Reality', *New York Herald Tribune Books*

6 December 1936, 40

Lechlitner (b. 1901) was a poet and reviewer.

Chiefly concerned with *Owl's Clover*, this review also deals briefly with *Ideas of Order*. The complete review is given for the theme development.

Of the two volumes under review, *Ideas of Order* contains the poems that appeared last fall in the Alcestic Press Limited edition, to which three new poems have been added: 'Farewell to Florida,' 'Ghosts as Cocoons' and 'Postcard. From the Volcano.' *Owl's Clover*, Wallace Stevens's latest work, is a group of poems in blank verse, which may be read as a single long poem with a philosophic theme in symphonic structure.

In *Harmonium* Stevens's first collection (1923), the poet's preoccupation with design – particularly with the eccentric as the base of design – was evident. An interwoven pattern repeating the color of hemlocks and the cry of peacocks might serve, or a recurrent death-sweet oriental note with a phrase of acrid irony in careful counterpoint. And the gay perfection of his simple melodious lyrics (one recalls with

delight 'Ploughing on Sunday') is nearer to pure poetry than
anything Stevens has since done. A definite theme, however,
underlines the work in *Harmonium* that imagination is the
'one reality' in the imagined world. It is a theme fulsomely
elaborated by that autobiographical pilgrim Crispin.

Ideas of Order which carries on this promise, further sets
forth the belief that the poet should be 'the exponent of the
imagination of society,' Stevens is not concerned with the
ideas of a political or social order, but of order arising from
'individual concepts.' The position of the poet caught
between the romantic and the factual, in 'Sailing After
Lunch', gives rise to an idea of order in the practice of an art.
'Sad Strains of a Gay Waltz' contemplates the non-existence
of order both in nature (in a further poem. 'Mars has Ruined
Nature, for the Moment') and in the masses of mankind.

> These sudden clouds of faces and arms.
> An immense suppression, freed.
> These voices crying without knowing for what.
> Except to be happy, without knowing how.
> Imposing forms they cannot describe.
> Requiring order beyond their speech.

As in *Harmonium* Stevens continues with his fondness for
epigram and metaphorical definition: 'life is an old casino in a
park.' 'One is most disclosed when one is most anonymous,'
and of romantic decadence. 'The twilight overfull of wormy
metaphors.' There is the further juxtaposition of contrasting
images, the sun and death; and the two forms of motion, that
fixed and suspended (stone, statue), that unbound and
flowing (the wind, the sea).

> To stand here on the deck in the dark and say
> Farewell and to know that that land is forever gone
> And that she will not follow in any word
> Or look, nor ever again in thought, except
> That I loved her once....

But the poems retain music as feeling, music as the analysis
of a mood; the brooding intensity of Brahms, the 'essential
prose wearing a poem's guise.'

Owl's Clover contains a fusion of the theme established in the two previous collections: the all-pervading power of imagination as reality, and the function of imagination alone in creating a sense of order. And imagination, to Stevens, must be considered as an individual as opposed to a mass or collective concept. The poem itself (the title is cryptic) is built up of separate units around a central symbol: a sculptured group of marble horses. As Marianne Moore has carefully noted, Stevens employs the 'principle of dispersal' common to music, a classical building up and recapitulation of sections in the movement. The first poem, 'The Old Woman and the Statue,' establishes the sculpture, an idea of order created by the imagination in harmonious accord with the windblown, autumn bronze trees surrounding it. This, as foreseen by the sculptor, makes for an ordered design, but there is an unforeseen intrusion: an old woman, black-cloaked, walking along the park path, seeing nothing but herself and her solitude. Hence, this intrusion reduces the mass of 'winged stone' to 'marble hulk,' light, confronted by 'black thought,' falls falsely.

'Mr. Burnshaw and the Statue' is in the nature of a reply to a review by Stanley Burnshaw of *Ideas of Order*, in which the reviewer took Stevens to task for his anti-collective view-point and the confusion of his ideas. Starting again with his sculptured marble horses, from a rather lamely satiric state-ment that they are not even Russian animals, Stevens pre-tends a future replacement of the statue by stones on which shall be carved, 'The mass appoints these marbles of itself to be itself.' He shudders at a time when politics will rule a poet's world – a world impossible for poets. In such a world, when the hopeless waste of the past merges with the waste to come, and from which the peacocks, doves and ploughman of yesterday are fled,

> ... buzzards pile their sticks among the bones
> Of buzzards and eat the bellies of the rich.
> Fat with a thousand butters, and the crows
> Sip the wild honey of the poor man's life.
> The blood of his bitter brain: and there the sun
> Shines without fire on columns intercrossed.
> White slapped on white, majestic, marble heads

Severed and tumbled into seedless grass.
Motionless, knowing neither dew nor frost.

The cooler, graver 'northward' moving voice of Stevens
becomes predominant. His statue is a part of northern sky,
the marble 'imagined in the cold.' His spiritual survey of
modern Europe (in contrast to Africa, where death sits on
the serpent's throne) is dispassioned analysis: the heaven of
Europe is empty, the heaven that was once the 'spirit's
episcopate,' in which man, walking alone, beheld truth.
Here, again, imagination on singular wings achieves the
'order' of solitude: the plural, or mass, represents chaos.
The question as to the desirability of man thinking his
separate thoughts, or not men thinking together as one, is
further propounded. 'Bomber Figuration,' the concluding
piece, is an apostrophe to the power of imagination transcending thought – imagination, 'the man below,' born within us as a second self. But

> Even imagination has an end
> When the statue is not a thing imagined, a stone
> That changed in sleep.

The somberly melodic final lines show the marked differences between Stevens's work in *Harmonium* and his present
mood and technique:

>   ... to feel again
> The reconciliation, the rapture of a time
> Without imagination, without past
> And without future, a present time, is that
> The passion, indifferent to the poet's hum,
> That we conceal? A passion to fling the cloak,
> Adorned for a multitude, in a gesture spent
> In the gesture's whim, a passion merely to be
> For the gaudium of being, Jocundus instead
> Of the black-blooded scholar, the man of the cloud, to be
> The medium man among other medium men.
> The cloak to be clipped, the night to be redesigned.
> Its land-breath to be stifled, its color changed.
> Night and the imagination being one.

By recognizing the importance of political and social change but refusing to admit the desirability of the union of the mass in an 'orderly' life, Stevens is obviously open to attack from the left. He takes his stand as a poet who prefers to suffer defeat by a cosmic rather than a Marxian law. He is aware that his is the philosophical liberal attitude, that he ironically admits his confusion and the anomaly of his position ('my old boat goes round on a crutch') is a point in his favor, but scarcely helps in resolving contradictions.

Stevens may well be remembered not so much for his ideas as for his superb mastery of form. In his present experimentation with the possibilities of the iambic pentameter of blank verse as a flexible instrument for modern prosody, he has made expert use of word-stress, internal rhyme, occasional inverted phrasing and – as in the above-quoted passage – variation in the metrical line itself to gain a finely integrated verbal texture.

Owl's Clover, limited to 105 copies signed by the author and beautifully designed by Vrest Orton, should be of particular interest to all lovers of fine editions.

40. Eda Lou Walton, 'Mr Stevens ... finds it exceedingly difficult to speak directly', *New York Times Book Review*

6 December 1936, 18

The introductory paragraph and review of *Ideas of Order* have been omitted.

... He has turned now to face the social scene, 'the colder climate' of man's struggle today. Since his technique has been, in a way, a technique of disillusionment, a way of writing in which words alone had life, a music fading out as the words were spoken, the poet must, in order to affirm something, alter his technique. In these last collections, therefore, Stevens is resorting more to statement. He is, in a way, arguing with himself....

Owl's Clover is a continuation of Mr. Stevens's arguments in *Ideas of Order* about the artist's position in the world today. This long, half-descriptive, half-narrative poem has to do with an equestrian statue, the symbol of art. In the first section, 'The Old Woman and the Statue,' this statue, a group of horses, is described. Then the old woman is introduced, a hopeless figure to whom the statue means nothing. The dark mind of the old woman changes the statue. Human fate alters the significance of art. In the end, however, the statue rises into beauty again. The second section, 'Mr. Burnshaw and the Statue,' has to do with the question of art's social significance. Obviously, this section was written in answer to Mr. Burnshaw's criticism of Mr. Stevens's earlier poems. The poet half concedes Mr. Burnshaw's argument that the horses of the statue are not beautiful if they have no social message for the people – that one must live in change. But he concludes by returning to the conviction that men need art to transfigure reality.

The third section, 'The Green Continent' is an argument as to whether or not naturalism or barbarianism will conquer our modern art forms. The poet concludes that art rises from the sensual and will remain changelessly great for any order of society. 'A Duck for Dinner,' the fourth section, places the statue, or art, against the thesis of economic determinism. Stevens concludes that art sums up the past, foretells the future, is the statement of the heart's desire even when we are hungry. The final section of the poem states that man causes change, but is himself never actually changed; that we are weary of the thinker and would be reconciled with the natural man again. Art is today just what it is; let it be what it may become in the future. Since we exist in change, we change, but art sums up the whole of what we, as man, have known.

This whole poem is a little weighted with thought, a little less successful than the lyrics in *Ideas of Order*. And Mr.

Stevens, who has always spoken through sensuous words, finds it exceedingly difficult to speak directly. For these reasons, though *Owl's Clover* is very interesting, it is not an entirely fine poem or series of poems.

Since Wallace Stevens is undoubtedly one of our best poets, it is interesting to trace the changes in his artistic position. He has been the pure epicurean, sophisticated and intellectual, but delighting most in the conjured mood of beauty. Today he is certainly taking account of a world in which this philosophy is antiquated. He is trying to evaluate the position of the artist in a world of struggle, of action. If this means, for a time, that his poetry is less surely perfect, it means also that his later poetry may be more significant than his earlier work. Stevens is trying to put aside mood and dream clothed in fine rhetoric for reality.

41. Ben Belitt, 'the edifice of a new technique begins to take shape', from 'The Violent Mind', *Nation*

Vol. 143, no. 24, 12 December 1936, 710

A poet, translator and editor, Belitt (b. 1911) is best known for his translations of Lorca's *Poet in New York* (1955) and *Selected Poems of Pablo Neruda* (1961). The present review also deals with *Ideas of Order*.

Though the poetry of Wallace Stevens has not lacked themes of commanding contemporary stature, these have not, until recently, constituted his major concern. His problem has been a curious one: moved to formal discourse in the quest for order and certitude, his art has not up to the present permitted him to pursue such discourse or his temperament to accept it. Instead, in an essentially evocative medium, he has continued to qualify definitions to their fractional parts, reducing ideas into images and images into sounds – and then neglected the full circle which returns both sound and image to experience and unites the fractional with the definitive insight.

In *Ideas of Order,* his last volume but one, now re-issued, the movement toward a poetry of statement was first discernible. From the initial 'Farewell to Florida,' it is a volume almost wholly transitional, telling off again and again a theme of halt and change and voicing a determination to abandon one aesthetic climate for another – to withdraw from 'Floridian' self-indulgence and calm and 'live by bluest reason in a world of wind and frost,' to 'return to the violent mind.' With a melancholy by turns bemused and ironic yet wholly lacking in truculence, Stevens recasts his theme in image after image, affirming, inferring, surmising – reticently as in 'There is no such thing as innocence in autumn, Yet, it may be innocence is never lost'; somberly as in 'Bare night is best. Bare earth is best. Bare, bare'; ironically as in 'Poet, be seated at the piano. Play the present, its hoo-hoo-hoo, Its shoo-shoo-shoo, its ric-a-nic'; and humbly:

No more phrases, Swenson: I was once
A hunter of those sovereigns of the soul....
These lions, these majestical images.
If the fault is with the soul, the sovereigns
Of the soul must likewise be at fault, and first.

The method, however, continues to be no less oblique than that of the earlier *Harmonium,* even though the labor of pruning is already under way. Like 'Decorations in a Nigger Cemetery,' the long sequence of three-and-four-line notations furnishes a convenient pattern of his approach in general: here we have, impinging upon a general mood, a series of epigrams, cryptic till the reader feels the centrifugal pull of mood fusing the fragments into proper focus.

With *Owl's Clover,* Mr. Stevens's most recent volume, the

edifice of a new technique begins to take shape amid the wreckage of the old. Essentially a blank-verse sequence of five soliloquies strung together on a prevailing symbol, it attempts to explore the 'violent mind' to which Stevens is now apprenticed, and weighs the consequences which an art like his own, 'manqué and gold and brown,' must be prepared to accept if it is to provide equal room for 'plowmen, peacocks, doves.' Unfortunately, however, the key symbol – here a statue representing a group of winged horses in flight – is neither felicitous, nor consistently employed, nor readily translatable in terms of its various contexts. In 'The Old Woman and the Statue', for example, the physical details of the marble are too vividly underscored to permit of symbolic analogy. In 'Mr. Burnshaw and the Statue,' where one is compelled to acknowledge a symbolic function, it is only very painfully that the meanings can be narrowed down from vaguely political contexts to an unclear gospel of living 'incessantly in change' in the stream of contemporary experience. And in 'The Greenest Continent,' the most complex section of the five, one is gratuitously presented with a companion symbol – that of 'the greenest continent', Africa – which one pursues through numerous levels of reference until one comes to rest in a discussion of art, the art of Wallace Stevens, and the ordeal of rediscovery that awaits the poet in the wilderness in which he has newly set foot.

It will not be necessary to inform Mr. Stevens's admirers in passing that *Owl's Clover,* like its predecessors, abounds in the kind of orchestrative cunning of which he remains our most knowing purveyor. The music is, moreover, as Stevens intended, of a somewhat more toughened sort, pruned of bravura and merging the logical with the lyrical. Yet it is also the least fluid which his instrument has given out so far. Doubtless, the same incongruities which induce him to address political reflections to imaginery 'mesdames' in terms of statuary and the pastoral dance recur to clot his rhetoric with gingerbread and stand in the way of a thoughtful wiriness. His position, at present, is not unlike that of the conductor Basilewsky of his poem, who performs concertos for airplane and pianoforte; and it is perfectly obvious that no

one surmises the fact more than Stevens himself. Yet his pact
with 'the violent mind' is one which is deeply felt, and has
been sealed in somber good faith, in the hope that

> The charts destroyed, even disorder may,
> So seen, have an order of its own, a peace
> Not now to be perceived yet order's own.

It remains to be seen, however, whether such a doctrine does
not cut the Gordian knot with a sword of two edges: one to
save and one to destroy.

42. Marianne Moore, 'Unanimity and Fortitude', *Poetry*

Vol. 49, no. 5, February 1937, 268–72

Cited as a review of *Owl's Clover* and *Ideas of Order*, this
piece is perhaps more interesting as a show of verbal
colourings; but, characteristically, Marianne Moore also
offers several original critical perceptions, not least the
comparison between Stevens and Eliot.

For some of us, Wallace Stevens is America's chief conjuror –
as bold a virtuoso and one with as cunning a rhetoric as we
have produced. He has, naturally, in some quarters been
rebuked for his skill; writers cannot excel at their work
without being, like the dogs in Coriolanus, 'as often beat for
barking As therefore kept to do so.' But for healthy
seductiveness, like the patterned correspondences in Handel's
Sonata No. 1, he has not been rivalled:

> The body dies; the body's beauty lives.
> So evenings die in their green going,
> A wave, interminably flowing.

His repercussive harmonics, set off by the small compass of the poem, 'prove' mathematically to admiration, and suggest a linguist creating several languages within a single language. The plaster temporariness of subterfuge is, he says,

> Like a word in the mind that sticks at artichoke
> And remains inarticulate.

And besides the multiplying of h's, the characteristically ironic use of scale would be noted, in 'Bantams in Pine Woods':

> Chieftain Iffucan of Azcan in caftan
> Of tan with henna hackles, halt!

The playfulness, that is to say humor, of such rhymings as egress and negress, Scaramouche and barouche, is just right, and by no means a joke; one's sense of humor being a clue to the most serious part of one's nature. But best of all, the bravura. Upon the general marine volume of statement is set a parachute-spinnaker of verbiage which looms out like half a cantaloupe and gives the body of the theme the air of a fabled argosy advancing.

A harmonist need not be proud of dominating us illusorily, by causing a flower in bloom to appear where a moment before there was none; and not infrequently Wallace Stevens' 'noble accents and lucid, inescapable rhythms' point to the universal parent, Shakespeare. A novice of verse, required in an examination to attribute to author or century the line, 'These choirs of welcome choir for me farewell' might pay Wallace Stevens a high compliment.

> Remember how the crickets came
> Out of their mother grass, like little kin,

has perfectly Shakespeare's miniature effect of innocent sadness, and the consciously pertinaciously following of a word through several lines, as where we see the leaves

> Turning in the wind,
> Turning as the flames
> Turned in the fire,

are cousin to the pun of Elizabethan drama. We feel, in the tentatively detached method of implication, the influence of Plato; and an awareness of if not the influence of T.S. Eliot. Better say that each has influenced the other; with 'Sunday Morning' and the Prufrocklike lines in 'Le Monocle de Mon Oncle' in mind,

Shall I uncrumple this much crumpled thing?
....
For it has come that thus I greet the spring—

and the Peter Quince-like rhythmic contour of T.S. Eliot's 'La Figlia Que Piange.' As if it were Antipholus of Ephesus and Antipholus of Syracuse, each has an almost too acute concept of 'the revenge of music'; a realization that the seducer is the seduced; and a smiling, strict, Voltaire-like, straight-seeing, self-directed humor which triumphs in its pain. Each is engaged in a similar though differently expressed search for that which will endure.

We are able here, to see the salutary effect of insisting that a piece of writing please the writer himself before it pleases anyone else; and how a poet may be a wall of incorruptibleness against any concessive violating of the essential aura of contributory vagueness. Such tense heights of the romantic are intimated by mere titles, that one might hesitate to make trial of the content lest it seem bathos, but Wallace Stevens is a delicate apothecary of savors and precipitates, and no hauteurs are violated. His method of hints and disguises should have Mercury as their patron divinity, for in the guise of 'a dark rabbi,' an ogre, a traveller, a comedian, an old woman, he deceives us as the god misled the aged couple in the myth.

Again, and moreover, to manner and harmonics is added a fine and exultant grasp of beauty – a veritable refuge of 'blessed mornings, meet for the eye or the young alligator;' an equivalence for jungle beauty, arctic beauty, marine beauty, meridian, hothouse, consciously urban or unconsciously natural beauty – which might be alarming were it not for the persistent foil of dissatisfaction with matter. This frugally unified opulence, epitomized by the 'green vine angering for life' – in Owl's Clover by the thought of plundered harassed Africa, 'the Greenest Continent' where 'memory moves on leopard's feet' – has been perfected stroke by stroke, since the period of 'the magenta Judastree,' 'the indigo glass in the grass,' 'oceans in obsidian,' the white of 'frogs,' of 'clays,' and in 'withered reeds,' until now, tropic pinks and yellows, avocado and Kuniyoshi cabouchon emerald-greens, the blent but violent excellence of ailanthus silk-moths and metallic breast-feathers – as open and unpretending as Rousseau's Snake-Chamber and Sleeping Gipsy – combine in an impression of incandescence like that of the night-blooming cereus.

Despite this awareness of the world of sense – which at some points, to a prudish asceticism, approximates wickedness – one notices the frequent recurrence of the word *heaven*. In each clime which the author visits and under each disguise, it is the dilemma of tested hope which confronts him. In *Owl's Clover* 'the search for a tranquil belief,' and the protest against the actualities of experience, become a protest against the death of world hope; against the unorder and chaos of this 'age of concentric mobs.' Those who dare to forget that 'As the man the state, not as the state the man', who divert 'the dream of heaven from heaven to the future, as a god,' are indeed the carnivorous owl with African greenness for its repast. The land of 'ploughmen, peacocks, doves,' of 'Leonardo,' has been 'Combating bushmen for a patch of gourds, Loosing black slaves to make black infantry;' 'the widow of Madrid Weeps in Segovia;' in Moscow, in all Europe, 'Always everything That is dead except what ought to be;' aeroplanes which counterfeit 'the bee's drone' and have the powers of 'the scorpion' are our seraphim.' Mr. Stevens' book is the sable requiem for all this. But requiem is not the word when anyone hates lust for power and ignorance of power, as the author of this book does. So long as we are ashamed of the ironic feast, and of our marble victories – horses or men – which will break unless they are first broken by us, there is hope for the world.

That 'The Men Who are Falling' should have received the Nation's prize for 1936 is gratifying, however natural we feel the acknowledgment to be. As R.P. Blackmur has said, 'The poems rise in the mind like a tide.' They embody hope, which in being frustrated becomes fortitude; and they prove to us that the testament to emotion is not volubility. It is remarkable that a refusal to speak should result in such eloquence and that an implied heaven could be made so definite. Unanimity of word and rhythm has been attained, and we have the seldom exhilaration of knowing that America has in Wallace Stevens at least one artist whom professionalism will never demolish.

THE MAN WITH THE BLUE GUITAR AND OTHER POEMS

New York, 1937

Knopf published a run of 1,000 copies.

---

43. Eda Lou Walton, from 'Wallace Stevens's Two Worlds', *New York Times Book Review*

24 October 1937, 5

... In this new group of poems Stevens has avoided all embroideries of language. In rhythms that precisely approximate guitar playing and singing, he talks out his ideas. At times the singer is himself completely identified with his instrument, at times he and the instrument are in syncopation. But under the influence of the rhythm, the informal and contradictory effects of life as the poet observes them, seem to take on an art form.

> Poetry is the subject of the poem,
> From this the poem issues and
>
> To this returns. Between the two,
> Between the issue and return, there is
>
> An absence in reality,
> Things as they are. Or so we say.

Wallace Stevens has always perceived the truth stated here, but in his earlier poems he saw the necessity of dwelling always, even though ironically, on beauty:

Beauty is momentary in the mind –
The fitful tracing of a portal
But in the flesh it is immortal

The body dies; the body's beauty lives
So evenings die, in their green going,
A wave interminably flowing.

This new collection of poems indicates, in other words, that a fine poet has come to devote himself to proving an interrelationship between fact and vision. He has forsaken any desire to devote himself to building beauty apart from life. Therefore, though this poetry is leaner, more casual, the collection is a distinct advance in Stevens's work. The skill of these plucked and strummed-out improvisations proves him again the master of the most subtle rhythmical effects.

44. Ruth Lechlitner, 'a master of form', *New York Herald Tribune Books*

14 November 1937, 2

... Wallace Stevens plucks at these strings with the assured, sensitively controlling fingers of the practiced artist. His suave mutations in component rhythms are a delight to the ear; his internal rhymes, and his studied effects in assonance, are distributed with the precision of delicate weights. His satire is never heavy; he can combine harmoniously a meta-physical image having a seventeenth-century aura with a jazz-note hot from the modern ether. There are touches, as in the following of his earlier happy humor.

Sombre as fir-trees, liquid cats
Moved in the grass without a sound.

They did not know the grass went round.
The cats had cats and the grass turned gray

And the world had worlds, ai, this-a-way:
The grass turned green and the grass turned gray.

In another poem he can show – and make you hear through sheer verbal technics – the wrangle between 'employer and employee,' so that it comes between the player and his music with the effect of distortion on a radio program.

The concluding poems, group-entitled 'A Thought Revolved,' continues the Guitar theme. The one about the lady dying of diabetes who listens to the radio is a neatly ironic comment upon modern life and death, and a superb exercise in verse-mechanics. As a master of form Wallace Stevens, who may be considered by some primarily a 'poet's poet,' should be studied by all aspirants to the art. His 'Romanesque Affabulation' is for-example not only a model of modern poetic technique but a good summation of Stevens's philosophy with its commentary on the poet in search of a belief in this our troubled time:

[Quotes Section III of 'A Thought Revolved', 'Romanesque Affabulation', *CP*, pp. 185–6.]

45. William Carlos Williams, on 'a troubled man who sings well', *New Republic*

17 November 1937, 50

Stevens was a long-time admirer of Williams' poetry and the two men, though of very different temperament, were friends. Williams, for his part, had reservations about Stevens' work, because Stevens had not fully abandoned traditional measure. There is evidence that the two poets were aware of each other as far back as 1915. In 1925, when Marianne Moore asked Stevens to review Williams' *In the American Grain* for the *Dial*, he refused, remarking however that, 'What Columbus discovered is nothing to what Williams is looking for' (see *Letters*, p. 246). Later Stevens wrote a preface for Williams' *Collected Poems 1921–1931* (New York, 1934) and a reference there to the 'anti-poetic' in Williams highlighted a fundamental difference in aesthetics between the two poets and, thereafter, the remark was a repeated irritation to Williams. In spite of this, the two sustained a lifelong understanding, though usually from a careful distance.

Williams, like Stevens, is one of the half-dozen most important American poets of the twentieth century. The range and depth of his work as a poet, dramatist, novelist, short-story writer, essayist, memoirist, editor and translator are widely known.

The story is that Stevens has turned of late definitely to the left. I should say not, from anything in this book. He's merely older and as an artist infinitely more accomplished. Passion he has, too often muted, but not flagrantly for the underdog. No use looking for Stevens there – without qualifications.

'The Man with the Blue Guitar,' the first poem, is one of the best. It is everything that we know as Stevens. There are thirty-three divisions of it, a longish poem arranged in couplets, four beats to the line – thirty-three virtual lyrics, a format which Stevens has always found congenial, for, though he seems at times not to wish to acknowledge it, he is primarily a lyric poet. But unlike some of his earlier variations on a theme, this progresses to a fairly definite conclusion. The Blue Guitar, or its master rather, argues with an objector who complains that he (the poet) does not speak of things as they are. The reply comes:

Nothing must stand
Between you and the shapes you take
When the crust of shape has been destroyed.
You as you are? You are yourself.
The blue guitar surprises you.

Stevens is a troubled man who sings well, somewhat
covertly, somewhat overfussily at times, a little stiffly but
well. If he were satisfied with that! He seems at his best
singing in the four-beat time and the lyric form of this
excellent poem. But this isn't enough for Stevens.

And so, to clinch the argument – for this book is in a way
one long argument to emphasize a point – Stevens goes on
and unfortunately overemphasizes what he has to say,
relative to the function of a poet, making a defense of the
poet, an apology for the poet, for Stevens himself, facing his
world. Because of this and the wordiness of its effect I don't
like the second poem, a long subdivided one also under the
general head, 'Owl's Clover.' It has its old woman very
effectively balanced against the heroic plunging of sculptured
horses, but nothing moves as it should.

Five beats to the line here, and that's where the trouble is
let in. These five beats have a strange effect on a modern
poet; they make him think he wants to think. Stevens is no
exception. The result is turgidity, dullness and a language,
God knows what it is! certainly nothing anybody alive today
could ever recognize – lit by flashes, of course, in this case;
for whatever else he may be Stevens is always a distinguished
artist. The language is constrained by the meter instead of
there being – an impossible peak it may be – a meter discovering itself in the language. We are still searching. Much
more might be said were there space for it.

The whole book shows the too rigid selection which
Stevens feels in his virtue. He does not want to overload a
book with merely excellent but repetitious lyrics.

Fortunately there are five shorter pieces standing more or
less alone at the book's close, the last of which, 'The Men
That are Falling,' is the most passionate and altogether the
best work in this selection – one of the best poems of the day.
Here Stevens has shown himself the man, the artist in all the

profundity of his aroused sensibilities, no longer fiddling with thoughts but embodying thought in an adult thrust with all his mature weight behind it. The five beats to the line are not an embarrassment here, while the invention of dealing with the head only in depicting a death, such a death as that of this poem, is something of which our literature may be proud – the real of that to which we sometimes facetiously refer as creative writing. It's a lesson for us all.

46. Robert Fitzgerald, 'Thoughts Revolved', *Poetry*

Vol. 51, no. 3, December 1937, 153–7

Fitzgerald (b. 1910) is an American poet, translator and teacher, best known for his translation of the *Odyssey* and (with Dudley Fitts) Sophocles' *Oedipus* cycle.

One surprises, and is a little surprised by, the eminence of these poems. Not their excellence, for that is customary in Stevens, but a passionate sharpness of authority which I do not remember having felt before. It is not merely that plain speech has been dovetailed more often into the life-giving rhetoric, for that in itself might be only a further sophistication; it is the public significance and earnestness of the result.

The metrical and divisional scheme of 'The Man with the Blue Guitar' was a particularly happy one, permitting Stevens every skilful kind of care and carelessness in the rumination his subject required of him. Stevens is always a 'masked amazer' whose clear character does not appear at once. After the reader has admired certain lines because Shakespeare might have written them, he begins to admire

them because only Stevens could. In this long poem, however, Stevens has given himself room to be explicit and
there is less elegance for its own sake.

Almost all of Wallace Stevens' poems might go under the
title here given to a set of four: 'A Thought Revolved.' In our
time any poetry which actually succeeds in being a thought
revolved, i.e., displayed by the fantastic mind in its true
facets and circling to a point of rest, seems extraordinary
because there is so little like it. Most poems start with the
need to objectify some fragment of reality, or to embody an
experience, or to declaim, or to work a fable out of the
imagination. In any case they seldom owe their form to
intellectual coherence....

On the blue guitar. This is a symbol characteristic of
Stevens, suggesting improvisation, which is the essence of
creation; a literally light tone and the profound overtones of
folk music; Bohemianism, and the abstraction of abstract
painting. It rhymes with 'things as they are.' That is
convenient, perfect, and the poem thus begins, insistently
rhyming these opposites as an introduction to the conflict
which the poet wishes to define.

> The man replied, 'Things as they are
> Are changed upon the blue guitar.'

> And they said then, 'But play, you must,
> A tune beyond us, yet ourselves...'

For the rhetorical variation within the following 32 sections,
each made up of four, five, six or seven couplets, there are
few if any parallels in this medium. The first six sections have
an alternating easy ring of dialogue which is somehow
majestic, like a chorus and principal in Sophocles on an issue
of behavior or justice. To the poet, who says:

> So that's life, then: things as they are?
> It picks its way on the blue guitar.

> A million people on one string?
> And all their manner in the thing,

> And all their manner, right or wrong?...

His audience replies:

> Do not speak to us of the greatness of poetry,
> Of the torches wisping in the underground,
>
> Of the structure of vaults upon a point of light.
> There are no shadows in our sun...

Poetry then proceeds to illustrate and at the same time to describe itself:

> ...the color, the overcast blue
> Of the air, in which the blue guitar
>
> Is a form, described but difficult,
> And I am merely a shadow hunched
>
> Above the arrowy, still strings,
> The maker of a thing yet to be made...

And in section XXII we get a statement in resolution of the conflict between poetry and 'things as they are.' I shall not quote this statement because there is a danger that people will scalpel it out of its context and hold it up all bloody as if it were the heart of the poem, which it is not, or as if it were Stevens' true resolution, which it is not either. The whole peom is that if anything is.

Writing in the *New Republic*, William Carlos Williams has criticized the second group of poems in this book, 'Owl's Clover,' for 'overemphasizing' the poet's argument. This means precisely nothing, and it soon appears that what Williams really objects to is the line of five beats, which 'have a strange effect on a modern poet; they make him think he wants to think.' Well, then they have been having that strange effect on Stevens for a long time, since most of his ambitious work has been in pentameter. It is true that 'Owl's Clover' has a more studied air than 'The Man with the Blue Guitar,' more, for instance, of that kind of side-slipping and shading in which Stevens resembles Edwin Arlington Robinson:

> She was that tortured one,
> So destitute that nothing but herself

Remained and nothing of herself except
A fear too naked for her shadow's shape...

But instead of being turgid and dull, as Williams says they
are, these poems again exemplify, with subject matter of
considerable grandeur, the luxuriant thoroughness of
Stevens' mind. The subject is the decline of the west. To read
Stevens on that subject should be a pleasure, and it is.

47. Selden Rodman, on Stevens' distance from 'the good earth', *Common Sense*

Vol. 7, January 1938, 28

This is part of a composite review which deals also with
Marya Zaturenska's *Cold Morning Sky, Letters from
Iceland* by W. H. Auden and Louis MacNeice, and *Poems*
by MacNeice.

In originality, as well as in sheer output, the younger poets of
old England seem to be outstripping those of new America.
To balance things, we have more latent vitality. There is less
'bone-structure' in Stephen Spender at his best – and his best
is great – than in Muriel Rukeyser; but our pace is slow. Two
much older poets, Carl Sandburg and Archibald MacLeish
have produced enough during the last couple of years to put
any five of their juniors to shame.

But so much cannot be said of Wallace Stevens, whose best
work seems to lie behind him, for *The Man with the Blue
Guitar* is pretty thin stuff. Always a deft handler of
abstractions and elusive colours, this poet's work would
profit from a choice of subject that might force him closer to
the good earth....

48. Dorothy Van Ghent, on Stevens as unwitting Marxist, *New Masses*

11 January 1938, 41–6

Van Ghent (b. 1902) is author of *The English Novel* (1961).

In 'When Poets Stood Alone', the long article from which this excerpt is taken, she assesses the contemporary American poetry situation from the point of view of a Marxist sympathizer. Her epigraph is two lines from Stevens' 'Anglais Mort à Florence':

> He stood at last by God's help and the police;
> But he remembered the time when he stood alone.

Prolix and not always clear, the writer appears to claim that Stevens and other American poets of consequence are unwittingly 'socialist'.

... At the head of this essay a couple of lines from Wallace Stevens stand as epigraph, announcing the bafflement and despair of a person who has lost orientation in a world where matter crowds out essence, quantity engulfs quality, and mechanized institutions seem to exist solely for the purpose of overreaching themselves day after day in vulgarity and aimlessness. Wallace Stevens's theme has always had to do with the imagination as an ordering function in a disorderly world. Like Santayana, the exponent of a creative skepticism, he has found satisfaction in the plasticity of apparitions, and he has found faith in the pure animation of nature.

The man who remembers the time 'when he stood alone,' when the police did not have to prop him up, is remembering the time when imagination was fresh, vigorous, and vivid, when seeming and being were the same thing, when

179

apparitions were valid by reason of their appearance, when the feeling of the animal was his right to the claim of existence. Now with the voracious encroachment of vulgar materialism, of capitalist materialism, animal feeling seems to have been swamped under an accumulation of useless goods. Goods, material goods, have piled up in huge heaps, and man, the animal, dwindles as they pile up. Similarly the imagination which was accustomed to feed on the plastic beauty of the material object is now stunned by the accumulation of useless objects, not only useless objects, but objects that are soul-destroying by the very aimlessness of their production. The poetry of Stevens, as its theme of decaying imagination becomes more overt, has also gradually lost much of the imaginative fervor it had before its subject-matter became more ideological, before its subject-matter became decadence itself.

And here comes the equation. Identifying the imagination with a materialist order that is human and naïve, he identifies the loss of personal integrity with the conditions of vulgar – that is, capitalistic – materialism; and according to this equation the more material that is aimlessly and wantonly heaped up, the fewer persons there are in the sense of persons of integrity and personality. The man who remembers the time when he stood alone is remembering the time when he could value things for what they were, intrinsically; for then he stood also as a thing among things.

And this, in its positive aspect, is the attitude represented in the poetry which has been dealt with in this paper. It is basic because it is *in* the poetry. It is not merely contingent, as are the philosophies of flux or escape which have been pointed out as conditioning our literary heritage. The poets who have been dealt with here were interested in observing the material fact, simply because that fact was interesting and beautiful in its own right. This is the human and the naïve point of view. It is the point of view of a socialist economy....

49. Delmore Schwartz, Stevens' 'special kind of museum', *Partisan Review*

Vol. 4, no. 3, February 1938, 49–52

Delmore Schwartz took a point of view ideologically opposite to that expressed by Dorothy Van Ghent (No. 48). In an essay written a few years after the present review, Schwartz said that the 'only life available to the man of culture has been the cultivation of his own sensibility' (see 'The Isolation of Modern Poetry' in *Selected Essays*, Chicago, 1970, p. 10).

Schwartz's first book, *In Dreams Begin Responsibilities* (1938), was an immediate success and his *Selected Poems: Summer Knowledge* was awarded the Bollingen Prize in 1959. Meanwhile, however, Schwartz had begun to suffer paranoid delusions and eventually abandoned his life as a literatus and academic, dropping out of sight for over a year. His last months were spent in a Times Square hotel which was a haunt for down-and-outs, and when he died there of a heart attack on 11 July 1966 his body was not claimed for three days. There is an excellent biography by James Atlas, *Delmore Schwartz: The Life of an American Poet* (1977) and a touching sketch of Schwartz's relationship with John Berryman in Eileen Simpson's *Poets in Their Youth* (1981).

Schwartz's further extended view of Stevens, 'The Ultimate Plato with Picasso's Guitar,' appears in the *Harvard Advocate*, December 1940.

The poems of Wallace Stevens present an elegant surface. It has been mentioned often, and misunderstood even more frequently, but its affiliations are fairly clear. The same dandyism of speech and the same florid irony is to be found in such writers as James Branch Cabell and Carl Van Vechten, in certain poems of J. C. Ransom and Conrad Aiken, even in the prose style of Santayana, in the poems of the forgotten Donald Evans, and going further back in time, in the moonstruck poems of Dowson, Laforgue, and Verlaine, the Verlaine of 'Fêtes Galantes,' and the Laforgue who sighs that existence is so quotidian. This is a formidable family, but the resemblances are unmistakable. They are also superficial; Stevens has made a significant virtue out of the dubious verbal habits involved in the tendency from which he seems, in some way, to have derived his style. He is unquestionably a much better writer than most of the above authors.

Perhaps it is worthwhile attempting to account for the kinship by relating Stevens to the *milieu* which must have surrounded him when he began to write. As a hypothesis, one may suppose that his style crystallized in the days when *The Smart Set* was the leading literary magazine, when one knew French with pride, discussed sophistication, feared to be provincial, and aspired to membership among the élite. The backwash or lag of that day is still apparent in the Greenwich Village tearoom, and one can scarcely doubt that among the admirers of Miss Millay, there are some who still exist in that period of time. To be a poet at that time was to be peculiar; merely to be interested in the arts was to take upon oneself the burden of being superior, and an exile at home. It may be that as a result of some such feeling, Stevens called his wonderful discourse on love 'Le Monocle de Mon Oncle,' thus resorting to French, and thus mocking, as so often in his titles, the poem itself, as if the poet were extremely self-conscious about the fact of being a poet. It ought to be added that the title of the poem in question does, nevertheless, have a distinct meaning in the poem.

In the present volume, Stevens provides another example, the best one perhaps, of how much there is in his poetry beneath the baroque decoration. The surface would seem to be a mask, which releases the poet's voice, a guise without which he could not speak. But the sentiments beneath the mask are of a different order. If we rest with our impression of the surface, we get nothing but a sense of play and jocular attitudinizing:

> To strike his living hi and ho,
> To tick it, tock it, turn it true,

If we dig into just such usages and then come back to the poem as a whole, we understand the justice of such verbalism, its necessity, and we are confronted with a mind of the utmost seriousness, aware and involved in the most important things in our lives.

The imagination and actuality, the blue guitar which is poetry and things as they are, constitute the antithesis to which Stevens devotes a varied discourse in the present book. In the title poem or suite of poems, there are thirty-three short lyrics in which the various relationships between art and the actual world are named, examined, turned upside down, and transformed into the terms of Stevens' personal vision. In the opening lyric, we are given the suggestion of some lack in the nature of poetry. The poet is addressed by his audience:

> They said, 'You have a blue guitar,
> You do not play things as they are'

The poet replies that the imagination must of necessity alter and distort actuality, and the audience then extends its demand:

> 'But play you must
> A tune beyond us, yet ourselves,
>
> A tune upon the blue guitar,
> Of things exactly as they are.'

The difficulty is that poetry is somehow insufficient. The incidence of that insufficiency, its present point, is made evident further on in the poem:

> The earth is not earth, but a stone,
> Not the mother that held men as they fell,
>
> But stone, but like a stone, no, not
> The mother but an oppressor

It is because of an enforced awareness that his time is one of immense conflict and derangement that the poet has been compelled to consider the nature of poetry in its travail among things as they are. The basic preoccupation, the apprehension which has produced two volumes in two years, was revealed most explicitly in the previous book, *Ideas of Order*:

> There is order in neither sea nor sun,
> There are these sudden mobs of men,
>
> These sudden clouds of faces and arms,
> An immense suppression, freed,
> These voices crying without knowing for what,
>
> Except to be happy, without knowing how....

This is the way, then, in which Stevens answers these sudden mobs of men, these sudden clouds of faces and arms: he justifies poetry, he defines its place, its rôle, its priceless value. Nothing could be more characteristic of this poet, of his virtues and also of his limitations, and one cannot think of an answer of greater propriety.

The second sequence of poems, 'Owl's Clover,' consists of five meditations in blank verse, all of them concerned with extending the theme of the fate of art amid terrifying change and destruction, and envisaging the kind of place toward which history is moving:

> Shall you,
> Then, fear a drastic community evolved
> From the whirling, slowly and by trial; or fear
> Men gathering for a final flight of men,
> An abysmal migration into possible blue?

The fear is in the foreground and is complicated by the themes which were Stevens' direct subject in *Harmonium*, the brutality and chaos of Nature, which is here figured forth in a new symbol, Africa; and also the absence of belief, the departure of God, the angels, and heaven. The attitudes towards what is to come are complex and ambiguous, as they ought to be. The poet can only regard the possibilities which he fears and state his hope:

184

> Basilewsky in the bandstand played
> 'Concerto for Airplane and Pianoforte,'
> The newest Soviet reclame. Profound
> Abortion, fit for the enchanting of basilisks ...
> What man of folk-lore shall rebuild the world,
> What lesser man shall measure sun and moon,
> What super-animal dictate our fates?
> As the man the state, not as the state the man.

But finally and unequivocally, in the last poem of the volume, the poet salutes the men that are falling, for whom God and the angels have become identical with the cause for which they are falling:

> Taste of the blood upon his martyred lips,
> O pensioners, O demagogues and pay-men!

> This death was his belief, though death is a stone
> This man loved earth, not heaven, enough to die.

This is clearly a poetry which flows from a mind in love not only with the beautiful, but also with the just.

There are, however, distinct limitations also. From beginning to end, in *Harmonium* as well as in the present volume, these poems are absorbed in 'responses' to various facts. They are absorbed to such an extent that the facts can scarcely get into the poems at all. We may compare Stevens to William Carlos Williams, whom he admires and who may be said to represent the other extreme, a poet whose whole effort is to get facts into his poem with the greatest exactitude and to keep everything else out. One beautiful line in particular in 'Owl's Clover' ('The sound of z in the grass all day') emphasizes by contrast how little direct observation there is in Stevens. There is no specific scene, nor time, nor action, but only the mind moving among its meanings and replying to situations which are referred to, but not contained in, the poem itself. 'Rocks, moss, stonecrop, iron, merds,' another poet writes, 'The woman keeps the kitchen, makes tea, Sneezes at evening, poking the peevish gutter.' By thus placing the fact within the poem, the response to the fact gains immeasurable strength and relevance. In Stevens, however, the poet 'strides' 'among the cigar stores, Ryan's

lunch, hatters, insurance and medicines' without convincing
the reader that he is walking on an actual street. There is
always an abstractness present; everything is turned into an
object of the imagination. Certain weaknesses result: the
word-play does not always escape the adventitious frivolity
for which it is always mistaken by the careless reader; the
poem is sometimes extended not by a progress of perception,
or of meaning, but one word and one phrase multiplies
others; and, to sum up these defects, the poet is 'too poetic.'
It may also be that the burden of this style is responsible for
the faults which have always been present in Stevens' blank
verse, a lack of variety in going from line to line, a difficulty
with overflow, and lately, in 'Owl's Clover,' a tendency to
anapestic substitution which unsettles the sonorous Miltonic
period.

Virtue and defect, however, seem to be inseparable. The
magnificence of the rhetoric necessitates an exclusion of
narrative elements, necessitates the whole weight of the
verbalism, and, on the other hand, makes possible the
extreme range and freedom of the symbols. The blue guitar,
the statue, the duck, the greenest continent, and above all the
bread and the stone presented here for the first time are
figures and metaphors of a richness and meaningfulness
which justify the method. The poems taken as a whole
constitute a special kind of museum, of a very familiar
strangeness, located, because of the extent of the poet's
awareness, in the middle of everything which concerns us.

50. Julian Symons, 'A Short View of Wallace Stevens', *Life and Letters Today*

Vol. XXVI, September 1940, 215–24

Symons (b. 1912) is a poet, novelist, playwright,
biographer, writer on criminology, and editor. A

versatile and able writer, Symons is best-known for his detective stories, such as *The Thirty-first of February* (1950), *The Man Who Killed Himself* (1967) and *The Plot Against Roger Rider* (1973).

This essay is of particular interest as an early British overview of Stevens' work.

Wallace Stevens is the author of three books of verse, *Harmonium, Ideas of Order,* and *The Man with the Blue Guitar,* none of which has been published in this country. In America he is regarded as the best American-born poet writing today, next to Eliot: in England his work is even less respected than read. These notes are the basis for a more comprehensive study: their primary purpose is to introduce to English readers a poet remarkably neglected in this country.

Harmonium was first published in 1923; another edition with fourteen new poems appeared in 1931, but the book as a whole represents the first, and less valuable part of Stevens' work. A great many of the poems are written in the Imagist manner, with the sharpness and sensitiveness characteristic of the Imagist poets, but not with an Imagist seriousness; most of them contain a slightly tittery joke, or if they do not contain a joke they contain a titter, something which might have been a joke, the idea of a joke; and the joke is on Mr. Stevens as much as anyone. Here are three parts of 'Thirteen Ways of Looking at a Blackbird':

[Quotes Parts I, II and III, *CP*, p. 92.]

This is nearly very gentle, very observant, very charming: but it is not serious, it is in a gentlemanly way a little absurd. Mr. Stevens strolls through a world of rosy chocolate and gilt umbrellas, making little ironic notes on shapes and colors ('The houses are haunted / By white night-gowns. / None are green, / Or purple with green rings, / Or green with yellow rings, / Or yellow with blue rings'), and the delicacy of his taste and the extreme Englishness of his American accent make him look uncommonly like Philo Vance. This is 'The Surprises of the Superhuman':

The palais de justice of chambermaids
Tops the horizon with its colonnades.

If it were lost in Übermenschlichkeit,
Perhaps our wretched state would soon come right.

For somehow the brave dicta of its kings
Make more awry our faulty human things.

Surely it is a Regie from which this cultivated American is flickin' the ash? The most successful poems in *Harmonium* are those in which the necessary irony is least obviously self-critical, 'Le Monocle de Mon Oncle,' 'Peter Quince at the Clavier,' and 'The Comedian as the Letter C.' This last long poem is indeed Stevens' most completely characteristic work, and conveys more nearly than any other single poem his skill and usual flippancy:

>   Crispin,
>   The lutanist of fleas, the knave, the thane,
>   The ribboned stick, the bellowing breeches, cloak
>   Of China, cap of Spain, imperative haw
>   Of hum, inquisitorial botanist,
>   And general lexicographer of mute
>   And maidenly greenhorns, now beheld himself,
>   A skinny sailor in the sea-glass.
>   What word split up in clickering syllables
>   And storming under multitudinous tones
>   Was name for this short-shanks in all that brunt?

This bears about the same relation to the best poetry of our time as the comedy of Lyly bears to the comedy of Ben Jonson. One may admire the virtuosity which is able to keep language on this level throughout a poem of more than five hundred lines: but still the whole poem remains a piece of virtuosity, a literary curio. Crispin is a comedian, he is not a serious person, and hardly a *person* even, Crispin is by his creator's account 'The Comedian *as the Letter C':* Crispin is Mr. Stevens playing gracefully with the letter C and employing this imperative haw of hum to probe very gently beneath the shell of that real world which he uneasily apprehends to exist somewhere outside Crispin's range: Crispin is a figure finally unsatisfactory, even to his creator.

Twelve years after *Harmonium*, *Ideas of Order* was published in a limited edition. In 1936 it was brought out by Knopf, with three new poems. On the dust-wrapper of the Knopf edition Mr. Stevens says:

We think of changes occurring today as economic changes, involving political and social changes. Such changes raise questions of political and social order.

While it is inevitable that a poet should be concerned with such questions, this book, although it reflects them, is primarily concerned with ideas of order of a different nature, as, for example, the dependence of the individual, confronting the elimination of established ideas, on the general sense of order; the idea of order created by individual concepts, as of the poet, in 'The Idea of Order at Key West'; the idea of order arising from the practice of any art, as of poetry, in 'Sailing After Lunch.'

This is clear, direct, and a little portentous: but the language of the poems in *Ideas of Order* is not strikingly different from that of the poems in *Harmonium*:

> Why seraphim like lutanists arranged
> Above the trees? And why the poet as
> Eternal *chef d'orchestre?*

Why indeed? Still, *Ideas of Order* represents an advance: it is less uselessly ironic, more accomplished all round. There is an increase in skill, not accompanied by any marked alteration in style.

The apparatus of Stevens' poems has changed little from 1923 to 1939; although he passed twelve years without publishing a book it is difficult to mark off his writing into periods, as the writing of Eliot and Yeats may easily (and usefully) be marked off. *Harmonium* is not noticeably less 'mature' than the later books; but the title poem of *The Man With the Blue Guitar*, published in 1937, is undoubtedly Stevens' most important work. This piece contains thirty-three short poems, written in couplets, which deal with 'the incessant conjunction between things as they are and things imagined.' The blue guitar, which is used as 'a symbol of the imagination' throughout the series of poems, is a piece of *chinoiserie*, as irritating as Yeat's occult symbols; yet Stevens' writing is so skillful, and the alternations from poem to poem are so deft, that admiration overcomes irritation, and the blue guitar is reluctantly accepted:

> I cannot bring a world quite round,
> Although I patch it as I can.
>
> I sing hero's head, large eye
> And bearded bronze, but not a man,
>
> Although I patch him as I can
> And reach through him almost to man.
>
> If to serenade almost to man
> Is to miss, by that, things as they are,
> Say that it is the serenade
> Of a man that plays a blue guitar.

That is the second poem; the third begins: 'Ah, but to play man number one', and touches the same theme a little differently; the fourth is a philosophical reflection:

> So that's life, then: things as they are?
> It picks its way on the blue guitar.
>
> A million people on one string?
> And all their manner in the thing,
>
> And all their manner, right and wrong,
> And all their manner, weak and strong?
>
> The feelings crazily, craftily call,
> Like a buzzing of flies in autumn air,
>
> And that's life, then: things as they are,
> This buzzing of the blue guitar.

The subject of the poems shifts lightly and with ease from politics to abstract morality, from abstract morality to the practical use of poetry; all the poems are written with the wit and care shown in the quotations given; and through them all the symbol of the blue guitar is maintained with wonderful ingenuity. 'The Man with the Blue Guitar' is certainly one of the most notable poetic achievements of the last twenty years, an achievement that may be compared with *The Waste Land* or 'Mauberley.' If the language used is rarely strong, it is always delicate; if the images are not frequently powerful, they are always pleasing; if the 'meaning' is sometimes flippant, it is rarely obscure: and of how many contemporary poems can one say so much?

Stevens has published several poems in the last two years, poems which seem rarely to approach 'The Man with the Blue Guitar' in wit and skill: but full comment on these new poems can hardly be made with justice until they are collected into a book. Some estimate of the value of his work up to 1937 may, however, be made the more justly because his writing shows little sign of further development.

There is a point of view from which Stevens makes the painful experiments with language and subject matter through which Eliot and Pound developed in the late 'teens and the early 'twenties, seem needless and even slightly ridiculous. For Stevens' 'method,' though sometimes allegorical, and demanding continual attention on the reader's part, successfully avoids the 'cultural-reference-rock-jumping' difficulties of *The Waste Land* and the metrical and linguistic trickery of 'Mauberley' and the *Cantos*. By using an eight- or ten-syllable iambic line for all his important poems, Stevens has been able to obtain as much variation as is necessary, or even desirable, in his verse. Great interest in the *alteration* of poetic structure (distinct from interest in the use and application of technique), like that shown by Eliot and Pound in their early work, and less subtly by Cummings and William Carlos Williams, is perhaps an indication of uneasiness rather than of self-confidence. The introduction of radical novelties in poetic structure is so dangerous, it may here be pointed out, that it should be attempted only after existing structural forms have been most carefully considered and rejected. I do not suppose that anyone thinks of Eliot and Pound primarily as craftsmen; whereas it is often difficult to think of Stevens as anything else. Several of Eliot's early poems, and certainly Pound's 'Mauberley,' become from this point of view almost elaborate evasions of technical problems; there are no such evasions in 'Le Monocle de Mon

Oncle' or 'Peter Quince at the Clavier.' Eliot and Pound have, in fact, always had *something* to *say*, and they are conscientious enough artists to be troubled about a way of saying it: an unfriendly criticism of Stevens would conclude that he has not much to say, but an unusual facility in saying it.

Such a criticism would be oversimple; but still, Stevens' weakness as a poet proceeds always from a point at which an *idea* is being communicated; communicated (from lack of a creative and critical background) in unsuitably flippant language. A long and interesting article on 'The Comedian as the Letter C' appeared recently in the American *Southern Review*.[1] The writer of the article (an enthusiastic admirer of Stevens) concludes that the poem

tells both how a representative modern poet tried to change from a romanticist to a realist and how he adapted himself to his social environment. The hero's development may be summarized as a passage from (1) juvenile romantic subjectivism, through (2) a realism almost without positive content, consisting merely in recognizing the stark realities of life, (3) an exotic realism, in which he sought reality in radical sensuousness, (4) a kind of grandiose objectivism, in which he speculated upon starting a sort of local-color movement in poetry, but which he presently saw as romantic, and finally, through (5) a disciplined realism that resulted in his accepting his environment on its own terms, so to speak, and (6) marrying and begetting children, to (7) an 'indulgent fatalis[m] and skepticism.'

If one accepts this definition, which is perhaps as near an estimate of the poem's theme as can be made, it becomes necessary to point out that there is a distressing lack of relevance between the language in which the poem is written, and the meaning which is given to that language. Nor is it possible to defend the poem on the ground that it is deliberately a comic piece. Mr. Stevens' intention was no doubt to write a comic poem, but certainly not to write a flippant poem; yet the flippancy of the language (which has already been indicated) can hardly be exceeded; and it is not less true now than in the eighteenth century that flippant language used throughout a lengthy poem must debase a serious theme. An elaborate faulty good taste mars even 'The Man With the Blue Guitar':

> He held the world upon his nose
> And this-a-way he gave a fling.
>
> His robes and symbols, ai-yi-yi
> And that-a-way he twirled the thing.

It is a grave artistic error to attempt to convey the 'incessant conjunction between things as they are and things imagined' in such terms.

This flippancy leads naturally to Stevens' second and most revealing fault. His work does not contain an objective view of life, nor does it express a philosophy of life; it gives instead an objective view of Mr. Stevens in various attitudes. This view may be most valuable and interesting; it may result in valuable and interesting poetry; it is still a poor substitute for a view of life. There is not one of Stevens' more important poems which does not have for its explicit or implied subject *the poet and his poetry*, rather than a consideration of a man as a social animal. The definition of 'The Comedian as the Letter C' is terribly clear; poem XXII of 'The Man with the Blue Guitar' begins 'Poetry is the subject of the poem'; and notice also 'The practice of any art, *as of poetry*' in the note on *Ideas of Order*. The reader will get a clear understanding of Stevens' approach to his material, and the nature of that material, by examining the second poem (already quoted) of 'The Man with the Blue Guitar' and by asking that always reasonable question: What is said in this poem? What is it about?

The poem is a statement on the poet's part of inability to come to terms with the 'real world,' the world which is 'quite round' (lines 1–2). He writes about man: but his writing turns man to a formal figure, a 'bearded bronze' (lines 3–6). So far so bad, one could think, for the poet; but then comes the conclusion (lines 7–10) that *if* inability to come to terms with the world, to be unable to write of men as men but only as bearded bronzes, is 'to miss, by that, things as they are' (there is now some doubt on that point, it seems!), then we should say that this is 'the serenade/Of a man that plays a blue guitar.' That is to say, since the blue guitar is 'a symbol of imagination,' the serenade of a man who has imagination. So that the position finally posed by Mr. Stevens here is that if you have 'imagination,' you will

be able to write about reality, about 'things as they are.'
'Imagination' and 'reality' are mutually contradictory; and
this leads the 'imaginative' man, the player of the blue guitar,
into all kinds of (poetic) difficulties, for he writes about
reality at one remove: and like a man who sees himself
reflected endlessly between two mirrors, he writes not about
life, but about the poet's reflection of life in his poetry; which
becomes before long the reflection of a reflection, and at
length the reflection of a reflection of a reflection.

'Poetry is the subject of the poem': if the statement were
true, so much the worse for poetry; but it is not true, or it is
not true of the best poetry. There is a limited sense in which
poetry is the poem's subject, that sense in which reading, and
not reading a book, is the object of reading, in which being a
butcher, and not making a living, is the object of being a
butcher; but that is not at all what Mr. Stevens means, or it is
not what he means in his own poetry, where poetry is too
often the subject of the poem, with results rarely sterile, but
sometimes absurd.

From the failure of American literature to evolve in a
hundred and fifty years a tradition useful to a poet inclined to
European dandyism; from a time and a country absorbed in
largely useless literary experiments; from his own natural
genius and limitations; comes the work of Wallace Stevens.
Eccentric and typical, irritating and urbane, his poems are
not less readable than unsatisfying: and if one pays the tribute
to his skill to say that they are always very well worth
rereading, one must make at the same time the motion of
regret that a poet with so fine a natural genius should be so
frequently a fribble of taste.

NOTE

1 Hi Simons, '"The Comedian as the Letter C": Its Sense and Its
Significance', *Southern Review*, Vol. V, Winter 1940, pp. 453–68.

PARTS OF A WORLD

New York, 1942

Knopf edition of 1,000 copies. A second edition of 330 copies was published in 1943.

---

51. Weldon Kees, 'Parts: But a World', *New Republic*

Vol. 107, no. 3, 28 September 1942, 387–8

Born in Beatrice, Nebraska, in 1914, Weldon Kees was a poet, abstract expressionist painter, jazz pianist, composer, photographer and documentary film-maker. He disappeared in San Francisco in July 1955, presumably a victim of suicide. His *Collected Poems* were published in 1962.

Wallace Stevens has been, and still is, very much what Van Wyck Brooks has blithely called a 'coterie writer.' His audience is probably more restricted than that of any other poet of his importance. A good many of the poets of Mr. Stevens' generation, and of the generation following, have, in their various ways – some after prolonged experimental maneuvers – entered doors of political discipleship, stale recapitulation, critical inflexibility or silence. Stevens has been one of the few to have escaped all of these easily available traps; and he has been publishing for more than forty years. Since 1899, the year in which his first uncertain verses appeared in the *Harvard Advocate*, he has irregularly but persistently continued to document the exploration of his fanciful, bizarre and original world, parts of which are on exhibition here.

Self-conscious, ironic, impersonal, Stevens produced in *Harmonium*, his first book, the most exhaustive poetic record we have had of the interrelationships of the world of fact and the artistic imagination. Almost every poem he has written has been an exercise in ransacking the shifting antagonisms of opposites, employing an imagery more varied and luxuriant than any other of the time. Opulent cataracts, apricots, pale parasols, bougainvilleas, peacocks and purple watermelons swarmed through his early poems; the 'literary' and the commonplace were juxtaposed in patterns of the most striking and lustrous variety. No other poet has displayed a greater facility for inventing diversified symbols for relatively similar purposes.

The world of this volume, extending and deepening the concern with society toward which Stevens has been moving ever since the publication of *Ideas of Order* seven years ago, bears a closer relationship to the objective world of today than that earlier world of *Harmonium* – civilized, elegant and lush – had to the Wilson – Harding – Coolidge world of its composition. Here one finds less of the Firbankian vaudeville, the dazzle, the oo-la-la, that skittered among the poet's earlier balancing between the luxuriant and the austere.

In the face of today's disintegration and chaos, a good deal of his earlier serenity and self-possession has gone. There are new tones of anguish, grief and disgust, and an awareness that our society is moving not to 'the bread and wine of the mind,' but to 'a falling and an end.' The accessibility of the imagination as a place of retreat has been blocked more and more by 'the bombastic intimations of winter,' 'the martyrs à la mode,' the 'soldiers ... marching and marching in a tragic time':

> It is shaken now. It will burst into flames,
> Either now or tomorrow or the day after that.

Stevens was never blind to threatenings of disaster; but his awareness of it, and the manner in which it was faced, were rendered a bit remote by a general air of languid fastidiousness – disaster faced in the drawing-room with a glass of sherry and a collection of Picassos. Now his speculations on a society in which the imagination may very well be liquidated conclude with the melancholy reflection that

> In a village of the indigenes,
> One would have still to discover. Among the dogs and dung
> One would continue to contend with one's ideas.

An increasing despair runs through these poems, and it is most marked in some of the finest lyrics, in 'The Dwarf,' 'Loneliness in New Jersey,'[sic] 'Dry Loaf,' 'Arcades of Philadelphia the Past,' in which mountains, at first recalled with nostalgia, become 'scratched and used, pure fakes'; 'The Common Life,' in which the bleakness of the objective world is scrutinized as a dimensionless horror; and in 'Cuisine Bourgeoise,' in which

> We feast on human heads, brought in on leaves,
> Crowned with the first, cold buds. On these we live,
> No longer on the ancient cake of seed,
> The almond and deep fruit. This bitter meat
> Sustains us.... Who, then, are they, seated here?
> Is the table a mirror in which they sit and look?
> Are they men eating reflections of themselves?

Stevens has never specialized in intensity; the absence of it, in many of the other poems, combined with the growing rhetorical monotony, accounts for most of his failures. There are mobs and masses in his poetry that were never here before; and there is even one fairly long poem that gives evidence of being the outcome of a brief tête-à-tête with Marxism. And there are a few poems looking like ill-at-ease revivals of standard Stevens favorites, but they are not frequent. His distinguished place in American poetry has never been more secure....

52. Louise Bogan, 'the whole question of Stevens' place in American poetry', *New Yorker*

10 October 1942, 61–2

Louise Bogan (1897–1970) was a poet and long-time reviewer for the *New Yorker*. Her chief work is *The Blue Estuaries: Poems 1923–1968* (1969).

... he has progressively become more and more philosophic, closed in, and obscure. His early work was produced in the heyday of the so-called American Poetic Renaissance, and he had the purest and most witty kind of talent in the more precious and Imagist vein of that poetry revival. Then as now, his ear was impeccable; and he wrote in the classically simple tone which is necessary to set off the color and movement of fanciful, ornate material. His early poems took influences from Mallarmé and Laforgue and Chinese translations of the period; something from Beardsley's prose and von Hofmannsthal's libretti; touches from the *commedia dell' arte*. A definite strain of rather bric-à-brac affectation ran through them, and they often occurred against a subtropical Floridian background. Their titles added a flourish; young enthusiasts knew by heart 'Peter Quince at the Clavier' and 'Thirteen Ways of Looking at a Blackbird.' Stevens' work, however, was not all glitter and arabesquing of the surface. He wrote many poems of piercing insight. Wit, in them, flashes one brief aspect of a situation and summons up the whole.

Of late years, from about 1936 on, Stevens has begun to write poems obliquely directed against the blundering obtuseness of 'politic man.' He has not dropped his early manner, and the effect of his almost automatic, lulling rhythm, when applied to a piece of argument, has been rather strange. Although his shorter poems, such as 'Study of Two Pears' and 'Arrival at the Waldorf,' continued to strike out their peculiar charm and his short ironic remarks are put down with the old exquisite conciseness, he now seems obsessed by his defense of the imagination against 'the world of fact.' In his earlier work, when that argument was implicit, his point was made more convincingly.

The appearance of this new book brings up the whole question of Stevens' place in American poetry....

53. Horace Gregory, on Stevens and the art of analogy, 'An Examination of Wallace Stevens in a time of War', *Accent*

Vol. 3, Autumn 1942, 57–61

Best known for his translations of Ovid and Catullus and for *A History of American Poetry 1900–1940* (written with his wife, the poet Marya Zaturenska), Gregory (1898–1982) was also a poet, teacher and biographer.

And although my mind perceives the force behind the
    moment,
The mind is smaller than the eye.
        'A Fish-Scale Sunrise' from *Ideas of Order, 1936*

For the past ten years the poetry of Wallace Stevens has been the occasion for a great quantity of excellent talk in critical reviews; it is to Mr. Stevens' credit that he has forced his critics to exercise their brains in searching out the superlatives of praise; he has driven them forth into many curious fields of speculation, and then, once they were well on their way, he has leaped ahead, leading them in small and closely herded droves into the bogs of metaphysical discussion. As a tribute to Mr. Stevens' gifts and to his wit, all this has been a gratifying spectacle, and I am willing to suppose that Mr. Stevens in his quiet fashion has enjoyed the show. Since the earliest publication of his work in *Poetry*, he has successfully created an atmosphere of high (and brilliantly serious) comedy wherever his poems have appeared; today he is a master of his art, and if his later work has shown a tendency to grow more diffuse with the passage of time, its sensibility remains untarnished, its wit continues to refresh the ear and eye, and in certain respects which I will speak of later, its present offering is the most important contribution that Mr. Stevens has made to American literature since the first publication of *Harmonium* in 1923.

Meanwhile a general question concerning the nature of Mr. Stevens' poetry is in need of being answered; it is a question that has its bearing upon the work of a half-dozen twentieth-century poets, including E.E. Cummings, T.S. Eliot, and Marianne Moore. The question is: Is Mr. Stevens a philosopher? Can we hook ladders to his Prester John's balloon with the hope of landing safely on a terrain peopled by Zeno, Plotinus, Socrates, George Santayana, William James, John Dewey, and Professor Whitehead? I think not, and more than that, I am convinced, allowing for a difference of some two thousand years, that Mr. Stevens is one of those who were kept in mind when poets were excluded from the ideal Republic. I would go further and insist that Mr. Stevens is not an intellectual, and that the value of his poetry cannot be measured in intellectual terms – in that sense, the poetry of both Thomas Hardy and Edwin Arlington Robinson is more profound than his; theirs has greater richness if not less austerity, and a greater depth of emotion as well as a more enduring tensile strength. In saying this, I do not mean that Mr. Stevens' poetry lacks intelligence or is without evidence of a finely tempered and inquiring mind, but the point I wish to make is that a distinction must be drawn between a so-called 'intellectual poetry' and the poetry that employs to the utmost the resources of poetic intelligence and wit. The distinction has particular relevance in reading Mr. Stevens'

Parts of a World because a number of his new poems make use
of terms that have their origin in philosophic discourse; one
might almost say that Mr. Stevens ruminates at large on the
lack of order in a world outside his vision; he thinks about it
and speculates upon it, but his true wisdom, his rightness, his
precision are always related to objects that are close at hand.
In *Ideas of Order* – 'Sad Strains of a Gay Waltz' – he identified
the future harmonies of the world with skepticism:

Too many waltzes – The epic of disbelief
Blares oftener and soon, will soon be constant.
Some harmonious skeptic soon in a skeptical music

Will unite these figures of men and their shapes
Will glisten again with motion, the music
Will be motion and full of shadows.

And in the sixth stanza of his 'Examination of the Hero in a
Time of War' from *Parts of a World,* the skeptical attitude
resumes its voice:

Unless, we believe in the hero, what is there
To believe? Incisive what, the fellow
Of what good. Devise. Make him of mind.
For every day.

Now, I am not at all certain that Mr. Stevens' skepticisms
should be advanced as his prime excuse for being; we accept
them only insofar as they exist within the poem for the
poem's sake – we may recognize and grant the intelligence
behind the questions and avowals, we may admire the wit or
the sensibility that endows them with poetic meaning, we
may even add them to our own store of critical observations
on the world around us – but as philosophy (and here I use
the word 'philosophy'in its intellectual sense, the sense which
implies the creation or the furtherance of a philosophic
system) that is another matter.

Mr. Stevens is not, of course, the first poet to use the
language of philosophic monologue for the expression of his
sensibility; to take one example out of many, Pope's grand
patchwork of theology, aphorisms and ideas, his *Essay on
Man,* was a response to the same purpose that enters the

longer pieces in Mr. Stevens' *Parts of a World,* and no one, I
think, would make the error of comparing Pope's *Essay,*
lively as it is, with *The Divine Comedy* or *Paradise Lost;* for the
same reason, one would not trouble to waste time comparing
and contrasting the virtues of Mr. Stevens' 'Extracts from
Addresses to the Academy of Fine Ideas' with Hardy's
portentous ruin of an epic drama, *The Dynasts.* It is all too
true that in reading Wallace Stevens' poetry 'The mind is
smaller than the eye'.

I hope that these remarks do not seem to retard an
enjoyment of Mr. Stevens' poetry, for I have been speaking
of it as it is not, in the hope of making a much-needed
distinction clear. The fact that Mr. Stevens thinks should not
occasion our surprise, but a thinking poet does not necessarily become transformed into a philosopher; some few of his
poems may embrace theological or philosophic terms – and
he may speak of angels or devils, or rabbis, or 'the flat
historic scale' – yet I believe that his ability to do so in a poem
is of quite another order from occupying Bishop Manning's
pulpit or writing a supplementary volume to Professor
Whitehead's *Process and Reality.*[1] I, for one, am happy to read
Mr. Stevens as a poet of sensibility, and there is no one today
writing poetry in English who can rival his high appreciation
of the comedy which exists in a civilized milieu. Naturally,
one would not care to be shipwrecked on a desert island with
one of Mr. Stevens' volumes of poetry; its consolations
would then soon become nostalgic, and nostalgia, I submit,
would be a weary and futile mood if it accompanied the
hunting of clams upon a sandy beach.

Mr. Stevens' comic genius has ideas as well as images for
its counters, and these are set as so many pawns upon a
board; Mr. Stevens, as he sets his pieces on their red squares
and black, is always at his best when an entire poem may be
read as an analogy. (It should be said that Marianne Moore's
poetry follows the same rule and that the parts of Mr.
Stevens' world touch on their peripheries the poetry of Miss
Moore, John Crowe Ransom, Conrad Aiken, William
Carlos Williams, E. E. Cummings, and John Brooks Wheel-
wright. This is not to say that his poetry is like theirs, nor
should one confuse the identities of seven poets, but it is true

that a reading of one of the seven would open a door,
however small or well-concealed, to a reading of the others.)
The first poem of Mr. Stevens' new book, which bears the
title of 'Parochial Theme,' should be read, I take it, as an
analogy to seven-eighths of the cocktail bar conversation
uttered and overheard during the 1930's. Mr. Stevens warns
his readers that the theme is parochial, and reserves for his
conclusion a word or two of salutary advice:

> Salvation there:
> There is no such thing as life; or if there is
> It is faster than the weather, faster than
> Any character. It is more than any scene:
>
> Of the guillotine or of any glamorous hanging,
> Piece the world together, boys, but not with your hands.

The same art of making the entire poem stand for an
observation of the world (and Mr. Stevens is always happiest
when he has brought his camera into clear foci of objects seen
within the poem, whether they are pink carnations or
acrobats, or pears or fish, or grapes or rubies) is demonstrated in some four or five short pieces in the new volume,
and in these, indeed, 'the part is the equal of the whole,' and
the poems themselves are without question among the finest
that Mr. Stevens has written in the past fifteen years. It is
only as one reads the longer pieces that the atmosphere
becomes thin, the argument diffuse and tenuous. I wish I
could say that his 'Examination of the Hero in a Time of
War' is as closely woven as his 'Le Monocle de Mon Oncle,'
but I cannot; the poem has excellent stanzas, and the last two
are in his most fortunate vein, and as he writes of 'true
autumn' and asks 'But was the summer false?' I begin to
wonder if he has read W.B. Yeats' query concerning the
existence of last season's vegetables in an introduction
written for 'Three Revolutionary Songs.' Yet the poem, as
poem, seems loosely overwritten, and the same charge may be
brought against 'Life on a Battleship'; it may seem an
impertinence to offer Mr. Stevens the loan of a blue pencil,
but the temptation to do so cannot be denied, and one would
welcome fewer of his non-verbal expletives, his 'Hurroos'

and 'da da doos' which lead on the road downward from high comedy into whimsy.

The danger which has beset Mr. Stevens' longer pieces, a danger that has been apparent ever since the publication of *The Man with the Blue Guitar* in 1937, has been the *reductio ad* whimsy of his totally serious and critical consideration of the relationship between two aspects of reality, the poet's imagination and the external world – the relationship exists, and no one would deny Mr. Stevens' pertinency in asking a few questions regarding his own or another man's position in respect to it. The difficulty arises in stating an intellectual problem in terms of fancy; in doing so, the Coleridgian distinctions between fancy and imagination become blurred beyond recognition and depart, and the various aesthetic values in the poem before our eyes become as incongruous in their relationship as the pairing of A. A. Milne's Winnie the Pooh with King Lear's Fool. A *tour de force* of this sort may still be possible, and in poetry the unpredictable always exists to shock or to terrify members of an elder generation, but so far, Mr. Stevens has walked with the constant danger of whimsy at his side, and he has progressed, at the cost of becoming diffuse, mildly argumentative, and, I suspect, unguardedly repetitious.

Some time ago, and the occasion happened to be the publication of the second and enlarged edition of *Harmonium,* I remarked that the poetry of Wallace Stevens had its analogy, and perhaps a predecessor, in the art of that American who succeeded so admirably in living away from home, James M'Neil Whistler, and who was – with the exception of Henry James and T.S. Eliot – the most fortunate of American expatriates. Today the analogy seems stronger than ever before, for Mr. Stevens in his new book is as fine a poet as Whistler was a painter; the same notes of elegance, charm, sensibility – and impressionism – are as lightly struck and as well controlled in Mr. Stevens' shorter poems as on the canvases of the man who wrote *The Gentle Art of Making Enemies.* Possibly Mr. Stevens' readings in French poetry of the mid- and latter half of the nineteenth century have contributed to the *fin de siècle* shading of his metrical nuances, and one can see how aptly many of his images fall within the period that embraced Laforgue as well as Mallarmé; but, if so, I believe the mere literary influence to be a matter of secondary importance. Mr. Stevens' alliance with that moment is one of temperament, not a desire to emulate the teachings of a master, and for us it is of greater profit to recognize in him the singular qualities he indubitably possesses – and the existence of the singular man is, of course, his primary concern. The singular Whistler and the singular Wallace Stevens – though Mr. Stevens spends his periods of exile in Key West instead of London – should be our concern in reading *Parts of a World*.

Among the memorable poems that the present book contains. I list in addition to those I have mentioned, 'The Glass of Water' and 'The Woman That Had More Babies Than That,' and I cannot resist the complete quotation of his 'Contrary Theses (I)' which is, I believe, one of his best poems, illuminating, as its lines make their progress down the page, the present 'consciousness,' as Mr. Stevens himself would say, 'of the violent reality of war':

> Now grapes are plush upon the vines,
> A soldier walks before my door.
>
> The hives are heavy with the combs.
> Before, before, before my door.
>
> And seraphs cluster on the domes
> And saints are brilliant in fresh cloaks.
>
> Before, before, before my door.
> The shadows lesson on the walls,
>
> The bareness of the house returns.
> And acid sunlight fills the halls.
>
> Before, before. Blood smears the oaks.
> A soldier stalks before my door.

NOTE

[1] Mention of Manning and Whitehead is largely a literary flourish, but it is worth noting that *Process and Reality* was influential in the thinking of William Carlos Williams and, later, Charles Olson.

54. Hi Simons, 'The Humanism of Wallace Stevens', *Poetry*

Vol. 61, no. 2, November 1942, 448–52

Simons was a Chicago publisher who became interested in Stevens' work, corresponded with him, and systematically examined Stevens' relationship to the French Symbolists. Simons' essay, 'Wallace Stevens and Mallarmé' (*Modern Philology*, May 1946), is seminal. Also relevant to the debate is his 'The Genre of Wallace Stevens', *Sewanee Review,* Vol. LIII, no. 4, Autumn 1945, where he takes issue with the views of Horace Gregory (No. 53) and Mary Colum (No. 56) (see also No. 50).

Of the present review, Stevens wrote to a correspondent in January 1943: 'I cannot imagine any of the reviews, except possibly the one by Simons, doing much in the way of helping one to be accepted' (*Letters*, p. 433).

Mr. Wallace Stevens is one of the few living poets who have constructed, each of them, a complete world for his imagination to inhabit. Minor men, half-poets, write out of more or less temporary adjustments between their personalities and their environments. Stevens writes from a unique, whole vision of life, that is revealed in *Parts of a World*.

We left him, as the fabulists say, in *Owl's Clover* and *The Man with the Blue Guitar,* working his way out of the dilemma which the coexistence of things imagined and things-as-they-are posed to him. This new book shows how he finally did so. It was by means of what he calls, in the metaphysical lyric, 'Connoisseur of Chaos,' 'a law of inherent opposites, / Of essential unity.' 'Law' is a metaphor for 'feeling,' a feeling of supreme pleasure in the recognition of the interrelationships of such contraries as the actual and the imagined, the real and the ideal, order and disorder, man and woman, life and death. Total reality comprises both opposites in each pair; it is not complete, hence not real, without them both. So the imagined is as truly part of reality as the actual. Such poems as 'On an Old Horn' in which the order of spirit prevails over the order of matter, and 'Poem with Rhythms,' where the image tends to become more valid than the thing to which it corresponds, seem merely to perpetuate Stevens' old principle, 'Imagination is the will of things'; and it isn't unfair to say of his world that, as with so many other idealisms, empathy is the cement that holds it together. It would be unfair, however, and incorrect, to consider it a wholly subjective construction: 'Dry Loaf' and 'Cuisine Bourgeoise' are among the most terribly realistic poems written in our times, and the book contains others devoted to the reality-pole of the reality-imagination dichotomy. But the most eloquent pages celebrate momentary resolutions of conflict. For Stevens never forgets that the world of incessant war, chronic economic crisis and social and cultural disintegration which we have made for ourselves is a chaos, in which only instants of tranquillity or exaltation are possible. Such moments are 'the weddings of the soul' in which one realizes the 'essential unity' of the 'inherent opposites.'

Traditionally, absolute idealists try to escape the confusion of the actual. But Stevens, though an idealist, is no absolutist: 'On the Road Home' is a parable of his discovery that 'There is no such thing as the truth ... There are many truths, / But they are not parts of a truth.' Thus, he is able to accept the chaos and be a connoisseur of its nuances of change and moments of equilibrium. In 'Landscape with Boat', he adds to his thesis of the relativity of truth the corollary,

> that if nothing
> Was divine then all things were, the world itself,
> And that if nothing was the truth, then all
> Things were the truth, the world itself was the truth.

That is the basis in reason of his latest position with regard to the problem of belief: as he puts it in 'Asides on the Oboe', 'final belief / Must be in a fiction.' One possible fiction of

faith is 'the idea of God.' But Stevens really finished with
theology in *Owl's Clover,* and his recent prolific activity may
be best understood as an effort to elaborate the distinctive
kind of humanism symbolized and incarnate in 'the hero,'

> The central man, the human globe, responsive
> As a mirror with a voice, the man of glass,
> Who in a million diamonds sums us up.

When this figure, or its prototype, first appeared in 'A Duck
for Dinner' as a 'super-animal' to 'dictate our fates' on the
principle, 'As the man the state, not as the state the man,' he
bore some suspicion of resemblance to a sort of *fuehrer.*
Things in the present collection like 'Life on a Battleship'
don't quite clear him of it. But the definitive characterization
appears in 'Montrachet-le-Jardin' and 'Examination of the
Hero in a Time of War' where the hero personifies those
capacities for noble living and thinking in which the average
man transcends himself. 'The common man is the common
hero,' but not in the sense of an individual raised to eminence
by circumstance, nor in that of 'the classic hero / And the
bourgeois.' 'There is a feeling as definition.'

> Instead of allegory,
> We have and are the man, capable
> Of his brave quickenings, the human
> Accelerations that seem inhuman.

Is that pure subjectivism? Or how does the hero manifest
himself? The statement,

> he studies the paper
> On the wall, the lemons on the table.
> This is his day.

does not mean that all the hero's acts are trivial, but rather
that he is heroic in even his most trivial doings, since even
them he performs heroically.

> He is the heroic
> Actor and act but not divided.
> It is a part of his conception,
> That he be not conceived, being real.

Real? – this idealization of the ordinary person, our common self? Stevens answers that challenge with another. When summer passes,

> True autumn stands then in the doorway.
> ....
> But was the summer false? The hero?
> How did we come to think that autumn
> Was the veritable season, that familiar
> Man was the veritable man?

In terms as close as may be to a literal description of an experienced feeling, Stevens writes:

> To meditate the highest man, not
> The highest supposed in him and over,
> Creates, in the blissfuller perceptions,
> What unisons create in music.

Thus, the hero symbolizes a conviction that life must be nobly lived to be worth living. That feeling pervades the finest poems of reflection and the most intense lyrics in *Parts of a World*. It gives its tone to Stevens' humanism, a humanism with an aesthetic instead of a moralistic basis, more yea-saying and better-humored than the humanism of Babbitt and More that went flat, a philosophy whose author can say, 'What more is there to love than I have loved?', an attitude insistently contemporary that yet makes place among contemporary tensions for a conception of noble living and noble imagining.

Only the main topographic outlines of Stevens' world are indicated in these few paragraphs. Space that might have been given to critical reservations has been added to that for exposition. Discussion of the potency of rhetorical means and effect in the verse has been omitted. This last, the most signal lack, is the most easily remedied. Often in the past fifteen years Wallace Stevens has been called the foremost living master of his art in America. The reader of this, his most deeply imagined work, may judge for himself the sense and the measure in which that is true.

55. Frank Jones, 'to wish, sometimes, that he were an eagle', *Nation*

7 November 1942, 488

Of this review, Stevens told Henry Church: 'last Thursday a man called me up on the telephone and said that he had been asked to review the book for the *Nation*. He is an instructor in the classics at Yale. I asked him to come out to the house and we had a good time, never mentioning the book' (*Letters*, pp. 418–19).

The toucan is an enchanting bird. He is perky and pensive by turns. His round eye flashes as he eats, but when he has swallowed, the long beak bends slowly down, now to one side, now to the other, and the head is the head of a skeptic. Wallace Stevens, who often writes of toucans, is the most entrancing of them. But now he seems to have swallowed his magical world for good, and to watch him sadly contemplate the darkening scene is to wish, sometimes, that he were an eagle.

For it takes an eagle, preferably a Yeats eagle, to be at ease on the heights to which Stevens here aspires. Of course, he may become one: his growth has been steadily manifest these past twenty years. In *Harmonium* he created an enchanted country, uniquely rounded, wholly credible. It has its pathos, but chiefly that of individual yearning for a more perfect imagined universe: the 'idea of a colony' in 'The Comedian as the Letter C,' the 'paradise' of 'Sunday Morning.' In the two subsequent collections, *Ideas of Order* and *The Man with the Blue Guitar,* the conflict of such longings with the increasingly cruel outer world is dramatized, and the poet's power grows with his theme. Once it was Crispin, the aesthete 'comedian,' 'green crammer of the

green fruits of the world,' who sought a 'mythology of self.'
Now it is 'all people,' those who 'cry and cry for help,' that
must find again 'the warm antiquity of self.' And when the
search leads to defeat and despair, Stevens approaches the
tragic, as in 'The Men that are Falling,' which I consider his
most intensely moving poem. But the present collection
reveals that he has been experimenting with that perilous
thing, the poet's answer to his own predicament.

Our time makes such answers peculiarly hard, because the
predicament is largely imposed by the very formation of a
poetic personality, a creative ambience. Colossal effort of
will is needed in order to dwell for the needed time 'where,'
as Henry James phrased it, 'in the dim underworld of fiction,
the great glazed tank of art, strange silent subjects float.' And
this effort necessitates a severance from the actual. How is the
artist to 'return,' to set his art right with the world, if to do so
he must employ the only creative processes he knows, those
which established his unique world, his true mythical self?

As with Yeats, Stevens's attempt involves some rejection
of former aims. Yeats 'banished heroic mother moon and
vanished, came to look upon the timid sun'; and Stevens
cries, in 'Montrachet-le-Jardin,' the most successful of these
poems: 'Bastard chateaux and smoky demoiselles, / No more
I can build towers of my own, / There to behold, there to
proclaim, the grace / And free requiting of the responsive
fact, / To project the naked man in a state of a fact,/As acute
virtue and ascetic trove.' But he doesn't build the towers, he
chiefly proclaims that he can. In the series entitled 'Examination of the Hero in a Time of War' he does make an
impressive effort at construction, developing – by his accustomed devious routes, but with fewer green vistas than
before – a concept of the hero as a redeeming, radiant force
inherent in humanity: neither the superior 'Leader' nor the
uncreative 'common man,' but 'Instead of allegory,/We have
and are the man, capable/Of his brave quickening, the
human/Accelerations that seem inhuman.' It is good doctrine, strongly and often beautifully stated, but not with the
light and music, pensive and perky by turns, that made his
other world so livable. These are more evident in the shorter,
more personal poems, many of which are extremely lovely,

notably 'On the Road Home' and 'The Hand as a Being,' utterances of a contemplative yet quickening love of the sensible world.

Stevens himself, as one would expect from so sure a critic of his work, seems disquieted by this development. He finds it necessary to append a comment stating that in war time 'consciousness takes the place of the imagination.' I assume that by 'consciousness' he means 'intelligence,' but the choice of words is revealing. As the 'unconscious' imagined world fades, the force that created it is supplanted by the endeavor to *understand* the total world – or so Stevens feels. But this feeling indicates that his is not the invincible imagination of the supreme poet, an imagination that always feeds peace or war, week day or holiday, on precisely that 'consciousness,' in Stevens's sense of the word. Why, as it increases, does a Yeats grow greater, a Stevens become unsure? For one thing: toucan or eagle, Stevens's imagination matured in a willed detachment, Yeats's in a willed togetherness with the past and present of his nation. Such factors may have nothing to do with the difference between talent and genius, but they certainly affect the capacity of self-renewal.

56. Mary M. Colum, on Stevens' 'separation from life', *New York Times Book Review*

29 November 1942, 12

Mary M. Colum (1887–1957) was an American-Irish literary journalist, and wife of the poet and playwright Padraic Colum (1881–1972).

This review is included because it marks a turning towards a view of Stevens as isolated aesthete, in contrast to the writings of the reviewers of the 1930s who found at least political inclination in Stevens' poems.

... So impressive is the mind behind *Parts of a World* that one hesitates to express dissatisfaction with its product. The author, we are told on the jacket of the book, is concerned with the relation between the imagination and the world, but he himself tells us that in our time consciousness takes the place of the imagination. It seems to us that what Wallace Stevens is really concerned with is the relation between one man's consciousness and the world, but a world in which humanity and its problems, desires and affections have hardly any place. The mind that the author projects into such careful and measured language is the philosophic speculative mind where the passions are of the intellectual rather than the sensuous order. We can have no great poetry without intellectual brooding, but when the speculative intellect is too dominating, as it is now among a certain type of writer, the result, no matter what command he has over rhythms and words, is something other than poetry. Consider these lines from 'The Poems of Our Climate':

> Say even that this complete simplicity
> Stripped one of all one's torments, concealed
> The evilly compounded, vital I
> And made it fresh in a world of white.
> A world of clear water, brilliant-edged,
> Still one would want more, one would need more,
> More than a world of white and snowy scents.

This is very accomplished writing, but one reader, anyway, gravely doubts if it has in it enough sensuous delight to be poetry. It reads a little like a piece of Thomas Aquinas. Wallace Stevens has been compared to a whole array of French poets, including Laforgue and Gautier. Actually there is something of Gautier in Stevens, but temperamentally he seems to this reviewer to be the opposite of Laforgue, whose concern was with people and with objects permeated with a sense of people. Wallace Stevens's concern is with objects, and when he writes about people they are simply other objects. He seems to be aware of his separation from life as it is commonly lived:

> To think of a dove with an eye of grenadine
> And pines that are cornets, so it occurs,
> And a little island full of geese and stars:
> It may be that the ignorant man, alone,
> Has any chance to mate his life with life
> That is the sensual, pearly spouse, the life
> That is fluent in even the winteriest bronze.

57. Louis Untermeyer, 'Departure from Dandyism', *Saturday Review*

Vol. 25, no. 51, 19 December 1942, 11

Wallace Stevens remains as much a problem for his troubled admirers as for his untroubled detractors. Friendly appraisers have indicated that Stevens's later work represents a departure from the once cultivated verbal dandyism, from an art that was insulated by its preoccupation with esthetics, and, like Yeats, from a dependence on a set of arbitrary symbols. Frank Jones,[1] for example, cites the new series entitled 'Examination of the Hero in Time of War' and several other poems in *Parts of a World* as 'utterances of a contemplative yet quickening love of the sensible world.' Horace Gregory,[2] differing from Jones and others, fails to find an analogy with Yeats, and establishes a connection with Whistler 'as a painter – the same notes of elegance, charm, sensibility, and impressionism.' According to the commentators, the growth has been away from pictures of a brightly abstract universe toward soliloquies on the darker world of desperate reality.

But Stevens agrees with his commentators (when he agrees at all) only by innuendo; he has by no means repudiated his fondness for the early 'absolute' poetry. In Whit Burnett's recently published anthology, *This is My Best,* Stevens significantly chose as his sole contribution the early 'Domination of Black.' Moreover, in the paragraph stating 'why' he selected the poem, Stevens declared: 'Poetry is neither politics nor philosophy. Poetry is poetry, and one's objective as a poet is to achieve poetry, precisely as one's object in music is to achieve music.' This old and always dangerous comparison leads Stevens to combine, and often to confuse, sounds, colors and 'effects' with metaphysical conclusions, to mix the program and the performance, to write (too often, it seems, poetry) poetry about poetry. More than a few of Stevens's ultra-fastidious pages concern themselves with writing which is elaborately virtuoso, with a maximum of form and a minimum of content, with the art of being an artist. The author, says the dust-jacket reassuringly, is occupied 'with the relation between the imagination and the world.' But (as if that were not true of every poet) what world? Stevens seems to be less anxious to establish a relation between imagination and 'the' world than making 'a' world – another world of the intellect; a forced creation, an incongruity of serious wit and irresponsible whimsy. Tragedy is not absent, but it moves the reader chiefly with the impact of its rhetoric, not with the depth of a persisting emotion.

It is as a poet of comedy that Stevens is most spectacular. It is not in the framing of a philosophy nor an esthetic but in a comedy of words and ideas that his singularity triumphs. This poet, as two of his new titles suggest, gives 'A Sense of the Sleight-of-Hand Man,' of 'Asides on the Oboe'; he is a 'Connoisseur of Chaos.' He can play with wayward non-sense:

> Under the eglantine
> The fretful concubine
> Said 'Phooey! Phoo!'
> She whispered, 'Pfui!'

That he still loves to toy with repetitive syllables (as in the familiar 'Chieftain Iffucan of Azcan in caftan') is proved by the new:

> I sang a canto in a canton,
> Cunning-coo, O, cuckoo-cock,
> In a canton of Belshazzar...

But if Stevens is concerned with man's bewilderment in a dissolving world and his desire 'to move in the direction of fact as we want to be,' he still mingles amazing luxuriance and mocking obscurity in what he once called 'the essential gaudiness of poetry.'

NOTES

1 See No. 55.
2 Horace Gregory, 'An Examination of Wallace Stevens in a time of War', *Accent*, Vol. III, Autumn 1942, pp. 57–61.

NOTES TOWARD A SUPREME FICTION

Cummington, Massachusetts, 1942

Cummington Press issued 273 copies.

58. R.P. Blackmur, 'An Abstraction Blooded', *Partisan Review*

Vol. 10, no. 3, May–June 1943, 297–301

Blackmur here captures what Marianne Moore called Stevens' 'affirming freedom of the mind'. (Her review, 'There is a War that Never Ends', first published in *Kenyon Review,* Winter 1943, is included in *Predilections,* London, 1956.) Blackmur himself comes up with an even better phrase below, in his playful reference to Stevens as 'free master of the fresh and rejoicing tongue of sensibility and fancy'.

In one of Mr. Stevens' early poems he made the simple declaration that 'Poetry is the supreme fiction,' and in another there was a phrase about 'the ultimate Plato, the tranquil jewel in this confusion.' Now, in *Notes Toward a Supreme Fiction,* he shows us a combination of the two notions with a development into a third thing, which if it is not reached is approached from all round. The poem is like a pie marked for cutting in three pieces, with an imaginary centre which is somehow limited, if you look long enough, only by the whole circumference. A triad makes a trinity, and a trinity, to a certain kind of poetic imagination, is the

217

only tolerable form of unity. I think the deep skills of imagination, by which insights, ideas, and acts get into poetry, thrive best when some single, pressing theme or notion is triplicated. It is not a matter of understanding, but of movement and of identification and of access of being. The doublet is never enough, unless it breeds. War and peace need a third phase, as liquid and ice need vapor to fill out and judge the concept of water, as God the Father and God the Son need the Holy Ghost, or hell and heaven need purgatory, or act and place need time. The doublet *needs* what it makes. This is a habit of creative mind.

Mr. Stevens has acquired that habit. Wanting, as we all do, a supreme fiction, wanting, that is, to conceive, to imagine, to make a supreme being, wanting, in short, to discover and objectify a sense of such a being, he sets up three phases through which it must pass. It must be abstract; it must change; it must give pleasure. Each phase is conceived as equal in dimension, each being given in ten sections of seven three-lined stanzas: and each phase is conceived as a version of the other two, that is, with a mutual and inextricable rather than with a successive relationship.

Let us see what the elements of the Fiction look like when taken separately. It must, the poet argues, be abstract, beyond, above, and at the beginning of our experience, and it must be an abstract idea of *being,* which when fleshed or blooded in nature or in thought, will absorb all the meanings we discover. That is to say, it must be arche-typical and a source, an initiator of myth and sense, and also a reference or judgment for myth and sense; it tends to resemble a Platonic idea in character and operation, and its natural prototype, its easiest obvious symbol, will be the sun. But it must change in its abstractness, depending on the experience of it, as a seraph turns satyr 'according to his thoughts'; for if it did not change it would tend to disappear or at least to become vestigial. You take character from what is not yourself and participate in what changes you. The process of change is the life of being, like abstraction, requires constant iteration and constant experience. Most of all the Fiction must change because change is the condition of perception, vision, imagination. 'A fictive covering / weaves always glistening from the heart and mind.' What changes is the general, the instances of the abstract, as they strike a fresh or freshened eye. That is why this fiction which changes, and is abstract, must give pleasure; it must be always open to discovery by a fresh eye, which is the eye of pleasure, the eye of feeling and imagination, envisaging the 'irrational distortion.'

> That's it: the more than rational distortion,
> The fiction that results from feeling.

In short, an abstract fiction can change and, if the abstraction was soundly conceived, the more it is the same the more it will seem to change, and by the feeling of change in identity, identity in change, give the great pleasure of access of being.

> The man-hero is not the exceptional monster,
> But he that of repetition is most master.

These are the bare bones of doctrine, and in another poet, most likely of another age, might exactly have been in control of the motion of the poem. In Stevens' poem the doctrine is not in control, nor does he pretend that it is; it is not a system, or even an organization, that he provides us with, but a set of notes brought together and graphed by the convention of his triad. If his notes are united, it is partly by the insight that saw the triad outside the poem, and partly by the sensibility – the clusters of perceptions, and the rotation of his rosary of minor symbols – into which he translates it. There is the great unity and the heroic vision in the offing, and they may indeed loom in the night of the poetry, but in the broad day of it there are only fragments, impressions, and merely associated individuations. Their maximum achieved unity is in their formal circumscription: that they are seen together in the same poem.

Whether a poet could in our time go much further – whether the speculative *imagination* is possible in our stage of belief – cannot be argued; there are no examples; yet it seems more a failure of will than of ability. Certainly Stevens has tackled Socrates' job: the definition of general terms. Certainly, too, he has seen one of the ways in which the poet in whom the philosopher has hibernated, muddled in sleep, can go on with the job: he has seen, in the sensibility, the relations between the abstract, the actual, and the imaginative. But he has been contented or been able only to make all his definitions out of fragments of the actual, seeing the fragments as transformations of the abstract: each one as good, as meaningful, as another, but bound not to each other in career but only to the centre (the major idea) which includes them. That is why, I think, so many of the fragments are unavailable except in passing, and the comprehension of what is passing depends too often upon special knowledge of fashion and gibberish in vocabulary and idiom.

Mr. Stevens himself understands the problem, and has expressed it characteristically in one of the segments of the decade requiring that the Fiction change. It is one of the segments, so common in so many poets of all ages, in which the poet assures himself of the nature and virtue of poetry: the protesting ritual of re-dedication.

> The poem goes from the poet's gibberish to
> The gibberish of the vulgate and back again . . .
> Is there a poem that never reaches words
> And one that chaffers the time away? . . .
> It is the gibberish of the vulgate that he seeks.
> He tries by a peculiar speech to speak
>
> The peculiar potency of the general,
> To compound the imagination's Latin with
> The lingua franca et jocundissima.

Granting the poet his own style, it could not be better expressed. Mr. Stevens, like the best of our modern poets, is free master of the fresh and rejoicing tongue of sensibility and fancy and the experience in flush and flux and flower; but he lacks, except for moments, and there, too, resembles his peers, the power of the 'received,' objective and authoritative imagination, whether of philosophy, religion, myth, or dramatic symbol, which is what he means by the imagination's Latin. The reader should perhaps be reminded that *gibberish* is not a frivolous word in the context; it is a word *manqué* more than a word mocking. One gibbers before a reality too great, when one is appalled with perception, when words fail though meaning persists: which is precisely, as Mr. Eliot suggested in a recent number of the *Partisan Review*, a proper domain of poetry.

One does what one can, and the limits of one's abilities are cut down by the privations of experience and habit, by the absence of what one has not thought of and by the presence of what is thought of too much, by the canalisation and evaporation of the will. What is left is that which one touches again and again, establishing a piety of the imagination with the effrontery of repetition. Mr. Stevens has more left than most, and has handled it with more modulations of touch and more tenacious piety, so that it becomes itself exclusively, inexplicably, fully expressive of its own meaning. Of such things he says:

> These are not things transformed
> Yet we are shaken by them as if they were.
> We reason about them with a later reason.

He knows, too,

> The fluctuations of certainty, the change
> Of degrees of perception in the scholar's dark,

which it is not hard to say that one knows, but which it is astonishing, always, to see exemplified in images of the seasons, of water-lights, the colours of flowers in the colours of air, or birdsong, for they make so 'an abstraction blooded, as a man by thought.'

It is all in the garden, perhaps, where the poet's gibberish returns to the gibberish of the vulgate, and where the intensity of the revelations of the single notion of redness dispenses, for a very considerable but by no means single occasion, with the imagination's Latin.

> A lasting visage in a lasting bush,
> A face of stone in an unending red,
> Red-emerald, red-slitted-blue, a face of slate,

> An ancient forehead hung with heavy hair,
> The channel slots of rain, the red-rose-red
> And weathered and the ruby-water-worn,

The vines around the throat, the shapeless lips,
The frown like serpents basking on the brow,
The spent feeling leaving nothing of itself,

Red-in-red repetitions never going
Away, a little rusty, a little rouged
A little roughened and ruder, a crown

The eye could not escape, a red renown
Blowing itself upon the tedious ear.
An effulgence faded, dull cornelian

Too venerably used.

59. Dudley Fitts, on 'one of the master verbalists of modern English', *Saturday Review*

Vol. 26, no. 35, 28 August 1943, 8–9

Fitts (1903–68) was an American classicist, translator and critic, noted chiefly for his translation of the plays of Sophocles (with Robert Fitzgerald, see No. 46) and Aristophanes.

Also reviewed are books by Dylan Thomas and Edward Doro.

... It is nonsense to attempt, in anything less ambitious than an extended essay, criticism of Mr. Stevens's latest book. One can only say that it represents the full flowering of a tendency which was visible in his work as far back as the revised edition of *Harmonium* – a tendency away from pure rhetoric, from decoration *sui causa* towards philosophical statement. Yet in moving so, it has at no point abandoned or even qualified the intricate melodic and harmonic invention that set Mr. Stevens with Eliot and Yeats and Pound, years ago, as one of the master verbalists of modern English: all this has been kept to adorn a steadily increasing depth. Certain affectations have been kept as well: the curious Whitman-like obsession (in how un-Whitman-like a setting!) of snìps of foreign languages; a certain preciosity which occasionally gets completely out of hand; the strange noises for instance: 'an Arabian in my room, / With his damned hoobla-hoobla-hoobla-how'. Thus, a fine apostrophe to the world ('Fat girl') precariously names the globe 'my fluent mundo'; the god's name inevitably produces such a phrase as 'Phoebus is dead, ephebe'; and when the ocean 'Howls hoo and arises and howls hoo and falls,' I am inclined to wish that the poet had never heard the mob jeering Coriolanus out of Rome. But when one has noted these flaws, as one notes the flaws in anything that one loves, what richness of art and matter remains! The poems are a many-faceted discussion of the esthetic of poetry and hence of the meaning of existence, of the Fictive and hence of the True: 'How simply the fictive hero becomes the real; / How gladly with proper words the soldier dies. / If he must, or lives on the bread of faithful speech.' And in a fairly strict form – each poem is composed of seven unrhymed or, at most, vaguely assonanced tercets – there is presented to us something better than a 'fluent mundo': it is a picture of the world itself....

60. Yvor Winters, 'Wallace Stevens, or the Hedonist's Progress', from *The Anatomy of Nonsense*

1943, 431–59

This well-known essay was reprinted in *In Defense of Reason* (1947) and *On Modern Poets* (1959), and contrasts interestingly with Winters' brief but highly complimentary reference twenty years earlier (see No. 8). Always strong-minded, though sometimes wrongheaded, Winters often penetrated to the most serious weaknesses of much twentieth-century poetry, both technically and spiritually. Here he attempts, to demonstrate how Stevens' philosophy undermines his poetry. Despite its importance and its profoundly negative conclusions, the essay did not undermine Stevens' writing reputation.

Though Wallace Stevens has published almost nothing in the way of criticism, he has nevertheless been very clear in stating his theories of life and of literature, and he may justifiably be treated, I believe, in a series of essays on literary theorists.[a]

His fundamental ideas are stated in 'Sunday Morning', an early poem, and in some ways his greatest. The poem consists of eight stanzas in blank verse, each containing fifteen lines, and it presents a clear and fairly coherent argument.

The first stanza sets the stage and identifies the protagonist. We are given a woman, at home on a Sunday morning, meditating on the meaning of death. The second stanza asks the question which provides the subject of the poem; it asks what divinity this woman may be thought to possess as a recompense for her ultimate surrender to death; and having asked the question, it replies that her divinity, which must live within herself, consists wholly in her emotions – not in her understanding of the emotions, but in the emotions as a good in themselves. This answer is not quite the orthodox romantic answer, which would offer us in the emotions either a true guide to virtue or a more or less mystical experience leading to some kind of union with some kind of deity. Any philosophy which offers the cultivation of the emotions as an end in itself, I suppose, is a kind of hedonism. In any event, that is the kind of philosophy which we find here.

The third stanza, by means of the allegory of Jove and his human loves, through his union with whom he crossed the heavenly strain upon the human, implies that man has a capacity which may at least figuratively be termed divine; the stanza is a subordinate commentary on the one preceding, and does not really advance the argument.

In the fourth stanza, however, the argument moves forward. The protagonist objects to the concept which has been offered her; she states that the beauties of this life are transient and that she longs to believe in a Paradise beyond them. The remainder of the stanza, and the greater part of it, is the poet's reply: in a passage of great rhetorical power, he denies the possibility of Paradise, at the same time that he communicates through the feeling of his language a deep nostalgic longing to accept the ideas which he is rejecting. In the first two lines of the fifth stanza, the woman repeats her objection, and the poet then replies with an explanation of the function of death: it is our awareness of the imminence of death which heightens our emotions and sharpens our perceptions; our knowledge of life's transience stimulates our perception of life's beauty.

In the sixth stanza the poet considers an hypothetical paradise, and, since he can imagine it only in terms of a projection of the good life as the hedonist understands the good life, he deduces that paradise would become tedious and insipid: we have in this stanza the first sharp vision of the ennui which is to obsess the later work of the poet and which is ultimately to wreck his talent, an ennui arising from the fact that emotion is not a good in itself, but that if cultivated for itself alone is merely a pleasant diversion so long as the novelty of a given experience endures, at most as long as new experiences can give us the illusion of novel excitement, and then becomes a disease of the spirit, a state of indifference in which there is neither novelty nor significance.

The seventh stanza presents a vision of a future race of men engaged in a religious ritual, the generating principle of which is their joy in the world as it is given them and their sense of brotherhood as 'men that perish.' The stanza contains suggestions of a pantheism which goes beyond the bounds of a strict hedonism, but they are merely suggestions and they appear nowhere else. The eighth and last stanza begins by denying the immortality of Jesus, and, by implication, of men; and it places the protagonist finally and irretrievably on a small but beautiful planet, floating like a tropical island in boundless space, 'in an old chaos of the sun.'

This summary, even as summaries go, is extremely skeletalized. It has been my intention, here, merely to isolate the hedonistic theme for future consideration; the theme is not thus isolated in the poem, but is complicated by its interconnections with other human problems from which not even a hedonist can escape. Whatever the defects of the hedonistic theme, and with the possible but by no means certain exception of a few short poems by Stevens and of two or three poems by E.A. Robinson, 'Sunday Morning' is probably the greatest American poem of the twentieth century and is certainly one of the greatest contemplative poems in English: in a blank verse which differs, in its firmness of structure and incalculable sensitivity of detail, from all other blank verse of our time save that of a few poems by Hart Crane which were in some measure modeled upon it, it renders the acute uncertainty of what we are inclined to consider the modern mind, but it does so with no uncertainty of method or of statement; it renders an acute consciousness of the imminence of death, of the sensory and emotional richness of life on this bewildering planet, and of the heroic magnificence of the religious myths which are lost to the poet and to many of the rest of us, except as memories of things long past. If Stevens' career had stopped with this

poem, or a few years thereafter, it might seem an unnecessary unkindness to insist upon the limitations of understanding which the poem discloses; but those limitations appear
very obviously in a few later poems, and they seem to me to
be very clearly related to the rapid and tragic decay of the
poet's style. As a poet in early maturity, Stevens brought to
this subject a style which was the result of a fine native gift
enriched by the study of English blank verse; the subject,
once formulated, and accepted as a guide to life and to
expression, destroyed the style in less than two decades. In
'Sunday Morning' itself, we detect the limitations of the
subject only by rational analysis; in the later work we see the
effect of those limitations.

We may consider briefly, and perhaps as a kind of footnote
to 'Sunday Morning', one of the more obscure poems, called
'The Stars at Tallapoosa.' As far as I can penetrate this poem,
I judge that it postulates the absolute severance of the
intellectual and the emotional: the lines between the stars are
the lines of pure intellect; the earth-lines and the sea-lines
represent the non-intellectual experience (loosely speaking) of
daily human life. Both modes of experience have beauty and
should be pursued, but they are disparate and unrelated to
each other; and it follows, although this is not stated in the
poem, that the intellectual experience, since it bears no
relationship to the rest of our life and hence is in no way
useful, is valuable simply for the independent emotional
excitement which one may derive from it.

If we turn to 'A High-Toned Old Christian Woman,' a
brief didactic and satirical poem, which is quite clear and
unmistakable as regards its theoretic import, we get an
additional step in the argument: we learn that the 'moral law'
is not necessary as a framework for art, but that 'the
opposing law' will do as well, and that in either event, the
artists,

> Your disaffected flagellants, well-stuffed,
> Smacking their muzzy bellies in parade,
> Proud of such novelties of the sublime,
> Such tink and tank and tunk-a-tunk-tunk,
> May, merely may, madame, whip from themselves
> A jovial hullabaloo among the spheres.

Stevens, in becoming thus explicit, states his final doctrine, as do certain other contemporary theorists, in language surprisingly reminiscent of Poe:

It may be, indeed, that here this sublime end is, now and then, attained in fact. We are often made to feel with a shivering delight, that from an earthly harp are stricken notes which *cannot* have been unfamiliar to the angels.[b]

Poe's statement is made, of course, in the tone of saccharine sentimentality which is Poe's nearest approach to sincerity; Stevens' statement is made ironically, but one should not be misled by this fact. For though Stevens is ridiculing himself and his artists, he is ridiculing his old Christian woman, the representative of the moralistic point of view, even more severely: he is offering his opinion as more nearly tenable than hers, notwithstanding the fact that he cannot offer his opinion with real seriousness. Stevens' self-ridicule is as irrational in its way as Poe's sentimentalism, and like that sentimentalism springs from a doctrine which eliminates the possibility of the rational understanding of experience and of a moral judgment deriving therefrom: since no idea is really tenable and since we cannot judge of the justice of a feeling but can only seek to heighten its intensity, all ideas and all feelings may fairly be, and sooner or later, in the history of a sensitive and witty man, are certain to be, subjected to merciless ridicule; but of this we shall see more interesting evidence later.

It is perhaps not important, but it is at least mildly interesting, to call attention at this point to a poem which has been at least twice misinterpreted by commentators who have not taken the trouble to understand Stevens as a whole. The poem is 'Anecdote of the Jar':

[Quotes *CP*, p. 76.]

Stanley P. Chase has written of this poem:

'Very likely the little poem is meant to suggest nothing more than the superiority, to an intensely civilized person, of the simplest bit of handicraft over any extent of unregulated 'nature' ...[c]

And Howard Baker writes with the same obtuseness, but with greater elaborateness:

Similarly a wild disorderly landscape is transformed into order by the presence of a symmetrical vase.... The jar acts in the imagination like one of the poles of the earth, the imaginary order of the lines of latitude and longitude projecting around the pole. The jar itself – simple and symmetrical, a product of the human consciousness and not of nature – is a very fitting symbol for man's dominion over nature...[d]

If the poem ended with the fourth line, there might be an imperfect justification of the interpretation offered by these writers, for in the first four lines the wilderness is not only dominated by the jar – as, in fact, it is dominated throughout the poem, – but it is called slovenly. If we examine the next two lines, however, we see that the phrase, 'the slovenly wilderness,' is in fact a slovenly ellipsis. The wilderness is slovenly after it has been dominated and not before: it 'sprawled around, no longer wild.' The jar is the product of the human mind, as the critics remark, and it dominates the wilderness; but it does not give order to the wilderness – it is vulgar and sterile, and it transforms the wilderness into the semblance of a deserted picnic ground. Its sterility is indicated in the last three lines, and if the jar is to be accepted as symbolic of the human intellect, then the poem is in part another example of the same theme which we found in 'The Stars at Tallapoosa,' but expressed this time with disillusionment and a measure of disgust. The poem would appear to be primarily an expression of the corrupting effect of the intellect upon natural beauty, and hence a purely romantic performance. To read any measure of neo-humanism into Stevens is as foolish as to endeavor, in the manner of certain young critics of a few years ago, to read into him a kind of incipient and trembling consciousness of the beauty of Marxism.

I have already pointed out that in the sixth stanza of 'Sunday Morning,' the stanza in which Stevens projects into the eternity of paradise the highest good which he can imagine, there appears a weary dissatisfaction with the experience, a hint of the dissatisfaction which might imaginably appear in our present life if the experience were too long protracted. This dissatisfaction is familiar to students of romantic literature under the name of ennui; it is the boredom which eventually overtakes the man who seeks for excitement instead of understanding. In the poem entitled 'The Man Whose Pharynx was Bad' we find a statement of this boredom which is both extreme and explicit. The poem as it appears in *Harmonium* lacks four lines of the original version, lines ten to thirteen inclusive, which appeared in the *New Republic* for September 14, 1921. Those lines are essential to the poem and to the understanding of Stevens, and I shall quote the entire poem in its original version:

> The time of year has grown indifferent.
> Mildew of summer and the deepening snow
> Are both alike in the routine I know;
> I am too dumbly in my being pent.
>
> The wind attendant on the solstices
> Blows on the shutters of the metropoles,
> Stirring no poet in his sleep, and tolls
> The grand ideas of the villages.
>
> The malady of the quotidian ...
> Perhaps if summer ever came to rest
> And lengthened, deepened, comforted, caressed
> Through days like oceans in obsidian
>
> Horizons, full of night's midsummer blaze;
> Perhaps, if winter once could penetrate
> Through all its purples to the final slate,
> Persisting bleakly in an icy haze;
>
> One might in turn become less diffident,
> Out of such mildew plucking neater mould
> And spouting new orations of the cold.
> One might. One might. But time will not relent.

The poet has progressed in this poem to the point at which the intensity of emotion possible in actual human life has become insipid, and he conceives the possibility of ultimate satisfaction only in some impossible emotional finality of no matter what kind. In fact, the figurative opposites of summer and winter here offered suggest the opposites of the moral and the anti-moral which appear in 'A High-Toned Old Christian Woman.'

The situation in which Stevens may here be observed is similar to a difficulty in which Poe found himself. Poe, like Stevens, sought only emotional stimulation in the arts, and hence he considered novelty, and novelty of a fairly crude kind, to be an essential of good art. He wrote:

Nothing is more clear than this proposition, although denied by the chlorine critics (the grass-green). The desire of the new is an element of the soul. The most exquisite pleasures grow dull in repetition. A strain of music enchants. Heard a second time, it pleases. Heard a tenth it does not displease. We hear it a twentieth, and ask ourslevs why we admired. At the fiftieth, it produces ennui, at the hundredth disgust.ᵉ

Both men are in search of intense feeling; neither is in search of just feeling, of feeling properly motivated. The poem as an exercise in just feeling is an act of moral judgment, as I have repeatedly indicated; and though all such judgments must of necessity be governed by general principles, yet each particular judgment, since it arises from an individual relationship between unique persons and events, will be, if truly just, unique, as individual men are unique, and will have its own inexhaustible fascination as a living entity. But if one does not recognize this principle of justice, then the poem can have no true uniqueness: the poet and the reader alike are bent, as are Poe and Stevens, on a quest for the new, which, in the realm of emotion divorced from understanding or any principle of propriety, can be found only in new degrees of intensity and of strangeness; and as each new degree achieved becomes familiar it is submerged in the monotone of that which is no longer new, so that the search is equally devoid of hope and of significance. Poe never had the wit to perceive the futility of this search; Stevens has the wit not only to see the futility but to be both depressed and ironic in consequence, yet he is unable to think himself out of the situation into which he has wandered.

Unless one change one's entire philosophy, having arrived

at this impasse, there can remain open to one only two modes
of action: one may renounce one's art and subside into a kind
of stoical silence; or one may pursue, not greater intensity of
experience, for human language and the human organism
alike set a certain limit to progress in that direction, but
experience increasingly elusive and incomprehensible.
Stevens has considered both of these possibilities, but since
he has chosen the latter, we may fairly examine first the
mode of action which he has considered and discarded. It so
happens, incidentally, that his meditation upon the possibility of renunciation has resulted in his longest single work.

'The Comedian as the Letter C' (the significance of the
title, I regret to say, escapes both my learning and my
ingenuity) is a narrative poem in six parts, dealing with a
poet who begins with romantic views of the function of his
art and who, in reforming them, comes to abandon his art as
superfluous. The first part of the poem deals with Crispin's
encounter with the sea, that is, with his realization of a
universe vast, chaotic, and impersonal beyond his power of
formulation or imagination, and rendering him contemptible
by contrast. In the second part, Crispin arrives in Yucatan,
disillusioned as to his old convictions, but finding a
heightened experience and new food for his art in the
barbaric violence of the tropical landscape; finding these, that
is, until he is overwhelmed by a thunderstorm, of which the
symbolic function is similar to that of the sea in the first part,
and is driven with the terrified crowd about him into the
cathedral. In the third part he returns to North America,
intent now, not on the extreme and unnatural excitements of
the southern landscape which he has left, but on the
discovery of reality:

> He gripped more closely the essential prose
> As being, in a world so falsified,
> The one integrity for him, the one
> Discovery still possible to make,
> To which all poems were incident, unless
> That prose should wear a poem's guise at last.

But he is bent on discovering not the reality of his own
nature, but rather the reality of his native country. Man is no

longer, as in the first line of the first part, the intelligence of his soil; but the soil, as we note in the first line of the next and fourth section, is man's intelligence. These statements do not have the philosophical lucidity which would delight the present simple paraphraser, but they seem to mean, in their relationship to this poem, that Crispin has been turned away first from the attempt to study himself directly, and second from the attempt to indulge in exotic experiences, and that he has been turned instead to the attempt to master his native environment – to master it, that is, for the purposes of poetry. The nature of this last procedure I do not pretend to understand, and since the words which I have just used are my own and are not quoted from Stevens, it is possible that my confusion is of my own contriving. But in general, I should say that Stevens appears to have slipped here into the Whitmanian form of the romantic error common enough in our literature, but current especially in Stevens' generation and espoused in particular by Stevens' friend W.C. Williams: the fallacy that the poet achieves salvation by being, in some way, intensely of and expressive of his country. A common variant of this notion is the idea that the poet should bear the same relationship to his time, and in fact the two versions are perhaps most commonly combined, as they are in Williams. Felt with sufficient intensity, they become indistinguishable, as in Crane or even in Whitman, from pantheism, and go quite beyond the bounds of hedonism; but the notions in question represent merely a casual subject for meditation in Stevens, a subject which he considers because he is confused but which involves a spiritual quality, a capacity for naively whole-hearted enthusiasm, which is quite foreign to his nature. The ideas are the attempt to justify a kind of extroversion: the poet, cut off from human nature, which is his proper subject-matter, seeks to find a subject in the description, or, as the saying goes, in the expression, of what is round about him. In practice, this results mainly, as in Williams, in a heavy use of the native landscape, sometimes as legitimate symbolism or background, sometimes as the subject of mere description, sometimes as false symbolism:[f] in the first of these three instances, the poet is actually intent on doing something not adequately explained by his theory;

in the second he is doing something relatively easy and unimportant; and in the third he is writing badly. Crispin seeks, then, an understanding not of himself but of his native landscape and his native landscape is a temperate one, which does not offer the flamboyant and succulent excitements of Yucatan:

> The spring came there in clinking pannicles
> Of half-dissolving frost, the summer came,
> If ever, whisked and wet, not ripening,
> Before the winter's vacancy returned.

This landscape is the one which appears in 'The Man Whose Pharynx was Bad,' and which Stevens there uses to symbolize his own frustration. But Crispin, having returned from Yucatan, hopes now to achieve the beatific pleasure reserved for the successful hedonist, not by extravagance of experience, but by the honesty and accuracy of experience: by honesty and accuracy, however, so far as we can judge from the poem, merely in describing the scenery which surrounds him, as if, perhaps, there were some ulterior virtue in this process which cannot quite be defined in words. The fourth section of the poem is really an elaboration upon the central ideas of the third, and it scarcely calls for comment at present. In the fifth and sixth parts, Crispin's concentration upon the normal world about him results in his marrying and begetting daughters; and finding that the facts which he had set out to describe with such exemplary honesty are more engrossing than the description of them, he abandons his art, in order, as very young people are sometimes heard to say, to live. This is not surprising, for the honest description which Crispin set out to achieve is in itself a moral experience, though of a very limited kind: honest description renders the feeling appropriate to purely sensory experience, and is hence a kind of judgment of that experience. But if Crispin had realized this, he would have realized the whole moral basis of art, and would have proceeded to more complex subjects; not realizing this, he lost interest in his simplified art, and found the art even in this simplified form to be the last element of confusion remaining in his experience: to achieve intelligent objectivity, Crispin is forced to abandon his description and merely enjoy the subject-matter of his description in the most naked possible of conditions:

> He first, as realist, admitted that
> Whoever hunts a matinal continent
> May, after all, stop before a plum
> And be content and still be realist,
> The words of things entangle and confuse.
> The plum survives its poems.....
> .... it survives in its own forms,
> Beyond these changes, good fat guzzly fruit.

We have now the complete argument, I believe, which leads to Crispin's renunciation. The passage in which the renunciation takes place, however, is interesting for another reason; for the quality of the rhetoric employed at this particular juncture helps us profoundly to understand Stevens himself. The passage follows closely upon the lines just quoted and will be found about half-way through the fifth section:

> Was he to bray this in profoundest brass
> Arointing his dreams with fugal requiems?
> Was he to company vastest things defunct
> With a blubber of tom-toms harrowing the sky?
> Scrawl a tragedian's testament? Prolong
> His active force in an inactive dirge,
> Which, let the tall musicians call and call,
> Should merely call him dead? Pronounce amen
> Through choirs infolded to the outmost clouds?
> Because he built a cabin who once planned
> Loquacious columns by the ructive sea?
> Because he turned to salad beds again?

What I wish the reader to note is this: that the passage describes Crispin's taking leave of his art, and describes also his refusal to use his art in the process of leave-taking, because the art is, after all, futile and contemptible. Yet for Stevens himself the entire poem is a kind of tentative leave-taking; he has not the courage to act as his hero acts and be done with it, so he practices the art which he cannot justify and describes it in terms of contempt. Furthermore, the chief instrument of irony in this passage, and throughout the

poem, and indeed throughout much of the rest of Stevens, is
a curious variant on the self-ridicule, the romantic irony,
with which we are familiar from Byron through Laforgue
and his modern disciples;[g] the instrument is self-parody, a
parody occasionally subtle, often clumsy, of the refined and
immutable style of Stevens at his best. To estimate at least a
part of the tragedy represented by Stevens' career, the reader
can scarcely do better than compare the lines quoted above
with the last section of the much earlier 'Sunday Morning':

> She hears upon that water without sound,
> A voice that cries, 'The tomb in Palestine
> Is not the porch of spirits lingering.
> It is the grave of Jesus where he lay.'
> We live in an old chaos of the sun,
> Or old dependency of day and night,
> Or island solitude, unsponsored, free,
> Of that wide water, inescapable.
> Deer walk upon our mountains, and the quail
> Whistle about us their spontaneous cries;
> Sweet berries ripen in the wilderness;
> And, in the isolation of the sky,
> At evening, casual flocks of pigeons make
> Ambiguous undulations as they sink,
> Downward to darkness, on extended wings.

Since the poet, having arrived at the predicament to which
we have traced him, however, is not to abandon, his art,
there remains only the possibility that he seek variety of
experience in the increasingly perverse and strange; that he
seek it, moreover, with no feeling of respect toward the art
which serves as his only instrument and medium. In the
poem entitled 'The Revolutionists Stop for Orangeade,' we
are given the theory of this type of poetry:

> Hang a feather by your eye,
> Nod and look a little sly.
> This must be the vent of pity,
> Deeper than a truer ditty
> Of the real that wrenches,
> Of the quick that's wry.

And from this point onward there remains little but the sly look and a perverse ingenuity in confusing the statement of essentially simple themes. *The Man with the Blue Guitar,*[h] for example, which is one of his most recent performances, is merely a jingling restatement of the old theme of the severance between the rational understanding and the poetic imagination. But the statement is never quite clear; and since the theme, though unsound, is far from difficult to understand, one is inclined to suspect that the lack of clarity is the result of a deliberate choice, a choice motivated, perhaps, by the hope that some note more moving than the poet has a right to expect may be struck from the obscurity. And if one does not always encounter such wilful semiobscurity in the later poems, one much too commonly encounters the kind of laborious foolishness to be found in the following poem, entitled 'The Mechanical Optimist,' published in *New Directions* for 1936:

A lady dying of diabetes
Listened to the radio,
Catching the lesser dithyrambs.
So heaven collects its bleating lambs.

Her useless bracelets fondly fluttered,
Paddling the melodic swirls,
The idea of God no longer sputtered
At the roots of her indifferent curls.

The idea of the Alps grew large,
Not yet, however, a thing to die in.
It seemed serener just to die,
To float off on the floweriest barge,

Accompanied by the exegesis
Of familiar things in a cheerful voice,
Like the night before Christmas and all the carols.
Dying lady, rejoice, rejoice!

The generating mood is one of ennui; the style represents an effort, half-bored and half desperate, to achieve originality; the victim of the irony is very small game, and scarcely worthy of the artillery of the author of 'Sunday Morning';

the point of view is adolescent. The author of 'Sunday Morning' and of 'Le Monocle de Mon Oncle,' the heir of Milton and of Jonson, is endeavoring, in his old age, to épater les bourgeois. The poem is the work of a man who twenty or twenty-five years earlier was one of the great poets of the English language.

This is the outline, I believe, of the sequence of ideas and states of mind which have debased the greatest American poetic talent of the twentieth century. The sequence is offered merely as a species of logical sequence; it is only imperfectly chronological. Stevens was a hedonist from the beginning, and the entire complex of ideas and feelings which I have recounted are to be found in his work from the beginning. But although it is possible to find some of his most wilful nonsense – 'Earthy Anecdote', let us say, or 'Metaphors of a Magnifico' – among his earlier poems, it is likewise true that all of his great poetry is early. 'Sunday Morning' is one of the earliest compositions; 'The Snow Man,' 'Le Monocle de Mon Oncle,' 'Of the Manner of Addressing Clouds,' 'Of Heaven Considered as a Tomb,' 'The Death of the Soldier' are all of the next few years. All of these poems were written and first published before 1923, the date of the first edition of *Harmonium;* and if there is a later poem as good I do not know it or cannot appreciate it. There are other poems, more or less early, less perfect or of smaller scope but still of considerable beauty, such as 'Peter Quince at the Clavier' or 'Cortège for Rosenbloom,' and such poems as these one may find equalled occasionally, though very rarely, at a later date; but these two surpass anything by the author which I have read in the past decade.

Some of the virtues of 'Sunday Morning' I have indicated in very general terms, but one cannot turn from the poem that may be the greatest American work of our century without considering briefly some of its more haunting beauties, if it be only as an act of piety.

I have already quoted the final stanza of the poem, and its beauty should be obvious; yet as removed from its context, the stanza loses much of its complexity. The 'water without sound,' the 'wide water inescapable,' is not only an image representing infinite space; it is an image, established in the first stanza, representing a state of mind, a kind of bright and empty beatitude, over which the thought of death may darken suddenly and without warning:

> She dreams a little, and she feels the dark
> Encroachment of that old catastrophe,
> As a calm darkness among water-lights.

The language has the greatest possible dignity and subtlety, combined with perfect precision. The imminence of absolute tragedy is felt and recorded, but the integrity of the feeling mind is maintained. The mind perceives, as by a kind of metaphysical sense, the approach of invading impersonality; yet knowing the invasion to be inevitable and its own identity, while that identity lasts, the only source of any good whatever, maintains that identity in its full calm and clarity, that nothing may be sacrified without need. This combination of calm and terror, in dealing with this particular theme, will be found in only one other poet in English, in Shakespeare as one finds him in a few of the more metaphysical sonnets.[1] The calm clarity of tone enables the poet to deal with a variety of kinds of feeling which would be impossible were the terror emphasized for a moment at any point, were the complete and controlled unity of the experiencing mind for a moment disordered by its own perceptions. The same poem, for example, is able to contain the following lines, of a sweetness of an illusory simplicity which again are scarcely less than Shakespearean:

> She says, 'I am content when wakened birds,
> Before they fly, test the reality
> Of misty fields, by their sweet questionings;
> But when the birds are gone, and their warm fields
> Return no more, where, then, is paradise?'

And out of this passage proceeds the great lament for the lost myths, which I have already mentioned. This passage and others similar, though beautiful in themselves, are a preparation for the descriptive lines in the last stanza, and when we finally come to those lines, they are weighted with meaning and feeling accumulated from all that has gone before. It is difficult for this reason to quote from the poem for the purpose of illustrating its beauty.

One aspect of the poem may perhaps be mentioned, however, with some small profit, and it may best be indicated, I believe, through a brief comparison with Bryant's 'Thanatopsis.' Bryant's poem is a great poem and is worthy of the comparison, and its resemblance to Stevens' poem in certain ways is both surprising and illuminating. Both poems are semididactic meditations on death, written in a firm but simplified Miltonic blank verse, the verse of Stevens, possibly, being somewhat smoothed and softened by the intervention of Tennyson. Both poems are pagan in their view: but that of Bryant, the New Englander of the early 19th century, is essentially stoical, whereas that of Stevens, the Pennsylvanian of the 20th century, is Epicurean. Both poems find man, a spiritual being, isolated in a physical universe: but for Bryant that universe is the Earth, hairy, vast, and almost against the eye; for Stevens it is the tropical Pacific of infinity, in which the earth appears as an infinitesimal floating island.

The poems resemble each other more curiously, however, in that each bears a particular relationship to an antecedent body of more or less decadent poetry.

The deistic philosophy of the 18th century had early generated in its numerous followers a combination of ideas and attitudes which was to mark literary style, and especially poetic style, more strongly, perhaps, than any other philosophy has ever done. Deism was an amateur philosophy, a fact which may account in part for its rapid rise to popularity among men of letters and gentlemen at large: it received its definitive philosophical outline from the third Earl of Shaftesbury and its definitive literary expression from Alexander Pope, in *The Essay on Man*. Roughly speaking, one may say that these writers taught:[j] that the world is ruled by a beneficent mind, that everything is as it must be, that what appears to be evil is actually good as relative to the whole, that because the ruling mind is beneficent man will find happiness in all his benevolent affections and beneficent actions and misery in their opposites. They taught likewise[k] that virtue is natural to man and that the instincts and emotions are more reliable guides to conduct than the reason, though training and cultivation may refine these guides; that, in the words of Robertson,[1] 'to be good humored and truly cultivated is to be right in religion and conduct, and consequently happy.' The contradictions in this philosophy have been so often recounted that I need scarcely remark upon them here. What I wish to point out is this: that in spite of all contradictions the philosophy represents an attack on the rational faculty and a fairly complete outline of later romanticism; that the attack is made by means of what purport to be the methods of the rational faculty – that is, the attack is composed of a small set of concepts which are supposed to explain all experience, and which are moved about in various pseudo-rational relationships in order that certain philosophical conclusions may be reached. The deists appear to have achieved the delusion that they were reasoning with a final and immutable clarity, at the same time that they were attacking with all their small but apparently sufficient intellectual powers the very foundations of reason itself.

Their ideas generated an attitude of smug imperception in at least two ways: they were sure, in the first place, that they had solved all the essential problems of philosophy, history,[m] and morals, with the result that moral ideas and feelings were with increasing regularity expressed in a fixed set of stereotyped expressions or literary counters, which of necessity had for the most part a somewhat sentimental quality; and the general tendency of their philosophy worked to destroy the belief in the value of rational criticism, so that in spite of the composition of a good deal of literary criticism in the period, most of it somewhat superficial, the virtue of these counters long passed unchallenged, and when the challenge came, it came, strangely enough, not in the name of the intellect but in the name of the sensibility. Christian doctrine, and to some extent the best classical philosophy preceding it, had taught man to examine himself according to sound and intricate rules, in order that he might improve himself, and, if a Christian, achieve salvation. Deistic doctrine taught him that he was fairly certain of achieving any salvation that there might be available if he would only refrain from examining himself: 'There needs but thinking right [i.e., deistically], and meaning well.'[n] The result was the 18th century cliché, the most obvious symptom of the neat and innocent reasoning and perceiving of so many 18th century writers.

The Age of Reason has won that name from its heirs: from those who have agreed with it so completely as to abandon its literary methods, which were merely the methods of the preceding age, and too often unduly simplified.[o] The reasoning of the Age of Reason was very largely directed toward the destruction of the authority of Reason. Later romantic writers accepted the notion of the essential baseness of Reason with no real argument, and, when they began to see the monotony of 18th century language at its worst, they had recourse to the standard romantic explanation of dullness, that it was caused by excessive intellectualism; and we have as a result the nineteenth century judgment, which still prevails, of eighteenth century poetry, that it is bad because too intellectual, whereas in reality eighteenth century poetry is commonly good and is often great but displays defects which are primarily due to intellectual deficiency. The eighteenth century poetic language had become so well established by the middle of the century that it could dominate men with no respect for the ideas which seem to have generated it: Samuel Johnson had nothing but contempt for deism, yet his style shows the influence of deism; the influence upon his prose was small, for that was the medium which he cultivated most assiduously, but the influence upon his verse was great. The prologues to *Comus* and to *A Word to the Wise*, which are probably his greatest poems, are stereotyped in almost every detail of language, but are poems of extraordinary power because of the conviction and intelligence of the author, which are expressed mainly in the plot and rational outline, and in a certain tragic irony with which the stereotypes are occasionally used: these poems are the work of a great genius employing a decadent language. The reason, at this time, was tending toward immobility; and in those who accepted the doctrine, the emotions were freed: the natural outcome was to be found in Gray and Collins, men who in a discreet and sophisticated manner cultivated the feelings for their own sake, who generalized about the feelings with facile elegance but with small understanding, and who in varying degrees were the victims of uncomprehended melancholy.

These men and others of less talent but closely related, such as Blair and Macpherson, formed much of the immediate background of Bryant. The influence of Blair is to be seen in the form and matter of 'Thanatopsis'; the influence of Ossian has been seen in Bryant's taste for panoramic landscape, though as a matter of fact Gray, Collins, and others of the period might be cited in this connection with equal justice. One of the most obvious relationships to these poets is to be seen in Bryant's early taste for the semi-epigrammatic epithet, which marks Gray's 'Elegy' so strongly, a type of phrase which seems to show the breaking down of the Popian epigram in the direction of the standard cliché of the period: Gray's 'mute inglorious Miltons' meet their milder descendants in Bryant's 'solemn brood of care.' The most interesting resemblance of Bryant to these romantic predecessors, however, is to be found in moments of a kind of melancholy, which though in a measure formal and even arbitrarily imposed upon the matter, is deeply felt by the poet.

> ... the vales
> Stretching in pensive quietness between...
> Where thy pale form was laid with many tears....

These lines are very beautiful in their way, but they are far from specific: a sadness deriving in part from the general theme of the poem, and in part from a traditionally fixed rhetoric and emotional approach, is spread like a fine haze across the whole body of detail. This rhetoric, with its cognate melancholy, which, though formulary, is none the less profoundly a state of mind, is the most obvious characteristic of early romanticism: it is obvious in Gray and Collins and faintly discernible in the early Bryant.

Blake and Wordsworth broke the somewhat narrow frame of this early romanticism by freeing new emotions, mainly the obscurely prophetic; Wordsworth freed himself from the rhetorical forms of the preceding century by scrutinizing with literal exactness not his own human nature but the external nature of landscape, and Blake and Coleridge achieved a comparable freedom by a similar literalness in treating the phantasmagoria of the supernatural. The scope of romantic poetry was thus widened, but it remained essentially romantic poetry: poetry, that is, which sought to free the emotions rather than to understand them. Romantic poetry developed in the nineteenth century in England more or less along the lines indicated by these poets, and with no radical innovations of method after their time: the English romantics sought to free the emotions by writing about them in a more or less emotional manner; Wordsworth, of course, became less consistently Romantic as he matured.

The next step in the development of romantic practice, though it was suggested by Coleridge in the doctrine of organic form, was first indicated more or less fully by Poe, and in the matter of actual poetic practice was perhaps first taken by Poe, though very haltingly. One sees its nature precisely in the great French Symbolists. If it is the business of the poem to 'express' emotion, then the form itself of expression should be expressive and if we are rigorously reasonable, as a few of the romantics are, in the pursuit of their unreasonable ends, we shall see that language can best be purely expressive of emotion if it is so used that all except emotional content is as nearly as possible eliminated. Mallarmé was quite clear as to the necessity of eliminating rational content from language[p] and was more brilliant and more elaborate than any other poet has ever been, in his technique of elimination. The later poems especially display extremely obscure symbolism and reference, stated in a syntax so perverse as to be barely and very uncertainly explicable, at the same time that the individual phrases communicate feelings and perceptions more sharp and interesting, when viewed in isolation, than they frequently have a right to communicate when viewed as a part of any deducible whole. The suggestiveness of the details is forced into startling isolation by the difficulty of comprehending the poems as wholes; and this effect appears, at least, to be deliberately sought. The reader who is curious may profitably study the three sonnets beginning respectively 'Tout Orgueil fume-t-il du soir,' 'Surgi de la croupe et du bond,' and 'Une dentelle s'abolit' in the Fry-Mauron edition.[q]

In the last of these, the technique of negation, by which gross matter is eliminated, and feeling, it is hoped, is preserved, approaches the quality of unintentional parody: 'A lace curtain is effaced in doubt of the supreme Game [the nature of the supreme Game, one should observe, is more than uncertain] to display like a blasphemy nothing but the eternal absence of any bed.' The same doctrine is stated, perhaps less clearly, but in terms approaching those of Stevens in 'The Revolutionists Stop for Orangeade,' by Paul Verlaine, in 'Art Poétique':

> Il faut aussi que tu n'ailles point
> Choisir tes mots sans quelque méprise:
> Rien de plus cher que la chanson grise
> Où l'Indécis au précis se joint....
>
> Car nous voulons la Nuance encor,
> Pas la couleur, rien que la Nuance![r]

And Rimbaud, in the version of 'Bonheur' which appears in *Les Illuminations,* informs us that the beatitude of which he has made a magic study has made his speech incomprehensible, has caused it to take wing and escape; and earlier in the same poem he states that he has eliminated rational control from his life as well, for the same beatitude has taken possession of his life, both body and soul, and dispersed all effort. Just as the first great English romantics released the new subject matter, these poets, who were in rebellion against the stylistic looseness of their immediate predecessors in France, released the method which was, essentially, the proper method of romantic poetry. They released it, that is, within the bounds imposed by more or less traditional forms and by their own considerable talents and training: in their less fortunate successors we can observe the rapid progression toward le surréalisme. Mallarmé, like Gray, is a scholarly and sophisticated enemy of Reason; the body of his work, like that of Gray, is small; and similarly its generative power is very great. Mallarmé and his coadjutors seem to have played a part in the career of the young Stevens similar to that of Gray and Collins in the work of the young Bryant.

Mallarmé and Verlaine resemble Gray and Collins in their

precise artistry and in their sophisticated melancholy, a melancholy which arises in both generations for much the same reasons, and which is kept within fairly close stylistic bounds in both pairs of poets by comparable sophistication of style. But the Frenchmen surpass the two Englishmen of a century earlier in the elusive fluctuation of their perception; they have come closer to writing not merely about their emotions but with their emotions, and in addition to being in certain ways more sensitive, they are harder to understand. In fact, they seem to exist very close to that precarious boundary beyond which meaning will become so diminished that sensitivity must rapidly diminish with it, since the feeling contained in language is indissolubly connected with the abstract sense of language and must vanish if that abstract sense is wholly destroyed.

It is in relationship to this resemblance and to this difference that it is most interesting to compare 'Thanatopsis' to 'Sunday Morning.' Both Stevens and Bryant in these poems were influenced perceptibly by the preceding decadent masters; both seem to have recovered from the influence to such an extent that the influence appears as a faint memory, as the supersensitivity of a kind of convalescence, in poets who are even more heavily influenced by antecedent and stronger tradition. But in Bryant this recovery was aided by more than mere literary tradition: he found his support in the skeletalized morality and etherealized theology of Unitarianism. From these he derived concepts over-simplified much as were those of deism, but over-simplified, at least, from something that was originally sound. The best of his later poems, 'To a Waterfowl,' 'The Past,' 'The Battlefield,' and 'The Tides,' are written on themes which are clear and reasonably sound but which he was able to apprehend only in terms so general as to approach without quite impinging upon vagueness. There is in these poems a good deal of the moral conviction that we find in the best poets of the English Renaissance, along with a remarkable gift for style, but there is very little left of the old moral intelligence, the diversity, the subtlety, and the precision. Bryant had not the intellect requisite to surpass the dominant ideas of his generation in New England and recapture anything of the earlier intelligence, but the ideas at least supported him, and he had enough either of simplicity or of stubbornness not to exchange them for anything worse. But Stevens appears to have been supported at this point in his career by little except literary tradition; like Bryant he accepted one of the current philosophies of his time, but one more beguiling and at the same time more dangerous than that of Bryant, and like Bryant he seems to have accepted it with no trace of scepticism, and with the result that we have seen. His history epitomizes that of four generations of French poets.

But we have done with the outline of Stevens' general history; it is with the moments of dangerous but successful balance in his earlier years that we are now concerned. I have spoken of the elusive fluctuation of perception in Mallarmé and Verlaine, and I have referred to the extraordinary subtlety with which Stevens perceives the impingement of death, as well as other matters, in 'Sunday Morning'; and I have compared this quality in Stevens to a similar quality in some of Shakespeare's sonnets. This particular kind of sensitivity is fairly common in modern poetry, but nowhere at so high a level of excellence, I think, except in Valéry, certainly nowhere in English: at a lower level, or in another language and rhetorical tradition, it would probably display nothing that we should think of as Shakespearean.

'Le Monocle de Mon Oncle,' a work produced a few years later than 'Sunday Morning,' endeavors to treat the subject of love in hedonistic terms and confesses ironically to encountering more than one difficulty. The poem is often obscure, and, perhaps because one cannot easily follow it, appears far less a unit than 'Sunday Morning'; it contains extraordinary writing, however. The second stanza may fairly illustrate what I have said:

> A red bird flies across the golden floor.
> It is a red bird that seeks out his choir
> Among the choirs of wind and wet and wing.
> A torrent will fall from him when he finds.
> Shall I uncrumple this much-crumpled thing?
> I am a man of fortune greeting heirs;
> For it has come that thus I greet the spring.

These choirs of welcome choir for me farewell.
No spring can follow past meridian.
Yet you persist with anecdotal bliss
To make believe a starry connaissance.

The first four lines are incomprehensible, except as description, and the claim of the fifth line is unjustified; the remainder of the stanza, however, displays a combination of bitterness, irony, and imperturbable elegance not unworthy of Ben Jonson.

'Of the Manner of Addressing Clouds' deals essentially with the same subject as the passage in which Crispin contemplates the plum, but deals with it in a different mood; that is, the poet sees much the same relationship between his art and his subject as does Crispin, but since he sees himself alone in the 'old chaos of the sun,' 'that drifting waste,' amid the 'mute bare splendors of the sun and moon,' he is glad to retain his art as a mitigation of his solitude: what kind of mitigation he does not venture to say, but the mere fact of mitigation suffices him. The opening lines of this poem display a faint suggestion of Stevens' self-parody in one of its most frequent forms, an excess of alliteration which renders the style perversely finical. If one will compare these lines to the opening of 'The Comedian as the Letter C,' he may readily see how rapidly the method can degenerate into very crude comedy. 'Of Heaven Considered as a Tomb' is a vision of death as extinction. These two poems deal with the evaluation of the central theme of 'Sunday Morning,' with the irremediable tragedy, and they are free from all in that poem which invites question as well as much that provides richness and variety. The style of both has a cold concentration, related to this purity of motive, which almost surpasses, for me, the beauty of the longer poem. 'The Snow Man' and 'The Death of the Soldier' deal respectively with life and with death in a universe which is impersonal and devoid of any comfort except that which one may derive from the contemplation of the mute bare splendors. They have great power, but probably less than the other short poems which I have just mentioned, perhaps because of the metrical form.[s]

There appears to be in the best of the early poems, as I have said, a traditional seriousness of attitude and a traditional rhetoric cognate with that attitude and precisely expressive of it. This traditional element in the early work enables Stevens' talent to function at its highest power; but it is not only unjustified and unsupported by Stevens' explicit philosophy, it is at odds with that philosophy. And the conflict between the traditional element and the element encouraged by the philosophy results little by little in the destruction of the traditional element and the degradation of the poet's style. It is extremely important that we understand Stevens for more reasons than one; he has written great poems, and we should know them and know why they are great; and we should know what is bad, and why it is bad, so that we may separate the bad from the good and the more surely preserve the good. But beyond this, he gives us, I believe, the most perfect laboratory of hedonism to be found in literature. He is not like those occasional poets of the Renaissance who appear in some measure to be influenced by a pagan philosophy, but who in reality take it up as a literary diversion at the same time they are beneath the surface immovably Christian. Stevens is released from all the restraints of Christianity, and is encouraged by all the modern orthodoxy of Romanticism: his hedonism is so fused with Romanticism as to be merely an elegant variation on that somewhat inelegant System of Thoughtlessness. His ideas have remained essentially unchanged for more than a quarter of a century, and on the whole they have been very clearly expressed, so that there is no real occasion to be in doubt as to their nature; and he began as a great poet, so that when we examine the effect of those ideas upon his work, we are examining something of very great importance.

A Postscript: 1959:

When this essay was written, Stevens had only begun the elucidation of his theory of the Imagination, and its outlines were not clear. They are not clear yet, but one can decipher them. Briefly, Stevens believed that we live in a nominalistic universe made up of unrelated and inscrutable particulars, and that the only order possible in such a universe is that created by the poetic imagination. This notion is discussed most fully, but far from clearly, in his volume of prose, *The Necessary Angel,* and it is discussed or illustrated laboriously in most of his later poems. The best poem dealing with the topic may be 'Idea of Order at Key West,' but the subject is thin and the style is largely decorative. The theory is partly an attempt at a philosophic foundation for the hedonism which I describe in my essay and partly an extension of this hedonism. The trouble with the theory is this: that the order in question is imaginary, whereas reality remains incurably nominalistic. In the *Hudson Review* for the spring of 1951, Stevens published a poem entitled 'The Course of a Particular,' in which he explicitly renounces the doctrine. This poem was omitted from the *Collected Poems,* but appears in the *Opus Posthumous.* In the latter publication, however, there is an error which ruins the poem: in the next to the last line the word *ear* is changed to *air,* and the alteration renders the poem meaningless. The poem in the correct form is one of the greatest of Stevens' poems, and perhaps the greatest.

NOTES

a All poems mentioned in this essay, unless otherwise identified, are to be found in the second edition of *Harmonium,* by Wallace Stevens, published by Alfred A. Knopf, New York, 1931. The book is small, indexed, and well known, and page references seem unnecessary.

b From 'The Poetic Principle,' page 12 of Vol. I of the three volumes of criticism in Poe's works, the edition of Stedman and Woodberry. Quoted and elucidated in my essay on Poe, in the present volume.

c 'Dionysus in Dismay', by Stanley P. Chase, in *Humanism and America,* edited by Norman Foerster, Farrar and Rinehart, New York, 1930, page 211.

d 'Wallace Stevens and Other Poets', by Howard Baker, *Southern Review,* Vol. I, Number 2, Autumn 1935, page 376.

e Op. cit. Vol. III, p. 107.

f This whole topic is discussed at length in the essay entitled 'The Experimental School in American Poetry' (the section on pseudo-reference) in [*The Anatomy of Nonsense*].

g This entire subject is discussed in the latter part of my second essay in *Primitivism and Decadence,* already mentioned.

h *The Man with the Blue Guitar,* by Wallace Stevens, Alfred A. Knopf, N.Y., 1937.

i I have discussed this attitude of Shakespeare and some of its historical background in *Poetry: A Magazine of Verse* for February, March, and April, 1939; and have analyzed the 77th sonnet with this attitude in mind on page 49 of the issue for April.

j *Shaftesbury's "Characteristics,'* edited by J.M. Robertson, London, Grant Richards, 1900; editor's introduction pp. xxix and xxx.

k Pope, *Essay on Man,* especially Epistle III, more especially section II thereof; e.g., lines 97–8: And Reason raise o'er Instinct as you can, / In this 'tis God directs, in that 'tis man.

l J.M. Robertson, op. cit., p. xxxi.

m See *The Art of History,* by J.B. Black, Methuen and Co., Ltd., London, 1926. This book, which I fear is out of print, is one of the most brilliant pieces of criticism of our century, and ought to be more widely available.

n Pope, *The Essay on Man,* Epistle IV, 1. 32.

o The conclusion of *The Dunciad,* though not unduly simplified, is an example of the continuance: it is the natural development of the procedure established by Gascoigne, Ben Jonson, Greville, Donne, and others, and is one of the greatest passages in English poetry. *The Essay on Man* discloses a related procedure weakened by nonsense and sentimentalism.

p See his Avant-dire to René Ghil's *Traité du Verbe.* An extensive quotation from this, with a brief commentary upon it, will be found on page 18 of [*The Anatomy of Nonsense*].

q *Poems by Mallarmé.* Translated by Roger Fry, with commentaries by Charles Mauron. 1936, Chatto & Windus, London.

r In spite of this statement Verlaine is more innocent than Mallarmé, and less capable of intellectual perversity, as he is less capable than Rimbaud of consistent anti-moral energy and passion. On pages 99 and 100 of [*The Anatomy of Nonsense*] I refer to Verlaine as primitive – that is, limited, or minor, but relatively sound in method – rather than decadent. Such a view is supported by some of his best poems – 'Malines' or 'Le piano que baise une main frêle,' for example – but not by all. The poem beginning 'Dans l'interminable' differs not at all in method from Rimbaud's 'Larme'; both employ a description of strange landscape to communicate a feeling; but what is more or less conventionally obscure melancholy in Verlaine – obscure in the sense that the motive of the melancholy is nowhere suggested – is pushed to pure hallucination in Rimbaud. And many other poems by Verlaine use the same method: 'C'est l'extase langoureuse,' for example, or 'Green.' And it is worth remembering that the title of his best collection is *Romances Sans Paroles*.

s The scansion of free verse and the influence of the meter on the total poetic result may be found discussed at great length on pages 103 to 150 of [*The Anatomy of Nonsense*]. The scansion of 'The Snow Man' is there marked. That of 'The Death of the Soldier' is similar in principle, but simpler in form.

ESTHÉTIQUE DU MAL

Cummington, Massachusetts, 1944

Cummington Press issued 340 copies.

61. Gerard Previn Meyer, on Stevens' 'equilibrium', from 'Wallace Stevens: Major Poet', *Saturday Review*

Vol. 29, no. 12, 23 March 1946, 7–8

Meyer, besides being a regular literary reviewer for the *Saturday Review,* was a poet, author of *Louder than the Drum* and *For George Herbert.*

The present review was followed by a portrait sketch by Will Vance, 'Wallace Stevens: Man Off the Street', worthy of notice for a couple of quoted remarks: Untermeyer on Stevens' poetry as 'a strangely fastidious and hermetic art' and the poet Arthur Davison Ficke's (1883–1945) description of Stevens: 'A big, slightly fat, awfully competent-looking man. You expect him to roar, but when he speaks there emerges the gravest, softest, most subtly-modulated voice I've ever heard – a voice on tiptoe at dawn!' Graphic, if a little precious.

'The imagination loses vitality as it ceases to adhere to what is real.' The fact is that Stevens, a self-confessed romantic and escapist, even defiantly proud of it, though completely aware of reality is not thrown into emotional or intellectual confusion by it; he maintains an equilibrium between imagination and reality, being possessed of a profound understanding of both these factors.

His latest book, *Esthétique du Mal,* would seem to balance the two, and to reflect in its very title Stevens' preoccupation with the external problem: that of finding some answer – however much of an evasion it may *seem* – for the question of evil in the world has always challenged the explanations of religion. The very existence of pain, the poet seems to say, can be laid at the door of humankind; nature, on the other hand, is serenely indifferent:

> Except for us. Vesuvius might consume
> In solid fire the utmost earth and know
> No pain (ignoring the cocks that crow us up
> To die). This is a part of the sublime
> From which we shrink. And yet, except for us,
> The total past felt nothing when destroyed.

Pain, human pain

> does not regard
> This freedom, this supremacy, and in
> Its own hallucination never sees
> How that which rejects it saves it in the end.

Here, truly, is a new, if less obvious, kind of salvation, perhaps no more difficult for the mind to accept today than the old kind based on the belief that nothing on earth is regarded with indifference in heaven – a belief sorely shaken by the existence of evil....

The health of the world is closely tied up with the physical: it can be defeated by 'the false engagements of the mind.' And again:

> The greatest poverty is not to live
> In a physical world.

This is a theme the poet has celebrated for a long time, as far back as 'Peter Quince at the Clavier,' in fact, with its 'Beauty is momentary in the mind – The fitful tracing of a portal; / But in the flesh it is immortal.' Because of the domination of this theme, his reaction to 'ideological' revolutions might have been predicted:

> Revolution
> Is the affair of logical lunatics.

62. Wylie Sypher, 'Connoisseur in Chaos: Wallace Stevens', *Partisan Review*

Vol. 13, no. 1, Winter 1946, 83–94

Sypher (b. 1905) is the author of *Four Stages in Renaissance Style* (1955), *Rococo to Cubism in Art and Literature* (1960), *Loss of the Self in Modern Literature and Art* (1962) and a number of other books.

I

At a time of determined anti-romanticism Wallace Stevens has never concealed his own romantic affiliations; the success of his verse must be measured against the recent vogue of the metaphysical. Allen Tate has formulated our distaste for poetry that does not integrate the denotative with the connotative, that slackens tensions through irresponsible denotations, that grasps the actual world feebly, and that communicates an affective state – what Shelley called remote and minute distinctions of feeling. A great deal of Stevens' verse, imperfectly articulating the denotative and connotative, conveys minute and remote distinctions of feeling. The denotative level in Stevens is imagist – an intensely visual statement with virtuoso sound, color, rhythm. This visual statement, however, may have little to do with the connotative, affective level of statement on which his fictions are his feelings. The speculative passages in Stevens belong in a category of pseudo reference, to use Yvor Winters' term; behind the intellectualized phrasing is an imprecision of thought almost unparalleled in modern verse, which has depended, it is said, upon the counterpoint of the intellectual against the affective, the definite against the indefinite.

In fact, Stevens has demonstrated the uses of imprecision. First, the very fictions that compose the world for him are emphatic states – fictions that are feelings. They are not, for example, what they are in Eliot, scriptural, ritualistic, doctrinal; the differences between 'Sunday Morning' and *The Waste Land* in this regard are notable. Nor is Stevens' poetry, except in its imagist, denotative, extensional moments, directed toward objects, or to living amid objects. The characteristic motion of Stevens is centrifugal, not centripetal: the nuances of feeling and association, as in 'The Idea of Order at Key West,' extend indefinitely outward from the statement; whereas in most modern verse the meanings tend to fall at once and heavily inward upon texture, upon the logic and precision of statement, then by repercussion to diffuse outward. The intimations of Eliot rise by opposition to the complex allusion to traditional denotations. In Stevens the intimations move directly toward the 'fiction' of feeling beyond and transcending the statement; the fiction dissociates itself from the object, but not by repercussion. Thus ocurs a tone of reverie that is anti-metaphysical. The reading of Keats' Nightingale Ode is an experience more akin to the reading of 'Peter Quince at the Clavier' than to reading Eliot.

The romantic dis-equilibrium and slackness of tension may be illustrated by the extreme imprecisions of passages that may be termed pseudo-Shakespearian:

> ... Although she strews the leaves
> Of sure obliteration on our paths,
> The path sick sorrow took, the many paths
> Where triumph rang its brassy phrase, or love
> Whispered a little out tenderness ...

> ... desire for day
> Accomplished in the immensely flashing East,

Desire for rest, in that descending sea
Of dark, which in its very darkening
Is rest and silence spreading into sleep.

In contrast is the imagism that does actually fall inward toward the object itself; but only toward a visual, auditory, tactile apprehension of the object, toward sensuous denotations. In brief, the essential romanticism appears in the fracture between Stevens' conceptual, affective and imagist phases. Objects themselves, sensuously realized, do not symbolize the 'fictions,' the affective evocations, radiating beyond them; nor do the equivocal concepts terminate in the senses. His evaluations are temperamental responses through which the world is 'felt.'

II

Esthétique du Mal, the latest variation upon Stevens' theme that by feeling we live 'as and where we live,' is scored more somberly than might be expected. There appears a new phrase that, if elaborated, might release him from the patterns of composition and conception that have bound him almost hypnotically:

Life is a bitter aspic. We are not
At the center of a diamond...

By this insight Stevens might translate the problem of the poetic imagination to levels of a humanism that has been claimed for him but that he has never actually attained. For a score of years in both verse and prose Stevens has set the issue in terms of the adequacy of landscape as fiction, the adjustment of desire to the object, of the sensibility to intellectual constructs, of the world to the ultimate Plato.

Stevens has spent his energies in evading the absolute, the total fiction. His dread of the glass man – the rational man – his contempt for metaphysicians sprawling under the August sun, means that he has set one human faculty – reason – over against another – sensibility – in a dichotomy that has deprived him of what the poet most needs, fictions themselves. His plea has always been for the 'fiction that results from feeling,' or, as he has lately put it, 'a sense that we live in the center of a physical poetry, a geography that would be intolerable except for the non-geography that exists there.' To Stevens philosophy has meant rationalism; he has disregarded the fact that the most illuminating philosophies always have been touched with that ultimate Platonic insight, the *aretê sôtêrias,* which is not rationality at all, but reason in its most exalted mood – wisdom. To substitute for any philosophic response ('official' is his word) an entirely temperamental one results in a hypertrophy of the 'poetic' sensibility at the expense of poetic intelligence. 'There are also,' Socrates is said to have remarked, 'misologists, or haters of ideas.' Stevens has always proclaimed himself a misologist. Yvor Winters, by his own hard analytics, complains of Stevens' system of thoughtlessness, his hedonism. In spite of hedonist impulses, Stevens is really a misologist; curiously, he is a misologist obsessed by a thesis.

At the very moments when he identifies himself as a native of the world he has been forced to contend with hateful ideas amid solid, static objects – the parts of his world. His resolution has been a law of inherent opposites: 'Two things of opposite natures seem to depend / On one another.' This law is fulfilled through a pagan, and at times orgiastic, humility before things as they are – the euphoria of being 'without a description of to be... being an ox.'

In *Esthétique du Mal* appears humility of another order, alien to the earlier Stevens even in his malcontent vein – 'Pain is human'; this too is 'part of the sublime' and involves an imaginative apprehension of the human situation in which he has been deficient. Then the theme is put aside as Stevens returns to his wonted improvisations, exercises in viewing the world:

> The greatest poverty is not to live
> In a physical world.

Thus the *Esthétique* reiterates the plea that 'the genius of the body, which is our world,' be not 'spent in the false engagements of the mind.' Yet it is difficult to accept the structure of things for the structure of ideas, and he stands in need of fictions by which to live 'as and where we live.'

III

Here is the central problem in Stevens: the imagination in the Waste Land. Essentially Stevens has remained a poet of the Waste Land – disillusioned as to the gods, June evenings and Moscow. Like Eliot, he has set the issue:

> The prologues are over. It is a question, now,
> Of final belief. So, say that final belief
> Must be in a fiction. It is time to choose.

Stevens cannot choose; his fictions are unreliable since they prove to be merely his sensitivities. Two alternatives are possible: to grip 'the essential prose' as his Crispin attempted, or to establish a fiction so absolute that its hegemony over the sensibilities is total. Stevens avails himself of neither because he devotes himself to paganism and obscurantism, 'the fiction that results from feelings.' The consequences are the optimism that causes Stevens uneasiness whenever he realizes that pain is human, and the futility of his turning to the spring sun while 'employer and employee contend.' His most concentrated effort is in seeing the world in a dish of peaches. He is deprived of nightingales, and is 'weary of the man that thinks'; so the poet must offer the supreme fictions.

As obscurantist and pagan Stevens belongs to the post-World-War-I era. His cynicism about the bourgeoisie, his uncertainty on larger social issues, his depreciation of the gods, his discovery that 'the door / of earth penetrates more deeply than any word,' his measuring the world by the eye suggest the practiced fleshliness of the 'twenties, paganism at Hartford. Often his deepest perception amounts to the seventh stanza of 'Sunday Morning,' a boisterous devotion to the sun as a chant of the blood. Stevens is not what Gorham Munson called him, a dandy; he is one of the more cogitative pagans of the 'twenties roving amid the sharper violences of the 'forties. His euphoria has at moments diminished.

He has not attempted, like Eliot, to adopt fictions that

seem to bring larger clarifications than they actually do.
'Sunday Morning', for example, is not doctrinaire or
mannered. Stevens has understood that these supremacies
cannot be re-established, at least in their old autonomy. The
speculative energy of his verse has served as a commentary
upon the disorganization of the poetic temperament in a time
destitute of fictions. Living in the 'immense detritus of a
world / that is completely waste,' knowing that we have been
offered stones, not bread, in Monday's dirty light, he
diagnoses himself as a man whose pharynx is bad because the
time is so indifferent; Marx, too, has spoiled the landscape
for him. Without being committed to dogma or abstractions
or the dialectics of a social program, he has betokened the
disabilities of the pure poetic fiction, which in ways has
proved a cul-de-sac narrower and drier than the letter of the
law.

Stevens has been perilously near making a great refusal. As
he has admitted, the contemporary poet cannot evade the
pressure of the anti-poetic – the anti-poetic in the streets of
Passaic and Rutherford. We may allow him an ivory tower
from which one gains 'such an exceptional view of the public
dump and the advertising signs.' The questions are whether
Stevens has not been too dimly aware of this essential prose,
and whether he considers Rutherford and Passaic anti-poetic
simply because of being Rutherford and Passaic, or because
their violence is inexorable.

In spite of his profession that the imagination must adhere
to reality – that the subject matter of poetry is the life
lived among the solid static objects of space (a scene composed by the very living in it) – precisely what we miss in
Stevens is this composing amidst objects themselves. His
view of the poetic imagination ultimately opposes to the
violence without a violence within, and identifies poetry
with counter-pressures. The violence of his pressure against
'mournful' objects imposes upon his experience of them
arbitrary and even too-abstract constructions. The blue guitar
does not right the balance between actuality and imagination.
The composition too autocratically determines the form of
the experience instead of serving as a coherence within
experience. These arbitrary constructions are of limited

reference, often retinal and auditory. Stevens has said that 'a poet's words are of things that do not exist without the words.' From this Crocean view it does not necessarily follow, however, that 'poetry is words' or that 'words, above everything else, are, in poetry, sounds.' Delmore Schwartz has remarked that Stevens takes an art-perspective. His interests are compositions. He has consumed his talents in formulating a poetical epistemology to define the categories by which the anti-poetic (and the poetic) are to be apprehended. He has been the connoisseur of his own responses to the chaos about him.

IV

Stevens has never determined whether the poem generates in situation or myth; whether the imagination really ought to triumph in the urgent 'endless struggle with fact.' To conclude, as he does, that nothing will resolve the dilemma 'except a consciousness of fact as everyone is at least satisfied to have it be,' is to conclude nothing, for the myth that brings such consciousness is wanting. Stevens is repelled by, and intoxicated with, the object:

> The poem of the mind in the act of finding
> What will suffice. It has not always had
> To find: the scene was set; it repeated what
> Was in the script.
>   Then the theatre was changed
> To something else. Its past was a souvenir...
>   It must
> Be the finding of a satisfaction, and may
> Be of a man skating, a woman dancing, a woman
> Combing. The poem of the act of the mind.

This instant penetration of process to the degree of identification of mind with object is not always possible, however, since our fictions perversely contend with objects; there are lions in Sweden: after majestic images of the soul – Fides, galled Justitia, Patientia – have become souvenirs in our leafless wintry day

> ...the whole of the soul, Swenson,
> As every man in Sweden will concede,
> Still hankers after lions, or, to shift,
> still hankers after sovereign images.

By reason of the souvenir, the nostalgia for myth, Stevens is a pseudo-hedonist, a savage troubled. His impulse to surrender to the object is cultivated with a violence prepense. The result is a falsetto optimism:

> The... plastic parts of poems
> Crash in the mind

with a resonance that seems a little contrived. Throughout we miss the melancholy of Eliot and find instead Stevens the misologist striving to think 'without the labor of thought,' to sustain 'a gaiety that is being':

> ...all
> Things were the truth, the world itself was the truth.

The poet is a virile youth whose ecstasy suffices for his fictions – unless there come somber figurations of social unrest, the pain of war, the essential prose.

Amid the violence of his mature desires the poet, in his 'radiant and productive atmosphere,' surrenders to the 'morality of the right sensation.' The green fish in the reeds will be his absolute; the supreme fictions will be revealed within experience, which itself is epiphany – 'ecstatic identities between one's self and the weather.'

This adequacy of landscape is an organic sensibility. By the 'heart's residuum' the war between mind and sky is suspended, for desire springs up within the object, and the concept within the experience of desire and the object. There are thirteen ways of looking at a blackbird. There are 'so many selves, so many sensuous worlds,' as in the private worlds of Bertrand Russell's realism. The identity of the conceptual with the experiential recalls Wordsworth's repudiation of reason as a false secondary power of multiplying distinctions:

> It may be that the ignorant man, alone,
> Has any chance to mate his life with life

That is the sensual, pearly spouse, the life
That is fluent in even the wintriest bronze.

Transcendentalism is, however, involved in the Wordsworthian situation. By the immediacy of the sense sublime,
Wordsworth transcended his organic sensibilities and
attained his supreme fiction. Stevens has of late known such
moments – when 'time flashed again' and by an immaculate
ecstasy he shared the first idea. Ordinarily he is so hotly
pursued by lions in Sweden that he cannot evade the
metaphysical question and accept 'to be without a description
of to be': the supreme fiction must not only change and give
pleasure, but must be abstract as well. He must impose an
order:

> ...But to impose is not
> To discover... to find,
> Not to impose, not to have reasoned at all...
> ...To find the real,
> To be stripped of every fiction except one,
> The fiction of an absolute.

The composition of things no longer reads legibly – the
myths of rose and ice are done; and Stevens is left to repine
for absolutes and to be tormented with a sense that the
very

> ...thought of her takes her away.
> The form of her in something else
> Is not enough...

Thus living in many sensuous worlds indicates a failure in
imagination. The supreme fiction becomes fictitious indeed, a
dizzy pluralism, a rage for order that cannot be spent:

> ...the vast repetitions final in
> Themselves, and, therefore, good, the going round
> And round and round, the merely going round,
> Until merely going round is a final good.

Stevens has established, in spite of his misology, the 'fiction'
of relativism. As Whitehead has explained, the isolated event
has lost its status in complexes of events until 'the whole is

evidently constitutive of the part.' By a fiction more available to science than to the imagination, Stevens theorizes that the whole cannot exist without the parts, that the part is the equal of the whole; under these sanctions he lives incessantly but reluctantly in change and accepts the law of chaos as the law of ideas.

Through one of the incongruities of the Waste Land, Stevens has in effect allied himself with so alien a figure as Paul Elmer More in resisting the Demon of the Absolute. In 1928 More announced: 'This Demon of the Absolute is nothing else but rationalism, what Francis Bacon called the *intellectus sibi permissus.*' Although the orthodox humanist would insist that landscape is not adequate, Stevens has devoted himself to elaborating More's thesis that 'there are no absolutes in nature; they are phantoms created by reason itself in its own likeness, delusions which, when once evoked, usurp the field of reality and bring endless confusion in their train.'

Stevens himself is troubled to utilize his relativism: whether he will or no, man 'must become the hero of his world.' The gusto of living incessantly in change is a paralyzing optimism, a denial of loneliness in Jersey City, of the old chaos of the sun. If, as Whitehead says, 'endurance is the repetition of the pattern in successive events,' Proust rather than Stevens has dispensed with fictions and lived in the texture of process with a neutrality and unremitting grasp of the essential prose.

Dispossessed of adequate fictions, Stevens at moments may be Prufrock – 'a most inappropriate man in a most unpropitious place.' From this unpropitious place and time of year, from promenades among ideas, Stevens resorts to bright landscapes, the 'majors of the August heat' – a nomad exquisite of the Waste Land whose philosophy is an exercise in viewing the world.

V

The exercise itself involves a paradox. To create from the poetic imagination those fictions by which man becomes the hero of his world, 'the world must be measured by eye' – 'the eye grown larger, more intense' – until one finds 'the world of the dazzle of mica, the dithering of grass.' The supreme fiction proves to be the gaudiest, most heightened imagist presentation of the object.

The violence of Stevens' imagination often imposes complicated brilliant patterns upon the texture of experience, its 'composition':

> At the time of nougats, the peer yellow
> Sighed in the evening that he lived
> Without ideas in a land without ideas,
> The pair yellow, the peer.

'Sea Surface Full of Clouds' is an exercise imposing the fictive imagination upon solid static objects; the fiction is the words, the sounds, their composition. A parallel from painting is at hand. The effort of Cézanne and early cubists to 'realize' the object completely, to penetrate its mass thoroughly to the depth of psychological and entirely 'felt' landscapes, did not demand these fictions. This stage of cubism was succeeded by a more violent resistance to solid objects in space, until the abstract, synthetic, two-dimensional surface evolved. Within the fictions of this *cubisme de conception*, its *déplacements*, its simultaneous perspectives, the painter began to 'resist' or 'evade' the object: cubism produced what Stevens calls the 'dilapidations' of Braque and Picasso. This painting sacrificed connotation in favor of denotation, as Stevens himself suggests – denotation of the mind's arbitrary compositions.

Contrast, however, Picasso's *Three Musicians* compositions with his *Guernica*, in which the abstractions identify themselves with an external situation in a symbolism rarely utilized by Stevens, who does not thus see Hartford in a purple light. The designs in Stevens' later work approximate abstractions with great virtuosity of arrangement, but without the 'correspondences' of symbolist verse. (Edith Sitwell has contrived similar patterns, that crystallize upon the sensuous and conscious level rather than upon the inward levels of Mallarmé.) The first improvisations – 'Carlos Among the Candles,' to choose an early one – are keyed in a 'suggestive' Maeterlinck-like range in which ellipses (...) are intended to be evocative:

The extinguishing of light is like the five purple palmations of cinquefoil withering.... It is full of the incipiences of darkness... of desolation that rises as a feeling rises... Imagination wills the five purple palmations of cinquefoil...

Then the texture becomes harder, closer, more geometric as Stevens finds his obsessive theme; the abstraction is drier, its presentation more intellectualized; and the decorative medium is more sophisticated. Certain images and colors – green, red, black, white, yellow – are used in disciplined constructions:

> Green is the night, green kindled and apparelled...
> The topaz rabbit and the emerald cat...
> The greenness of night lies on the page...
> That elemental parent, the green night...
> Fat cat, red tongue, green mind, white milk...
> The lion sleeps in the sun...
>   ...Light
>
>   Is the lion that comes down to drink...
>   Ruddy are his eyes and ruddy are his claws...
>   Red-emerald, red-slitted-blue, a face of slate...
>   Red-in-red repetitions never going...

Images of horse and rider, pine boughs casting sibilant shadows, the sun, the moon, and even phrases like 'washed in his imagination' or 'washed the imagination clean' become frequent in the prose as well as the verse. The composition is in precise figurations:

> To feed on the yellow bloom of the yellow fruit
> Dropped down from turquoise leaves...

Even the insatiable big bird revolving under the glare of the clownish yellow sun (*Esthétique du Mal*) remains so entirely upon the surface of the composition that its evocations are conceptual and ornamental. The complications are exquisite, and sometimes, as in 'The Poems of Our Climate' and 'Woman Looking at a Vase of Flowers,' the gaudiness and synaesthesia of imagism are intellectualized into pseudo-philosophic statement.

Such violently retinal, auditory, tactile effects are foreshortened by the 'cultivated,' whimsical, even half-academic fastidiousness and punctilio of Stevens' language. In their references the poems are forever alternating between civilization and savagery, the *coterie* and the jungle. There are equatorial passages – the thunders of Yucatan, stars at Tallapoosa, the litter of tropical seas. Stevens has said farewell to Florida in all but his imagery, which indicates how he has remained not only a pagan but a fauve of the sort represented by Dufy or by the douanier Rousseau, who treats the 'green vine angering for life' with such bland vitality. Neither Stevens nor Rousseau can transcendentalize 'that alien, point-blank, green and actual Guatemala' beyond an affirmation of image that is at times almost sinister. The colors are as brutal as they are sonorous. The sensuous density is barbarous – but ordered into austere statement.

The cast of primitivism in the imagery is odd: in the early poems one moved in the atmosphere of the cruise ship. There was a resort primitivism, perhaps as if *Fortune* were reporting upon the Waste Land. One can thus distinguish levels of the primitive in Stevens: a 'social' one and one of temperament. Gorham Munson spoke of Stevens' 'flair for bright savagery,' and the voluptuousness of his language used to be called exotic. It is more important to remark the polarities in his imagery, swinging as it does between the basic slate and red weather, dilettantism and instinct. Stevens has remarked that feeling accumulates readily 'in the abnormal ranges of sensibility.' The extraordinary fierceness of Stevens' response to the cockerel's shriek and hen's shudder, or to our bourgeois cuisine of human heads 'brought in on leaves, crowned with the first, cold buds,' suggests that his fictions course in his blood.

VI

Stevens' vitality is not of the blood only, of the animal spirit. For a poet living amid a 'hacked-up world of tools' he carries himself with a gaiety that will break through his soberest causeries, in indiscreet language, at least, or else in a laughter of the mind. He may have mistaken his talent. His abundance of spirit finds its pitch within the range of high comedy, a range particularly Stevens' own. His ideas of order amid the Waste Land may be misconceived; but Stevens is endowed, as Eliot with his chill humor is not, with the Meredithian comic spirit, a mocking awareness of our absurdities and our pretense. He might even, with his malice against our Trimalchios, have become the Petronius of the Waste Land. Not by the ironic – a metaphysical tone – but by the comic does Stevens comment pertinently upon our desolation; things may not be as he says they are on his blue guitar; but his less grave addresses to all academies of fine ideas are welcome. Within this range he moves with entire competence; here he lives 'as and where we live.' Neither by blood nor by fiction can he achieve total belief, but by transcendental comedy – 'a laughter, an agreement, by surprise' – he affirms 'a gaiety that is being, not merely knowing.' The dramatic in Stevens is most immediate in the casual attack of his comic mood:

> A long time you have been making the trip
> From Havre to Hartford, Master Soleil,
> Bringing the lights of Norway and all that...
> An opening of portals when night ends,
> A running forward, arms stretched out as drilled,
> Act I, Scene 1, at a German Staats-Oper.

The comedy of the first and last periods is ringing with the silver laughter of the Meredithian faun; there are often the eruptive imagery, the riotous language, the springing delight over the victim, the intellectual tensions of *The Egoist*. The moments of high comedy in 'Le Monocle de Mon Oncle' indicate how defensive are the ironies of 'The Love Song of J. Alfred Prufrock.' The gaucherie of Prufrock is Eliot's gaucherie–Stevens, without being so ironic, is perhaps more completely the master of absurdity. 'The Comedian as the Letter C' may, indeed, mistake pomposity for wit, but even here the buoyancy of spirit carries the elephantine Carlylese jargon.

The euphoria of Stevens is least forced when, surprised by the pleasures of merely circulating, he contends with his ideas in the guise of fat Jocundus.

His commitment to 'a land beyond the mind,' however,

and to going round and round is failure to possess a myth. The task was in any case impossible. One understands why Stevens seizes upon the thesis of the late Henri Focillon that

Unless and until it actually exists in matter, form is little better than a vista of the mind, a mere speculation upon a space that has been reduced to geometrical intelligibility.... Without matter art could not exist.... The old antitheses, spirit-matter, matter-form, obsess men.... The first duty of any one who wishes to understand anything whatsoever about the life of forms is to rid himself of these contradictions of pure logic....

These forms can be equated with the fictions that are feelings – delusive fictions when one meets essential prose, and becomes aware that

There are these sudden mobs of men...
An immense suppression...
These voices crying without knowing for what...

Here is 'fact' as Stevens is presumably not contented to have it. He cannot 'evade' or abdicate what Eliot calls moral responsibility; nor can his mind find itself in an alien world. He can offer only notes toward a supreme fiction.

63. George Dillon, 'A Blue Phenomenon', *Poetry*

Vol. 68, no. 2, May 1946, 97–100

Editor of *Poetry* from 1937 to 1950, George Dillon (1906–68) was a poet, translator and editor, who was awarded a Pulitzer Prize for *The Flowering Stone* (1931). With Edna St Vincent Millay (1892–1950) he translated Baudelaire's *Les Fleurs du Mal*.

In recent years Wallace Stevens has not been delimited by the world of 'wide, accurately barbered lawns, white yachts with bright awnings, the silvered motor car, the small regiment of obsequious servants' which Gorham Munson once described as this poet's habitat. His new long poem, however, has been made into something which belongs to the décor of opulence. It is a superb bookmaking job, proving that our experts can sometimes equal the best European artisanship. Wightman Williams has supplied bold and fascinating decorations – they might be the marginal doodlings of his Satanic Majesty.

The poem, some three hundred lines on the classic theme of evil, could perhaps be most easily and honestly reviewed by quoting from Eliot:

> Oh, do not ask 'What is it?'
> Let us go and make our visit.

But while we do still sometimes ask what a poem *means*, we often do not feel sure that such a question is relevant. So powerful and so persistent has been the symbolist reaction, and so powerfully aided by the proliferation of what Hayakawa has called 'venal poetry,' i.e. advertising copy, that we have come to value especially the original, gratuitous, or 'absolute' effects of language. Without necessarily going to the Dadaist extreme, we have been quite willing to accept Newton's definition of poetry as an 'inspired nonsense.'

We may find, of course, that the apparent nonsense of poetry acquires meaning as the words are remembered and lived with; or that, even without meaning, it corresponds to an emotional 'truth' – as, for instance, the famous lines of Stevens beginning 'Beauty is momentary in the mind.' The question of obscurity has in fact not often arisen in connection with Stevens, whose earlier poems have been as frankly arbitrary 'arrangements' as certain modern paintings. We have expected from him nothing but a learned and beautiful galimatias: the sensuous verve, the ironic word-play, the musical ad-libbing on a chosen theme, where emotion largely resolved itself into the poet's delight in his medium. The formal plan, which might be some elaborate fable or the pretense of philosophical discourse, was often nothing but a palpable and amusing device to provide a framework for the glittering non-sequiturs, at the same time baffling the Philistine.

The question of obscurity, however, does seem relevant to Stevens' later work, including this poem, because in it we feel an effort toward more explicit communication. This effort almost constantly loses itself in the old verbal arabesques, which get rather blurred in the process. We still have some fine typical passages:

> The death of Satan was a tragedy
> For the imagination. A capital
> Negation destroyed him in his tenement
> And, with him, many blue phenomena.

But at times the ironic, smiling guitarist, who doesn't care whether or not he is overheard, seems momentarily replaced by an earnest business executive who is trying to clarify and expound his ideas in a staff meeting but finds that everything he says comes out as double talk. How far this can go may be seen in the following seven lines of blank verse which, to do them the least injustice, are here printed as prose:

Is it himself in them that he knows and they in him? If it is himself in them, they have no secret from him. If it is they in him, he has no secret from them. This knowledge of them and of himself destroys both worlds, except when he escapes from it. To be alone is not to know them or himself.

At such moments we are inclined to say, in the words which Stevens quotes from Victor Serge,

> I followed his argument
> With the blank uneasiness which one might feel
> In the presence of a logical lunatic.

And there are other passages, some of which should have been the best parts of the poem, which are coherent enough but where the serious feeling, rejecting the poet's natural idiom, has masked itself in a cold and heavily prosaic rhetoric:

Concentric circles of shadows, motionless
Of their own part, yet moving on the wind,
Form mystical convolutions in the sleep
Of time's red soldier deathless on his bed.

On the other hand, we are after all in the presence of a
master of language, and need only be a little patient. When
there is co-ordination, when thought and emotion do not
outrun the allusive style, the result is inevitably good, and we
realize that no poet has brought to philosophical meditation a
more engaging and natural manner. One of several instances
is the whole passage beginning 'His firm stanzas hang like
hives in hell' and containing the lines:

The fault lies with an over-human god,
Who by sympathy has made himself a man
And is not to be distinguished, when we cry

Because we suffer, our oldest parent, peer
Of the populace of the heart, the reddest lord,
Who has gone before us in experience.

If only he would not pity us to so much,
Weaken our fate, relieve us of woe both great
And small, a constant fellow of destiny...

Stevens, at any rate, has not been content to rest on his
prewar fame; he is, vaguely but sympathetically, among
those present. He can no longer say, 'All right, have it your
way. The world is ugly and the people are sad,' and then turn
to his natural themes, the musings of a wise and accomplished hedonism. He has been forced to recognize the
Adversary. In a world coming always closer, and which
surpasses in its stupidity and ferocity any quondam 'imagined world,' he has set himself to consider how evil may be
endured and how it may be opposed. In his view, the plight
of man is not so bad that a 'revolution' would not make it
worse; not does he omit, in this poem, his usual yawn at the
expense of the radicals. But his *Esthétique du Mal* is also an
expression of the familiar *mal d'esthète*, which is not particular
to this or to any century.

64. Louis L. Martz, 'Wallace Stevens: The Romance of the Precise', *Yale Poetry Review*

Vol. 2, Autumn 1946, 13–20

As noted on p. xii of Martz's *The Poem of the Mind* (New Haven, 1966), Chapter X of that book incorporates some passages from this review.

It is notable that the past year has seen two attempts to define the genre of Wallace Stevens. Notable, because they mean that the body of Stevens' poetry has now achieved the range and complexity and richness which demand a summing-up. His range is wryly indicated by the absolute diversity of the two pronouncements. Mr. Simons (*Sewance Review*, Autumn, 1945)[1] insists that Stevens is an 'intellectual poet' akin to Donne and aligns him with the Metaphysical Poets of the seventeenth century. But Mr. Sypher (*Partisan Review*, Winter, 1946)[2] sees 'essential romanticism' in Stevens and declares that 'the success of his verse must be measured against the recent vogue of the metaphysical.' Clearly, both critics cannot be right; the fact is, I think, that both are essentially wrong.

Mr. Simons applies to Stevens the definitions of Metaphysical Poetry made by Eliot, Williamson, and Grierson, and applies them in a way that may seem plausible until one considers the poetry of the Metaphysicals. Compare Donne's 'Canonization,' Marvell's 'Garden,' and Herbert's 'Collar' with Stevens' 'Asides on the Oboe,' which Mr. Simons would prove in detail a Metaphysical poem. One can see that Mr. Simons has not read his definitions accurately in the light of the poems themselves: he has misunderstood Eliot's distinction between 'the intellectual poet and the reflective poet.' The intellectual poet, as defined by the practice of Donne, pursues his poetry by heated ratiocination expressed in concrete details; as he thinks, he reconciles conflicting ideas or feelings by a logical sleight-of-hand imbedded in deftly manipulated metaphors. He does not state, then expand and define the statement by images. The image is the statement. Donne at his best thus achieves a double unity: the imagery is fluently associated and yet is also bound together by logic or the semblance of logic.

Stevens does nothing of the sort. Sometimes he thinks, he states the problem abstractly, as in 'Asides on the Oboe':

> If you say on the hautboy man is not enough,
> Can never stand as god, is ever wrong
> In the end, however naked, tall, there is still
> The impossible possible philosophers' man,
> The man who has had the time to think enough ...

and then he enforces and develops these statements by imagery:

> The central man, the human globe, responsive
> As a mirror with a voice, the man of glass,
> Who in a million diamonds sums us up.

Or the procedure may be reversed, as in 'The Bagatelles the Madrigals,' where the image of the serpent is first developed in two stanzas, and then the parallel with humanity is drawn rather baldly in the next three stanzas. These examples are extreme; Stevens' better verse is more closely knit; but the method is representative of a large part of his poetry. It is not the method of Donne. Where Stevens is not working in quite this way he uses a method of implication related to French Symbolism, a method which, as Mr. Simons concedes, has no parallel in Donne. Furthermore, Stevens has no ability to sustain an argument. Among his longer poems only 'Sunday Morning' and 'The Comedian as the Letter C' have beginning, middle, and end; and in these the progression is basically associative.

Mr. Sypher is right, then, in saying that there is in Stevens 'a tone of reverie that is anti-metaphysical.' Stevens is a *reflective* poet, 'the pensive man.' But it does not follow that there is in Stevens the 'essential romanticism' which Mr. Sypher claims to find in a 'fracture between Stevens' conceptual, affective and imagist phases,' a fracture accompanied by 'romantic dis-equilibrium and slackness of tension,' and by 'extreme imprecisions.' Setting aside the question whether this is a valid description of English poetry of the nineteenth century (the romanticism which Mr. Sypher is considering), one ought first to query Mr. Sypher's declaration that 'Stevens has demonstrated the uses of imprecision' in poetry. Surely if a passage is imprecise in terms of a given poem, it is a bad passage, it is not poetry. There is no poetry of imprecision. If Stevens is imprecise he is writing badly; and let us say at once that Stevens, like every other poet, does write badly at times. He is in places so inexact, so incoherent, that one listens impatiently until the rant subsides. But his weaknesses must not blind us to his strength.

It is a question of what one means by precision in poetry. Looking, apparently, for precision of plain statement and precision of simple detail, Mr. Sypher ignores Stevens' mastery of the higher reaches of precision in poetry: precision of complex implication, precision of complex association, precision of ambiguity, such as Mr. Winters has admired in his acute analysis of 'Sunday Morning' (see his otherwise pejorative essay on Stevens in *The Anatomy of Nonsense*). Mr. Blackmur more than a dozen years ago demonstrated Stevens' broad mastery of these higher precisions (see his essay in *The Double Agent*); and there is nothing in Stevens' poetry since *Harmonium* to make us alter Mr. Blackmur's conclusions, except to say that *Notes Toward a Supreme Fiction* shows equally precise control of more difficult materials, as I hope to prove by some of the following passages.

Mr. Sypher's main difficulty lies in a central misunderstanding: he does not see the unifying theme which permeates Stevens' poetry. Emptied of its theme, any writing will appear imprecise and fractured. Stevens' central problem has always been the same: the adjustment of man to a universe from which the supernatural and mythical have been drained, and in which the human imagination is consequently starving. The moon, his constant symbol of the imagination, throws her 'old light' now 'at the wearier end of November,'

When the body of Jesus hangs in a pallor,
Humanly near, and the figure of Mary,
Touched on by hoar-frost, shrinks in a shelter
Made by the leaves, that have rotted and fallen.

(Note the preciseness of 'pallor' in moonlight, and the underlying imagery of deserted wayside shrines.) The Virgin, the One of Fictive Music, is gone:

Unreal, give back to us what once you gave:
The imagination that we spurned and crave.

This is the setting of his poems: man, the disinherited, wandering without belief through a mechanical, insentient universe. 'How to live What to do' –

From this the poem springs: that we live in a place
That is not our own and, much more, not ourselves.

Somehow, by his own mind and senses, man must find order, must make terms with earth, must establish some relation between himself and the world about him. The 'war between the mind / And sky, between thought and day and night,' must be resolved: this is the poet's mission.

Amid this 'moving chaos that never ends,' amid these repetitions of eternal change, order is found by the poet in moments of supreme awareness, when one object, one scene, one person, one idea, is firmly grasped in all its possibilities by integrated mind and sense. Then round that one thing the world will compose itself, relation will be established, as, to take a simple instance, in 'Woman Looking at a Vase of Flowers,' when 'the inhuman colors fell Into place beside her, where she was,' like 'An affirmation free from doubt.' The affirmation is the momentary experience of unity and stability. These experiences range from such simple compositions to large physical landscapes and finally to the realm of the pure idea. Let us be clear about this last point, for Stevens is often called a hater of ideas and of reason. Though some of his less guarded exclamations may seem to bear this out, *Notes Toward a Supreme Fiction* should dispel any misconception. His apparent hatred of reason is only a hatred of what he calls 'reason's click-clack, its *applied* / Enflashings.'

The 'practical,' systematic application of rational power destroys imagination, limits sensitivity, crushes men into 'the common life,' 'A black line beside a white line,' a place where 'The men have no shadows / And the women have only one side.'

> Rationalists, wearing square hats,
> Think, in square rooms,
> Looking at the floor,
> Looking at the ceiling,

missing the significant landscapes. But his 'major man,' poet, prophet, philosopher, or all three in one, comes

> from reason,
> Lighted at midnight by the studious eye,
> Swaddled in revery.

This speculative reason, 'This warmth in the blood-world for the pure idea,' stirs his admiration, for reason striving to conceive the Platonic Idea is a fictive power.

This union of poetry and philosophy is declared in the late poem, 'Asides on the Oboe,' but had already been implied in the early 'Homunculus et la Belle Etoile,' where he says of the starlight:

> It is a good light, then, for those
> That know the ultimate Plato,
> Tranquillizing with this jewel
> The torments of confusion

The poem on page 12 of *Notes Toward a Supreme Fiction* sums it all up:

> The poem refreshes life so that we share,
> For a moment, the first idea ... It satisfies
> Belief in an immaculate beginning
>
> And sends us, winged by an unconscious will,
> To an immaculate end. We move between these points:
> From that ever-early candor to its late plural
>
> And the candor of them is the strong exhilaration
> Of what we feel from what we think, of thought
> Beating in the heart, as if blood newly came,

An elixir, an excitation, a pure power.
The poem, through candor, brings back a power again
That gives a candid kind to everything.

Candor, in its root meaning, here signifies the thing grasped
in its radiant essence, the full, clear, white, pure, dazzling
realization of the world and all things in it. The 'ever-early
candor' is the original Idea of the thing, or the thing as it
should be. 'Its late plural' is the varied manifestation of that
essence as now exhibited in the world about us – often a
sorry assortment of objects encrusted with the dirt of time,
but, seen in their first idea, radiant. Then 'Life's nonsense
pierces us with strange relation,' and the Imagination has, for
the moment, achieved its constant function, for 'The first
idea is an imagined thing.'

Such perceptions are hardly to be planned, but they come
to the man who trains his imagination to perceive them.
Perhaps, says Stevens,

> The truth depends on a walk around a lake,
>
> A composing as the body tires, a stop
> To see hepatica, a stop to watch
> A definition growing certain and
>
> A wait within that certainty, a rest
> In the swags of pine-trees bordering the lake.

Note here the interaction of precise generality and precise
concreteness, each supporting and enriching the other, as if
the abstract definition were a flower or a grove. And indeed it
is: the flower, the grove, perceived in candor, define
momentarily the observer's place in the world. It is a delicate
and complicated skill, this realization of candor:

> ...the difficult rigor is forthwith,
> On the image of what we see, to catch from that
> Irrational moment its unreasoning.

Then,

> We reason of these things with later reason
> And we make of what we see, what we see clearly
> And have seen, a place dependent on ourselves.

But modern man is too often dependent on the place, defeated by his environment. The fine poem on page 14 of *Notes Toward a Supreme Fiction* puts this failure as precisely as possible, by contrast with the animal kingdom:

> The lion roars at the enraging desert,
> Reddens the sand with his red-colored noise,
> Defies red emptiness to evolve his match,
>
> Master by foot and jaws and by the mane,
> Most supple challenger.

Red, symbol of anger and violent blood, dominates and fills the emptiness of inanimate nature. And the elephant 'Breaches the darkness of Ceylon with blares,' while the bear snarls 'At summer thunder and sleeps through winter snow.'

> But you, ephebe, look from your attic window,
> Your mansard with a rented piano. You lie
>
> In silence upon your bed. You clutch the corner
> Of the pillow in your hand. You writhe and press
> A bitter utterance from your writhing, dumb,
>
> Yet voluble of dumb violence. You look
> Across the roofs as sigil and as ward
> And in your centre mark them and are cowed...

The piano, along with other musical instruments, is used by Stevens as a symbol of the imagination; in this context 'rented piano' is both literally right and symbolically and exact expression of decayed imagination. The roofs from a *sigil* – a seal, an enchanting talisman; or a *ward* – a guard, a prison; both words also suggest a legal bond.

Only the imagination can achieve the desired freedom and domination, as the singing woman beside the sea creates the Idea of Order at Key West. The sea, as the woman sings, becomes a part of her song: she creates, she composes the scene:

> She was the single artificer of the world
> In which she sang. And when she sang, the sea,
> Whatever self it had, became the self
> That was her song, for she was the maker. Then we,

As we beheld her striding there alone,
Knew that there never was a world for her
Except the one she sang and, singing, made.

And as the listeners leave the spot, it seems that 'The lights in the fishing boats at anchor there'

Mastered the night and portioned out the sea,
Fixing emblazoned zones and fiery poles,
Arranging, deepening, enchanting night.

Thus man dominates, if only for a moment, 'The meaningless plungings of water and the wind.''Blessed rage for order,' says Stevens, rage, that is, for more than the mechanical order of the sea, whose

merely revolving wheel
Returns and returns, along the dry, salt shore.
There is a mother whose children need more than that.

The human need – to realize and thus compose and dominate the world by imagination:

Poet, patting more nonsense foamed
From the sea, conceive for the courts
Of these academies, the diviner health
Disclosed in common forms. Set up
The rugged black, the image. Design
The touch. Fix quiet.

Note the preciseness of that opening parenthesis – the poet, modeller of clay (or sand), pats the meaningless variety tossed up by the sea of physical life and another Venus emerges from the foam.

I am aware that there are places in Stevens' poetry where he seems to assert or desire a merely passive connection with the world about him. See, for example, 'Theory,' 'Anecdote of Men by the Thousand,' and 'The Latest Freed Man,' especially the lines where he wishes 'To have the ant of the self changed to an ox / With its organic boomings.' These bathetic lines, however, are modified at the close of that poem, where the central conception of Stevens reasserts itself:

It was everything being more real, himself
At the centre of reality, seeing it.

Thus, even in such an apparently slight poem as 'The Load of
Sugar-Cane,' 'The red turban / Of the boatman' pulls together
the whole fluent scene. Hibiscus on the Sleeping Shores does
not invade the man – he seeks the flower. His mind may at
times be passive, but its essence is action, creation; thus the
mind is imaged as a roaming moth:

Then it was that that monstered moth
Which had lain folded against the blue
And the colored purple of the lazy sea,

And which had drowsed along the bony shores,
Shut to the blather that the water made,
Rose up besprent and sought the flaming red

Dabbled with yellow pollen.

This flaming red hibiscus is an absolute, a fixity, like the ripe
pear with which 'Autumn beguiles the fatalist,' or the
chrysanthemums whose fragrance disguises 'the clanking
mechanism / Of machine within machine within machine,' or
like the lilacs from which 'we breathe / An odor evoking
nothing, absolute.'

This is not the treatment of nature usual in romantic poetry
of the nineteenth century. Stevens does not feel the 'sense
sublime / Of something far more deeply interfused.' He
does not moralize the flower or the pear. Stevens, it is true,
refers to himself as a 'romantic,' but there is a basic difference between the 'romance' which Stevens represents and
nineteenth-century romanticism. This may be illustrated by
comparing Stevens' 'Idea of Order at Key West' with
Wordsworth's 'Solitary Reaper.' In Wordsworth's poem the
superbly precise imagery draws the reader away from the
figure of the girl during the two central stanzas: the poet's
main effort is bent toward moving outward by connotation
from the particular Highland girl and spot into the breadth of
the world and the depth of history. The girl's song suggests
immense distances of space and time. This is, I think, the
peculiar greatness of nineteenth-century Romantic poetry at

its best. But in Stevens' poem the whole effort is bent toward realizing the particular spot and girl: the scene focuses inward upon the singer. The particular, though radiant, is fixed in its place: the pear is only ideal pear, the star is only ideal star. The object, thus realized and glorified, implies an attitude toward human life, as in 'Nuances of a Theme by Williams,' where he tells the star,

> Shine alone, shine nakedly, shine like bronze,
> that reflects neither my face not any inner part
> of my being, shine like fire, that mirrors nothing.

> Lend no part to any humanity that suffuses
> you in its own light.

This is an Imagist poem, but the image stabilizes the affections, and the image is an ideal. There is no 'fracture between Stevens' conceptual, affective and imagist phases.' All are part of one central need: to fix a relation between man and the world about him. His total work is 'The poem of the mind in the act of finding What will suffice.'

For Stevens nothing will suffice but the satisfaction of continually renewing, by imaginative insight, his relation to the world of physical objects. For him, man's greatest tragedy is 'To lose sensibility.' 'The greatest poverty is not to live In a physical world,' as he tells us in his recent *Esthétique du Mal*.

> And out of what one sees and hears and out
> Of what one feels, who could have thought to make
> So many selves, so many sensuous worlds –
> As if the air, the mid-day air, was swarming
> With the metaphysical changes that occur, Merely in
> living as and where we live.

This satisfaction, this stabilization, constitutes the 'romance of the precise,' as Stevens has called it in his recent 'Adult Epigram,' where he reminds us that

> The romance of the precise is not the elision
> Of the tired romance of imprecision.

Precise candor establishes precise relation, which, for the poet, resides primarily in the precise poetic word, in 'his

Virgilian cadences.' Such awareness of relation produces 'the redeeming thought' shown at its best in the delicately modulated end of 'Sunday Morning':

> Deer walk upon our mountains, and the quail
> Whistle about us their spontaneous cries;
> Sweet berries ripen in the wilderness;
> And, in the isolation of the sky,
> At evening, casual flocks of pigeons make
> Ambiguous undulations as they sink,
> Downward to darkness, on extended wings.

The pigeons, thus seen, exemplify one of the satisfactions of the physical world, and at the same time suggest an attitude, an approach, toward death.

If, then, Stevens is neither a Metaphysical nor a nineteenth-century Romantic, what is he? Can his genre be defined? There is space for only the barest suggestion. In his devotion to poetic craftsmanship, in his view of life and the resultant subject-matter (bright moments set against man's sombre fate), he suggests an affinity with Herrick, Ben Jonson, and the Roman and Greek poets who nourished these English representatives of pagan poetry. Read Horace. The parallels are there.

NOTES

1 See headnote to No. 53.
2 See No. 62.

TRANSPORT TO SUMMER

New York, 1947

Knopf edition of 1,750 copies, reprinted in November 1950 in a run of 1,500 copies.

65. Robert Lowell, on Stevens the 'improvisor', *Nation*

Vol. 164, no. 14, 5 April 1947, 400–2

A notable translator and playwright, Robert Lowell (1919–77) was awarded the Pulitzer Prize in 1946 for *Lord Weary's Castle*. Probably his most influential single work is *Life Studies* (1959), a book of autobiographical poems, and a landmark in a phase of American poetry which also included poets as various as John Berryman, Allen Ginsberg and Sylvia Plath.

Wallace Stevens is one of the best poets of the past half-century. If he has never had the popularity of Robert Frost, or the international reputation of T. S. Eliot or Ezra Pound, he has, nevertheless, been fortunate in the criticism that he has received. R. P. Blackmur's essay in *The Double Agent* is a masterpiece of imaginative elucidation. Ivor Winters's essay in *The Anatomy of Nonsense* is less brilliant, and its dismissal of Stevens's later work appears to me to be overdone. But Winters's evaluation is a corrective to Blackmur's appreciation; and by combining the two essays one can come to a calmer and more objective understanding of Stevens than is, perhaps, possible with any other contemporary American writer.

A few poems in *Transport to Summer* are better than anything that Stevens has written since *Harmonium*, but the earlier book is far more exciting and successful as a whole. Before I praise what is wonderful in Stevens, I shall try to describe briefly what I think are his principal themes, his faults in general, and the ways in which he has developed or deteriorated.

The subject throughout Stevens's poems is the imagination, and its search for forms, myths, or metaphors that will make the real and the experienced coherent without distortion or simplification.

> You must become an ignorant man again
> And see the sun again with an ignorant eye
> And see it clearly in the idea of it.

This is a threefold process: the stripping away of dead forms, the observation of naked reality, and the construction of new and more adequate forms. In his later poems Stevens often uses an elaborate machinery of abstractions, but what he is saying has changed very little. His world is an impartial, hedonistic, speculative world – he is closer to Plato than to Socrates, and closer to the philosophy and temperament of George Santayana than to Plato. Directly or indirectly much of his thought is derived from the dialectical idealism of Hegel.

The detachment and flexibility of a poet who can say in one place that Christianity is too nebulous, in another that it is too rigid, and in another that 'the death of Satan is a tragedy/for the imagination' are disarming. But perhaps Stevens is too much the leisured man of taste. As with Santayana, one feels that the tolerance and serenity are a little too blandly appropriated, that a man is able to be an imagination and the imagination able to be disinterested and urbane only because it is supported by industrial slaves. Perhaps if there are to be Platonists, there must always be slaves. In any case, Stevens has little of the hard ugliness and virtue of Socrates. His places are places visited on a vacation, his people are essences, and his passions are impressions.

Many of his poems are written in a manner that is excessively playful, suave, careless, and monotonous. And their rhetoric, with its Tennysonian sound effects, its harmonious alliteration, and its exotic vocabulary, is sometimes no more than an enchanting inflection of the voice.

The later poems are more philosophical, and consider many things in this world of darkness ('Lenin on a bench beside a lake disturbed/The swans. He was not the man for swans') which the Stevens of *Harmonium* would have excluded as unpoetic. His language is simpler and more mature. But structural differences make all that has been gained precarious. Nothing like the dense, large-scale organization of his 'Sunday Morning,' or even the small perfection of his 'Peter Quince at the Clavier,' is attempted. The philosophy is not exhaustive and marshaled as in Lucretius; and it is seldom human and dramatic as in Donne. When one first reads this poetry that juggles its terminology with such lightness and subtlety, one is delighted; but as one rereads, it too often appears muddled, thin, and repetitious. How willingly one would exchange much of it for the concrete, gaudy wit of *Harmonium*.

The points that I have been making are probably overstated, and they are necessarily simplified. But few poets of Stevens's stature have tossed off so many half-unfinished improvisations. Underneath their intellectual obscurity and whimsey, their loose structures, their rhetorical and imagistic mannerisms, and their tenuous subject matter, there seems to be something in the poet that protects itself by asserting that it is not making too great an effort.

The best poems in *Transport to Summer* are as good as anyone is writing in English. 'Notes Toward a Supreme Fiction,' the longest poem in the book, is a sequence in three parts, entitled: It Must Be Abstract, It Must Change, and It Must Give Pleasure. Each part has ten sections consisting of twenty-one blank-verse lines arranged in groups of three. In spite of a few beautiful sections – particularly Begin, ephebe, by perceiving; The first idea was not our own; Not to be realized; It feels good as it is; The great statue; and A lasting visage – and many fine moments, the whole seems to me to be unsuccessful. Its structure is sloppy, idiosyncratic,

and repetitious. It rambles and rambles without gathering
volume, and many of the sections are padded to fill out their
twenty-one lines. Much of the rhetoric is extremely mannered. Certain details, such as Canon Aspirin, and Nanzia
Nunzio confronting Ozymandias, seem written for
Stevens's private amusement. Of the shorter poems, I think
the best is 'No Possum, No Sop, No Taters.' It is objective
and subtle in its rhythms and perceptions, and is certainly one
of Stevens's most magical and perfect slighter pieces. Other
small poems in *Transport to Summer* approach it in excellence
but are imperfect, or have much less to them. 'Dutch Graves
in Bucks County' is much grander and more ambitious. The
past and the present are opposed thematically:

> Angry men and furious machines
> Swarm from the little blue of the horizon
> To the great blue of the middle height.
> Men scatter throughout the clouds.
> The wheels are too large for any noise...
> And you, my semblables, in gaffer-green,
> Know that the past is not part of the present.

It is written with tremendous feeling, pathos, and power. I
think that no living poet would be able to match the
magnificence of its rhetoric and resonance. A few lines are
slightly mannered, and there is something a little long,
formless, and vague about its development. But it is a very
large undertaking wonderfully executed.

'Esthétique du Mal' is a sequence in fifteen blank-verse
sections. It is about as good and important a poem as T. S.
Eliot's *Four Quartets* or 'Ash Wednesday.' Its subject is: How
shall the imagination act when confronted with pain and evil?
The structure is not very tight, two or three sections are not
particularly good, and several others have a great number of
bad or over-written lines. The good parts can be detached,
but they lose some of their momentum. But 'Esthétique du
Mal' is more in the grand manner than any poetry since
Yeats's; and is reminds one of parts of *Cymbeline* and *The
Winter's Tale* – slow and rapid, joining the gorgeous with the

very simple, wise, elaborate, open, tolerant without apathy, understanding with the understanding of having lived long.

> The death of Satan was a tragedy
> For the imagination. A capital
> Negation destroyed him in his tenement
> And, with him, many blue phenomena.
> It was not the end he had foreseen. He knew
> That his revenge created filial
> Revenges. And negation was eccentric.
> It had nothing of the Julian thunder-cloud:
> The assassin flash and rumble.... He was denied.
> Phantoms, what have you left? What underground?
> What place in which to be is not enough
> To be? You go, poor phantoms, without place
> Like silver in the sheathing of the sight
> When the eye closes....

66. F. O. Matthiessen, 'Wallace Stevens at 67', *New York Times Book Review*

20 April 1947, 4, 26

...At 67 his subject, like that of the later Yeats, is increasingly the imagination itself. Indeed, some of the titles here – 'The Motive for Metaphor,' 'The Creations of Sound,' 'The Pure Good of Theory' – might suggest that he has veered over the line into being more critical esthetician than poet. But the full-bodied connotations set up by the book's title are reinforced by the excitingly physical expectations of 'The Dove in the Belly' or 'Mountains Covered with Cats.'

Stevens' thoughts are generally drenched with the life of his senses. This vibrant fact forms the core of his exploration of the interplay between the mind and reality. He approaches that interplay from a variety of angles and stances. Sometimes, in the poems that are most analogous to a painter's still life, he says: 'Let's see the very thing and nothing else.' Sometimes he is absorbed with the differences between the observed thing and what the imagination can make of it, a contrast which calls out his recurrent symbol of the differences between sunlight and moonlight, between the stark actual and the release given by soft shadows and oblique half-tones. (Nathaniel Hawthorne, whose many days in a customs house are comparable to those spent by Stevens in his insurance office, often used the same symbols for the same purpose.)

Most frequently and most characteristically this poet of nuances is given over to speculations upon what the imagination can be said to add to reality. He knows, as the true artist must, that

> Description is revelation. It is not
> The thing described, nor false facsimile.

Rather it produces a heightened reality, 'intenser than any actual life could be.' In such speculations Stevens often seems closely akin to Santayana's conception of 'essences.'

'Notes Toward a Supreme Fiction,' running above six hundred lines, is the longest and most ambitious poem in this collection, and provides the most numerous variations upon Stevens' central theme. Its division into three parts of exactly equal length, entitled It Must be Abstract, It Must Change, It Must Give Pleasure, suggests again the dangers risked by Stevens' latest manner. The development of these propositions in unrhymed three-line stanzas of Stevens' formal pentameter can become such a set-piece as the more varied liveliness of 'The Man with the Blue Guitar' fully escaped being.

Stevens is often more completely successful in his shorter poems, as in the happily named 'Holiday in Reality.' For there, to express his conviction that the artist must always make a fresh and personal discovery, he brings into play his lightness and ebullience:

After all, they knew that to be real each had
To find for himself his earth, his sky, his sea.
And the words for them, and the colors they possessed.
It was impossible to breathe at Durand-Ruel's

The sense of unexpected deadness that can overtake you in
a gallery, that can make a museum and a mausoleum akin, is
what Stevens develops in the second of the three propositions
for his 'supreme fiction.' He is at his best in those poems
which embody his conviction that a work of art is a moment
of stasis out of movement, an equilibrium as difficult as it
is delicate. The heaviness of spirit that can descend from the
period pieces in Durand-Ruel's is because 'nothing had
happened because nothing had changed.'

Stevens knows that a poem is not a proposition, or, as he
puts it in 'Man Carrying Thing': 'The poem must resist the
intelligence/Almost successfully.' He conveys the value of
change most compellingly, not by direct statement, but by
such devices as his wonderfully effective recurrent symbol of
the endlessly fascinating movement of clouds. His greatest
resource has always been in the gaiety of his language, in the
way he employs also the nonsensical and the grotesque to
break through the restrictions of the fixed and dry rational
into what he calls 'the lingua franca et jocundissima.'

All of Stevens' later work has been written against the
realization that we live in a time of violent disorder. The
most profound challenge in his poems is his confidence that
even in such a time, even on the verge of ruin, a man can
recreate afresh his world out of the unfailing utilization of his
inner resources. The value of the creative imagination, of
'supreme fictions' in their fullest abundance, lies in the
extension, even to the point of grandeur, that they add to our
common lives. I suppose that Wallace Stevens, in expressing
such truths with the mellowness and tang of a late-summer
wine, has about one reader to every hundred of the latest
best-seller. Yet Stevens, who did not publish a poem until he
was 35, will increasingly be recognized to belong in the
company of Henry Adams and Henry James, with that small
body of important American artists who have ripened as
they matured, and who have been far more productive

beyond their middle years than during their green twenties or thirties.

67. Louise Bogan, Stevens' poetry 'a luxury product', *New Yorker*

Vol. 23, no. 11, 3 May 1947, 101

... Wallace Stevens... has of late years elaborated a style and an attitude that almost entirely destroy the possibility of any sustained emotion or idea. Stevens' poetry, musical and filled with occasional touches of beauty though it is, becomes more and more a luxury product, and his mannerisms are frequently affectations.

68. Richard Eberhart, 'Notes to a Class in Adult Education', *Accent*

Vol. 7, no. 4, Summer 1947, 251–3

Eberhart (b. 1904) is a noted American poet, whose books include *Collected Poems 1930–76* (1976) and *Selected Prose* (1978).

He was a close friend of Stevens' last years, and Stevens once wrote to him that 'whatever exists in common between us comes from a fundamental likeness' (*Letters*, p. 851).

Harmonium appeared in 1923 when Stevens was forty-four (1879 was the year Hopkins' aspens were 'all felled'). He was thus perhaps saved twenty years of trying to arrive at the singleness of aim with which he was fortunate to begin. Compared with certain other poets (cf. my remarks on *Notes Toward a Supreme Fiction* in this magazine, Winter, 1943)[1] he has shown no major change in growth, so that his late poems partake of the same type of sensibility as his early ones, the whole work over the years presenting a remarkable consistency.

In that review I posited an Ideal Reader (subsequently knocked down) who desired the tragic poet. It is negative to criticize poets for what they are not. Comparisons are valid indicators, but do not help much while enjoying a particular poetry. It is no use regretting that Stevens has not the sardonic realism of Beddoes. We may read Beddoes. Nor that he is not of whole areas of Baudelaire. We may read Baudelaire. He is not Milton. Sometimes we may put down his book with regret that in him this country has not produced the great tragic poet, but we should be ill-advised in that regret.

The way is open for the appearance and persistence of the tragic poet, should the times permit. There is none (or few, depending on how you look at it) to dispute him when he comes. But our expectations are inordinate and it is negative to expect Stevens to satisfy other cravings than those enlarged in his orbit. There are profound areas of life he does not touch, but the area of his use is illumined, not darkened, by a kaleidoscopic magic; his magic plays upon our sensibilities not violently, but with seduction. He lures us into imaginary delectations in realms of new correspondences. (He calls it Resemblance.) These correspondences abound as, among multifarious possibilities, exegetical filibusters for hopeful adumbrations of unfitful scholars. Salute to his irrepressible high spirits.

Perhaps a word about the dark places. 'It is almost time for lunch. Pain is human.' (38) 'Life is a better aspic.' (48) He does not evoke pain or convince us about the bitterness. Elsewhere he refers to 'fatal disasters' but these are never divulged, only posited. We do not experience the fatality and are not sure of the actuality of the disasters. There are imaginary fatalities and imaginary disasters. The poetry is constant skirmishes around the point, elusive and suggestive. 'Life's nonsense pierces us with strange relation.' (120)

An aesthetic principle is always present. This gives large play to our own shoots and flares of imagination and contemplation. The poems are a dream-map to a country of essences. The names are there, but you do not know how your foot will feel on the terrain. The terrain is 'rugged roy.' You might have lost the map on the way. For instance, in *Esthétique du Mal* the first term is more indicative than the second. Stevens has made no study of evil in man comparable to that of Baudelaire; he has not allowed himself so close, so devastating an inspection; instead there is always an aesthetic principle of guidance into imaginative states of being, into beautiful, often tenuous situations of the mind; into a subtle music giving subtle pleasure; even into an euthenics of the mind, for if everybody lived in the mental atmosphere of the poems it would be a better world. No doubt Stevens would be the first to decry any such intention, for the purity of his aesthetic argues a uselessness, a rarity, the pleasure of ideal contemplation. But it is art for life's sake. Every understanding of excellent poetry takes away part of our grossness. By the enlarging of our perceptions we become less ignorant. And thus it can be argued that poetry has a moral value, perhaps in spite of the lack of this intention on the part of a poet like Stevens. Surely to absorb and know the heart of his verse for ten years will make larger the soul, as it will make more sensitive the mind, and thus, descending into the realm of conduct, by actually transforming to some mysterious extent our natures, it will make us less gross in conduct (out of wariness against the ponderous arguments counter to this proposition I state it negatively), thus rebuke, to whatever extent, in whatever manner, with whatever quality, ugliness in the world. Conversely, as adults being educated, you should not study poetry, nor read Stevens in this case, if you think it will make you worse a moral being. There is a fascination of evil, and there are the lives of Poe or Rimbaud for readers to contemplate. The question of action for creators is in another category. I am talking to you as adult readers of poetry, not as creators who may have to enter worlds of the most violent action to find what they seek, and may be compelled, as was Crane, literally to jump into the ocean. The responsibility is much heavier on the maker.

These are only general notations before your meticulous study of the verse. A general notion is the idea in Stevens of the validity of repetition. 'The man-hero is not the exceptional monster, / But he that of repetition is most master.' (146) Note the weaving of repetitive phrases, the subtle changes, how the meaning runs back and forward through meshes of sounds, the neatness and formality of the presentations. Take quite at random lines, as on p. 110 (VIII), or pp. 63–64, and note how the major terms are repeated. Repetition is one of the modes of the freedom of his mind, an air-flow, a shift of currents, poems and poems, repetitions of controlled changes, repetition and repetition all through the years. The mind is a bee that searches through the airs of summers. The world of mental images and sensuosity moves irresistibly with 'flor-abundant force.'

Stevens would not catch an absolute if he could. The worlds are delicious approaches. The result is that many are caught, but he moves on, 'beau linguist.' Poetry is 'an elixir, an excitation, a pure power.' (119) 'The obscure moon lighting an obscure world / Of things that would never be quite expressed.' (6) 'Chocorua to Its Neighbor': 'I hear the motions of the spirit and the sound / Of what is secret becomes, for me, a voice / That is my own voice speaking in my ear.' (19) He would hold off the absolute:

> And not yet to have written a book in which
> One is already a grandfather and to have put there
> A few sounds of meaning, a momentary end
> To the complication, is good, is a good.

Yet in 'Repetitions of a Young Captain':

Secrete us in reality.

....

In a beau language without a drop of blood.   (33)

Note, in 'Holiday in Reality':

Spring is umbilical or else is not spring.
Spring is the truth of spring or nothing, a waste, a fake. (36)

Phenomena 'grow out of the spirit.' 'These are real only if I make them so.' The poem ends: 'And I taste at the foot of the tongue the unreal of what is real.' Many examples can be found of this reluctance to accept the real. It is the 'unreal of what is real' that is his tireless and wonderful search.

It is the human that is the alien,
The human that has no cousin in the moon.   (55)

As the platonic person, in Description of a Platonic Person (II of 'The Pure Good of Theory' 57–61) is 'unhappy about the sense of happiness,' the question arises 'Was it that – a sense and beyond intelligence?' We must become attuned to the nth sense: 'closely the ear attends the varying / Of this precarious music.' (59) Debris of Life and Mind (66) begins 'There is so little that is close and warm' and this magical poem is close and warm with wish and representation. While in Description Without Place the future must be 'seeming to be / Like rubies reddened by rubies reddening,' a felicitous example of repetition increasing contemplation to an abstraction, a spring to further contemplation. (VII, 76)

Of the mode of repetition you are invited to see its use and play in his prose in 'The Realm of Resemblance' read at Harvard in February, 1947, antecedent to the poetry (Partisan Review, May-June 1947, pp. 243–249). The ideas go back to Plato; should be compared with the nineteenth-century notions of correspondences; as indeed this piece should be studied in relation to the total practice of the poet.

It would be tedious to locate the interests of Stevens in a long list of words and names pointed up by him, the importations from French and Spanish (and Latin) – no Bengali, no Chinese – , the inventions; but a few may indicate colour and tone: Eulalia, Mrs. Pappadopoulos, Projection A, Projection B, Projection C, x, z, on-dit, Ha-eé-me, palabra, rou-coo, Descartes, Lenin, Nietzsche, selvages, effendi, ai-ai, anima, exhumo, millefiori, bandeaux, wiggy book, paisant, oh beau caboose, ithy oonts, Jacomyntje, Vertumnus, anonymids, coulisse, megalfrere. *Notes Toward a Supreme Fiction*, 1942, appears at the end of the book while *Esthétique du Mal*, 1944, begins on page 35. In the former, two periods are omitted from the former printing, 11, 12 and 15 of p. 120. A comma is added at the end of 1. 20 on p. 139. The word 'to' is left out altogether as if by printer's error at the beginning of the last stanza on page 143.

No final words about Stevens, no estimation, no totality of appreciation. Only a term or two in an index for your explorations. You should study the life in relation to the type of writing. You should not ignore the gothic, baroque, and whimsical elements, nor the bizarre and grotesque. You should recognize that limitation is strength, and speculate on the reasons for the limited view of Stevens. Remember that this century killed Lawrence, which allows to triumph quite other ideas, as orthodox religious ones in Eliot, or intellectual ones in Stevens. Perhaps because of our disbelief in the integrity of the individual, and of our mid-century chaos in a world situation of wars, these two poetical answers, as two only among possibilities, are not only likely, but seem inevitable once presented over decades. We cannot expect a whole view of man, a tragic poetry, in the present state of affairs.

NOTE

1 *Accent*, vol. III, Winter 1943, 121–2.

69. Delmore Schwartz, on 'an inspired minister in a small church', from 'Auden and Stevens', *Partisan Review*

Vol. 14, October 1947, 531–2

The review is in two separate parts, and this extract is taken from the second. The first and considerably longer section is a discussion of Auden's *The Age of Anxiety*.

Transport to Summer continues, extends, and enrichens the themes which dominated Wallace Stevens' previous books. He is writing again of the nature of poetry, of the way in which the imagination struggles with reality, of the necessity and ultimate poverty of ideas face to face with the darkness, variety, and endlessness of reality. To think of this new book and of his work as a whole within the arena or circus tent of modern literature is to come upon a fabulous image: Stevens is like an inspired minister in a small church (the church, however, is within the circus tent) who preaches sermons in celebration and in praise of poetry, reality, and their various relations. His listeners are other poets, but not all other poets. No one else appears to be interested enough to attend, and if anyone else did, he would be perplexed by what Stevens is saying and how he is saying it. For only poets remember that a good book must be conquered like a foreign language, and he who runs cannot read. It is true that there are times when Stevens' tropes are too tangential or peculiar to his own sensibility: he speaks once of 'Marianna's Swedish cart,' an allusion which can only be fully understood if one has read and remembered a recent poem by Marianne Moore. But this example is extreme. R. P. Blackmur has remarked that Stevens' poems 'grow in the mind.' At each new reading or new memory of them, one comes upon an astonishing lucidity, while metaphors and references which seem private or opaque become clear, necessary, fresh, and original as a discovery or an invention. The texture of Stevens' poetry is often visual, gay, and verbal in such a way that the reader may easily miss the seriousness and the passion of the attitudes and the emotions which are its substance. The starting point of so many poems is so often poetry itself, poetry as such, that Stevens may often seem to be merely the poet who is writing poetry about poetry. But it is as if a man who started to dig a well dug so long and so deeply that he dug his way to China. Stevens seeks out so many of the inexhaustible connections of poetry that he unearths a great deal of the actual world. Which is what one would expect: if you study anything closely enough, you find yourself studying a great many other things, of necessity. As Stevens says in one of his new poems, 'Adam in Eden was the father of Descartes.' Or, as in the motion of many of his poems, poetry brings one to the imagination which brings one to what is not imagined but actual which brings one to wonder which is which or Descartes, and whether Adam was as metaphysical and critical as Descartes, and in the end the poet has written a new poem in which the actual world becomes new again....

70. Louis L. Martz, 'the unique bird, inimitable', *Yale Review*

Vol. XXXVII, no. 2, December 1947, 339–41

Martz also reviews books by George Barker, Joan Murray, John Frederick Nims, Elizabeth Bishop, and Auden's *The Age of Anxiety*.

... Finally we come to the unique bird, inimitable. The new volume by Wallace Stevens may well stand as another landmark in American literature, along with his first volume, *Harmonium* (1923). It is true that, unlike this early volume, *Transport to Summer* is marred by a number of labored and muddy pieces. But this is not because Stevens has declined as an artist in his later years (he is now sixty-eight); it is because, having mastered one mode, he has tried to develop in new directions, impelled by a growing vision and by the cataclysmic events of the last twenty years. *Ideas of Order* (1935) marked a turning point; here, along with the 'essential gaudiness,' the vivid apprehensions of concrete experience, characteristic of *Harmonium*, we had a dominant interest in establishing something like a philosophy of the imagination. But theorizing was here still tightly integrated with concrete detail, to produce a distinguished (and neglected) volume. In *The Man with the Blue Guitar* (1937) and *Parts of a World* (1942) it was clear that Stevens was in the throes of working out a considerably different style, dealing explicitly and often abstractly with 'the role of the imagination in life, and particularly in life at present.' These volumes were interesting failures: good patches and fine poems were imbedded in an obscure, incoherent, and sometimes prosy mass. Fortunately for Stevens' admirers, 1942 also produced, in a limited edition, the reassuring *Notes Toward a Supreme Fiction*, while in 1945, in another limited edition, came the impressive *Esthétique du Mal*, both of which are now included in *Transport to Summer*, along with a large number of other poems which Stevens has evidently written since 1942.

All his essential substance is given at its best in these two long and brilliant sequences, where Stevens has mastered a conversational, meditative style, and also in two shorter sequences, almost as good, entitled 'Description without Place' and 'Credences of Summer.' The vision here expressed is briefly this: in a world of 'calculated chaos,' the human imagination remains a power for pleasure and victory, since the imagination can create its own intense and ordered world from materials provided by the world of physical objects. The 'transport to summer' consists in seizing with the imagination some pleasurable physical object, and then, by metaphor, clarifying it and relating it to other objects, until one has formed an integrated composition of the 'ideal' and the 'real'.' By such man-made 'credences' we dominate and enjoy our environment, though such domination cannot be sustained for long, and must be vigilantly re-established from moment to moment. This 'summer' is no easy flight from ugliness. *Esthétique du Mal* shows clearly that such pleasures are strenuously achieved and depend upon a thorough, unblinking recognition of the existence of pain. That recognition is in itself a work of the imagination:

> Except for us, Vesuvius might consume
> In solid fire the utmost earth and know
> No pain (ignoring the cocks that crow us up
> To die). This is a part of the sublime
> From which we shrink. And yet, except for us,
> The total past felt nothing when destroyed.

These things once understood, it is possible for us to build up imaginative compensations against the fact of pain, through establishing full, acute relationships with other human beings and with the external world. The utter tragedy for man, says, Stevens, is to become so 'Spent in the false engagements of the mind' that he falls into 'the greatest poverty':

> To lose sensibility, to see what one sees,
> As if sight had not its own miraculous thrift,
> To hear only what one hears, one meaning alone....

Certainly we are 'Natives of poverty, children of malheur,' who must face 'the unalterable necessity Of being this unalterable animal.' Yet, through the exercise of imaginative sensibility, we may create a metamorphosis such as Stevens describes in the witty, gay mood that marks some of the best parts of his *Notes Toward a Supreme Fiction*.

When the poems in these four sequences have so eloquent-ly expressed the theme, one finds rather tedious the presence of inferior pieces striving towards the same end. This reader, at least, would wish to keep only about a score of these other poems – among them 'Dutch Graves in Bucks County,' 'Holiday in Reality,' 'The Red Fern,' 'Men Made out of Words,' 'The House was Quiet,' and 'A Lot of People

Bathing in a Stream.' Stevens has been in the past sufficiently praised as an 'able virtuoso' with a 'cunning rhetoric.' It has seemed more important to stress here the fact that the superb craft of his best poems grows out of a deep concern for the role of the imagination in a world preoccupied with the tragic plans of the materialist.

71. R. P. Blackmur, from 'Poetry and Sensibility: Some Rules of Thumb', *Poetry*

Vol. 71, no. 5, February 1948, 271–6

Transport to Summer is here reviewed along with Herbert Read's *Collected Poems*. The essay is included in *Language as Gesture*.

... Mr. Stevens has grown prolific, and sometimes prolix. There is therefore in *Transport to Summer* no great amount of work truly alive; but there is some, and it adds ....

Looking at the late poems of Wallace Stevens, and at the same time thinking of the state of poetry as a whole, the following observations seem plausible. They note something in Stevens and are useful elsewhere.

This is a poetry which ad libs with relation to a centre, sometimes around it, sometimes to find it. If you ad lib having statement as your intention, you must have rhythm to begin with. If you ad lib having rhythm as your intention you must have statement to begin with.

Or put the whole thing the third way. This is a poetry which habitually moves by a mutual exchange of tokens or counters. If you have a set of counters to shove around they must have (and somehow deploy) whole sets of associations not your own, or your meanings will be merely assigned and will disappear with use.

This is a poetry of which an unusually high number of the words are recognizably a part of a special vocabulary. A specialized vocabulary, not charged and fixed by forces outside the vocabulary, will obliterate the perceptions it specializes. A live taxonomy must be idiomatic; it must survive its uses into another life – the life it taps.

This is a poetry which purports to wear a prose syntax. If you write your verse with a prose syntax, the statement itself must have a force of phrasing (in the musical sense) beyond the syntax. The line-structure must guide, and conform to, the movement of phrase. This is a particularly sound rule if it happens that your line averages the norm of blank verse. For blank verse to be as well-written as prose it must be very different from prose: precisely in the phrasing....

This is a poetry of repetitions, within the poem and from poem to poem. Rebirth in the individual (poem or person) can be only a little repetition. It is the misery and the force not ourselves that is reborn; it is the music of these which is repeated everlastingly.

This is a poetry of hocus-pocus; there is a ritual who shall say how. You must not ever remove hocus-pocus that you feel; you must not ever add hocus-pocus to what you feel. Hocus-pocus has an ancestry not yours; nor can you father it.

> We say ourselves in syllables that rise
> From the floor, rising in speech we do not speak.

This a poetry unusually high with the odor of 'poets' and 'poetry.' Poems about poetry and poets, except when they are invocations or testaments of failure, hide or obliterate what the poet ought to see. Only exemplary invocations should leave the note-book, one for each volume. It is true that nearly one-tenth (62 out of 600 odd) of Rembrandt's paintings are self-portraits – let alone etchings and drawings; but they are all of a man – or all but one, the one you choose – not of the artist....

This is a poetry nevertheless. 'The Dove in the Belly'; II, vi and III, iii of 'Notes Toward a Supreme Fiction'; 'Dutch Graves in Bucks County'; and part VII of 'Esthétique du Mal'

(beginning 'How red the rose that is the soldier's wound') –
all these, and no doubt others missed, go into that canon
against which other poems merely beat; the canon of poems,
no matter what their idiosyncrasy, which create sensibility in
desperation.

What is the desperation? Ask a haunted man what is a
haunt. – Holding in mind as much of Mr. Stevens' poetry –
all thirty-five years of it – as possible, does it not seem that
he has always been trying to put down tremendous statements; to put down those statements heard in dreams? His
aesthetic, so to speak, was unaware of those statements, and
was in fact rather against making statements, and so got in
the way. It is rather as if Lucretius had been compelled to
write his invocation to Alma Venus in the aesthetic of *The
Rape of the Lock*. Thus the statements come out as lyric cries,
all the more moving because we feel in them a craving for a
fuller being than they can ever reach. Of such privations, in
our place and time, is our actual drama made: 'an ancient
aspect touching a new mind.' However inappropriate to its
purpose, it was Mr. Stevens' own aesthetic which gave his
poems achievement. There is the desperation....

72. Victor Tejera, on Stevens' 'largely philosophical attitude', *Journal of Philosophy*

Vol. XLV, February 1948, 137–9

Of interest here is the linking by a professional
philosopher, a non-expert in the field of modernist
poetry, between Stevens and Santayana.

... Wallace Stevens' work evinces a largely philosophical attitude to both experience as the matter of poetry, and to poetry as the best issue of experience (he has also written as a critic). This attitude can be read into, and accounts for, the abstract and reflective manner of his work. It also accounts for the freedom and conviction with which he creates inasmuch as in his critical statements he has taken, as the justification of his use of metaphor, an explicitly realistic epistemological position. He believes, like some interesting contemporary philosophers, in the objectivity of the relation of similarity. He sees metaphor as a way of things; his poetry is realism asserted, in operation.

In this respect Stevens is symptomatic of the ever more keenly felt community of subject-matter between poetry and metaphysics. The methods of these two pursuits are obviously quite different; but can it be said that the purposes of poetry as implied by Stevens are so different from those of metaphysics as suggested in the work of Santayana, for example? It is a question of more than the coexistence, observable in both these men and in other poets and metaphysicians, of richly developed imagination with an explicit degree of ontological realism. It is a question of Stevens' novel way of handling metaphor and analogy in such a manner as to make them the bases of his view of the world.

Thus, if it can be said that metaphysics consists in the analysis of the differentiate of being, then it may also be said that poetry is the quest for similarities in the same domain. Seen in this light poetry becomes a complement, a transliteration of metaphysics. Stevens, of course, does not set out to illustrate in the denser, more vivid, medium of his poetry, philosophical theories. But while the relation of his poetry to metaphysics is not quite one of subalternation, he does avow that his subject is the search for forms, myths, or metaphors that will reduce the chaos of man's experience to an interesting order. He attempts, in other words, to invest the world with form for a practical as well as a purely esthetic purpose, i.e., his purpose is practical in the sense a working, say, skeptical or spectator, metaphysics is practical, and esthetic in the sense that his method of presentation is vivid and sensuous. This attempt has three stages, each of which to be effected successfully requires the exercise of a specific virtue. The first stage is Pyrrhonic: *skepticism* clears away the rubble of old and dead forms. The second is empirical and devoted to *observation* of the now naked and consequently stark reality. The third stage is the strictly poetic one and represents a reconstruing of experience through the *invention* of new and adequate forms; forms which are, to one reader at least, a guide to the feelings and a stimulus to the imagination. More important perhaps to other readers will be Stevens' habit, over and above the previously mentioned virtues, of reacting to the presented world with simultaneous irony and wonder.

73. Peter Viereck, that Stevens has become 'brilliantly trivial', from 'Some Notes on Wallace Stevens', *Contemporary Poetry*

Vol. 7, no. 4, Winter 1948, 14–15

A writer on politics and political history, and a poet, Peter Viereck (b. 1916) has specialized in explaining the Nazi mind, in such books as *Metapolitics* (1941) and *The Roots of the Nazi Mind* (1961). His first book of poems, *Terror and Decorum* (1948) was awarded a Pulitzer Prize.

... Almost the only part of the new book worthy of being placed alongside the book of 1923 is 'Notes Toward a Supreme Fiction' – and perhaps parts of 'Esthétique du Mal'. But it is precisely these two poems that have already been published (by the Cummington Press) and are merely being reprinted in *Transport*. The rest of *Transport* is new, and this is what we had particularly looked forward to, and this is what is particularly disappointing. It is unrewarding not because it is 'bad' – it isn't – but because it is trivial. Every great poet, if he has the zest to experiment, will at times be 'bad'. Or will seem to be so to the myopia of contemporary critics until the future rebukes them. But to be brilliantly trivial, to repeat mechanically the effects that were once achieved vividly, this is what will disturb Stevens's sincerest admirers.

Earlier than the 'blue guitar' symbol, the most interesting of Stevens's parables to 'tease us into thought' is his jar-in-Tennessee (from the poem 'Anecdote of the Jar', included in *Harmonium*). His new poetry of 1947 is summed up by his own description of that jar:

> The jar was round upon the ground ...
> The jar was gray and bare.
> It did not give of bird or bush.

The meaning of the jar's triumph ('it took dominion everywhere') is anti-artifice and pro-nature according to the interpretation given the poem by Yvor Winters in *Anatomy of Nonsense* (re-issued by the Swallow Press as part of *In Defense of Reason*, 1947). Earlier, other critics, ... had suggested a directly opposite interpretation: pro-art, anti-nature. But is there not a third possibility, that of ironic neutrality between art and nature? If so, then perhaps in this particular poem the poet is viewing with Olympian detachment and Janus-faced malice the taming of a wilderness that is too 'slovenly' by a creative process that is too 'gray':

> The wilderness rose up to it,
> And sprawled around, no longer wild.

In any event, Stevens's own artifacts, his own Tennessee jars, are never of the natural, spontaneous, effusive school of poetry but are the product of the most conscious, deliberate craftsmanship. Whatever lip service he may pay to nature in theory (even assuming that he was wholly pro-wilderness and anti-jar), in his own practice Stevens fortunately leaves all folksy primitivism to the ghost of Rousseau.

Fortunately and yet, beyond a certain point, unfortunately. In each of his successive works since *Harmonium* (*Ideas of Order* 1936, *The Man with the Blue Guitar* 1937, *Parts of a World* 1942), the jars have become increasingly polished, competently but mechanically, and in color an increasingly opaque 'gray'. In *Transport* the point is reached where we have endless polish and almost no jar. 'But if we have such another victory,' said Pyrrhus, 'we are undone'. One more such Pyrrhic victory over adjectives (over his own tools) by Wallace Stevens, and he will have no more language left with which to write....

THREE ACADEMIC PIECES

Cummington, Massachusetts, 1947

An edition of 246 copies.

74. M. L. Rosenthal, on Stevens as 'hedonist, pluralist and Platonist', *New York Herald Tribune Weekly Book Review*

9 May 1948, 21

An editor, critic and poet, Rosenthal (b. 1917) is Director of the Poetics Institute at New York University. Besides a number of volumes of his own poetry, his publications include *The Modern Poets: A Critical Introduction* (1960), *The New Poets* (1967) and *Sailing into the Unknown* (1978).

The second book reviewed is C. Day Lewis's *The Poetic Image*.

That poetry, technically speaking, is essentially compressed and patterned metaphor is the practicing definition of most modern poets of stature. Of course, the phrase 'patterned metaphor' contains whole labyrinths of implication which many critics have explored and will explore ever more deeply. But it is always helpful to learn what poets themselves say on their art, particularly when, like both Wallace Stevens and Cecil Day Lewis, they refuse to lose

308

themselves in the labyrinths, but try honestly to keep sight of the relation between what they do and what goes on in the rest of the world of life and thought.

Stevens's little book contains a prose essay ('The Realm of Resemblance') and two poems, all on the subject of metaphor. Poetry, says the essay, has reality as its central reference, for the resemblance between things is one of the 'significant components of the structure of reality.' In the imagination, as in nature, fortuitous relationships are created by such qualities and concepts as color, sex, time; they bind parts of reality together, suggesting an underlying unit. Stevens has been called hedonist, pluralist and Platonist, and this essay curiously justifies all three labels, especially the last. The point he so beautifully makes about the difference between resemblance and imitation, the poet as pleasure giver and as revealer or transformer of reality, and the true value of ambiguity are basically Platonic; so too are the consideration of what narcissism really is (the ego's search for resemblance in the outside world) and, by way of this consideration, of the relation between metaphor and the ideal.

The first of the two poems that follow is an exact poetic equivalent of the essay. Stevens had suggested a close relation between euphuism and the 'school of metaphor.' The poem, a long one entitled 'Someone Puts a Pineapple Together,' does, by its ingenuity and profusion, its attempt to show the total sum of meanings and impressions of a simple object, exemplify this kinship with an overflow of wit that surpasses Cyrano's moon speech. But neither here nor in the next poem, 'Of Ideal Time and the Choice,' is Stevens content merely to produce an infinite series of imagistic and intellectual variations on a single theme. He explains, in the 'Pineapple' poem, that the multiple meanings seen by the imagination, the tangents of himself, are used to 'protect him in a privacy,' but that nevertheless the 'incredible subjects of poetry' have their special function; 'the incredible,' as he puts it, 'gave him a purpose to believe.' This idea, together with the concern for resemblance, becomes in the third poem a program for idealists who would free themselves from the limitations of ordinary life.

309

The orator will say that we ourselves
Stand at the centre of ideal time,
The inhuman making choice of a human self.

75. Marius Bewley, on the relation between Stevens' early and later poetry, from 'The Poetry of Wallace Stevens', *Partisan Review*

Vol. 16, September 1949, 895–915

Bewley (1918–73) is author of *The Complex Fate* (1952), *The Eccentric Design* (1959) and *Masks and Mirrors* (1970).

A key document of what may be called the 'middle period' of Stevens criticism, the full text of Bewley's wide-ranging essay is readily available in *The Complex Fate* and elsewhere. Here, the substantial exegetical centre of the essay is omitted. The opening paragraphs and several pages at the close are included because they provide a useful summary of the prevailing critical position and one account of the relationship between *Harmonium* and Stevens' later work.

A good deal of criticism has been written by this time on the poetry of Wallace Stevens; and it is poetry that requires extensive analysis in the beginning if it is finally to be read with much intelligence. But that criticism has not been consistently accurate or helpful, and some of the best of it – an essay by the late Hi Simons in *Sewanee Review*, for example – is now forgotten in the files of literary periodicals. R. P. Blackmur's essay in *The Double Agent* is still illuminating, and, fortunately, still available; but the only other easily accessible extended essay is Yvor Winters' acrid attack, 'Wallace Stevens, or the Hedonist's Progress,' which is extremely misleading in its conclusions. And even these articles (Blackmur's and Winters') were written early, and deal almost exclusively with *Harmonium*. The result of this critical situation is that there has been a persistent bias in favour of Stevens' first volume, and this has led to an underestimation of the importance of meaning in his work as a whole. Yet Stevens deserves his reputation partly because his meaning is an important one, and because that meaning has been consistently developing from *Harmonium* towards the maturity of the late work. I do not wish to imply that the central meaning in Stevens' poetry is not present in *Harmonium* just as much as in *Transport to Summer*, but it is present in a hidden way, and also in a less mature way, and it is sometimes extremely difficult to come by. Marianne Moore once wrote: 'Wallace Stevens: the interacting veins of life between his early and late poems are an ever-continuing marvel to me.' It is only by tracing out some of these veins of interaction that one can ever be *quite* sure, at least in the early poems, that one knows in fulness of detail what Stevens is talking about.

The relation, then, of Stevens' late work to his early work is not one of conflict or supersession. But neither would it be correct to say that the late work related to the early as the sum of a problem relates to the digits it totals, for something has been added in the late work that was not present, in however piecemeal a state, before. What this addition is may be only a complex balance, an infusion of remarkable poise, but it *is* new. And despite those critics who think *Harmonium* the best of the volumes, it was needed. Its presence may have contributed to that sense of change in Stevens' work that led some critics in the late 'thirties to think he had taken up the social burden; but actually what was being taken up were the familiar meanings of the early verse, but taken up in a new way by the imagination – taken up, in fact, into what was sometimes a new dimension of poetic reality (new, at any rate for Stevens), and occasionally one could turn aside and look downward from the new use to the old use of an identical image, and realize with a sense of delicious discovery that one now, perhaps, really read the earlier poem for the first time....

But if Mr. Winters and others have frequently thought of Stevens as an aesthete, and even a Hedonist – Stevens has not always been prudent about the poetry he has allowed to be published. Stevens used to be thought of as an unvoluminous writer, but in recent years, despite the excellence of *Transport to Summer* (undoubtedly his best volume), and what he has published since, he has allowed too many of his practice poems to appear. *Parts of a World* seems to me to number among its sixty-five titles very little of genuine distinction. For one thing, Stevens had progressed far enough in the expression of his meaning in his early volumes that a group of miscellaneous poems, all intent on saying, willy-nilly, pretty much the same thing in a wide (but related) variety of metaphors could add nothing to his achievement, and I frequently find the monotonous shadow of these poems falling over the real quality of his late work, and marring the purity of response. 'A Dish of Peaches in Russia,' for example, seems regrettable to me:

> The peaches are large and round,
>
> Ah! and red; and they have peach fuzz, ah!
> They are full of juice and the skin is soft.
>
> They are full of the colours of my village
> And of fair weather, summer, dew, peace.
> ....
> I did not know
>
> That such ferocities could tear
> One self from another, as these peaches do.

No doubt peaches can strike off imaginative feats in the proper observer, but that 'and they have peach fuzz, ah!' leaves me uneasy. It doesn't seem to be leading up to the 'ferocities' in the last verse. But Stevens' subject-matter cannot be condemned because it happens, in this poem, to have failed disastrously. A good artist is entitled to his failures (if only he wouldn't publish them), and the failure here is not one of theory but one of practice. Imagination as subject-matter (implicit here, of course) is bound to look a little mauve and decadent if, in a given instance, it is unable to strain beyond Fancy.

I have made a point of this poem because it seems suggestive in several ways about Stevens' development as a poet. The enamelled images of *Harmonium* had carried certain limitations of expression with them, but they were sometimes of great beauty and peculiar subtlety. If in the late 'thirties Stevens did not actually, as some competent critics imagined, acquire a social consciousness, there does appear to have been a shift in his mode of experiencing – a gradual change in his verse rhythms. What was happening had nothing to do with taking up the social burden, but there was a withdrawal in Stevens' poetry from the predominance of the image, and Stevens (perhaps partly because of the shock of the war, although the change had begun earlier) began to feel increasingly in terms of an inquisitive and flexible line – a line capable of making deeper explorations and wider applications of his images to social reality than had been possible in many of his earlier saffron-starched verses. *Parts of a World* is unsuccessful (but this is said with a view only to explaining the success of his later work) because the conspicuous metaphor is still making a strong bid for controlling interest, but is steadily being supplanted by a new rhythmical interest which follows more closely the movements of the questioning and generous mind. And yet neither a balance nor an interesting tension is usually achieved in this volume between the two elements. They behave towards each other with the easy nonchalance of bar companions, and this is the more remarkable in that some of the poems treat of the nature of poetry itself with unusual insight. In *Transport to Summer* (although the dates of the composition of the poems in these two volumes must have overlapped) the balance is righted, and 'Notes Toward a Supreme Fiction,' reprinted in this book, will possibly be Stevens' greatest achievement, and it should be one of the great adornments of American literature – a set of thirty meditations on the nature of the imagination.

Finally, we have another of Stevens' best poems, 'A Primitive Like an Orb.' In this poem the transition he has been making from an imagistically to a rhythmically controlled consciousness (this in itself implies something that might be mistaken for a social consciousness) is triumphantly completed; but not, it is interesting to note, without the assistance of Eliot's late poetry, which, without being derivative, it yet somehow resembles. It might be repetitious here to discuss this poem at any length, but I cannot drop the matter without commenting on the singular propriety of the title. We have seen how the adjective 'primitive,' as a term of general application, signifies the triumph of the imagination in the world of Stevens' meaning. As a work of art, 'primitive' carries the same meaning, but focussed more insistently on the imagination's goal of operation. In this sense its opposition to the academic and conventional is almost rhetorical. But since the 'Primitive' of the title aims at achieving an imaginative unity in diversity, at seeing the wholeness behind each fragment of experience, it is a primitive shaped like an orb. And the 'orb' is nothing less than the age-old circle of perfection which can be symbolized even in a little drop of dew, of which Marvell wrote:

> ...the clear Region where 'twas born
> Round in itself encloses:
> And in its little Globes extent
> Frames as it can its native Element.

Harmonium, good as it is, has been praised excessively at the expense of the late work, and the late work has a habit of being confused with 'transition' work; but in spite of all such confusions Stevens is almost certainly (after the two exceptions earlier noted) the most considerable figure that American poetry has produced in this century. His meaning, insofar as it is operative within the fabric of his verse, has none of the immaturity that Winters accused it of, and it is large and coherent enough to form the basis of an important body of expression. Furthermore, its meaning is traditional, and it relates, in a way unusual in American art, to a European past. I do not mean that Stevens' poetry is a sycophant of Europe, but only that the tradition in which he thinks and feels and writes is not a provincial backwater. It is part of the main current, and one does not feel strange in speaking of him in relation to the great traditional non-American poets. He is validly related.

And he has a particular significance for our time. He has been immediately and painfully aware of the cultural disintegration that has closed in with such vehemence since the end of World War I. Perhaps in as intense a way as Yeats (the subject-matter of his poetry has been even more directly concerned) he has known that 'the centre does not hold,' and his Princeton lecture contains one or two of the most anguished passages dealing with our cultural tragedy that come to mind. It is in relation to his sense of the catastrophic fragmentariness of the contemporary world that his belief in the unifying power of the imagination has achieved such rare distinction. It cannot, in the nature of the case, offer a solution theoretically as complete as Eliot's Christianity, but it does offer a reality that sometimes seems to be almost the unbaptized blood-brother of Eliot's reality – and it is a reality that finds frequent, but by no means invariable, realization in the poetry itself.

THE AURORAS OF AUTUMN

New York, 1950

Knopf published 3,000 copies. A second printing of 1,000 copies followed in November 1952.

76. Louise Bogan, 'His emotions seem to be transfixed', *New Yorker*

Vol. 26, no. 36, 28 October 1950, 111–12

Also mentioned briefly is the first book-length study of Stevens, William Van O'Connor's *The Shaping Spirit* (New York, 1950) (see No. 77).

Wallace Stevens is the American poet who has based his work most firmly upon certain effects of nineteenth-century Symbolist poetry. The title of his latest volume, *The Auroras of Autumn* (Knopf), indicates that his powers of language have not declined; here is one of those endlessly provocative, 'inevitable' phrases that seem to have existed forever in some rubied darkness of the human imagination – that imagination with whose authority and importance Stevens has been continually occupied in his later period. This preoccupation was once implicit in what he wrote; his images performed their work by direct impact. Stevens' later explicit, logical, and rather word-spinning defense of the role of the imagination has weakened or destroyed a good deal of his original 'magic.' The whole texture and coloration of his later verse is more austere; his subjects are less luxuriant and eccentric; even his titles have quieted down. What has always been true of him is now more apparent: that no one can describe the simplicities of the natural world with more direct skill. It is a natural world strangely empty of human beings, however; Stevens' men and women are bloodless symbols. And there is something theatrical in much of his writing; his emotions seem to be transfixed, rather than released and projected, by his extraordinary verbal improvisations. Now that he is so widely imitated, it is important to remember that his method is a special one; that modern poetry has developed transparent, overflowing, and spontaneous qualities that Stevens ignores. It is also useful to remember (as Apollinaire knew) that since the imagination is part of life, it must have its moments of awkwardness and naïveté, and must seek out forms in which it may move and breathe easily, in order that it may escape both strain and artificiality.

77. William Van O'Connor, Stevens' narrowing theme, 'that we are haunted by the idea of death', *Poetry*

Vol. 77, no. 2, 19 November 1950, 109–12

O'Connor (1915–66) was the author of the first book-length study of Wallace Stevens, *The Shaping Spirit: A Study of Wallace Stevens* (1950), chiefly notable for drawing attention to Stevens' theories about poetry. O'Connor wrote a number of other books, including *Sense and Sensibility in Modern Poetry* (1948).

When *Harmonium* was issued in 1928 Wallace Stevens was forty-four years old. In October of 1950, shortly after the publication of *The Auroras of Autumn*, he will be seventy-one.

Because he was older than most poets publishing a first book and because he worked inside the same subject matter, enlarging and qualifying it, there is a remarkable consistency among his volumes. But there are differences too. There is a touch of melancholy in *Harmonium*, but it is the melancholy of *Twelfth Night* or *The Merchant of Venice*, the pleasant melancholy, partly satiety, that comes with knowing and enjoying the richness of the world:

> I do not know which to prefer,
> The beauty of inflections
> Or the beauty of innuendos,
> The blackbird whistling
> Or just after.

With *Transport to Summer* (1947) the melancholy is deeper:

> Time is a horse that runs in the heart, a horse
> Without a rider on a road at night.
> The mind sits listening and hears it pass.

In *The Auroras of Autumn*, it is deepest of all. We live as in the earlier volumes in a theatre of trope, of changing appearances:

> It is a theatre floating through the clouds,
> Itself a cloud, although of misted rock
> And mountains running like water, wave on wave,
>
> Through waves of light. It is of cloud transformed
> To cloud transformed again, idly, the way
> A season changes color to no end, ...

It is the same wondrous world, made out of words, but it is a more frightening world:

> There is nothing until in a single man contained,
> Nothing until this named thing nameless is
> And is destroyed. He opens the door of his house
>
> On flames. The scholar of one candle sees
> An Arctic effulgence flaring on the frame
> Of everything he is. And he feels afraid.

In 'Disillusionment of Ten O'Clock,' from *Harmonium*,

Stevens was saddened by a world without imagination – the people going to bed in their, white nightgowns would not 'dream of baboons and periwinkles.' He himself dreamed of a world of lutes, wigs, parasols, masques, peristyles, duchesses and barouches, a world of elegant decor. The man with imagination is more completely alive. But, as Conrad knew, and as Stevens of *The Auroras of Autumn* knows, the man with imagination lives not only in a more magnificent but in a more terrifying world:

> Is there an imagination that sits enthroned
> As grim as it is benevolent, the just
> And the unjust, which in the midst of summer stops
>
> To imagine winter? When the leaves are dead
> Does it take its place in the north and enfold itself,
> Goat-leaper, crystalled and luminous, sitting
> In highest night?

The Auroras of Autumn has a more persistently held to and perhaps narrower theme than any of the earlier volumes. It is that we are haunted by the idea of death, when we will cease to create the world in which we live. The theme is fairly explicit in 'Puella Parvula':

[Quotes the poem, *CP*, p. 456.]

The one stability is the imagination, the agent of change; we live in the world she shows us: 'The fire burns as the novel taught it how,' or 'words of the world are the life of the world,' or 'what we think is never what we see.'[1]

Selden Rodman says that despite the references to the physical world, even the catalogues of insects, birds, trees and fruits, he is not convinced of Stevens' preoccupation with the physical world.' Reading Yeats, on the other hand, he is 'convinced of a passionate interest in both the physical world and man.' Certainly there is an essential difference between the two poets. Stevens' reality is not Yeats' 'blood and mire of human veins' or 'this pragmatical, preposterous pig of a world, its farrow that so solid, seems.'[2] But in the long poem 'An Ordinary Evening in New Haven' Stevens has written his own answer to this argument:

319

It is not in the premise that reality
Is a solid. It may be a shade that traverses
A dust, a force that traverses a shade.

The American world of William James, John Dewey, Theodore Dreiser, Ernest Hemingway, Carl Sandburg, Vernon Parrington, *et al.*, has insisted that this 'is a pragmatical, preposterous pig of a world' – and it is. But it is also Mr. Stevens' world –

The less legible meaning of sounds, the little reds
Not often realized, the lighter words
In the heavy drum of speech.

Yeats too of course was keenly aware of those meanings that seem to be 'too subtle for the intellect.'

The aesthetic with which Stevens has been allied has never been popular in America, although we are now much more appreciative of it and willing to grant that it too is involved with 'reality,' probably in crucial ways. In France it was summarized by Anatole France, in England by Pater in the famous 'Conclusion' to his *Renaissance*, and in America it had its beginnings with Edgar Saltus, James Huneker, Lafcadio Hearn, Percival Pollard, and Vance Thompson. Later it belonged to the magazine *Others*, to James Branch Cabell, to Elinor Wylie, Carl Van Vechten, to the young F. Scott Fitzgerald – and to Wallace Stevens. It was an aesthetic which did very well in France, rather poorly in England, and for the most part very badly in America. In America it produced mostly wax flowers and undoubtedly destroyed certain careers. But Fitzgerald in fiction and Stevens in poetry were able to modify it, to make it thoroughly their own, to adapt it to American subjects, to their own themes, and to make it live. For the twenty-seven years since the publication of *Harmonium*, which as is generally known sold fewer than a hundred copies before being remaindered, Stevens has continued, usually with no very loud applause in his ears, to perfect his art. The Bollingen Prize for Poetry in 1950 was the first 'big prize' he has received. *The Auroras of Autumn* is in the same tradition, of elegance, of unique observations, of wit, of discriminations pushed at least two removes beyond what was expected – an art that still respects the highly individualized imagination:

> Likewise to say of the evening star,
> The most ancient light in the most ancient sky,
> That it is wholly an inner light, that it shines
> From the sleepy bosom of the real, recreates,
> Searches a possible for its possibleness.

NOTES

1 The source of this remark has not been traced.
2 These phrases from Yeats, both somewhat misquoted, are from 'Byzantium' and 'Blood and the Moon'.

78. David Daiches, on 'a master of poetic artifice, perhaps the most perfect in our time', *Yale Review*

Vol. 40, no. 2, December 1950, 355–6

Daiches (b. 1912) was Professor of English and American Literature at the University of Sussex, 1961–77. His many books include *A Critical History of English Literature* and studies of Milton, Burns, Scott and Stevenson.

Also reviewed are collections by E. E. Cummings, Delmore Schwartz, Howard Nemerov, Peter Viereck and John Frederick Nims.

...Wallace Stevens is, in his own way, a master of poetic artifice, perhaps the most perfect in our time. He is not one of the most versatile of our poets: his lines show little variety in weight and cadence, and his devices are relatively few, if always cunningly used. In his work it is the *imagery* that makes the poems, and the imagery is presented, for the most part, in slowly marching lines, to produce a sequence that mysteriously yields a revelation both utterly strange and utterly familiar. In this combination of strangeness and familiarity, achieved by imagery, lies much of the secret of his appeal.

This kind of poetry has its own dangers. It can go on and on, and we are spellbound, convinced that there is a deep poetry there if only we could locate it. But sometimes it is only a trick, a cunningly cultivated mannerism, the work of a man who has written much effective poetry in this style and can now (he thinks) depend on the style alone. 'This,' we say as we read, 'has the accent of poetry: I must return to it sometime and see what it really is.' But though Stevens has his own 'Parnassian' (to use one of Gerard Hopkins' terms), he rises above it often enough in this volume to make it a valuable as well as a fascinating collection, though not so valuable as *Harmonium* or *The Man with the Blue Guitar*, which remain his most consistently exciting books....

79. Jean Garrigue, on Stevens' 'essential prose', 'Search for Reality in New Haven', *Saturday Review*

Vol. 34, no. 6, 10 February 1951, 17–18

Jean Garrigue (1914–72), a poet and short-story writer, was the author of *A Country Without Maps* (1964).

In a dandaical poem entitled 'The Novel,' where he is rather playfully engaged with the toughness of equating perception against what is but why is it, Wallace Stevens says: 'The fire burned as the novel taught it how.' This is playfulness. But it is playfulness on a theme central to this book: the old theme of Art versus Reality, the Real versus its twin, the Non-Real, the old theme of the World versus the Mind that must regard the World faithfully. Stevens has wrought as many subtle variations on this pliant theme as might a painter choosing to interpret the same subject under differing lights from differing vantage points over and over again. 'Like a book at evening beautiful but untrue / like a book on rising beautiful and true.'

Years ago in *Harmonium* Stevens announced his poetic intention: 'He could not be content with counterfeit / With masquerade of thought, with hapless words... No, no, veracious page on page, exact.' Until 'He gripped more closely the Essential prose / As being, in a world so falsified, / The one integrity for him.' So be it. These poems are that – 'essential prose' of philosophical wit, working with 'sharp informations, sharp, free knowledges' – poems on the mind considering the world ... 'That which thinks not, feels not, resembling thought, resembling feeling.'

There are also poems about the poem, and then there are sheer lyrics, pure, weighty, marvelous. The muse of these lyrics is still 'purple.' But in general the muse of this sixth volume wears white and dictates in shades upon shades of white. Of course she too is still playful: with the old wordmaking – the boo-ha of the wind, the miff-maff-muff of water, the tink-tonk of the rain; the old dude words that gather around them the charm of being really untranslatable, words such as 'tournamonde,' for example; the old Latinities like *fulgor* that make such an awesome glitter in the midst of Saxon nouns. There are the old eccentric, oblique metaphor – 'The sun stands like a Spaniard' – the virtuoso phrases – 'fidgets of a fire,' 'a qualm of cold' – the operatic sighs of 'bella,' 'buffo,' 'perdu' – and then sheer Stevensiana – 'Effete green, the woman in black cassimere.'

There are the old personae – Professor Eucalyptus has now joined the ranks of those like Crispin or Nanzia Nunzio who boldly clap on masks of this lonely orator in space and clouds. But note: it is Professor Eucalyptus now, not merely a Polish Aunt, Peter Quince, or the lesser stage hands. And Professor Eucalyptus is not residing in Yucatan nor on the venereal soil of Florida. Professor Eucalyptus, like 'a philosopher practising his scales,' resides in New Haven, town of most essential prose, and he ruminates celestially, with just that prose purity and classic respect for things that Crispin went all out for in *Harmonium*. Above all he ruminates in a 'prose' of poetry so pure that it is like a music to be sung in the mind only. It has divested itself of caracole-cutting and figured somersault-turning, of delicate quiddities, and secretive, half-concealed antics. It is round now and out in the open, quiet, *white*, it is to be repeated, not *purple*. But why not?

For what is the subject of this 'prose'? It is what Professor Eucalyptus said: 'The search / For reality is as momentous as / The search for god.' And the search for that is not in Yucatan or Florida but in New Haven, closest to home, where it always hurts the most. 'Not grim Reality / But reality grimly seen / And spoken in paradisal parlance new.' That is it; a part of the clue, too, to this old quest by the new Eucalyptus. Consider this dialogue in which the Visitor declares: I am the angel of reality . . . I am one of you and being one of you / Is being and knowing what I am and know. / Yet I am the necessary angel of earth / Since in my sight you see the earth again, / Cleared of its stiff and stubborn, man-locked set.'

Such is the subject matter of these still, quiet poems, so musical in meditation, as ever so removed from the speaker, delivered from so serene and radiant a distance.

Stevens has long been known as the esthetician of the eye, of the way things look. But he has always been as interested in the philosophy of looking at the apple of his eye, the object. 'The plum survives its poems,' he has said. The plum is still doing that. But the Word, too, is still transforming by redescribing a part of the plum. But the Word must see, and see hard, the essential integrity of the plum. Read Stevens, who is talking of roses (but it could be plums!): 'We are two that use these roses as we are / In seeing them. This is what makes them seem / So far beyond the rhetorician's touch.' So

324

the angelic battle for the faithful way, the realest way of
seeing things is sustained. While it is not to be forgotten that
against that –

> The plainness of plain things is savagery,
> As: the last plainness of a man who has fought
> Against illusion and was, in a great grinding
>
> Of growling teeth, and falls at night, snuffed out
> By the obese opiates of sleep.

80. M. L. Rosenthal, 'Stevens in a Minor Key', *New Republic*

Vol. 124, 7 May 1951, 26–8

> Swatara, Swatara, black river,
> Descending, out of the cap of midnight,
> Toward the cape at which
> You enter the swarthy sea...

Had we but world enough and time, we would try to prove
the assertion that *The Auroras of Autumn* is the most
nostalgically philosophical of Wallace Stevens' volumes. The
title itself suggests a paradoxical alliance of joy and sorrow,
beauty and death (to reduce the unreducible to a crude
formula); and the first poem-sequence culminates in much
imaginative play around the idea of 'an unhappy people in a
happy world.' This sequence – the key to the book – begins
with a poem on the relation of reality to pure idea, and of
both to imagination, presenting the illusive shifting aspect of
these associations in the metaphor of a serpent:

> This is form gulping after formlessness
> Skin flashing to wished-for disappearances...

Slippery, dangerous shedding its old skin with each new insight, reality or meaning appears in many lights. Sometimes it seems to imply the existence at a higher level, of a 'master of the maze,' a comfortably Platonic guarantor of ultimate happiness and knowledge, at other times it seems decisively to deny any such possibility. Throughout the sequence, and for the rest of the book, there is a rich and complex poetic treatment of these basic motifs.

Readers familiar with Stevens' verse may gather from all this something of the manner in which he is working the same vein as before, and something of slightly changed emphasis of this book. The amazing image-making power, the musical skill, the subtle toying with words are as engaging as ever. There are still the off hand precision of phrase ('Wearing hats of angular flick and fleck'), the humorous formulations ('We'll give the week-end to wisdom, to Weisheit, the rabbi'), the self-ironies:

> This day writhes with what? The lecturer
> On this Beautiful World of Ours composes himself
> And hems the planet rose and haws it ripe...

But there is now probably more *argument*, with a relative subordination of the other elements. And a harder, darker note runs through the volume, a tragic note like that of the lines quoted at the head of this review. There is a new, less malleable pessimism:

> The day is great and strong –
> Pat his father was strong, that lies now
> In the poverty of dirt.

There is a bitterness – see 'In a Bad Time' at the sentimental assumption that to imagine an order in nature is to establish it or become part of it. In several pieces, Yeats' early poem 'The Lake Isle of Innisfree' is deliberately echoed' quoted, almost parodied as Stevens mercilessly worries the kind of romantic assumptions it embodies. It is to the savagely passionate older Yeats that Stevens (though his work rarely approaches such intensity) seems to feel most akin.

Like Yeats, for instance, he invents his deity. But Stevens' god, 'the spectre of the spheres,' is contrived in his own image – a proliferator of resemblances and connoisseur of distinctions in experience and definition that would drive a conscientious Rorschach tester haggard to his final rest. He is a pragmatic sort of god, who has created an expanding, unpredictable, impersonal universe so that its endless possibilities of delight and honour can be a challenge to his probing imagination:

> ... he meditates a whole
> The full of torture and the full of fate,
> As if he lived all lives, that he might know.

But in contriving such a god, Stevens is managing to kid his own facile curiosity just a little. Thus, he explains the tragic dilemma of mankind as the poet-god's device for balancing off all conceivable meanings so that he can understand them 'down to a haggling o wind or weather.' Obviously, he could not have gained half so much by arranging 'a happy people in a happy world' ('Buffo! a ball, an opera, a bar') or 'an unhappy people in an unhappy world' ('too many mirrors for misery'). The old Platonic scale of values was much more dependable than this experimental, fifty-fifty universe. The poet is nostalgic for it, as he is nostalgic for that other frail edifice against things as they really – probably – are: the family of his childhood, with its remembered security, love and innocence:

> Farewell to an idea.... The mother's face,
> The purpose of the poem, fills the room.
> They are together, here, and it is warm.

Though a number of these poems have the force of personal memory, none is autobiographical in much detail. Rather they bring into strong emotional focus the pathos and the bravery of man's desire to read something human into the intractable system of nature, that 'color of ice and fire and solitude,' by seeing it as a progression of ideas or memories or projections of his own needs. Yet the paradoxes of will and fatality are such (and this is another link with Yeats) that the slightest adjustment of the poet's sights can lead to a reversal of this focus. It suddenly becomes possible to defy the too-scientific god of perhaps and probability:

The meanings are our own –
It is a text that we shall be needing.
To be the footing of noon,
The pillar of midnight,
That comes from ourselves, neither from knowing
Nor not knowing, yet free from question,
Because we wanted it so
And it had to be.

And it becomes equally possible, in the sad speech of the 'angel of reality' that concludes the book, to dissolve once more that mood of courage in the acid of truth's essential 'tragic drone.' Stevens may not be able to tell us (and we doubt that he ought to try) where to go from here; *here* is, and how good and evil and true and untrue it is, he can help us to discover.

81. Randall Jarrell, 'Reflections on Wallace Stevens', *Partisan Review*

Vol. 18, May–June 1951, 335–44

Jarrell (1914–65), an American poet, translator, novelist and children's writer, has written some of the most distinguished critical commentary on American poetry. Of his several critical collections, still the best-known and most influential is *Poetry and the Age* (1955), which includes the present essay. His *Complete Poems* was published in 1969.

As he did with William Carlos Williams' *Paterson*, Jarrell became progressively less enchanted with Stevens' poetry, until he came to make his final overview of *Collected Poems* (see no. 106).

Let me begin with a quotation from Stendhal: ' "What I find completely lacking in all these people," thought Lucien, "is the unexpected...." " He was reduced to philosophizing.' In my quotation Lucien stands for Stevens, 'these people' for America and Business, 'the unexpected' for Culture, the exotic, the past, the Earth-minus-America; 'philosophizing' stands for, alas! philosophizing.... But before Stevens was reduced to it, he drew the unexpected from a hundred springs. There has never been a travel poster like *Harmonium*: how many of its readers must have sold what they had, given the money to steamship agents, and gone to spend the rest of their lives in Lhasa. Yet there was nothing really unusual in what Stevens felt. To have reached, in 1900, in the United States, the age of twenty-one, or fifteen, or twelve – as Stevens and Pound and Eliot did – this was so hard a thing for poets, went so thoroughly against the grain, that they emigrated as soon as they could, or stayed home and wrote poems in which foreignness, pastness, is itself a final good. 'But how absurd!' a part of anyone protests. 'Didn't they realize that, to a poet, New York City means just as much as Troy and Jerusalem and all the rest of those *immensely overpaid accounts* that Whitman begged the Muse, *install'd amid the kitchenware*, to cross out?' They didn't realize it; if one realizes it, one is not a poet. The accounts have been overpaid too many years for people ever to stop paying; to keep on paying them is to be human. To be willing to give up Life for the last local slice of it, for all those Sears Roebuck catalogues which, as businessmen and generals say, would be the most effective propaganda we could possibly drop on the Russians – this is a blinded chauvinism, a provincialism in space and time, which is even worse than that vulgar exoticism which disregards both what we have kept and what we are unique in possessing, which gives up *Moby Dick* for the Journals of André Gide. Our most disastrous lacks – delicacy, awe, order, natural magnificence and piety, 'the exquisite errors of time,' and the rest; everything that is neither bought, sold, nor imagined on Sunset Boulevard or in Times Square; everything the absence of which made Lorca think Hell a city very like New York – these things were the necessities of Stevens' spirit. Some of his poems set about supplying these lacks – from other times and places, from the underlying order of things, from the imagination; other poems look with mockery and despair at the time and place that cannot supply them, that do not even desire to supply them; other poems reason or seem to reason about their loss, about their nature, about their improbable restoration. His poetry is obsessed with lack, a lack at last almost taken for granted, that he himself automatically supplies; if sometimes he has restored by imagination or abstraction or re-creation, at other times he has restored by collection, almost as J.P. Morgan did – Stevens likes something, buys it (at the expense of a little spirit), and ships it home in a poem. The feeling of being a leisured, cultivated, and sympathetic tourist (in a time-machine, sometimes) is essential to much of his work; most of his contact with values is at the distance of knowledge and regret – an aesthetician's or an archaeologist's contact with a painting, not a painter's.

Many of Stevens' readers have resented his – so to speak – spending his time collecting old porcelain: 'if old things are what you want,' they felt, 'why don't you collect old Fords or Locomobiles or Stutz Bearcats, or old Mother Bloors, right here at home?' But, for an odd reason, people have never resented the cruel truths or half-truths he told them about the United States. Once upon a time Richard Dehmel's poems, accused of obscenity, were acquitted on the grounds that they were incomprehensible – and almost exactly this happened to Stevens' home-truths. Yet they were plain, sometimes. Looking at General Jackson confronting the 'mockers, the mickey mockers,' Stevens decided what the 'American Sublime' is: the sublime 'comes down / To the spirit itself, / The spirit and space, / The empty spirit / In vacant space.' Something like this is true, perhaps, always and everywhere; yet it is a hard truth for your world to have reduced you to: it is no wonder the poem ends, 'What wind does one drink? / What bread does one eat?' And in 'The Common Life' the church steeple is a 'black line beside a white line,' not different in any way from 'the stack of the electric plant'; in the 'flat air,' the 'morbid light,' a man is 'a result, a demonstration'; the men 'have no shadows / And the women only one side.' We live 'no longer on the ancient cake of seed, / The almond and deep fruit ... We feast on human heads'; the table is a mirror and the diners eat reflections of themselves. 'The steeples are empty and so are the people,' he says in 'Loneliness in Jersey City'; the poem is full of a despairing frivolity, as Stevens looks from Room 2903 out over that particular countryside which, I think, God once sent angels to destroy, but which the angels thought worse than anything they could do to it. And 'In Oklahoma, / Bonnie and Josie, / Dressed in calico, / Danced around a stump. / They cried, / "Ohoyaho, / Ohoo" ... / Celebrating the marriage / Of flesh and air.' Without what's superfluous, the excess of the spirit, man is a poor, bare, forked animal. In 'Country Words' the poet sits under the willows of exile, and sings 'like a cuckoo clock' to Belshazzar, that 'putrid rock, / putrid pillar of a putrid people'; he sings 'an old rebellious song, / An edge of song that never clears.' But if it should clear, if the cloud that hangs over his heart and mind should lift, it would be because Belshazzar heard and understood:

> What is it that my feeling seeks?
> I know from all the things it touched
> And left beside and left behind.
> It wants the diamond pivot bright.
> It wants Belshazzar reading right
> The luminous pages on his knee,
> Of being, more than birth and death.
> It wants words virile with his breath.

If this intellectual is 'isolated,' it is not because he wants to be.... But Stevens' most despairing, amusing, and exactly realized complaint is 'Disillusionment of Ten O'Clock':

> The houses are haunted
> By white nightgowns.
> None are green,
> Or purple with green rings,
> Or green with yellow rings,
> Or yellow with blue rings.
> None of them are strange,
> With socks of lace

And beaded ceintures.
People are not going
To dream of baboons and periwinkles.
Only, here and there, an old sailor,
Drunk and asleep in his boots,
Catches tigers
In red weather.

Any schoolboy (of the superior Macaulayish breed) more or less feels what this poem means, but it is interesting to look at one or two details. Why *ten o'clock?* They have all gone to bed early, like good sensible machines; and the houses' ghosts, now, are only nightgowns, the plain white nightgowns of the Common Man, Economic Man, Rational Man – pure commonplace, no longer either individual or strange or traditional; and the dreams are as ordinary as the night-gowns. Here and there a drunken and disreputable *old sailor* still lives in the original reality (he doesn't dream of catching, he *catches*): *sailor* to bring in old-fashioned Europe, old-fashioned Asia, the old-fashioned ocean; *old* to bring in the past, to make him a dying survival. What indictment of the Present has ever compared, for flat finality, with 'People are not going / To dream of baboons and periwinkles'? Yet isn't this poem ordinarily considered a rather nonsensical and Learish poem?

It is not until later that Stevens writes much about what America has in common with the rest of the world; then he splits everything differently, and contrasts with the past of America and of the world their present. In *Harmonium* he still loves America best when he can think of it as wilderness, naturalness, pure potentiality (he treats with especial sympathy Negroes, Mexican Indians, and anybody else he can consider wild); and it is this feeling that is behind the conclusion of 'Sunday Morning':

She hears, upon that water without sound,
A voice that cries, 'The tomb in Palestine
Is not the porch of spirits lingering.
It is the grave of Jesus, where he lay.'
We live in an old chaos of the sun,
Or old dependency of day and night,

Or island solitude, unsponsored, free,
Of that wide water, inescapable.
Deer walk upon our mountains, and the quail
Whistle about us their spontaneous cries;
Sweet berries ripen in the wilderness;
And, in the isolation of the sky,
At evening, casual flocks of pigeons make
Ambiguous undulations as they sink
Downward to darkness, on extended wings.

Here – in the last purity and refinement of the grand style, as perfect, in its calm transparency, as the best of Wordsworth – is the last wilderness, come upon so late in the history of mankind that it is no longer seen as the creation of God, but as the Nature out of which we evolve; man without myth, without God, without anything but the universe which has produced him, is given an extraordinarily pure and touching grandeur in these lines – lines as beautiful, perhaps, as any in American poetry. Yet Stevens himself nearly equals them in two or three parts of 'Esthétique du Mal,' the best of his later poems; there are in *Harmonium* six or eight of the most beautiful poems an American has written; and a book like *Parts of a World* is delightful as a whole, even though it contains no single poem that can compare with the best in *Harmonium*. But *Auroras of Autumn,* Stevens' last book, is a rather different affair. One sees in it the distinction, intelligence, and easy virtuosity of a master—but it would take more than these to bring to life so abstract, so monotonous, so overwhelmingly *characteristic* a book. Poems like these are, always, the product of a long process of evolution; in Stevens' case the process has been particularly interesting.

The habit of philosophizing in poetry – or of seeming to philosophize, of using a philosophical tone, images, constructions, of having quasi-philosophical day-dreams – has been unfortunate for Stevens. Poetry is a bad medium for philosophy. Everything in the philosophical poem has to satisfy irreconcilable requirements: for instance, the last demand that we should make of philosophy (that it be

333

interesting) is the first we make of a poem; the philosophical poet has an elevated and methodical, but forlorn and absurd air as he works away at his flying tank, his sewing-machine that also plays the piano. (One thinks of Richard Wilbur's graceful 'Tom Swift has vanished too, / Who worked at none but wit's expense, / Putting dirigibles together, / Out in the yard, in the quiet weather, / Whistling behind Tom Sawyer's fence.') When the first thing that Stevens can find to say of the Supreme Fiction is that 'it must be *abstract*,' the reader protests, 'Why, even Hegel called it a *concrete* universal'; the poet's medium, words, is abstract to begin with, and it is only his unique organization of the words that forces the poem, generalizations and all, over into the concreteness and singularity that it exists for. But Stevens has the weakness – a terrible one for a poet, a steadily increasing one in Stevens of thinking of particulars as primarily illustrations of general truths, or else as aesthetic, abstracted objects, simply there to be contemplated; he often treats things or lives so that they seem no more than generalizations of an unprecedentedly low order. But surely a poet *has* to treat the concrete as primary, as something far more than an instance, a hue to be sensed, a member of a laudable category – for him it is a always the generalization whose life is derived, whose authority is delegated. Goethe said, quite as if he were talking about Stevens: 'It makes a great difference whether the poet seeks the particular in relation to the universal or contemplates the universal in the particular ... [In the first case] the particular functions as an example, as an instance of the universal; but the second indeed represents the very nature of poetry. He who grasps this particular as living essence also encompasses the universal.'

As a poet Stevens has every gift but the dramatic. It is the lack of immediate contact with lives that hurts his poetry more than anything else, that has made it easier and easier for him to abstract, to philosophize, to treat the living dog that wags its tail and bites you as the 'canoid patch' of the epistemologist analyzing that great problem, the world; as the 'cylindrical arrangement of brown and white' of the aesthetician analyzing that great painting, the world. Stevens knows better, often for poems at a time:

334

> At dawn,
> The paratroopers fall and as they fall
> They mow the lawn. A vessel sinks in waves
> Of people, as big bell-billows from its bell
> Bell-bellow in the village steeple. Violets,
> Great tufts, spring up from buried houses
> Of poor, dishonest people, for whom the steeple,
> Long since, rang out farewell, farewell, farewell.

This is a map with people living on it. Yet it is fatally easy for the scale to become too small, the distance too great, and us poor, dishonest people no more than data to be manipulated.

As one reads Stevens' later poetry one keeps thinking that he needs to be possessed by subjects, to be shaken out of himself, to have his subject individualize his poem; one remembers longingly how much more individuation there was in *Harmonium* – when you're young you try to be methodical and philosophical, but reality keeps breaking in. The best of *Harmonium* exists at a level that it is hard to rise above; and Stevens has had only faintly and intermittently the dramatic insight, the capacity to be obsessed by lives, actions, subject-matter, the chameleon's shameless interest in everything but itself, that could have broken up the habit and border and general sobering matter-of-factness of age. Often, nowadays, he seems disastrously set in his own ways, a fossil imprisoned in the rock of himself – the best marble but, still, marble.

All his *tunk-a-tunks,* his *hoo-goo-boos* – those mannered, manufactured, individual, uninteresting little sound-inventions – how typical they are of the lecture-style of the English philosopher, who makes grunts or odd noises, uses homely illustrations, and quotes day in and day out from *Alice,* in order to give what he says some appearance of that raw reality it so plainly and essentially lacks. These 'tootings at the wedding of the soul' are fun for the tooter, but get as dreary for the reader as do all the foreign words – a few of these are brilliant, a few more pleasant, and the rest a disaster: 'one cannot help deploring his too extensive acquaintance with the foreign languages,' as Henry James said, of Walt Whitman, to Edith Wharton.

Stevens is never more philosophical, abstract, rational, than when telling us to put our faith in nothing but immediate sensations, perceptions, aesthetic particulars; for this is only a generalization offered for assent, and where in the ordinary late poem are the real particulars of the world – the people, the acts, the lives – for us to put our faith in? And when Stevens makes a myth to hold together aesthetic particulars and generalizations, it is as if one were revisited by the younger Saint-Simon, Comte, and that actress who played Reason to Robespierre's approving glare; Stevens' myths spring not from the soil but from the clouds, the arranged, scrubbed, reasoning clouds in someone's head. He is too rational and composedly fanciful a being to make up a myth – one could as easily imagine his starting a cult in Los Angeles. When one reads most eighteenth-century writing one is aware of some man of good sense and good taste and good will at the bottom of everything and everybody; but in Stevens – who is always swinging between baroque and rococo, and reminds one of the eighteenth century in dozens of ways – this being at the bottom of everything is cultivated and appreciative and rational out of all reason: the Old Adam in everybody turns out to be not Robinson Crusoe but Bernard Berenson.

Metastasio began as an improviser and ended as a poet; as one reads the average poem in *Auroras of Autumn* one feels that the opposite has been happening to Stevens. A poem begins, revealingly: 'An exercise in viewing the world. / On the motive! But one looks at the sea / As one improvises, on the piano.' And not the sea only. One reads a book like this with odd mixed pleasure, not as if one were reading poems but as if one were reading some 'Travel-Diary of an Aesthetician,' who works more for pleasure than for truth, puts in entries regularly, and gives one continual pleasure in incidentals, in good phrases, interesting ideas, delicate perceptions, but who hardly tries to subordinate his Method to the requirements of any particular situation or material. The individual poems are less and less differentiated; the process is always more evident than what is being processed; everything is so familiarly contrived by will and habit and rule of thumb (for improvisation, as Virgil Thomson says,

'among all the compositional techniques is the one most
servile to rules of thumb') that it does not seem to matter
exactly which being is undergoing these immemorial metamorphoses. Stevens' passagework, often, is so usual that we
can't believe past the form to the matter: what truth could
survive these pastry-cook's, spun-sugar, parallel qualifications?

> It was like sudden time in a world without time,
> This world, this place, the street in which I was,
> Without time: as that which is not has not time,
> Is not, or is of what there was, is full....

And on the shelf below:

> It was nowhere else, it was there and because
> It was nowhere else, its place had to be supposed,
> Itself had to be supposed, a thing supposed
> In a place supposed, a thing that reached
> In a place that he reached....

It is G.E. Moore at the spinet. And it looks worst of all when
one compares it with a passage from that classic of our prose,
that generalizer from an Age of Reason, that hapless victim
of Poetic Diction, that – but let me quote:

> As Hags hold Sabbaths, less for joy than spite,
> So these their merry, miserable Nights;
> Still round and round the Ghosts of Beauty glide,
> And haunt the places where their Honor died.
>   See how the World its Veterans rewards!
> A Youth of Frolics, an old Age of Cards;
> Fair to no purpose, artful to no end,
> Young without Lovers, old without a Friend;
> A Fop their Passion, but their Prize a Sot;
> Alive, ridiculous, and dead, forgot!

The immediacy and precision and particularity, the live touch
of things, the beauty that exists in precarious perfection in so
many poems in *Harmonium* –

>   the beauty
> Of the moonlight
> Falling there,

Falling
As sleep falls
In the innocent air –

this, at last, is lost in rhetoric, in elaboration and artifice and contrivance, in an absolutely ecumenical method of seeing and thinking and expressing, in *craftsmanship:* why has no loving soul ever given Stevens a copy of that *Principles of Art* in which Collingwood argues at length – many people might say *proves* – that art is not a craft at all? (I hardly dare to quote one great poet's even more sweeping 'But I deny that poetry is an art.') In *Auroras of Autumn* one sees almost everything through a shining fog, a habitualness not just of style but of machinery, perception, anything: the green spectacles show us a world of green spectacles; and the reader, staring out into this Eden, thinks timidly: 'But it's all so *monotonous.'* When Marx said that he wasn't a Marxist he meant, I suppose, that he himself was not one of his own followers, could not be taken in by the prolongation and simplification of his own beliefs that a disciple would make and believe; and there is nothing a successful artist needs to pray so much as: 'Lord, don't let me keep on believing *only this;* let me have the courage of something besides my own convictions; let me escape at last from the maze of myself, from the hardening quicksilver womb of my own characteristicalness.'

I have felt as free as posterity to talk in this way of Stevens' weaknesses, of this later mold in which he has cast himself, since he seems to me – and seems to my readers, I am sure – one of the true poets of our century, someone whom the world will keep on reading just as it keeps on listening to Vivaldi or Scarlatti, looking at Tiepolo or Poussin. His best poems are the poetry of a man fully human – of someone sympathetic, magnanimous, both brightly and deeply intelligent; the poems see, feel, and think with equal success; they treat with mastery that part of existence which allows of mastery, and experience the rest of it with awe or sadness or delight. Minds of this quality of genius, of this breadth and delicacy of understanding, are a link between us and the past, since they are, for us, the past made living; and they are our surest link with the future, since they are the part of us which the future will know. As one feels the elevation and sweep and disinterestedness, the thoughtful truthfulness of the best sections of a poem like 'Esthétique du Mal,' one is grateful for, overawed by, this poetry that knows so well the size and age of the world; that reminds us, as we sit in chairs produced from the furniture exhibitions of the Museum of Modern Art, of that immemorial order or disorder upon which our present scheme of things is a monomolecular film; that counsels us – as Santayana wrote of Spinoza – 'to say to those little gnostics, to those circumnavigators of being: *I do not believe you; God is great.*' Many of the peoms look greyly out at 'the immense detritus of a world / That is completely waste, that moves from waste / To waste, out of the hopeless waste of the past / Into a hopeful waste to come'; but more of the poems see the unspoilable delights, the inexhaustible interests of existence – when you have finished reading Stevens' best poems you remember once more that man is not only the jest and riddle of the world, but the glory.

Some of my readers may feel about all this, 'But how can you reconcile what you say with the fact that *Auroras of Autumn* is not a good book? Shouldn't the Mature poet be producing late masterpieces even better than the early ones?' (They might ask the same thing about *The Cocktail Party.*) All such questions show how necessary it is to think of the poet as somebody who has prepared himself to be visited by a daemon, as a sort of accident-prone worker to whom poems happen – for otherwise we *expect* him to go on writing good poems, better poems, and this is the one thing you cannot expect even of good poets, much less of anybody else. Good painters in their sixties may produce good pictures as regularly as an orchard produces apples; but Planck is a great scientist because he made one discovery as a young man – and I can remember reading in a mathematician's memoirs a sentence composedly recognizing the fact that, since the writer was now past forty, he was unlikely ever again to do any important creative work in mathematics. A man who is a good poet at forty *may* turn out to be a good poet at sixty; but he is more likely to have stopped writing poems, to be doing exercises in his own manner, or to have reverted to whatever commonplaces were popular when he was young. A good poet is someone who manages in a lifetime of standing out in thunderstorms, to be struck by lightning five or six times; a dozen or two dozen times and he is great.

82. Vivienne Koch, 'The Necessary Angels of Earth', *Sewanee Review*

Vol. LIX, no. 4, October–December 1951, 664–7

Vivienne Koch (1914–61) was the author of *William Carlos Williams* (1950) and *W.B. Yeats: The Tragic Phase* (1952).

In this review she goes on to assess volumes by W.S. Graham, Nicholas Moore, Basil Bunting, Alfred Hayes, Kenneth Rexroth, Delmore Schwartz, Howard Nemerov, Oliver Evans, Sidney Alexander, Richard Wirtz Emerson, J.V. Cunningham and Pedro Salinas.

I agree with Mr. Wallace Stevens when, in angelic garb, he tells the *paysans* in 'Angel Surrounded By Paysans'

> Yet I am the necessary angel of earth,
> Since, in my sight, you see the earth again.

But not all poets are *necessarily* angels, and some, when they are, can be very irritating angels indeed. But Mr. Stevens is not one of these as my subsequent comments should make clear. He is an angel who does make us see the earth again.

We do not think of Mr. Stevens as a 'metaphysical' poet in the modern and strict sense of that word, yet the title of this collection of poems written since *Transport to Summer* (1947) points a paradox. Auroras, as possessed by Autumn, renders an unconventional association, something a bit like Yeats's 'Dawn, or the terrible novelty of light!' The progress of the seasons charted by Stevens' recent title is, of course, a progress toward winter. I think we can be confident the metaphor will continue into his next work. The obvious biographical correspondence which is one part of the metaphor produces in this reader, at any rate, a kind of shock. It is hard to remember, hearing the vibrance of his voice, that Stevens is 72 years old, the eldest living poet of the great renascence of poetry in our time.

The theme of *The Auroras of Autumn,* a theme that has engaged other poets, perhaps most notably Yeats, has been so searchingly isolated by Stevens and so swarms with possibilities for his interest that it seems to have become uniquely his. It is the theme of the mind creating its own reality and by this process – art – asserting an autonomy of the will which gives meaning to the vulgar 'real.' This theme inhabits a range of metaphysical speculation which, when barely stated, *without the poetry* (and here and dangers of this kind of discussion are evident), may seem alarmingly close to a jejune solipsism. But the lie is given by the poems. They are *there;* they are not merely the fictions of the monarch, mind, but the actual objective translation of its action. No modern poet has been more engaged by this dilemma, solved for Stevens each time he makes a poem. No other poet's total work is so cohesive in its intellectual consistency. It is the problem enunciated in *Harmonium* (1923), which secures its most meticulous statement in *The Man with the Blue Guitar* (1937) and is now recapitulated in this elegiac and beautiful – if a little too iterative – collection.

The aesthetic of the creative morality now appears deceptively as a subtle modulation of it. The title piece, a long poem, and the even longer 'An Ordinary Evening in New Haven,' present sequences of short lyric variations on this theme. It is one which in all of Stevens' work for thirty years reveals the wish in it. There is such a desperation of elegant straining after the 'actual' that sometimes the beautiful ritual of the search seems a vain beating with nets, webby nets of desire and want. But the poet who in the middle period was 'rex and imperator,' destroying the 'real' in order to create a new 'actual,' who later sang 'How simply the fictive hero becomes the real,' now attempts to say 'Farewell to an idea,' or the ideas of order expounded in grave archetypal images of Mother, Father, Home; for the responsibility put upon him for constructing so many parts of a world is terrifying:

> ... The scholar of one candle sees
> An Arctic effulgence flaring on the frame
> Of everything he is. And he feels afraid.

Against this chilling and death-like brilliance there is, nevertheless, a solace:

> There may always be a time of innocence.
> There is never a place. Or if there is no time,
> It is not a thing of time, nor of place,
>
> Existing in the idea of it, alone,
> In the sense against calamity, it is not
> Less real....

And in 'An Ordinary Evening in New Haven,' a sequence of 31 lyrics in identical form which move to a religious illumination of Stevens' whole poetic past, he begins with a simple 'placing' of the eternal question:

> The eye's plain version is a thing apart,
> The vulgate of experience. Of this,
> A few words, an and yet, and yet, and yet –
>
> As part of the never-ending meditation,
> Part of the question that is a giant himself:
> Of what is this house composed if not the sun,
>
> These houses, these difficult objects, dilapidate
> Appearance of what appearances.
>
> ...

But the process is never-ending for a second giant may kill the first, and the mythological form, 'A great bosom, beard and being, alive with age,' continually replenishes and re-creates its necessity. And in a passage curiously reminiscent of *Four Quartets.* (although the first and always present memory in Stevens is of Yeats),[a] only one of several in this collection echoing that source, he roots this necessity in a mystical progress:

> The point of vision and desire are the same
> It is to the hero of midnight that we pray
> On a hill of stones to make beau mont thereof.
>
> . . .
>
> Say next to holiness is the will thereto
> And next to love is the desire for love,
>
> . . .

Thus 'Real and unreal are two in one' and, in the end, all the parts of Stevens' 'mille-flored' world are fitted into a magical ritual intended to 'prove' 'that the theory / Of poetry is the theory of life.'

The Auroras of Autumn employs to this end every cunning art in Stevens' vast repertoire of rhetorical effects. The melodic line is Olympian in the grand final manner of Yeats, but the vocabularly is peculiarly Stevens' ('choses,' 'frere,' 'collops,' 'meta-men,' and 'ditherings,' for example, rubbing elbows in a choice fraternity of the holy and the profane) 'as if to know became / The fatality of seeing things too well' . . . .

NOTE

a See an overt token of this in 'Page from a Tale,' a charming idyll which weaves in whole lines from – of all things – 'The Lake Isle of Innisfree.'

83. Joseph Bennett, on 'a lifetime of patient devotion to the highest standards', from 'Some Notes on American Poetry', *Nine*

No. 8, Spring 1952, 261–4

A more diffuse version of these comments had already appeared in the *Hudson Review* (Spring 1951). In the present notes, Bennett goes on to consider the poetry of Cummings, Williams, Lowell and Wilbur, and ends by mentioning several poets who have 'lapsed' into confessionalism.

With regard to Bennett's remark that 'his verse remains unpublished in England', this was by no means the case; from 1922 on, Stevens' work had been included in a number of anthologies published in Britain. From 1944 on, the Fortune Press had made efforts to publish a Stevens collection. Half a year or so before the appearance of Bennett's notice, Faber & Faber had made arrangements to publish a selection in England. Subsequently, volumes were printed both by Fabers and the Fortune Press, though the latter was almost immediately withdrawn. The circumstances are outlined by George S. Lensing in 'Wallace Stevens in England', in *Wallace Stevens: A Celebration,* edited by Frank Doggett and Robert Buttel (Princeton, N.J., 1980).

The *Pisan Cantos* of Ezra Pound, the most important book of verse to appear in the United States since the war, are familiar to English readers. And both Allen Tate and John Crowe Ransom, fairly well known abroad, have been inactive as poets in the past years. But Wallace Stevens, who ranks with these men as a poet, has continued to produce without interruption. Unfortunately, his verse remains unpublished in England.

His recently published book *The Auroras of Autumn,* written entirely since the war, contains some of the finest work of his career:

[Quotes Section II of 'The Auroras of Autumn', *CP*, pp. 412–13.]

The cold pyrotechnics of the climax show an intensity unusual in Stevens, flaring up at the end of a line of subdued and unobtrusive movement – a line qualified and underplayed, but moving and shifting always forward from the first 'Farewell' until the harmonies are resolved and the final chord is ready to be spread in full orchestral color across the keyboard. Metrically faultless, the verses provide us with some of the finest music in the poetry of our time.

Throughout his volume, Mr. Stevens returns to the image of the aurora borealis, producing again and again an uncanny emotional identification with the glacial beauty of the northern sky, which suggests in its overtones the Land of Death, the Regions at the back of the North Wind. For effects of tranquillity,

> And yet she too is dissolved, she is destroyed.
> She gives transparence. But she has grown old
> The necklace is a carving not a kiss.

for the separating out of subtly differentiated keys which cluster around a central, abstracted poise, formation finesse, Stevens has no rival in modern verse. He can round out and detach material which resists definition to the point of being intractable to any other instrument but his own,

> Sleep realized
> Was the whiteness that is the ultimate intellect,
> A diamond jubilance beyond the fire

and structurally his work is extremely tight; the positioning, down to each comma, is of the inevitable. A lifetime of patient devotion to the highest standards lies behind this book, a book which is evidence of Stevens' extraordinary creative power in his late period of full mastery. The great show-pieces of his first volume *Harmonium* (1923) burn on undiminished in the poetic memory of our time, but the new work shows a greater subtlety, a quieter manipulation of effects, and an economy of means that give it an increasingly dexterous emotional range and an intellectuality that is markedly more luminous....

THE NECESSARY ANGEL

New York, 1951

A Knopf edition of 3,000 copies.

---

84. Winfield Townley Scott, 'Stevens and the Angel of Earth', *Providence Journal*

2 December 1951, Section VI, 8

Scott (1910–68), an American poet, was the author of *Collected Poems* (1962).

In a recent review the critic Cleanth Brooks touched upon a point which would in fact bear pages of investigation; Brooks remarked on the frequency with which the art is itself the subject of contemporary poetry. He cited Eliot and 'even Frost' as poets whose central concern, whose subject almost, is poetry. Oddly Brooks did not mention Wallace Stevens who, beyond any other poet eminent in our times, is obsessed in his verse with aesthetic theory. His poems are notably self-conscious, from the first of some decades ago – increasingly in these later years.

So it is not surprising that Stevens has also from time to time sought through addresses and essays to formulate his personal perceptions of the character and activity of poetry. Seven such papers are here gathered from the past 10 years to make Stevens' first prose book. He himself puts very well the difference between the aesthetic approach through poetry and through criticism; in poetry the poet, he says, will consciously or inadvertently reveal what he believes poetry

347

to be, but these 'are disclosures of poetry, not disclosures of definitions of poetry;' these chapters, then, 'are intended to disclose definitions.'

'The Necessary Angel' of the title is the 'angel of earth,' the imagination; ('necessary ... since, in my sight, you see the earth again'). 'What is the poet's subject? It is his sense of the world,' Stevens says. And for Stevens the method of poetry – indeed of all art – is a balance between 'the real' (which he uses in the everyday sense) and the artist's imaginative power. Disbalance is bad art. Stevens is especially concerned with the degeneration of the imagination into the merely 'romantic' or the merely fanciful. 'The imagination is the liberty of the mind. The romantic is a failure to make use of that liberty. It is to the imagination what sentimentality is to feeling.'

Poetry and philosophy, poetry and painting, the implements of poetry – analogy, and others – are all approaches to the central concern of these chapters, the nature of poetry. The prose is that of an earnest, devoted, sometimes humorous man, meticulous in the presentation of his thought. It is not, I suppose, the kind of book guaranteed to fetch hordes of readers; but readers interested in any of the contemporary arts will find Stevens' concepts widely applicable and his expression simple. Now that Eliot and Auden have made it fashionable to regard poetry as a sort of 'game,' it is heartening to hear from Wallace Stevens that poetry is 'one of the enlargements of life.'

85. Babette Deutsch, from 'Pastures of the Imagination', *New York Herald Tribune Books*

9 December 1951, 4

... In these papers, all but one of them read before critical audiences during the critical years of this past decade, Stevens is repeatedly pondering his favorite theme, that of the supreme fiction. He offers a number of definitions of poetry, as nearly satisfying as any such definitions can be. All of them gain by the richness of the context in which they are placed. All of them have obviously been composed by a man who understands not alone the craft but the endless interest, the superlative significance of the art that he practices so beautifully. If his poems occasionally suffer from his fondness for intellection and lean a little too much toward metaphysics, his prose gains by his ability to fetch up a thought from the deeper reaches of the mind with the rod of a poet and to play the flashing fighting thing in the sunlight before he swings it onto the bank....

There are some plummy aphorisms, such as the remark that the romantic 'is a failure of the imagination precisely as sentimentality is a failure of feeling.' There are a few dubious pages, such as that on which he mistakenly commends Stalin for being free from the 'cult of pomp,' or where he speaks of nobility as 'conspicuously absent from contemporary poetry.' Has Stevens never read his contemporary, St.-John Perse? What chiefly fills his mind and reverberates for us, however, is nothing at all doubtful. It is the give and take between reality, things as they are, life in all its physical and spiritual violence, on the one hand, and, on the other, imagination, which he somewhere defines as 'the sum of our faculties' and elsewhere as 'the power that enables us to perceive the normal in the abnormal, the opposite of chaos in

349

chaos.' He knows that 'the world about us would be desolate except for the world within us,' and he makes the most of both worlds. He writes about imagination almost as Coleridge might have done, could that great mind have divorced itself from its religious provincialism. He writes about the significance of poetry as Arnold might have, could he have stepped out from under the shadow of the Victorian schoolroom. He writes, of course, and most happily, like no one but Wallace Stevens, and we can only rejoice to attend.

86. Rolf Fjelde, 'from … the hieratic to the credible', *New Republic*

Vol. 126, 4 February 1952, 19–20

Fjelde (b 1926) was founding editor of the *Yale Poetry Review* and editor of *Poetry New York*. He has translated a number of Ibsen's plays.

The angel that presides over this collection of essays and addresses is the angel of reality. Perhaps this will surprise some readers already acquainted with Wallace Stevens' opulent, often difficult poems, disciplined (in his own phrase) to 'resist the intelligence almost successfully.' Certainly it should disturb anyone who interprets his work via Yvor Winters' impressive essay in *The Anatomy of Nonsense*, wherein the whole apparatus of English poetry since Pope rumbles through two centuries into its simultaneous culmination and decay in the figure of Wallace Stevens, the bankrupt hedonist. Such interpreters may have to amend their ideas.

The seven papers assembled here are mostly occasional

pieces, composed to be understood at a hearing. For this reason they are a body of notes rather than a systematic *ars poetica*. Nevertheless, they include some of the most incisive and useful insights into the nature of poetry given us by a modern master. Many of these cluster about Stevens' persistent, possibly central theme: the dilemma of the active imagination in a world drained of myth which the poet can elaborate. This provides the focus for his attitudes, the impulse for his Jacob-like wrestlings with the earthly angel; even his mode of prose discourse relies on the tactics of the imagination – quizzical, discursive, forever revolving the subject at hand to release fresh aspects of its truth.

To state summarily the main theme and method of the book is scarcely to exhaust its richness. It abounds in felicitous expression and in wit, the product of Stevens' elegant irony. For example, this parenthetical reflection on current writing: 'Democritus plucked his eye out because he could not look at a woman without thinking of her as a woman. If he had read a few of our novels he would have torn himself to pieces.'

The most welcome attribute of the book, however, is its humane good sense, equally manifest whether Stevens is discussing a desolate Pennsylvania churchyard, Plato's images or the personalities of those who prefer 'a drizzle in Venice to a hard rain in Hartford.' I believe it is now possible to see, as it was not when Winters wrote his essay, that Stevens' poetic tendency has always been from what he terms the hieratic to the credible, and even beyond this toward, in some measure, the imaginative regeneration of the life of his times. In that sense, his commitment as revealed in this book is deeply in the real word, and his elegance itself is the victory.

87. Paul Dinkins, 'Stevens is no esthete; he is a thinker', *Dallas Morning News*

2 March 1952, part 6, 6

Presumably Dinkins' sense of 'esthete' here is pejorative. The point of including such a review is that it provides the limiting context for Stevens' reputation. At the time of writing, Dinkins was a teacher at Texas Christian University.

To misuse Mr. Stevens' metaphor – it may be said that his angels do not sing or fly: they perform an intricate and elegant ballet on the point of a needle. He is one of our major poets, as 'major' goes these days; which is to say scarcely more than that he is admired by the kind of critics and poets called serious, and that his audience, numerically considered, is a small one, whatever varieties of superiority it may possess. Such is poetry's situation now; and we have the choice of blaming the public for being lazy and imperceptive, or the poets for being obscure and difficult – or the twentieth century for being the twentieth century.

Be that as it may, the reviewer of such a book as *The Necessary Angel* must make clear at the outset that a special audience is being addressed. Admirers of Stevens' poetry will almost surely find many satisfactions in these essays. Perhaps the best advice for those to whom the poetry is a puzzle or a bore would be: Keep away.

It is not that the essays are 'precious' – that cheap and favorite jibe. Their author's concerns are proper ones: The relationship between reality and imagination, between poetry and painting, between the poet and his society. Stevens is no esthete; he is a thinker. His brilliance and subtlety are by no means merely verbal. In this prose capacity he does not go as far as greater poet-philosophers have gone – Wordsworth

352

and Coleridge, say, or his own contemporary, T. S. Eliot. In *The Necessary Angel* he remains primarily a poet discussing poetry. He is not (in Wordsworth's phrase) 'a man speaking to men' of their most basic and universal concerns, to which the relationship of poetry, though important, can only be referential.

88. Hayden Carruth, 'Stevens as Essayist', *Nation*

Vol. 174, no. 24, 14 June 1952, 584–5

Carruth (b. 1921) is an American poet, editor, critic and fiction writer. His books include *Journey to a Known Place* (1961), the anthology *The Voice that is Great Within Us* (1970), *Brothers, I Loved You All* (1978) and a book of criticism, *Working Papers* (1981).

Among casual readers of poetry, one sometimes hears: 'Ah, yes, Wallace Stevens. A very fine poet, no doubt, but how can you account for a man who persists in writing about such silly subjects?' On the one hand, this. On the other, the incredible injustices Stevens has suffered from those who take him seriously, from critics who have written admirably about Chaucer and Keats and Hart Crane and have had nothing but twaddle to say about Stevens. In this predicament – between the devilishly uninformed and the deep blue connoisseurs – it has been up to Mr. Stevens to save himself, and he has made a long stride in that direction by collecting in one volume, where they will be ineluctably accessible to even the laziest of us, seven of his important essays in prose.

Stevens is a poet who still believes that poetry is the supreme activity. Unlike many of his colleagues, who have turned to traditional dogmas or positivisms, Stevens refuses the opinion that art is a game, propaganda, or a ceremony. For him, poetry – he can say this unabashedly – is a means toward truth. It is man's best means, for its instrument is man's greatest faculty, the imagination, which surpasses indubitably the philosopher's reason and the scientist's inductive technique. And poetry, if it succeeds, possesses also the power to bestow upon its participants an automatic by-product – ennoblement.

Yet the poet's imagination is useless unless he brings it to bear squarely upon reality, and for Stevens reality is the vastly differentiated, sometimes discouraging reality of our own world, a world untinctured by intimations of any supernal intelligence. It is a reality of almost unlimited beauty for those who deal with it imaginatively and in its own terms. The poet who can enhance, organize, and make comprehensible an aspect of reality participates in the discovery of a truth. He enables himself and his readers; to him belong the moral and intellectual rewards of nobility. Reality is for the poet, as for all men, 'the necessary angel,' without a high regard for whom the poet would be only another radio announcer, howling in the wind.

As a poet, Stevens's primary duty has been to write poetry, to explore reality. He has written many poems, most of them admirable, some of them truly great. But as a poet who feels the poet's position in the modern world insecure – not economically or socially, but intellectually – Stevens has given himself the secondary duty to write about poetry. He has made a definition of poetry; he has studied the way poetry works. He has given us several theories of the processes of imagination, theories which elucidate the properties of metaphor, analogy, and resemblance. He has been especially concerned with the way poets look at reality, the way each man sees a tree differently, for these various views comprise what we can apprehend of truth, and they are our *raison d'être* as sensible beings.

How different are these ideas from those we usually hear of Stevens! Among his admirers, he is a high romantic, a direct descendent of French impressionism, a mage of the poetic ritual. Among his critics, he is a funambulist, an *élégant*, a hedonist, a decadent, even a dude. Both parties have been too much impressed by the externalities of Stevens's poetic style, his very precise rhetoric and his occasionally rococo vocabulary. They have seized upon and exaggerated those poems in which Stevens has presented an exotic view of the world, poems of Florida and Tehuantepec, and they have neglected the poems which extol the august and even austere beauty of mundane things. They have forgotten, in other words, what has always been true: a poet's observations, if they are valid, must be his own, and his style, if it is effective, must be original.

The fact is, the ideas Stevens expresses in these essays and has always expressed in his poems bear a much closer affinity to Wordsworth, to Sidney, or to the men of the ancient world than they do to the decadents of the late nineteenth century. In so far as our world is decadent in comparison with the ancient or any other world, Stevens is too, though I should prefer to use some such word as 'refined' or 'elaborate.' The nobility that Stevens has sought is not Homer's; it is a modern nobility, intellectual and subtle; it is heroic only in its spiritual or aesthetic staunchness. Perhaps it is not nobility at all, but a kind of very good intelligence or very intelligent goodness that we in our moral sedentariness can still aspire to. But whatever it is, it is not foolishness or frippery. It is earnest, though not deadly earnest, and its products – Stevens's poems – are serious works, constructed to a measure which would allow no extraneous or supercilious ornament. It is inconceivable that a poet whose concept of poetry is the one enunciated in these essays could be vulnerable to affectation or preciosity. Stevens has created a theory of the value of poetry which surpasses in seriousness the more insistent dicta of all his contemporaries, and his poems are hard grapplings with reality, out in the open, away from the *culs-de-sac* of spiritual remoteness that have trapped so many of the rest.

The development of Stevens's thought has been, if one hesitates to say logical, at least consistent and true to its own problems. The questions raised in his latest essays go back directly to his early poems, 'Sunday Morning,' 'Sea Surface Full of Clouds,' and so on. Most of his ideas are not original – his close affinity to Wordsworth has already been pointed out by J.V. Cunningham – but they have been rigorously tested by all the poetic conditions of modernity. Nor has Stevens tried to write criticism or aesthetic theory. His essays are more nearly an operating program for poets, for one poet particularly – Stevens himself. As such their greatest importance will be as an adjunct to, or defense of, his poetry. To this end – the real appreciation of Stevens's poetic achievement – they are indispensable.

I do not want to turn from noticing these essays without saying a word about their extraordinary qualities as literature. Like his poems, Stevens's prose contains many prodigious remarks: 'The centuries have a way of being male.' 'The supreme example of analogy in English is *Pilgrim's Progress.*' 'When we look back at the period of French classicism ..., we have no difficulty in seeing it as a whole.' These will probably scare small scholars half out of their wits. So much the better. A little area must be reserved. But we know that Stevens likes to shock us, and we laugh and look for the most outrageous and exotic surmises, until, all at once, they are no longer outrageous and exotic but the astute and respectable thoughts of a man who lives in Hartford, Connecticut. These are rich essays, simply constructed yet richly and elegantly written. They contain many references, an anthology full of quotations from the most various and delightful authors, all very much to Stevens's purpose, but all exciting and pleasant to come across for their own sake. I do not mean to be altogether frivolous when I suggest that the best way to read this book is to invest in a bottle of the best sherry one can afford and a twenty-five-cent cigar. At least I found them the appropriate accessories and not at all antagonistic to the seriousness I have spoken of.

89. Edwin Honig, from 'Three Masters', *Voices*

Vol. 148, May–August 1952, 34–5

Honig (b. 1919), who teaches at Brown University, Rhode Island, is a poet, academic writer and translator of Calderon and Lorca.

Also reviewed are Marianne Moore's *Collected Poems* and William Carlos Williams' *Paterson*. Of the three poets, Honig says, 'it is their merit as innovators of a living language and their enduring sense of craft that have made them masters.'

... The whole book is a description of the imagination, 'the necessary angel,' seen in different forms of engagement with the Jacob-figure of reality. In each form there is a central text or series of texts providing the strategic grounds for what seems the crucial bout. But each bout becomes crucial in itself as the view of truth which is the reason for the particular bout is clarified. 'The Noble Rider and the Sound of Words' uses Plato's image of the soul as a charioteer to assess the idea of nobility transmuted by the poet into the quest for figures of speech in a living language. In 'The Figure of the Youth as Virile Poet,' 'three scraps' from Henry Bradley, Paul Valéry and William James introduce the question of the relationship between the artistic personality and the truth that is expected of him in any age. Stevens emerges more and more as a mock metaphysician fired by the aim of posing, in order deliberately to destroy, definitions that would otherwise kill the subject under inquiry. It is the force and play of the tentative credence he gives to such definitions that keep the subject, even the idea that there is a subject, alive. The pretense of objectivity is the clearest road to the most supple subjectivity. For his staunchest conviction is that 'there can be no poetry without the personality of the poet, and that, quite simply, is why the definition of poetry has not yet been found and why, in short, there is none.'

In three shorter essays ('Three Academic Pieces,' 'About One of Marianne Moore's Poems,' and 'The Relations Between Poetry and Painting'), Stevens is most epicurean, most epigrammatic, and hence most removed from his subject. And the mood which thus detains him into examining surfaces does not involve him or his angel.

But in 'The Effects of Analogy' and 'Imagination as Value,' the two most basic discussions of the book, Stevens comes closest to formulating an experiential poetics on the principles that poetry is 'a science of allusions' and 'a rhetoric in which the feeling of one man is communicated to another in words of the exquisite appositeness that takes away all their reality.' The antagonism of the terms, science and rhetoric, hints at the sort of tension which quickens the sense and practice of poetry for Wallace Stevens, and which, through his discussion, is bound to keep the reader remarkably alert. As a poetic document, *The Necessary Angel* is more revealing of Stevens' practice than are Yeats' *A Vision* or Eliot's *Selected Essays* of their respective practices. With Malraux's *Psychology of Art*, it seems the most virile critical production of a creative mentality in this century....

90. Bernard Heringman, 'The Critical Angel', *Kenyon Review*

Vol. XIV, no. 3, Summer 1952, 520–3

Heringman submitted a Ph.D. thesis on Stevens to Columbia University in 1955 and published some articles and reviews on Stevens' work. *Letters of Wallace Stevens* includes thirteen letters to Heringman written between 1949 and 1954. The present review has been judged 'the best' on *The Necessary Angel*, 'because Heringman, unlike many Stevens' reviewers, understands the convolutions of the poet's thought, and . . . is able to specify how Stevens' constructs – reality, imagination, poetry – metamorphose and interchange in their definitions'. (See Abbie F. Willard, *Wallace Stevens: The Poet and His Critics* (Chicago, 1978), p. 237.)

In his introduction to these essays, Wallace Stevens says all but one 'were written to be spoken, and that affects their character.' He leaves it to us to see how; if my guess is right, it is in the same manner as his poetry is affected, with respect to the development of ideas; and it is a different effect than one might expect. The development is less rather than more explicit and systematic. He will, for example, lead up obliquely to the statement of a theme in a striking phrase, then weave around it in a free association of ideas and phrases, or simply leave it to form its own nexus in his hearer's mind and go directly to the statement of counter-subjects in a condensed fugal pattern. Then the one or the several themes will recur every few pages, exploiting the associations which have arisen, leading them into relation with new themes, building a complex harmony of sounds and ideas. When Stevens read at the Museum of Modern Art in New York last year, first a paper (the last in this collection) on 'The Relations between Poetry and Painting,' and then a group of poems, it was possible to listen to both halves of the program with the same ear. I found it necessary, in fact, to remind myself of the difference in the second part, until the intenser rhythms and denser language of the poetry had worked on me for a while.

Partly by reason of this similarity in construction, Stevens' prose is as much illuminated as his poetry by its context, his whole work. When he says in one place that reality is the source of poetry, one must remember that in another he says poetry is the source of reality. Even remembering both remarks, and perceiving their neatness as a summary of his thought, one is obliged to remain dissatisfied with the neat refrain, obliged to persist in exploring the delights of the context. The dialectic, the elaboration, the play of ideas and tropes, all this is nearly as dazzling in the prose as in the poetry, and equally necessary to an understanding of Stevens' meanings.

These essays, like many of the poems, are about poetry. Like the poems, they work a continuous dialectic between reality and imagination, and reflect sometimes their possible synthesis, the 'supreme fiction.' This is what Stevens says poetry does, and that is why he has been able to find in poetry 'the sanction of life.'

Two statements, among the earliest and the latest respectively in the book, will at least indicate the range and strength of this view. The first: '... what makes the poet the potent figure that he is, or was, or ought to be, is that he creates the world to which we turn incessantly and without knowing it and that he gives to life the supreme fictions without which We are unable to conceive of it.' The other: '"(Poetry) is an illumination of a surface, the movement of a self in the rock." A force capable of bringing about fluctuations in reality...' This is the rock which becomes 'the rock of summer' in Stevens' poem, 'Credences of Summer.' It is reality and imagination identified; nature at its most physical, but given a moving self, illuminated, invented by the poet.

Reality, imagination, poetry: these are the major terms of Stevens' discourse in these essays; in his poetry, too, though there he more often gives them other names. In the course of an examination of his work, a certain fluidity becomes apparent in the meaning and relation of these terms, ponderous as they are. They become, at times, nearly interchangeable, particularly baffling to any attempt such as I have made to fix them in some kind of pseudo-mathematical formula. A typographic device may do better, distinguishing between small and large meanings for each term and allowing them to be not always simultaneous. Thus, REALITY for Stevens equals *reality* (nature, the physical, the actual) plus *imagination*. This is the synthesis, the invented rock. Poetry (in general, or his own) concerns itself with *imagination* (poetry, music, art, the ideal) or with *reality,* or with the varying relations between the two. *Poetry* represents *imagination* at work on *reality,* or resisting the pressure of *reality* (war, appetite, chaos), or attempting a reconciliation with *reality.* IMAGINATION, as art or as metaphysics, transforms *reality,* transforms life, makes them bearable and fruitful, gives them meaningful form or finds the form which they have. To complete the circle, POETRY, as the synthesis of *imagination* and *reality,* equals REALITY.

These are the bones which take on flesh in the course of Stevens' work in prose and in poetry. The last equation, for instance, becomes such solid substance in his essay, 'The Figure of the Youth as Virile Poet,' or in his great poem, 'Notes Toward a Supreme Fiction,' that one accepts as a natural corollary the equation of poetics and metaphysics; one accepts Stevens' absolute dedication to poetry as a dedication to life. 'What our eyes behold may well be the text of life but one's meditations on the text and the disclosures of these meditations are no less a part of the structure of reality.'

Stevens' explicit ontology, when it appears in remarks like this one, proceeds not from systematic philosophical construction but from discussion, quite tentative often, of the nature of poetry and of imagination. The inference is that, insofar as there is an argument leading to the metaphysical conclusion, it is a circular one. Which is as it should be, with metaphysics, particularly in the case of a poet. Stevens begins with this view of reality, and he ends with it; he has spent about 35 years constructing magnificent circles of poetry around it, and at least the decade represented in this book on comparable circles of prose. The earliest (1942) and most splendid of the essays takes off, nominally, from an idea of nobility. It becomes immediately an idea of poetry and leads to a consideration of the opposition and interdependence of imagination and reality. The latest essay (1942) begins with a way of looking at paintings and goes through the same process. This means, of course, that Stevens is repetitive. It means that his ontology is constant and pervasive. But as a basic view of the nature of reality it is applicable to every phase of human life and culture. Only a certain sympathy with the metaphysics is needed to sustain one's interest in the varied applications Stevens makes, to poetry, painting, human nature, language, politics.

Stevens' definition of 'the structure of reality' and his concern with its two elements, both in dichotomy and in synthesis, manifest themselves quite clearly in each of the essays. His poetry differs on this score, treating the two in large part separately, in fairly regular alternation, often touching on the idea of synthesis but seldom dealing with it directly. As he put it himself in a letter, 'Sometimes I believe most in the imagination for a long time and then, without reasoning about it, turn to reality and believe in that and that alone. But both of these things project themselves endlessly and I want them to do just that.' It seems significant, however, that the poem ('Angel Surrounded by Paysans') from which he took the title and epigraph for his essays does deal directly with the synthesis. The angel calls himself both 'the angel of reality' and 'a man of the mind.' He is the imagination which is necessary to reality, to life. He is another of Stevens' figures for poetry, which, as he says in his first essay, 'helps us to live our lives.'

The angel brings a kind of epiphany which Stevens also represents in his prologue to the 'Notes Toward a Supreme Fiction':

> In the uncertain light of single, certain truth,
> Equal in living changingness to the light,
> In which I meet you, in which we sit at rest,
> For a moment in the central of our being,
> The vivid transparence that you bring is peace.

But the illuminating appearance of the angel is only momentary; the peace and the joy of realization of the 'supreme fiction' – poetry – the synthesis of imagination and reality – come only in an occasional flash, when the poet transcends his usual distractions, on one hand the world's chaos and on the other the sterile order of the rationalist.

Stevens has been much concerned with these distractions, not only as they affect poetry but also as they affect humanity, though he specifically denies, in the first of these essays, that any 'social obligation' should be attached to the poet. To appreciate his 'social consciousness' it is necessary to understand Stevens' use in his work of 'the poet' and 'poetry.' Often, nearly always, I think, he uses the terms to mean much more than the maker of verses and his product, to mean substantially what he means by *imagination*. 'Poetry is the imagination of life.' It is a way of life and a part of life, pervasive, necessary, inevitable. The poet speaks to and for the imagination of every man. Thus, when Stevens concerns himself with the fortunes of poetry, he concerns himself with what he deeply believes is essential to the fortune of man. In these essays, as well as in his poems, he has deeply searched our possibilities. He has made a powerful case for the possible synthesis of imagination and reality which should be our best fortune. And, with some of his poems, he has won it for us, achieving himself the quality he attributes to 'the venerable, the fundamental books of the human spirit.' His words, like theirs, 'have made a world that transcends the world and a life livable in that transcendence.'

91. Harry Levin, 'candidly and classically aristocratic', *Yale Review*

Vol. XLI, no. 4, June 1952, 615–6

Levin (b. 1912) has had a long career of teaching English and comparative literature at Harvard. Among his books perhaps best-known are *The Overreacher: A Study of Christopher Marlowe* (1952), *The Power of Blackness: Hawthorne, Poe, Melville* (1958) and *The Question of Hamlet* (1959). A more recent publication is *Memories of the Moderns* (1980).

In this review Levin goes on to consider Graham Greene's *The Lost Childhood and Other Essays* and E.M. Forster's *Two Cheers for Democracy*.

... the first volume in prose by Wallace Stevens seems at last to function on middle ground between the two careers of that distinguished poet-executive – or rather, following his terminology, between reality and imagination. Imagination, as might be expected and even desired, has the upper hand. A series of somewhat oracular 'contributions to the theory of poetry,' controlled less by logic and rhetoric than by association and suggestion, is animated by Mr. Stevens' flair for citing the concrete image and discerning the pictorial example. Thus a poem of Marianne Moore's is illuminated more by his description of a Pennsylvania Dutch church than by his cross-reference to an article on the epistemological nature of poetic truth. Statements like 'The centuries have a way of being male' or 'the namby-pamby is an intolerable dissipation' have the ring of lines from Mr. Stevens' poem, while two of the 'Three Academic Pieces' lapse into delightfully characteristic verse. (But when the invocation reads 'O juventes,' does Mr. Stevens mean 'O juvenes' or 'O juventas?') Perhaps his most effective discussion is that of 'The Noble Rider and the Sound of Words,' where the poet's relation to life is traced through Plato's charioteer, Cervantes' uneasy horseman, Verrocchio's famous statue, and other equestrian portraiture less dignified and more recent. Mr. Stevens' tastes are candidly and classically aristocratic; he addresses himself to an imaginative elite and welcomes the circumscriptions of the ivory tower; above all, he relies upon the arts to compensate for what our age has lost in the form of belief....

SELECTED POEMS

London, Fortune Press, 1952
London, Faber & Faber, 1953

As noted in the headnote to No. 83, the Fortune Press edition, published in December 1952, was quickly withdrawn. Stevens apparently acquired Austin Clarke's review copy of this edition through John L. Sweeney (v. Edelstein, *Wallace Stevens: A Descriptive Bibliography*, p. 100). No figure is available for the Faber first run, but runs of 1,000 were printed in 1954 and 1965.

92. Richard Murphy, 'The Music of Poetry', *Spectator*

13 February 1953, 191–2

Richard Murphy (b. 1927) is an Irish poet whose works include *Sailing to an Island* (1963), *The Battle of Aughrim* (1968) and *Selected Poems* (Faber, 1979).

Wallace Stevens is the most musical poet of this century. Not only does he write poetry about music, but style is infected with cadences that attain the purity of music as nearly as we can conceive it in words. This is remarkable in an age when many have complained against the pollution and decay of the language since the period of the Authorised Version. Neither the *Four Quarters*, nor Ezra Pound's *Cantos*, both of which are modelled on forms of musical composition, echo the technique of music so perfectly as the variations of 'The Man

with the Blue Guitar.' This beautiful poem, and the perhaps
finer 'Peter Quince at the Clavier,' extract the most melody
possible from the language. They are what we generally and
rightly call 'pure poetry.' It is the type of poetry that reflects
the age by what it leaves unsaid.

Wallace Stevens was born in 1879, and his earliest work
was composed in the period before the First World War,
when he contributed with Ezra Pound and T.S. Eliot among
others to *Poetry (Chicago).* His most recent volume was
published in America in 1950. Stevens's work is familiar to us
only through anthologies, and this selection made by the
author from all his works is his first book to be published in
England. This is surprising. He is not by any means in the
native or the Whitman tradition of American poetry, which
would make it naturally difficult for us to appreciate his
outlook, or be sufficiently interested in his observation. In
most of these poems he is not recognisably American. He is a
symbolist, at his best in the style and character of Yeats's
early poem 'Adam's Curse,' a style which has since lost its
social context in Europe:

> We sat together at one summer's end,
> That beautiful mild woman, your close friend,
> And you and I, and talked of poetry,

The symbolists tended even if they were tone-deaf, like
Yeats, to regard poetry as music. They did not regard it, as
Yeats eventually did, as the expression of a people. Except
for Stevens's beautiful treatment of colour, even under the
shadeless glare of the sun at Key West, the visual quality of
his poetry is unimportant. Its locality, its social context,
appear to be irrelevant. His visual technique is that of a
would-be impressionist, but the formation of any definite
mental portrait or landscape or characterisation is destroyed
by the abstractness of his mind. Often this spoils his vision,
but leaves his music unimpaired. His

> Birds that came like dirty water in waves

are indeed visible and memorable, and sometimes he achieves
a superb orchestration of the senses:

Now is midsummer come and all fools slaughtered
And spring's infuriations over and a long way
To the first autumnal inhalations, young broods
Are in the grass, the roses are heavy with a weight
Of fragrance and the mind lays by its trouble.

In the longer forms the weakness of the pure poet is more
noticeable: not an inability to sustain the sounds he sets out to
elaborate, but to sustain the interest in what he is saying. We
reach in Stevens the limit to the value of poetry which
over-emphasises the musical element in language. How easy
it is to enjoy, but how difficult to receive the statement
within the sound! One does not complain of lines such as:

It may be that in all her phrases stirred
The grinding water and the gasping wind;
But it was she and not sea we heard.

But one criticises without complaining – admittedly from a
puritanical outlook – that the beauty of his sounds and his
colours are not enough. The shadowy note of desire, the
muted tones of elegy, the exquisite sensuality of his lyric, and
the sophisticated concealment of the world from his poetry,
leave us wondering: 'How is it that you live, and what is it
you do?' The question does not destroy or degrade the
pleasure of his verse. In fact this is great enough in its own
tradition to make the question seem, well, a little ill-
mannered. Indeed, his poetry corrects the extremes of prosy
journalism to which the other tradition has often been
driven. Such elegance as he possesses has a permanent value.
It lacks, however, the immediacy and the impurity of
ordinary life. It extracts and refines but does not reflect.

They said, 'You have a blue guitar,
You do not play things as they are.'
The man replied, 'Things as they are
Are changed upon the blue guitar'

His method is to reduce experience to a few principles, and
rare sensations which suffuse the principles, then refine both
to a phrase that he varies and repeats till it becomes rich with
meaning through the intricate alternation of its echoes.

367

Wallace Stevens has been a good influence on the work of at least one English poet, and this edition should give him the wider reputation he deserves in this country. He will probably have more influence now than he might have had before the war, when the current of poetry was flowing in a less aesthetic direction. He ought also to be an example to all of the limitations of poetry considered primarily as music, when his work is set against the events of our time. His publishers should be encouraged to prepare a collected edition, which may modify the extent of these limitations.

93. G.S. Fraser, 'The Chameleon's Dish', *New Statesman*

Vol. 45, no. 1145, 14 February 1953, 181

Fraser (1915–80) was a British poet, critic and teacher. His books include *The Modern Writer and This World* (1958), *Vision and Rhetoric* (1959) and *Essays on Twentieth-Century Poets* (1977).

'How fares our cousin Hamlet?' 'Excellent, i'faith; of the chameleon's dish; I eat the air, promise-crammed; you cannot feed capons so.' In his own country, Mr. Wallace Stevens has as high a reputation as any living American poet, but over here his work has proved too much of a chameleon's dish for most of our gross-feeding critics. Indeed its ingredients are largely colour and space. It is not, in fact, that Mr. Stevens is by any means blind or numb to the sensuous world, or that his thought is too simple for us, or his emotions not sufficiently intense. But the world his senses respond to is not that in which we ordinarily, rather imperceptively, move; and the realm of his more urgent self-questionings is a less grossly moral and practical one than ours. Apples grow on his trees to be looked at, not to be eaten; young women lean out of his balconies to form elements in a total composition, not to pick up young men. He wanders through our world, which, grips most of us so painfully, like an alert philosophy lecturer through an art gallery. For him the world is, in fact, compositional:

> He often thought of the land from which he came,
> How that whole country was a melon, pink
> If seen rightly and yet a possible red.

'If seen rightly': that is perhaps the phrase to hang on to there; Mr. Stevens's world is one of shifting total patterns, arranged, and stressed by the observer's eye. That world's modes of dissolution, the possible shifts of inclusive aesthetic perception, are his central theme. Thus the emotional urgencies of his poetry are not, on the whole, even poeticised versions of the urgencies of ordinary living; they are those of a mind pondering about the ultimate nature of aesthetic experience and, especially latterly, about the shifts of a poem from trickery to revelation under the poet's hands: how far is Prospero the dupe, how far the master, of his own wand?

Two famous early short poems by Mr. Stevens are worth quoting, both to indicate the way he has gone, and the way he has not. 'Anecdote of the Jar' is a concrete presentation of a problem in general aesthetics:

[Quotes *CP*, p. 76.]

This poem has puzzled better critics than myself; but one must give one's own answers even if they seem to come too easily, and what it seems to me to say is that the framework, the perspective, that gives nature aesthetic significance (or by wider analogy, human significance) is put there by ourselves. There is no 'picture' there without our 'frame': no 'pattern' without our arbitrary selections and stresses – the line about the jar, which has almost a strut or a swagger,

> And tall and of a port in air,

suggests that there is a certain proud wilfulness (and that

Mr. Stevens approves of it) in the way we dominate the world just by looking at it. Both Wordsworth and Coleridge, both 'nature's life' and 'our life' as unconsciously projected into nature, are very far away: it is *our consciousness* that makes nature interesting. My second quotation is from 'The Emperor of Ice-Cream':

> Take from the dresser of deal,
> Lacking the three glass knobs, that sheet,
> On which she embroidered fantails once,
> And spread it so as to cover her face...

My point there is that for the 'ordinary reader' these lines have a 'human pathos' which has not in fact proved to be one of Mr. Stevens's developing qualities; I agree with the ordinary reader in thinking he would have been a larger writer—not necessarily a finer artist – if it had. In the later poems the meditation is more prolonged and abstruse and the empirical element, clouds and birds and colours, more schematic. These later poems are at once a meditation and a making, and a meditation about what is being made:

> The poem is the cry of its occasion,
> Part of the res itself and not about it,
> The poet speaks the poem as it is,
> Not as it was...

Each new attempt to write a poem, in fact, especially when the nature of poetry is the poet's central theme, raises anew the question of what a poem is. Thus these late meditations of Mr. Stevens can be, and tend to be, indefinitely prolonged; their mode is self-questioning repetition, as in music. It is hard to say anything clear or helpful about so rich and complex a poet in a short space; but I hope I have conveyed two things: my immense respect for Mr. Stevens; and my conviction that if *all* poetry were of his kind, we should not perhaps consider poetry, as those of us who like it tend to, as being *centrally* important to human experience.

94. William Empson, on Stevens the 'beau linguist', *Listener*

Vol. 49, no. 1256, 26 March 1953, 521

Sir William Empson (1906–84) was a poet, editor, and influential scholar and critic. His *Collected Poems* was published in 1955 and his works include *Seven Types of Ambiguity* (1930), *The Structure of Complex Words* (1935) and *Milton's God* (1961).

This selection made by Mr. Wallace Stevens from his poetry ought certainly to be welcomed in England; he has been highly admired in America for thirty years, and it is time he was better known here. There is one unfortunate feature of his style which ought to be noticed, what he calls 'beau-linguist' perhaps (page 106), as in the line 'I call you by name, my green, my fluent mundo' (page 128). Walt Whitman also liked throwing in foreign words, to the effect 'Comes the dawn, *camerados*; pre-sophisticate your *tief toilettes'*, but Henry James, having more actual foreign contacts, said it was rather a pity Whitman knew all those bits of foreign languages. It is not offensive in Whitman once you realise that he is trying to be all-inclusively democratic; a reader is supposed to feel personally welcomed, in the new dawn, when he meets a bit of his quaint old mother-tongue, though it is out of date because American English is somehow taking over the whole world. But other writers, English as well as American of course, have taken a very different attitude to Europe and felt themselves raw by contrast to it; then the suggestion becomes 'just look at our Wallace, bandying the flashing bon-mot with the foreign lady of title; doesn't he seem at home?' It was also a fault of Oscar Wilde to be startlingly at home in high society, and Mr. Wallace Stevens, very well-to-do it appears, and growing up in the hey-day of Oscar Wilde, was perhaps more influenced by him than by Whitman. But then again, though one can pick on examples which seem definitely mistaken, it is obviously a good thing for a poet to be aware of foreign languages; maybe the English-speakers are no longer learning them enough.

Actually there isn't a great deal of this foreign-language trick in his poetry, but there is a lot of something rather like it; an idea that it is enough entertainment for the reader to see the poet trying on a new fancy dress. There is also a good deal of philosophising, which the reader dare not say he has quite understood, but the main point of it, and indeed the reason why it is hard to follow, seems to be an idea that a person like this doesn't really need to philosophise. One need not object to this attitude in principle, in fact it can make good poetry, but it comes to feel very airless. One can't help wishing he had found more to say, if only because he could evidently say it.

He is not however such a narrow poet as these remarks might suggest; the elegant pungency of the nature-descriptions (birds especially) is invigorating, and the fine poem 'Dry Loaf', with the line

Regard the hovels of those that live in this land,

is after all more unselfcentred than most poets nowadays care to be. He is also a master of what is perhaps needed most for poetry in English, a long delicate rhythm based on straight singing lines. The long poem 'Sunday Morning' has this all through, and ends with a splendid example of it:

Deer walk upon our mountains, and the quail
Whistle about us their spontaneous cries;
Sweet berries ripen in the wilderness;
And, in the isolation of the sky,
At evening, casual flocks of pigeons make
Ambiguous undulations as they sink,
Downward to darkness, on extended wings.

95. Donald Davie, ' "Essential Gaudiness": The Poems of Wallace Stevens', *Twentieth Century*

Vol. 153, no. 916, June 1953, 455–62

Davie (b. 1922), a British poet and critic of note, is Professor of English at Vanderbilt University. He is the author of *Purity of Diction in English Verse* (1952), *Articulate Energy* (1955), *Ezra Pound: Poet as Sculptor* (1964) and *Thomas Hardy and British Poetry* (1973). Davie's *Collected Poems* appeared in 1972. *Pound,* his second study of the American poet, was published in 1976, and *The Poet in the Imaginary Museum: Essays of Two Decades* in 1978. He is an editor of *PN Review*. His article here covers both volumes of *Selected Poems* (i.e. the Faber edition and the withdrawn Fortune Press edition).

For nearly thirty years the Americans have been claiming, in Wallace Stevens, one of the great poets of our age. It seems inexcusable that the English reader has had to wait so long before he could judge this poet for himself. It is especially exasperating when one discovers that Stevens deserves nearly everything that his admirers have claimed for him. He is indeed a poet to be mentioned in the same breath as Eliot and Yeats and Pound. That is his place, and that is the company he must keep. We are called upon now not to assign a status but to define an excellence. And now, at last, generous selections from his work come at the same time from two different publishers. What a pity one or other of them did not appear fifteen years ago.

The third poem in the Fortune Press selection, one of the most important works of Stevens's early period, is entitled 'Le Monocle de Mon Oncle'. (The title is a silly one, like many of Stevens's titles.) The second stanza runs as follows:

> A red bird flies across the golden floor.
> It is a red bird that seeks out his choir
> Among the choirs of wind and wet and wing.
> A torrent will fall from him when he finds.
> Shall I uncrumple this much-crumpled thing?
> I am a man of fortune greeting heirs;
> For it has come that thus I greet the spring.
> These choirs of welcome choir for me farewell.
> No spring can follow past meridian.
> Yet you persist with anecdotal bliss
> To make believe a starry *connaissance*.

I think it was Yvor Winters who first drew attention to the
felicities here. 'Much-crumpled', for instance, gives us (1) a
sensuous impression of the wet woods, (2) the difficulty of
distinguishing the bird-song from its accompaniments of
sounding rain and wind, (3) the staleness for the poet of the
hackneyed theme that the bird represents – 'Spring', the
topic handled so many times by so many poets before.
But now consider a stanza, later in the same poem:

> If sex were all, then every trembling hand
> Could make us squeak, like dolls, the wished-for
>   words.
> But note the unconscionable treachery of fate,
> That makes us weep, laugh, grunt and groan, and
>   shout
> Doleful heroics, pinching gestures forth
> From madness or delight, without regard
> To that first, foremost law. Anguishing hour!
> Last night, we sat beside a pool of pink,
> Clippered with lilies scudding the bright chromes,
> Keen to the point of starlight, while a frog
> Boomed from his very belly odious chords.

This is thoroughly late-Victorian, poor Browning or poor
Meredith. Activity masquerades as agility; violence as
energy; it is hectic and monotonous. Refusal to use abstractions brings about locutions neither abstract nor concrete,

but fussy blunt gestures – 'pinching gestures forth...', 'to that first, foremost law'. And the point is that this stanza differs from the stanza about the red bird, only in degree. The stuff is the same, and in the later stanza it has worn threadbare, that's all.

In fact, 'Le Monocle de Mon Oncle', for all its precious title and a few jazzy superficialities ('connaissance'), is a strikingly old-fashioned poem. This is as true of the movement of thought, as of the versification. 'At forty,' the poet asks, 'is it time to grow "spiritual" or "platonic"? To abjure the world of sense now that in so many ways (e.g. sex) that world is becoming easier to abjure, because it is less insistent and intoxicating?' He answers that this is not the case, because the imagination does not decay with the senses, but can create a world as 'real' as the actual world. The poet thinks in Keatsian terms throughout, and the movement of thought is Keatsian too. For instance, between stanzas viii and ix the thought turns upon itself and abdicates the path it had embarked upon, in just the fashion of – 'Forlorn! The very word is like a bell...' We can imagine the student's painstaking account: 'The poet's mood suddenly changes...' It hardly needs to be pointed out that one cannot read *The Waste Land* in this way, or 'Hugh Selwyn Mauberley.' When we try to understand 'Le Monocle de Mon Oncle' or 'Sunday Morning', it is a question of 'Do you follow? Have you hold of the thread?' Eliot does not ask us to 'follow' in this way. The process of understanding *The Waste Land* is not a process of pursuit, but of harking back and forth. In short, Stevens's poem, like an ode by Keats, is still *discursive;* it moves from point to point, always forward from first to last. Lose the thread, and you may go back and look for it. In *The Waste Land,* by contrast, it is only when the poem is grasped as a whole that each part of it falls into place.

The difference between 'Sunday Morning' and 'Le Monocle' on the one hand, *The Waste Land* and 'Mauberley' on the other, can be put in another way. Except at certain key-points, like the image at the very end of 'Le Monocle' ('That fluttering things have so distinct a shade'), the poetry and the meaning do not coincide. To get at the meaning, you have to go *behind* the poetry, whereas if you go behind Eliot's poetry you have gone behind the meaning too. Understanding 'Le Monocle' is a matter of groping through a dazzle, or stripping off the caparisons, until you come, behind the rhetorical magnificence, at a structure of plain sense that is quite lean and skeletal. It is possible to write a prose paraphrase of the poem, without quoting from it more than once; it is not possible to do this with *The Waste Land* or 'Mauberley' or Yeats's 'Byzantium'. The gorgeousness, we cannot help but feel, was laid on afterwards, the flesh upon the skeleton, the clothes on top of that. So, if this verse at its best recalls the Keats of the Odes, it is not surprising that at its worst is sounds like some uninspired Victorian imitating the Keatsian manner:

> Death is the mother of beauty; hence from her,
> Alone, shall come fulfilment to our dreams
> And our desires.

Stevens has written, of his poem 'The Emperor of Ice Cream':

This wears a deliberately commonplace costume, and yet seems to me to contain something of the essential gaudiness of poetry; that is the reason why I like it.... I dislike niggling, and like letting myself go.

Once again, the echo is there. For this recalls nothing so much as the Keatsian tag about how poetry should 'surprise by a fine excess'. Stevens has insisted repeatedly that he is a 'Romantic' poet. This, together with what we find in the verse of 'Le Monocle de Mon Oncle', for instance, advises us of one way in which 'Romantic' may be understood. Stevens is a Romantic in the sense that Keats was Romantic – his is to be a poetry of excess, among other things of rhetoric in excess of meaning, rhetoric for its own sake, for its 'essential gaudiness'.

Consider, for instance, this poet's thoroughly old-fashioned concern for the beautiful. It is surely plain that his poems are, or aspire to be, 'beautiful' in a quite straightforward way, winning and seductive. If we were pressed, presumably we should have to maintain that 'Hugh Selwyn

Mauberley' is as 'beautiful' as Stevens's 'Sunday Morning'; but in saying that of Pound's poem we need to use quotation marks, while in applying the word to Stevens's poem we can let it stand unqualified. Stevens, like Keats, is saying something and also 'being beautiful'; Pound and Eliot are saying something as exactly as possible, and the beauty is in the exactness. The beauty of their poetry is in the relation of rhetoric to meaning; in Stevens the rhetoric aspires to be beautiful for its own sake. So Stevens's obscurity is of a kind familiar to readers of Keats; it derives from what he puts into the poem. Pound's and Eliot's obscurity derives from what they leave out.

Marius Bewley remarks,[1] of a poem called 'Bantams in Pine-Woods,' 'The rather brassy appeal of this poem exists at a more superficial level than its meaning which is extremely difficult to excerpt.' This is no more than I have argued for, in Stevens's poetry, the meaning and the 'appeal' are on different levels. the 'appeal' is the appeal of 'beauty' and it exists in the rhetoric; the meaning is somewhere else, behind or below. The question is, of course, whether this is typical of Stevens's procedure in general, or peculiar to this poem and a few others which are less than his best. I differ from Mr Bewley in finding this feature typical of all Stevens, even at his best. But then I am not so shocked by it as Mr Bewley is. 'Brassy' and 'superficial', taken together, show that the critic is rather contemptuous or afraid of this sort of 'appeal'. I am simply grateful for it. Marius Bewley, being more of a purist, has to draw attention to 'the ultimate failure of this poem', and to decide 'if the poem means what I think it does, the meaning fails to be realized in the body of the verse. It is disowned by the very images that proclaim it.' That 'the meaning fails to be realized in the body of the verse' is true; 'it is disowned by the very images that proclaim it' is another matter, and not true at all. The images will serve, they serve splendidly, and proclaim loudly. They 'own' the meaning all right. All one feels is that they were not the only images, the inevitable choice, to proclaim this meaning: the poet chose these rather than others, and chose well – still, he chose; the images did not choose themselves.

Perhaps the most striking thing about the poetry of

Stevens is its metrical conservatism. 'To break the pentameter,' said Pound, 'that was the first heave.' Stevens has
never made the break; the greater part of his poetry is written
in quite regular iambic pentameters. One can read critic after
critic without finding this really striking feature even
acknowledged. Yet there can be no adequate account of
Stevens that does not take note of one of his most striking
eccentricities – his extreme metrical conservatism in an age of
revolutionary metrical experiment. If I am right in thinking
that a Keatsian allegiance is the clue to Stevens, then his
metres are accounted for – his conservatism in this department is part and parcel with his conservatism in structure and
in rhetoric. It used to be said that Stevens's poetry could only
be appreciated if one were familiar with the poetic experiments of French symbolism. But I do not think that Stevens
is 'post-symbolist' in this sense, as T. S. Eliot is. His novelty
is all on the surface; he is really very conservative.

By 'Keatsian allegiance' I mean nothing so crass as Keatsian
'influence'; nor do I mean that, for Stevens, Keats is the poet
of poets. I take him only as the most distinguished
representative of the kind of poetry that Stevens seems to
favour. And perhaps, after all, Keats is not the most
distinguished name that can be found. It has been said of a
line from 'Le Monocle de Mon Oncle' that it has 'the
Shakespearean note':

> I am a man of fortune greeting heirs.

This sounds like a line from a play, but this should not make
us suppose that it recalls, in its context, Shakespeare the
dramatist. If it is true that Stevens at his best can compass 'the
Shakespearean note' (and I think it is), what he gets is the note of
the sonnets, not of the plays. It is the note of:

> the prophetic soul
> Of the wide world dreaming on things to come.

F. W. Bateson says that what this means is 'professional
soothsayers'. If he is right, then surely the splendour of the
language is something in excess of the sense, adding
enormously to our pleasure but not assisting (rather,
obstructing) our understanding. The same can be said of

Stevens at his most splendid:

> We live in an old chaos of the sun
> Or old dependency of day and night.

To twist and reverse T. S. Eliot's remark on Dryden, this is poetry that suggests enormously but states little. Consider just the repeated 'old'. Is the repetition necessary to the sense? Or can we say of 'dependency', even, that on scrutiny, it yields as much by way of meaning as it does in terms of euphony and rhythm? This is florid poetry, a poetry of excess; but in saying so, we are saying no more than must be said sometimes of Shakespeare.

And Stevens needs no sponsors. To defend his methods, we need appeal to no authority beyond the poet himself. His view of life is comprehensive and consistent. As critic and as poet, he defines this one inclusive vision. Up to this point, we have examined that part of his vision which may be called his aesthetic, arriving at it in the surest way by seeing how it works out in his artistic practice. But he has, too, a metaphysic, an ethic, an epistemology; and the aesthetic can be seen truly only when it finds its place in the whole structure of the poet's thought. If we see it in that way, we see that his rhetoric of excess corresponds to an ethic of excess, even (the expression is a queer one but may be clearer later) an epistemology of excess. As according to him the best language is excessive language, so the best, the noblest sort of conduct is action in excess. And so the clearest, the truest sort of perception is the perception that exceeds its object, elaborating upon it.

We do not think of Stevens as an ethical poet. William Van O'Connor[2] agrees with Marius Bewley in finding Stevens's central pre-occupation to be with imagination, with the role that imagination plays, or should play in the apprehending of reality. That is, they see him first and foremost as epistemologist; and I think they are right – this is indeed the point of leverage. But as one can speak of imaginative perception and imaginative language, so one speaks of 'imaginative' behaviour. And if we understand what Stevens means by 'imagination', we understand not only what perception he trusts and what language he tries for, but also what behaviour he recommends. Marius Bewley has brilliantly demonstrated how Stevens has gradually built up for himself in his earlier poems a vocabulary of personal symbols which is, by the time he does his later work, astonishingly copious, and finely articulated. One advantage of such a symbolic vocabulary is in the way it provides the poet with deliberate ambiguities. When he has perfected such a personal symbolism, he can write sentences which have meaning on more than one level, so that a statement about the conditions of human perception is also a statement about the conditions of human action.

Both Mr. Bewley and Mr. O'Connor compare Stevens's view of imagination with Coleridge's. Mr. O'Connor throws out, apparently at random, a valuable observation:

Coleridge believes the power of imagination is denied to 'the sensual and the proud;' there is no reason to think that Stevens does.

Indeed, there is not. There is, on the contrary, every reason to think that Stevens takes one sort of pride as the surest evidence of imagination. For him, as for many Romantics, the imaginative man is the proud man. He esteems in men the quality of *panache*, the capacity for making large gestures, conspicuous self-expression, in manner and clothes as in language. The grand manner expresses itself in action as in speech. One may live with style, as one may write with style, and Stevens in his criticism has set great store by this fruitful ambiguity. As Mr O'Connor remarks, of a poem called 'The Weeping Burgher':

The verities are 'sorry verities'. We are reconciled to them by 'excess', by style.

Yes, we come to terms with the world by going beyond it, by wearing our hat at a rakish angle, by elaborate movements of the arm or the wrist. It is only so that we perceive it truly, by letting our imagination colour our perceptions. In the same way it is only so that we act in the world with dignity, by letting our imagination colour our actions in excess of what circumstances force upon us. And it is only so that we recreate it in the beauty of poetry, by letting our imagination colour our words in excess of what bare meaning demands of us. Style, imagination, rhetoric, excess – these are the basic terms of Stevens's ethic, as of his epistemology and his aesthetics.

We see this in Stevens's own life. Mr. O'Connor heads his first chapter 'Stevens as Legend'. Precisely. Stevens is a legendary figure; he has taken care that he should be, as Byron and Yeats did before him. Perhaps some of the legend was built up around him, wished upon him by others. But not all. It is surely clear, for instance, that some of the early poems that have not worn well, the self-consciously cryptic or culpably ambiguous pieces like 'Anecdote of a Jar', 'Metaphors of a Magnifico', even 'Bantams in Pine-Woods', are Stevens's contributions to the legend. They are good for the legend, if they are not good poems – again, like many poems by Byron. Each of these poems is 'a grand gesture', a too elaborate bow, a too exquisite formality; they are Stevens's substitutes for the cape and the flowing tie.

At this point I must take issue with Marius Bewley. He quotes himself, and analyzes, 'The Pastor Caballero', where –

> The sweeping brim of the hat
> Makes of the form Most Merciful Capitan
>
> If the observer says so: grandiloquent
> Locution of a hand in rhapsody.

He quotes from 'Infanta Marina':

> She made of the motions of her wrist
> The grandiose gestures
> of her thought.

And yet he can write of the jar in 'Anecdote of the Jar', 'It had style (more properly, manner or affectation) rather than reality.' This diminuendo, from 'style' through 'manner' to 'affectation', seems to me at variance with the whole course of Stevens's thought, as of his poetic practice. For Stevens, 'style', whether in life or literature, is only 'affectation' or 'mannerism' that succeeds. Admittedly the splendid hat of 'The Pastor Caballero' is examined from the point of view of the beholder, not the wearer. But observe that 'Infanta Marina' makes gestures of thought not *with* the motions of her wrist, but *of* those motions. The movement of the wrist does not express the motions of the mind; it invokes them and creates them. She behaves grandly not because she thinks grandly, but in order to do so. So, in 'Le Monocle de Mon Oncle', the poet's solution for the drabness and sterility that comes upon him, is 'bravura', 'the music and manner of the paladins'. If a man can no longer think and feel grandiosely, then he acts grandiosely or he makes a grandiose speech, and this renovates and exalts his thinking and his feeling. The cure for sterility is to act and speak as if it did not exist; by so doing, one destroys it.

Stevens is always mannered and affected. The affectation of his poorer poems reflects back out of the poetry upon Stevens the private individual; in his better pieces the affectation succeeds and becomes style because it stays in the poetry and builds up the public and representative figure of the poet. Where the affectation is a way of dealing with experience, with the theme of the poem, it justifies itself as poetic style; where it is a way of dealing with society, represented by the reader, it may be justified in terms of social behaviour, but not in terms of poetry.

This account, I fear, will appear laboured. And yet it is the merest scratching of the surface, over-simplifying at every point a weave so rich and ramifying that it calls for volumes of explication. I hope that at least it will show I am nothing if not profoundly grateful for the significant beauty that Stevens so generously provides. Only if that point is taken, can I go on to admit that, for my own part, I think the very greatest poetry is more chaste, less florid than this. It would seem to follow that I prefer an ethic more austere, a heroism less counfounded with 'panache'. That inference, too, I do not refuse. Yet it is Stevens's achievement that whenever we pick up his poems, he makes such reservations seem graceless and niggling. He is a great poet indeed.

NOTES

1 Marius Bewley, *The Complex Fate*. Part of Bewley's essay is included above (No. 75), but this passage is omitted.
2 William Van O'Connor, *The Shaping Spirit: A Study of Wallace Stevens* (Henry Regnery Company, Chicago, 1950).

96. Unsigned review, Stevens as 'the figure on the high-wire attempting balance amid disorder', *Times Literary Supplement*

19 June 1953, 396

This long review, of which perhaps one-sixth is quoted here, professes to admire Stevens as a 'master', but eventually (and somewhat coyly) hints that Stevens, in fact, lacked the concentration to make the profound spiritual discovery so nearly available to him.

...A poet who has spent a lifetime trying his best to say what he thinks deserves to have his thoughts regarded. To compliment Mr. Stevens, as one must, on the devotion he has given to his writing, so obvious in that insouciant grace which may deceive anyone who has never attempted it, is no more than politeness. To say further that he loves words for their sound and 'colour,' as every good poet should do, is but to prolong talk of the weather. Let it be taken for granted that Mr. Stevens is the best poet writing in America, and one of the best poets now writing in English. But these superlatives must be qualified: most often Mr. Stevens's excellence is of statement rather than idea, of sound rather than sense. It is as a 'singer' that he is outstanding. His initial gift may not have been so great as that of others; but how tirelessly he perfected it, with what care he made certain that the notes were pure and truly placed. If Mr. Stevens has for long been a poets' poet, it is just because so often he triumphantly bring off the apparently impossible, says something so remarkably well that criticism stops for a moment, breathless:

You know how Utamaro's beauties sought
The end of love in their all-speaking braids.
You know the mountainous coiffures of Bath.
Alas! Have all the barbers live in vain
That not one curl in nature has survived?
Why, without pity on these studious ghosts.
Do you come dripping in your hair from sleep?

It would be pleasant to continue the hunt for other ways of praising work so greatly liked, but something more is owing to a master. That sort of praise, what does it mean, in the end? There is no insolence in considering this openly: Mr. Stevens's poems are concerned with himself – his life, and what it may be worth. Like most puzzled people he gives half of his heart first to one conclusion and then to the other. At moments he tells himself that ours is a dog's life: 'Darkness, nothingness of human after-death.' But there are other moments in which resolute gloom is lightened by strange uncovenanted gleams: 'Where Do I begin and end?'... 'A dream (to call it a dream) in which I can believe'... 'What am I to believe?'... 'He wanted his heart to stop beating and his mind to rest In a permanent realization.'... Those are the stanchions; the high-wire is strung between; on it Mr. Stevens tries to balance himself with a very bright parasol: 'Poetry / Exceeding music must take the place of empty heaven and its hymns....' Engaged in such a testing work, is the aerialist to be blamed for clutching the jade handle hard, even for blinking at the taut coloured paper so as to make it look like parachute silk?

Thus portrayed, Mr. Stevens's position may not seem dignified, but neither is the similar position of the many for whom he is so remarkable a prototype. Their parasols may be inscribed 'Gloria mundi' or, more splendidly, 'Omnia vincit Amor,' but the wavering movement from uncertainty to uncertainty is the same. It might seem, then, that this subjective, exquisite poetry, inclining easily to the frivolous, the *recherché*, the *chic*, but then as suddenly tending toward the ominous, the superstitious, the mystic wonderland of religious terms divorced from religion, would find a wide and appreciative audience in England to-day. But even with

the best will in the world towards the confused sentiments of
Mr. Stevens's work, the average man is going to find
that – charmingly stated or not – confusion differs from
order, and that these poems, if full of meaning, leave much of
their meaning merely noted....

97. Bernard Bergonzi, 'The Sound of a Blue Guitar', *Nine*

No. 10, Winter 1953–4, 48–51

Bergonzi (b. 1929), Professor of English at the University of Warwick, has published studies of H. G. Wells and
T. S. Eliot and *Heroes' Twilight: A Study of the Literature
of the Great War* (1965).

English readers have had to wait a long time for the
publication of Stevens' poetry in anything other than
anthologies, for his first book appeared in America in 1923.
This need not cause too much surprise, regrettable though it
might be. English and American literary cultures are distinct
entities, and traffic between them, particularly in poetic
matters, is imperfect and limited – despite the exchange of
Mr. Eliot for Mr. Auden. But if Karl Shapiro and Kenneth
Patchen have already been published in this country, it is
clear the first English publication of Stevens is long overdue.
English readers will no longer have any excuse for remaining
ignorant of the work of a writer who is widely regarded in
America as one of the great poets of this century....
    Stevens was never an Imagist, but his early work shows
the influence of that discipline. Its ingenuity and wit and
colourfulness are reminiscent of the poetry that Edith Sitwell

was writing at about the same time, but this is at best a superficial comparison, and Stevens' subsequent development has been very different. It is these poems – from *Harmonium* – that have been most widely anthologized, and by which Stevens is probably best known: such work as 'Peter Quince at the Clavier,' 'Anecdote of the Jar,' 'The Emperor of Ice Cream' or 'To the One of Fictive Music.' It is understandable that Stevens' early work should be his most popular, for it is, on the whole, more approachable than his later poetry. The early poems tend to be concise, concrete, and fairly close to the world of things, while the later ones, and particularly those written since *The Man with the Blue Guitar* (1937), which marks something of a watershed in his development, are, in comparison, often long, complex, rarified, and concerned less with external reality in itself than with the relation between that reality and the mind. A concentration on the early poems may be unfortunate if it gives only a partial view of his development. Nevertheless, and despite his impressive recent poetry, much of the verbal felicity in his first volume remains unsurpassed. Here are the closing lines of 'Sunday Morning':

> And, in the isolation of the sky,
> At evening, casual flocks of pigeons make
> Ambiguous undulations as they sink
> Downward to darkness, on extended wings.

Stevens has almost certainly the purest diction of any living poet. It is possible to read poem after poem simply for the excellence of their style. Whether it is advisable to do this is another matter, for Stevens is a poet to be read in depth rather than in breadth, and, as Edmund Wilson pointed out in his original review of *Harmonium,* his work is seen to better advantage in single poems than *en masse.* Even with the early poems, considerable application is needed for the proper understanding of many of them. The well-known 'Emperor of Ice Cream' is a fundamentally baffling poem, despite its directness and bareness of language, and one can contrast the grace and lucidity of 'Peter Quince at the Clavier' with the elegant impenetrability (for one reader, at least) of 'Le Monocle de mon Oncle'. Like Valéry, Stevens has never made any concessions to his audience; sometimes his symbols are readily accessible, and at other times they will require a skilled explication to attach any meaning to them. And often such an explication will be beyond the scope of even a reasonably experienced reader of modern poetry, especially a non-American. The elaborate patterns of sound and imagery in 'Sea Surface full of Clouds,' for instance, must obviously contain a great deal of significance, but the key is missing, and one must remain outside the structure.

Mention of Valéry recalls that, if Stevens is not an imagist, he can with more justification be called a symbolist. If the aesthetic of continental symbolism had an American source in Poe, Stevens may be said to have reimported it, for he has consistently looked towards Europe, and particularly to France, for his manner, if not his subjects. His stylish, withdrawn, meditative muse has little connection with the tradition stemming from Whitman. To call Stevens a symbolist does help to place him, but it is a term of limited usefulness; strictly a description rather than an interpretation. Much of his theory of imagination leads back beyond Mallarmé directly to Coleridge. In one major respect, however, Stevens resembles the European symbolists: the tendency to Music, described in Pater's famous phrase about all art tending to the condition of music. Images of music and musical instrument, such as the Blue Guitar, the symbol of the poetic imagination, occur constantly in Stevens' poetry; and there is an extraordinary musical sense in the actual quality of his writing. Much of his verse has a *cantabile* loveliness rare in modern poetry; lines will sing themselves into the mind and remain there. At times Stevens betrays a certain impatience with conventional language; a desire to move more completely into the abstract world of music would perhaps explain the recurrent passages of onomatopoeia, and lines where the referential function of words is kept at a minimum:

> I sang a canto in a canton,
> Cunning-coo, Oh, cuckoo cock.

Stevens' favourite verse form, particularly in his recent work, is a two or three line stanza, usually without rhyme, and employing extensive *enjambement,* as well as alliteration, to which he is somewhat over-addicted. This is an admirable form for shorter poems, but in the long poems the absence of more elaborate architectonic devices tends to lead ultimately to monotony, despite the consistent excellence of the poet's musical diction. It is conceivable that after hearing too many concertos by Vivaldi one might wish instead for a page or two of, say, the *Symphonie Fantastique.* Occasionally Stevens will break the flow of his verse by an abrupt shift in rhythm, or by introducing what seems to be a deliberately cacophonous line. This is presumably an attempt to prod the reader into a closer attention to the matter as opposed to the style of the poem. Stevens' consistent mellifluence is in fact a disadvantage in the close reading of his long poems, which deal with philosophical themes of some complexity, for the mind becomes diverted by the suave movement of the verse, and some effort is required to bring the analytical faculties to bear, whereas a poet in the Metaphysical tradition, such as Empson, will organize his verse so that its movement helps to develop the argument of the poem. And, with Stevens, it is necessary to take careful note of his philosophising. It would be a pity if a poet of his seriousness were to be considered only as the 'maladif, mandarin-miened, mauve melody-man' of David Gascoyne's witty parody.

It has been said that all Stevens' poems are about poetry. This is probably inaccurate, though he has written in section XXII (a highly significant passage) of *The Man with the Blue Guitar:*

> Poetry is the subject of the poem,
> From this the poem issues and
> To this returns.

His recurring pre-occupation is the attempt to penetrate by absolute self-consciousness into the nature of the poetic act. For Stevens poetry is nothing less than the intelligible apprehension of reality; much of his work can be described as an attempt at a poetic epistemology. As already mentioned, one has to go to Coleridge to understand Stevens' exalted view of the imagination. Indeed, he appears to abolish Coleridge's distinction between the Primary imagination, 'the living power and prime agent of all human perception' and the Secondary, presumably the creative imagination of the artist. If reality is fundamentally unintelligible in itself, then the poetic imagination itself will impose 'Ideas of Order' (the title of one of Stevens' books) upon the external chaos. One is inevitably reminded of the Kantian categories.

> And things are as I think they are
> And say they are on the blue guitar.

Pursued far enough, this attitude could mean that poetry becomes a religion, though not necessarily in the somewhat crude Ricardian manner. And Stevens does not evade this point; the poet must construct a 'supreme fiction' by which man can live.

> Poetry

> Exceeding music must take the place
> Of empty heaven and its hymns.

And in the final poem in this selection occur the lines:

> We say God and the imagination are one.
> How high that highest candle lights the dark.

No doubt Stevens has been accused of being cut off from reality, as were so many of the earlier symbolists. In one sense it is a rather foolish charge, for it is not possible to be literally severed from reality: one cannot contract out of Being. 'Everything possible to be believ'd is an image of truth' – considered ontologically, at least. Nevertheless, one can sympathize with the attitude behind this accusation. Though it is not to be expected that Stevens would be very much concerned with the events of the market-place, the life of humanity and human emotions play only a small part (though they are entirely absent, particularly in *Harmonium*) in his universe. His phenomenal world of forms and colours is lonely and depopulated:

> The human
> Reverie is a solitude in which
> We compose these proportions, torn by dreams.

One must compare this with Yeats lamenting the death of his friends, with the voices in Eliot's rose-garden, or even with the long arguments and the history-lessons in the *Cantos*. That the comparison can be made is an indication of Stevens' stature.

His poetry, and even the selection of it under review, represents a lifetime of magnificent achievement. But it is, alas, essentially a barren magnificence (which is not to imply that younger poets cannot learn much from Stevens about the art of poetry). If this is a harsh verdict, it is perhaps the penalty of viewing the world purely as an aesthetic phenomenon, and so trying to make poetry do more than can be reasonably expected of it. Stevens has reached a post-symbolist pinnacle of great purity and splendour, but there can be no going beyond it. It will be necessary to retrace one's footsteps, and make the long and troublesome descent to a world that may not be intrinsically unintelligible after all, and where a poetic 'supreme fiction' may be unnecessary. As Maritain once remarked, 'It is a deadly error to expect poetry to provide the super-substantial nourishment of man'; and ultimately one will read Stevens' poetry less for pabulum than for style. And, as style, it is superb.

98. William Carlos Williams, from 'A Celebration for Wallace Stevens', *Trinity Review*

Vol. 8, no. 3, May 1954, 10–11

To mark Stevens' seventy-fifth birthday, this celebration includes contributions from T.S. Eliot, Marianne Moore, Archibald MacLeish, Conrad Aiken, Alfred

Kreymborg, Norman Holmes Pearson and a dozen or so others.

Stevens knew Williams from the early years of the century, in Greenwich Village circles, where, despite Stevens' characteristic reserve, as Williams wrote of him later, 'He really was felt to be part of the gang'. (This remark is quoted by William Van O'Connor in *The Shaping Spirit*, p. 15.) Stevens, for his part, said of Williams, 'One never detects paraphrase in anything you do, either personally or in your writing, so that there really is live contact there' (*Letters*, p. 246).

It is instructive to contrast the tone of this celebratory piece of Williams' with Eliot's note on the same occasion (part of which is in Ehrenpreis, *Wallace Stevens*, 1972).

I'll never forget 'Peter Quince at the Clavier' nor the admonishment to some dignitary wearing 'a caftan of tan' and 'with henna hackles' to 'halt'. 'I placed a jar in Tennessee' is a line with which I am as familiar as with my own name. All these things which I learned from the poems of Wallace Stevens in the early 20's or before have become part of my life. As distinct is the memory I have of my first trip to Hartford to pay him a visit. I had been to Vermont on a vacation and had my dog Bobby along. He was an intelligent dog and knew how to behave before strangers. Stevens had reserved quarters for us in a hotel. He spoke that night of having a friend who every Christmas made a point of sending him a present, from Paris, some candied violets! and what a kick he always got from it. Stevens is a big man and obviously intelligent. He was friendly but aloof and not in the least effeminate. Nor did he give ground under attack but continued to celebrate his own peculiar view of the world. There was always something forbiddingly formal about Stevens; that was perhaps his parental background.

If you knew him you couldn't help liking him howbeit with an admixture of awe for his accomplishments, especially if you knew how he had fought his way from being news reporter on the *New York Tribune,* I think it was. Finding himself licked there and reversing his field he gave himself to his present position in the law.

He wanted to be a writer, perhaps a poet. It took a certain adroitness and perseverance to cling to that while changing face to become proficient in something else. He, apparently, was not dismayed but took it as an occasion for sharpening his wits. His poetry has not suffered. He has made a success of both professions. After all, you cannot spend all your life writing, there come moments when you might as well be otherwise employed. It's bracing and returns the writer to his words with a rather sharper eye for detail.

What has Stevens accomplished with his life? Or better put, what has been his aim and how far has he succeeded in achieving it?

It's the infinite variety of resource in the phrasing of his poetic ideas that has kept Stevens alive for us the past thirty to forty years. It was there in the first poems and is still there in *The Auroras of Autumn,* one of his most recent books. There is a verbal quickness, a love for alliteration and other grace notes which are clearly used to enhance the charm of what is being said, but what I refer to goes further than that. It is what undoubtedly has made him all his life a poet. It is the music of his lines, the overall music of his phrasing, that has been the thing that has kept Stevens perennially at the top of his game, always ready to carry it further. If it were not for that he could not have gone on.

Stevens has a quick mind and, as becomes a lawyer, it is full of verbal quiddities. His imagination fills his poems with an infinite variety of birds and beasts, trees and flowers, lakes and seas with their presence and as like as not with their movements. His language is distinguished by a superb choice of words, unusual words aptly used in a normal but never dull order. There is never an inversion of phrase but on the contrary a directness of every day speech, livened by wit. You feel that underneath, a thought exists and if you are not alert it will trip you – as it leads to a rewarding conclusion.

Unlike prose, which means what it says, poetry is the music of words, it doesn't at all mean what it says and that is the reason for its rejection by a practical world. What it means is much more than can be spoken at least in prose just as music cannot be given an articulate meaning. The music of a poem transcends the words, always linked with them, surpasses them. The poems of Wallace Stevens show well this music. They show it on two levels, a playful fascination with the words, an affectionate caressing of the horse's neck which is to be easily understood; followed by the surge that takes hold of the man when the beast upon whose back he is mounted plunges with him into space.

This power did not come to Stevens at once. Looking at the poems he wrote thirty years ago, charming as they are, 'Peter Quince at the Clavier' etc., Stevens reveals himself not the man he has become in such a book as *The Auroras of Autumn* where his stature as a major poet has reached the full. It is a mark of genius when an accomplished man can go on continually developing, continually improving his techniques as Stevens shows by his recent work.

Many long hours of application to the page have gone into this. A word has to be taken out and transposed. A redundant word first has to be detected in its redundancy and when a man's fascination with it has been cured, finally, he appears with an axe and cuts it off. This takes intelligence and above all, courage. Some never achieve that courage. But the man destined to be a major artist has to sacrifice many easy triumphs to emerge at his full stature. Stevens shows today that he has known these battles and has survived them.

Look alone at the inversion of phrases in his first book, *Harmonium,* and this is a work of major importance. It has all disappeared in the later years. A smoothness, a mastery of the line has taken its place. It is Stevens' devotion to the music of his measures that has brought this about. Patiently the artist has evolved until we feel that should he live to be a hundred it would be as with Hokusai a perspective of always increasing power over his materials until the last breath.

COLLECTED POEMS

New York, 1954; London, 1955

Knopf published a first printing of 2,500 copies.

---

99. Samuel French Morse, 'A Poet who Speaks the Poem as It Is', *New York Times Book Review*

3 October 1954, 3, 21

Samuel French Morse (b. 1916), a poet, critic and scholar, edited Stevens' *Opus Posthumous* (1957) and was co-editor (with Jackson R. Bryer and Joseph N. Riddel) of *Wallace Stevens: Checklist and Bibliography of Stevens Criticism* (1963). He also wrote *Wallace Stevens: Poetry a Life* (1970).

Off-hand, in the manner of improvisation, Wallace Stevens once wrote, 'It is life that one is trying to get at in poetry.' It is a characteristic remark, impersonal almost to the point of diffidence, and still colloquial: an obvious fact charged with conviction that amounts to more than mere feeling. Without the feeling, the words become sententious, as proverbs are likely to be, and obiter dicta. The difference between a remark about poetry and the thing itself, however, is worth noting, as a few lines from 'An Ordinary Evening in New Haven' will make clear:

The poem is the cry of its occasion,
Part of the res itself and not about it.
The poet speaks the poem as it is,

Not as it was: part of the reverberation
Of a windy night as it is, when the marble statues
Are like newspapers blown by the wind. He speaks

By sight and insight as they are...

Doctrine in prose becomes the veritable thing in verse, dramatized completely by feeling. Sense becomes truly a matter of the senses, seeing and hearing, and that X which defines itself as 'insight' or imagination. In no other poet of our time have 'the secretions of insight' been more persuasive or more often achieved.

The Collected Poems of Wallace Stevens is a triumph for the imagination, the faculty that William James felt was some-how less than the rational faculty, that Freud opposed to the intellect, and that philosophers and theologians have dispara-ged ever since Plato banned the poets from his Republic and the lineage of musicians was traced to Jubal Cain. From 'Peter Quince at the Clavier,' first published nearly forty years ago, to 'Not Ideas about the Thing but the Thing Itself,' written this year, these poems assert the goodness of the imagination. They are proof, as their author has said, that Poetry is one of the sanctions of life.

The poems of *Harmonium*, published in 1923, have acquired the verisimilitude of life. They have become part not only of the way we look at things, but also of what we see. They are part of the reality of our century, all the more valuable because in them 'the torments of confusion' are composed and tranquilized. Reading these early poems again is in experience like that of Crispin, the hero of 'The Comedian as the Letter C,' whose marvelous voyage to Carolina 'made him see how much / Of what he saw he never saw at all.' To re-read 'The Comedian' is to discover almost as if for the first time the only major poem (in English, at any rate) of our age which is deeply rooted in the tradition of intellectual comedy. Complicate with a dazzlingly sensuous apprehension of fact and a lucid and humorous awareness of its own limitations, 'The Comedian' defies literal exegesis as completely as it repays loving attention to its richly sustained details.

This is not to say that Stevens has escaped the exegete; but a good deal of the criticism, favorable and otherwise, lavished upon the poems has been written from a point of view which seems to imply that for all their deftness they are either trivial or morally suspect. A comic view of life, criticism suggests, is a romantic falsification. The truth would seem to be that Stevens' chief 'argument' is to demonstrate that 'what we see is what we think':

> Inescapable romance, inescapable choice
> Of dreams, disillusion as the last illusion,
> Reality as a thing seen by the mind,
>
> Not that which is but that which is apprehended,
> A mirror, a lake of reflections in a room,
> A glassy ocean lying at the door,
>
> A great town hanging pendent in a shade,
> An enormous nation happy in a style,
> Everything as unreal as real can be,
> In the inexquisite eye...

Imagination, not mere sensibility, is thus the real measure of value. A poet who can synthesize the sum total of his experience, even if only momentarily, is for Stevens the poet who matters, although it may be true that

> ...his mastery
>
> Left only the fragments found in the grass,
> From his project, as finally magnified.

These words, from a recent poem, 'Two Illustrations That the World Is What You Make of It,' like almost everything else he has written, assert in context at least that taking the world apart is for Wallace Stevens only preliminary to seeing the world whole. The world is one defined almost exclusively by esthetic values; for this reason it sometimes seems remote and private, too much of a joke, and too pure to furnish real sustenance. There are times when Stevens becomes garrulous; and especially in a good many of the recent short poems he counts heavily on manner at the expense of matter.

In one sense, then:

This endlessly elaborating poem
Displays the theory of poetry
As the life of poetry. A more severe,

More harassing master would extemporize
Subtler, more urgent proof that the theory
Of poetry is the theory of life,

As it is, in the intricate evasions of as,
In things seen and unseen, created from nothingness,
The heavens, the hells, the worlds, the longed-for lands.

In a sense, too, Wallace Stevens has spent a lifetime writing a single poem. What gives his best work its astonishing power and vitality is the way in which a fixed point of view, maturing naturally, eventually takes in more than a constantly shifting point of view could get at.

The point of view is romantic, 'almost the color of comedy'; but 'the strength at the center is serious.' Behind Wallace Stevens stand Wordsworth and Coleridge as well as Rimbaud and Mallarmé, and, surprisingly enough, La Fontaine and Pope. This poetic lineage is important only in so far as it proves that a master can claim the world as ancestor. Knowing where he stands, the poet can move as a free man in the company of free men.

Perhaps this kind of freedom, demanding as much discipline of the reader as of the poet, proved too austere when *Harmonium* was first published. Whatever the explanation, the book sold almost not at all. Hindsight makes one wonder how, except for a few anthologists' favorites (which include some of the best), the poems survived at all. Contradictorily, it seems impossible to account for the neglect of so much that we should now be unwilling to lose. The *Collected Poems* includes the whole of *Harmonium* in the 1931 edition, which added the extraordinarily beautiful 'Sea

Surface Full of Clouds' and a handful of other poems to the original text; *Ideas of Order, The Man with the Blue Guitar, Parts of a World, Transport to Summer, The Auroras of Autumn,* and twenty-five new poems.

Of these last, half a dozen reveal that 'words of the world are the life of the world.' 'To an Old Philosopher in Rome' and 'The Rock' surpass almost all the poems that precede them. Only the fabulous anecdote, 'The Comedian as the Letter C' and the superb longer meditations, such as *Notes Toward a Supreme Fiction, Esthétique du Mal,* can equal them. The artifice that in some of the shorter poems occasionally seems excessive, has been wholly transformed to 'a festival sphere.' ...

100. John Ciardi, from 'Wallace Stevens' "Absolute Music"', *Nation*

Vol. 179, no. 16, 16 October 1954, 346–7

Ciardi (b. 1916) is an American poet, teacher, editor and translator, whose work includes a well-known version of Dante's *Divine Comedy* and *How Does a Poem Mean?* (1959).

...Joking with Robert Frost once in Florida (I report the exchange from Mr. Frost's account of it), Stevens said, 'The trouble with you, Frost, is that you write on subjects.' Frost replied, 'The trouble with you is you write bric-à-brac.'

The exchange was in play, but the center of the play locates a real difference. Some poets, Frost notable among them, write poems which have their references, at least in large part, in a recognizable external world; to the extent that we knew beforehand something at least about what they are describing, our understanding of the poems is made easier. Stevens, on the other hand, insists on the poem as its own imagination and subject; a thing made of itself in the saying; a self-entering, self-generating, self-sealing organism, a thing of its own nature.

> The sound of that slick sonata
> Finding its way from the house, makes music seem
> To be a nature, a place in which itself
> Is that which produces everything else.

In the pursuit of that absolute music, that music which rises from itself and follows itself, Stevens has gone farther than any other man in English to achieve his sound effects. So in 'Bantams in Pine Woods'.

> Chieftain Iffucan of Azcan in caftan
> Of tan with henna hackles, halt!

The reader who does not stay around long enough to realize that this is good play beginning with the comic effect of saluting a champion bantam rooster (significantly strutting about a pine woods as if he meant to knock over the trees) by the ridiculous name he bears in the pedigree book – such a reader will simply find himself puzzled here, especially if he is one of those literalists who must always know at once where he stands. For that matter, even the most devoted admirer of Stevens is likely to find himself swallowing hard to take down some of the decorative French tags and quasi-Elizabethan lolly-lilly cicanics Stevens so often runs in while pursuing his 'absolute music.'

It is not for such devices, or for the philosophy of the imagination, that one falls in love with Stevens, but for the magnificence of his ear. Let any reader begin with such a poem as 'Le Monocle de Mon Oncle,' or 'Sunday Morning,' and simply ask himself if English or American speech has ever been made overflow with such music as this. Stevens teaches the language its own singing possibilities....

101. Delmore Schwartz, from 'In the Orchards of the Imagination', *New Republic*

Vol. 131, 1 November 1954, 16–18

... The starting-point of Stevens' poems is often the aesthetic experience in isolation from all other experiences, as art is isolated from work, and as a museum is special and isolated in any modern American community. And if one limits oneself to the surface of Stevens' poetic style, one can characterize Stevens as the poet of Sunday: the poet of the week-end, the holiday, and the vacation, who sees objects at a distance, as they appear to the tourist or in the art museum. But this is merely the poet's starting-point. Stevens converts aestheticism into contemplation in the full philosophical and virtually religious sense of the word. The surface of his poetry is very often verbal, visual, and gay; beneath the surface, it is a deadly earnest scrutiny of attitudes toward existence, of 'how to live, what to do.' The reader begins with the impression that Stevens is a dandy and virtuoso of language, and too many readers have stopped with that impression; but the reader who persists discovers that Stevens is literally a poet of ideas, a philosophical poet; his discourses on thought, existence, nature, and destiny are suave and elegant – and also profound, uniting an underlying seriousness with an ultimate gaiety. The point of view of the man of art, the concert-goer, the student of French poetry – the point of view, in short, of the aesthete – has been transformed from a limitation into a window with 'a good light' as the poet says, 'for those who know the ultimate Plato.'

Stevens has often been much underrated because readers fail to perceive this transformation. The reader begins with such sensuous observations as

The sound of z in the grass all day....

A crinkled paper makes a brilliant sound....

With my whole body I taste these peaches....

Each perception is in itself valuable and beautiful; hence it is
understandable enough that the careless reader does not see
how often the perceptions are essentially springboards
leading to ultimate generalizations, to such formulations of
insight and wisdom as

The greatest poverty is not to live
In a physical world....

Adam in Eden was the father of Descartes....

If sex were all, then every trembling hand
Could make us speak, like dolls, the wished-for words....

Perhaps the best illustration is one of Stevens' best and most
ambitious poems: 'Le Monocle de Mon Oncle.' The title
itself is ironic and flippant and misleading; and the poem is
written chiefly in the bravura style of such verses as

Is it for nothing, then, that old Chinese
Sat titivating by their mountain pools
Or in the Yangtze studied out their beards....

and

...A frog
Boomed from his belly odious chords....

But the poem is, in fact, a serious meditation on the nature of
love. When the middleaged protagonist describes himself and
his wife as 'Two golden gourds distended on our vines....
We hang like warty squashes, steaked and rayed,' the
mocking ironic grotesqueness is necessary to bring one to the
conclusion, the delicate statement of the difficult belief that
love makes human beings important and unique, no matter
how they look in middle age or at any other time.

R. P. Blackmur was the first to remark (in a pioneer essay
on Stevens, in 1932)[1] that Stevens' poems 'grow in the

mind.' They do. The growing continues, astonishing and inexhaustible, and comparable to the experience of living with paintings. And as his poetry grows in one's mind, the greater the abundance of comment which it seems to require. Clearly the primary comment must be the conviction that Stevens is a great poet, that his work as a whole is as important as that of Frost and Eliot. There are so many other things to be said about his work (naturally enough, since it is the fruit of fifty years) that, in a brief essay, one can hardly attempt to do more than name some of them. There is the complex neglected fact that Stevens is a New England poet, like Robinson and Frost, and like Emerson, Thoreau, and Emily Dickinson also. Exhibiting the strains of solitude, exoticism, and Puritanism, his poems are at times comparable to the precious and strange objects which Yankee skippers acquired in the China trade. Then there is Stevens' assimilation and mastery of the lessons of modern painting, *vers libre* and imagism, of the traditional norms of the blank verse style in Shakespeare and Milton, his inventive and original use of place names, of foreign and archaic words, and his witty coinages, his relationship to Whitman and to Baudelaire (two poets who almost never are a combined influence upon any modern poet). And then there is the triumph of his reputation, which like that of Marianne Moore and Williams Carlos Williams, has been slow but irresistible....

Interpretation is the key – and the glory of Stevens' poetry: the power and richness of interpretation is made infinite by the poetic imagination. Writing interpretation with imagination, Stevens arrives at a system of perspectives which makes or can make anything and everything poetic; everything which exists can be a rich instance of the poetic, once it is seen from the right bias, angle, or attitude of interpretation....

So too the poetry of Stevens will modify the speech and consciousness of many generations indirectly. His inventions, his discoveries, his long labor in the orchards of the imagination will directly affect other poets more and more in the future, giving a new, unintended and triumphant meaning to a pronouncement in his first book which was merely meant to be witty: 'I am a man of fortune greeting heirs.''

NOTE

1 See above, No. 28.

102. Lawrence Ferlinghetti, on a poetry of 'cerebral phosphorescences', *San Francisco Chronicle*

28 November 1954, 22

The complete review is titled 'Two Different Types of Poetry' and, in general, compares Stevens' work to that of E. E. Cummings, whose *Poems 1923–54* is also reviewed. The review was written when Ferlinghetti was still using his family's anglicized surname of 'Ferling', but it shows already his desire to 'put poetry back on the streets', an endeavour to implement which was to make him (and his City Lights Books) famous just a few short years later as publicist, impresario and publisher for the Beat Generation.

... there is no doubt that his *Collected Poems* prove him to be the most immaculate master of poetics, and it would take a book to do justice to the range of his poetic music, to the rare combination of his eye and ear. As a poet's poet he is perfect.

His poetry gives, almost exclusively, intellectual pleasure. It is poetry, to use his phrase, of 'cerebral phosphorescences.' He is most concerned with 'the poem of the mind' or 'the poem of the act of the mind.' And, as he says halfway through the present volume, poetry itself becomes the subject of the poem.

Stevens has also said that the poem really should be 'the cry of its occasion.' But this is just what Stevens' poems usually are not, almost always lacking the directness that any cry must have....

103. Randall Jarrell, 'a book like this is truly an occasion', *Harper's Magazine*

Vol. 29, November 1954, 100

... One might as well argue with the Evening Star as find fault with so much wit and grace and intelligence; such knowledge of, feeling for, other times and places, and our own; such an overwhelming and exquisite command both of the words and of the rhythms of our language; such charm and irony, such natural and philosophical breadth of sympathy, such dignity and magnanimity. (Toynbee often has the calm and generosity of a visitor from a better age, and you feel that Stevens would like nothing better than to be such a traveler through time.) Little of Stevens' work has the dramatic immediacy, the mesmeric, involving humanity, of so much of Yeats' and Frost's poetry: his poems, if they were ideally successful, might resemble the paintings of Piero della Francesca. But some of these cool, clear, airy poems, which tower above us in the dazzling elegance, the 'minute brilliance,' of yachts or clouds, ought to be sailing over other heads many centuries from now.

104. Hayden Carruth, 'Stevens is Elizabethan in his attitude toward language', *Poetry*

Vol. 85, no. 5, February 1955, 288–93

This article appears in *Poetry* under the title 'Without the Inventions of Sorrow'.

Opulence – it is the quality which most of us, I expect, ascribe before all others to the poetry of Wallace Stevens: profusion, exotic abundance and luxuriance. We carry in our minds an image of poems which teem with rich, strange, somehow forbidden delights, omnifarious and prodigious. Just to read the titles of his poems is to acquire again this sense of the extraordinary: 'Tea at the Palaz of Hoon,' 'The Bird with the Coppery, Keen Claws,' 'Sea Surface Full of Clouds,' 'The Man with the Blue Guitar,' 'Mrs. Alfred Uruguay,' 'The Owl in the Sarcophagus,' 'Angel Surrounded by Paysans,' 'The Irish Cliffs of Moher' – and hundreds more, of course. They are everywhere, extending round one, as it were, like an incredible, incomparable gallery.

Nor is the idea of a gallery out of place in speaking of the collected edition of Mr. Stevens' poems. I was continually impressed, as I wandered – no other word will do – among the hundreds of poems in this volume, by the way in which they present to us the whole movement of this century in art; no exhibition of paintings could be more expressive of the modern artist's aims and methods. Of course, the poet's very graphic way with imagery reminds one naturally of painting; the bright, Mediterranean colors and the dramatic interiors, as in the opening lines of 'Sunday Morning,' recall to me most clearly, I think, Matisse, though other readers undoubtedly have other associations. The chief point is, however, that in these poems the many influences on the art of our time can be seen clearly: French, pastoral, metaphysical, Homeric, etc.; and the many aims: to originate, to shock, to re-examine, to analyse, and above all to deal uncompromisingly with the realities of the contemporary world.

In point of time, Stevens' career as a writer has been co-extensive with the development of modern art, at least as it has occurred in this country, and the career itself, as recorded in these poems, reveals the stages through which we have come to believe the masters must always pass. The chronology is not definite and, for my purpose, perhaps not important. But there are the early masterpieces of conventional technique – 'Sunday Morning' and a few shorter poems in regular but marvelously controlled blank verse. There are the poems in which this technique begins to shift under an experimental impetus; of many examples, 'The Comedian as the Letter C' is one. There are the sheer experiments, often fragmentary and uncharacteristic. There are the variations on a constant theme – many of them apparently impromptu – of the middle period, when the poet was working toward a strong and individual style, a technique with which he could master any material, no matter how complex or 'unpoetic.' And there are the later poems which sometimes revert to an old simplicity. The progression has, of course, been accompanied – quickened, pervaded, impelled – by a relentless amendment and elaboration of the poet's theme, and the lavishness of his invention has never diminished.

But why? Why do we inevitably come back to this impression of opulence? One thinks immediately of the abounding images from the natural world, quick glimpses of land and water:

> The rocks of the cliffs are the heads of dogs
> That turn into fishes and leap
> Into the sea.

> It is true that the rivers went nosing like swine,
> Tugging at banks, until they seemed
> Bland belly-sounds in somnolent troughs.

On an old shore, the vulgar ocean rolls
Noiselessly, noiselessly, resembling a thin bird,
That thinks of settling, yet never settles, on a nest.

The cricket in the telephone is still.
A geranium withers on the window-sill.

But do they really abound? It was much more difficult than I
had expected it would be to find these four detachable
examples, and even they are not truly representative. The
fact is, most of the poems are single metaphors, short,
whole, compact, even spare; the images are used frugally and
pointedly; they are never merely decorative. Even the long
poems are generally composed of short sections, separated
and numbered, which each conform to this pattern of lyric
rigor, and the few long poems which do comprise sustained
passages of narrative or exposition are surprisingly un-
adorned. In other words, the poems themselves, when we
examine them without our preconceptions, contain neither
denser nor more ornate imagery than we should expect to find
in 534 pages of poetry by any other author, and in many cases
the comparison, especially if it were with the work of his
contemporaries, would show Stevens' poems to be the
simpler in design, structure, and figuration.

Perhaps, then, it is a question of the poet's subject, his
materia. Many of the poems, true enough, and especially the
earlier ones, convey an exotic scene, Caribbean radiance of
sun-drenched seas and forests. 'Hibiscus on the Sleeping
Shores,' 'The Idea of Order at Key West,' 'O Florida,
Venereal Soil' – these and many others, most of them from
Harmonium, the poet's first book, are clearly visions of
splendor. But the first poem in the second book is called
'Farewell to Florida,' and thereafter Stevens' characteristic
scene is not tropical but northern, and there are as many
celebrations of drab and wintry occasions as of summer.
Again I was surprised to find how few of the poems are in
fact given to outright flourishes of terrestrial glitter.

The earlier poems, those which appeared in *Harmonium*,
are undoubtedly the best known. They have been repub-
lished many times in anthologies and repeatedly discussed by
the critics. They have become a regular part of university

courses in modern literature. And many of them, of course, are undeniably brilliant; it is not surprising that they are used as displays. But they are not as good as the later poems, and emphatically they do not reveal the qualities of Stevens' whole accomplishment. The advantage of this collected edition is the prominence which it gives to the main body of poems.

I think we conclude finally that, in the texts themselves, the language is the only constant ratification of our sense of the poet's opulent invention. There is nothing new in the idea of Stevens as a master of language. But to explore the pages of this collection is to be astonished, quite literally, by the extraordinary range and intensity of his rhetorical genius. It is not virtuosity, for the virtuoso's superlative performance must be theoretically attainable by anyone, whereas Stevens excels at that which only he can do. It is a perfection, a pressing extension within the formulations of his own strict style and prosody, of the aptitude for naming which must be fundamental to any writer's talent. Someday, perhaps, an industrious scholar will count the number of different words Stevens has used; I hope so, for although I am sure his poems incorporate by far the largest vocabulary among contemporary poets, it would be instructive to have the difference measured. Stevens delights in odd words, archaic words, foreign words which he can wrest to an English meaning. In this respect he is like Whitman, but, to my ear, better than Whitman, for I am never embarrassed by Stevens' importations: he dominates and controls the foreign words with an authority which Whitman could never achieve. More exactly, Stevens is Elizabethan in his attitude toward language, high-handed in the extreme. When all else fails, he derives words anew, gambling with the recognizable roots and associations:

> The grackles sing avant the spring
> Most spiss – oh! Yes, most spissantly.

Such delight in language is infectious, and we are convinced, as we should be, when Stevens says to us,

> Natives of poverty, children of malheur,
> The gaity of language is our seigneur.

Stevens is the delighted craftsman whose delight is, in part, the access of gratification which comes upon the exercise of mastery. His pleasure is endless because it is part of his work, past and present; it is transmissible because we too, in reading his poems, share that mastery.

True poetry is instinct with this delight – and with much more, of course. With meaning which transcends its verbal properties. With a passion which makes whole the verbal elements. As it happens, Stevens' delight in language is concomitant to his entire vision, his argument. If there is space in this short tribute for only a glance at one or two technical aspects of his poetry, I think we can be sure that scholars and critics for many, many years will be engrossed by the problems of the larger content. As their work progresses and our appreciation grows, we shall see more and more clearly how *humane* is the desire which has given us, in these poems, a delight that is interpretative of our world. Even now, of course, we have in this book poems which are beautiful, impeccable, and famous, poems which are so intimate a part of our time and scene that we are almost persuaded to say, appropriatively: 'This is what we have been able to do; by these works we are willing to be known.'

105. R. P. Blackmur, from 'The Substance that Prevails', *Kenyon Review*

Vol. XVII, no. 1, Winter 1955, 94–110

Blackmur used the occasion of Stevens' *Collected Poems* to provide another overview of the work. 'The Substance that Prevails' was presented first, in an earlier form, as a Braden Lecture at Yale University on 8 October 1954. The excerpt here is part of a paragraph on pp. 102–3 of the *Kenyon Review* version. It is included

as it affords the opportunity for comparison of Blackmur's views on Stevens' work early and late in the poet's
career (see No. 28).

.... Being a dandy, he is not a symbolist, either as Yeats or
Valéry was: the iconography of his mind is immediate and
self-explanatory *within* his vocabulary. You need no special
key, only a dictionary and a sense of life and the willingness
to assume his role. He is not a symbolist, but he may be a
parodist: both dandy and connoisseur make a parody of their
other selves: that is how they touch the quick of their
other – their previous and their final – selves. Even as a
parodist, he is not given to any secret meanings, nor to any
meanings not present in immediate words and attitudes
under the shaping influence of his role. In the deepest possible
sense his thought is in the action of his role. So he writes of 'a
few things for themselves,' and again – as near as he comes to
the statement of mystery – he says 'The only emperor is the
emperor of ice-cream.' His ambiguities are of the nature of
consciousness not of intent, of sensibility not of aspiration.
There is nothing he wishes to create, there is everything he
wishes to meet; nothing to transcend, much to mirror; in the
clashed edges of the things his poems see. Hence he is not an
allegorist, but a connoisseur of the absolute in the phenomenal; everything is said as expressly as possible in the medium
of his vocabulary, in the resources of the dictionary of his
mind. The mystery of his senses is enough....

106. Randall Jarrell discovers 'a great poem of a new kind', *Yale Review*

Vol. XLIV, Spring 1955, 340–53

The first half of Jarrell's article is especially valuable for its discussion of 'The Rock', but the whole is included because it ends with his interesting 'shopping-list'. The article is included in Jarrell's *Third Book of Criticism* (1969). In a briefer note on the book, which appears in *Harper's Magazine*, October 1955 (and is included in Jarrell's *Kipling, Auden and Co:* (1980)), Jarrell says: 'His last poems, "The Rock," show better than any other poems, perhaps, what the world looks like as we leave it.'

Back in the stacks, in libraries; in bookcases in people's living rooms; on brick-and-plank bookshelves beside studio couches, one sees big books in dark bindings, the *Collected Poems* of the great poets. Once, long ago, the poems were new: the books went by post – so many horses and a coach – to a man in a country house, and the letter along with it asked him to describe, evaluate, and fix the place in English literature, in 12,000 words, by January 25, of the poems of William Wordsworth. And the man did.

It is hard to remember that this is the way it was; harder to remember that this is the way it is. The *Collected Poems* still go out – in this century there have been Hardy's and Yeats's and Frost's and Eliot's and Moore's, and now Stevens' – and the man who is sent them still treats them with rough, or rude, or wild justice; still puts them in their place, appreciates their virtues, says *Just here thou ail'st*, says *Nothing I can say will possibly . . .* and mails the essay off.

It all seems terribly queer, terribly risky; surely, by now, people could have thought of some better way? Yet is it as different as we think from what we do to the old *Poems* in the dark bindings, the poems with the dust on them? Those ruins we star, confident that we are young and they, they are old – they too are animals no one has succeeded in naming, young things nothing has succeeded in aging; beings to which we can say, as the man in Kafka's story says to the corpse: 'What's the good of the dumb question you are asking?' They keep on asking it; and it is only our confidence and our innocence that let us believe that describing and evaluating them, fixing their places – in however many words by whatever date – is any less queer, any less risky.

The *Collected Poems* of such a poet as Stevens – hundreds and thousands of things truly observed or rightly imagined, profoundly meditated upon – is not anything one can easily become familiar with. Setting out on Stevens for the first time would be like setting out to be an explorer of Earth. Fortunately, I knew some of the poems well, and the poems I didn't know at all – the new ones in 'The Rock' – I fell in love with. I have spent a long time on the book, and have made lists (of what seemed to me the best poems, and the poems almost as good) that I hope will be of help to those who want to get to know Stevens' poetry, and of interest to those who already know it. But I too want to say *Nothing I can say will possibly* . . . before I mail my essay off.

This *Collected Poems* is full of extraordinary things, and the most extraordinary of all is the section of twenty-eight new – truly new – poems called 'The Rock.' One begins

It make so little difference, at so much more
Than seventy, where one looks, one has been there
                                                    before.

Wood-smoke rises through trees, is caught in an upper
                                                    flow
Of air and whirled away. But it has been often so.

In 'Seventy Years Later,' Stevens can feel that 'It is an illusion that we were ever alive'; can feel that the old, free air 'is no longer air' – that we, the houses, our shadows, their sha-dows, 'The lives these lived in the mind are at an end. They never were.' To him, now, 'The meeting at noon at the edge of the field seems like/An invention, an embrace between one desperate clod / And another in a fantastic consciousness, / In a queer assertion of humanity ...' Custom, the years, lie upon the far-off figures, and the man remembering them, 'with a weight / Heavy as frost, and deep almost as life'; and this weight and depth are in the poems, but transfigured, transcendent – are themselves a part of the poems' life. When Stevens says, as he looks at an old man sleeping, that 'The two worlds are asleep, are sleeping now. / A dumb sense possesses them in a kind of solemnity,' the motion of his words is as slow and quiet as the sleep of the worlds. These are poems from the other side of existence, the poems of someone who sees things in steady accustomedness, as we do not, and who sees their accustomedness, and them, as about to perish. In some of the poems the reader feels over everything the sobering and quieting, the largening presence of death. The poems are the poems of a very old man, 'a citizen of heaven though still of Rome'; many of their qualities come naturally from age, so that the poems are appropriately and legitimately different from other people's poems, from Stevens' own younger poems. These poems are magnanimous, compassionate, but calmly exact, grandly plain, as though they themselves had suggested to Stevens his 'Be orator but with an accurate tongue / And without eloquence'; and they seem strangely general and representative, so that we could say of them, of Stevens, what Stevens himself says 'To an Old Philosopher in Rome':

> each of us
> Beholds himself in you, and hears his voice
> In yours, master and commiserable man.

How much of our existence is in that 'master and commiserable man'! When we read even the first stanzas of this long poem,

> On the threshold of heaven, the figures in the street
> Become the figures of heaven, the majestic movement
> Of men growing small in the distances of space,
> Singing, with smaller and still smaller sound,
> Unintelligible absolution and an end—

413

The threshold, Rome, and that more merciful Rome
Beyond, the two alike in the make of the mind.
It is as if in a human dignity
Two parallels become one, a perspective, of which
Men are part both in the inch and in the mile.

How easily the blown banners change to wings...
Things dark on the horizons of perception,
Become accompaniments of fortune, but
Of the fortune of the spirit, beyond the eye,
Not of its sphere, and yet not far beyond,

The human end in the spirit's greatest reach,
The extreme of the known in the presence of the extreme
Of the unknown....

It seems to us that we are feeling, as it is not often possible for us to feel, what it is to be human; the poem's composed, equable sorrow is a kind of celebration of our being, and is deeper sounding, satisfies more in us, than joy; we feel our natures realized, so that when we read, near the end of the poem,

It is a kind of total grandeur at the end
With every visible thing enlarged, and yet
No more than a bed, a chair and moving nuns...

Total grandeur of a total edifice
Chosen by an inquisitor of structures
For himself. He stops upon this threshold...

We feel that Santayana is Stevens, and Stevens ourselves – and that, stopping upon this threshold, we are participating in the grandeur possible to man.

This is a great poem of a new kind. The completeness and requiredness of the poem's working-out; the held-back yet magically sure, fully extended slowness with which these parallel worlds near each other and meet, remind one of the slow movements of some of Beethoven's later quartets and sonatas. But poems like these, in their plainness and human rightness, remind me most of a work of art superficially very different, Verdi's *Falstaff*. Both are the products of men at once very old and beyond the dominion of age; such men seem to have entered into (or are able to create for us) a new existence, a world in which everything is enlarged and yet no more than itself, transfigured and yet beyond the need of transfiguration.

When Stevens writes, in 'The World as Meditation,' of Penelope waiting for Ulysses, it is not Penelope and Ulysses but Stevens and the sun, the reader and the world – 'two in a deep-founded sheltering, friend and dear friend.' At dawn 'a form of fire approaches the cretonnes of Penelope,' a 'savage presence' awakes within her own 'barbarous strength.' Has Ulysses come? 'It was only day. / It was Ulysses and it was not. Yet they had met, / Friend and dear friend and a planet's encouragement'; and she combs her hair, 'repeating his name with its patient syllables.'

Some of the phrases of the poems describe the poems better than any I can invent for them. 'St. Armorer's Church from the Outside' shows us the stony majesty of the past, man's settled triumphs:

> St Armorer's was once an immense success.
> It rose loftily and stood massively; and to lie
> In its church-yard, in the province of St. Armorer's,
> Fixed one for good in geranium-colored day...

but it leaves them for 'the chapel of breath,' for 'that which is always beginning because it is part / Of that which is always beginning, over and over,' for the new creation that seems to us 'no sign of life but life, / Itself, the presence of the intelligible / In that which is created as its symbol.' And the poems' wish for themselves, at the end – 'It was not important that they should survive. / What mattered was that they should bear / Some lineament or character, / Some affluence, if only half-perceived, / In the poverty of their words, / Of the planet of which they were part' – is touching as Keats' 'writ in water' is touching, and endears them to us more than our own praise.

Stevens has always looked steadily at the object, but has looked, often, shortly and with a certain indifference, the indifference of the artist who – as Goethe says – 'stands above art and the object; he stands above art because he utilizes it for his purpose; he stands above the object because he deals with it in his own manner.' But now that the unwanted, inescapable indifference of age has taken the place of this conscious indifference, Stevens is willing to be possessed by 'the plain sense of things,' and his serious undeviating meditation about them seems as much in their manner as in his. His poetry has had 'the power to transform itself, or else / And what meant more, to be transformed.' The movement of his poetry has changed; the reader feels in it a different presence, and is touched by all that is no longer there. Stevens' late-nineteenth-century orchestration has been replaced, most of the time, by plain chords from a few instruments – the stir and dazzle of the parts is lost in the sense of the whole. The best of these late poems have a calm, serious certainty, an easiness of rightness, like well-being. The barest and most pitiable of the world's objects – 'the great pond, / The plain sense of it, without reflections, leaves, / Mud water like dirty glass, expressing silence / Of a sort, silence of a rat come out to see' – have in the poems 'the naked majesty... of bird-nest arches and of rain-stained vaults,' a dignity and largeness and unchangeableness; on the winter day 'the wind moves like a great thing tottering.'

I had meant to finish this section on 'The Rock' by quoting the marvelously original 'Prologues to What Is Possible,' but it is too long; I had better quote 'Madame La Fleurie,' a particularly touching treatment of a subject that is particularly Stevens':

> Weight him down, O side-stars, with the great
>   weightings of the end.
> Seal him there. He looked in a glass of the earth and
>   thought he lived in it.
> Now, he brings all that he saw into the earth, to the
>   waiting parent.
> His crisp knowledge is devoured by her, beneath
>   a dew.
>
> Weight him, weight, weight him with the sleepiness
>   of the moon.
> It was only a glass because he looked in it. It was
>   nothing he could be told.

It was a language he spoke, because he must, yet
    did not know.
It was a page he had found in the handbook
    of heartbreak.

The black fugatos are strumming the blacknesses
    of black . . . .
The thick strings stutter the final gutturals.
He does not lie there remembering the blue-jay,
    say the jay.
His grief is that his mother should feed on him,
    himself and what he saw,
In that distant chamber, a bearded queen, wicked
    in her dead light.

When the reader comes to aberrant poems like 'Page of
a Tale' and 'A Rabbit as King of the Ghosts,' he realizes how
little there is in Stevens, ordinarily, of the narrative, dramatic, immediately active side of life, of harried actors
compelled, impelled, in ignorant hope. But how much there
is of the man who looks, feels, meditates, in the freedom of
removedness, of disinterested imagining, of thoughtful love.
As we read the poems we are so continually aware of Stevens
observing, meditating, creating, that we feel like saying that
the process of creating the poem is the poem. Surprisingly
often the motion of qualification, of concession, of logical
conclusion – a dialectical motion in the older sense of
dialectical – is the movement that organizes the poem; and in
Stevens the unlikely tenderness of this movement – the one,
the not-quite-that, the other, the not-exactly-the-other, the
real one, the real other – is like the tenderness of the sculptor
or draftsman, whose hand makes but looks as if it caressed.

Few poets have made a more interesting rhetoric out of
just fooling around: turning things upside-down, looking at
them from under the sofa, considering them (and their
observer) curiously enough to make the reader protest, 'That
were to consider it too curiously.' This rhetoric is the
rhetoric of a kaleidoscope, a kaleidoscope of parts; and when
it is accompanied, as it sometimes is, by little content and less
emotion, it seems clear, bright, complicated, and inhuman.
When the philosopher is king, his subjects move like prop-

ositions. Yet one is uneasy at objecting to the play – to the professional playfulness, even – of a large mind and a free spirit.

I have written, in another essay, about the disadvantages of philosophizing (in verse) as inveterately and interminably as Stevens has philosophized. But his marvelous successes with his method, in its last bare anomalous stages in 'The Rock', make me feel that the hand of the maker knows better than the eye of the observer, at least if it's my eye. Without his excesses, his endless adaptations and exaggerations of old procedures, how could he ever have learned these unimaginable new ways of his? A tree is justified in its fruits: I began to distrust my own ways, and went back to the poems (in *The Auroras of Autumn*) that had seemed to me monumental wastes; transcendental, all too transcendental études; improvisations preserved for us neither by good nor by bad, but by middle fortune. I read them over and over, relishing in anticipation the pleasures of an honest reformation. I could see how much familiarity this elaborate, almost monotonously meditative style requires of the reader; I managed, after a while, to feel that I had not been as familiar with the poems, or as sympathetic to the poems, as I ought to have been. And there I stuck. Whatever is wrong with the poems or with me is as wrong as ever; what they seemed to me once, they seem to me still.

Stevens' poetry makes one understand how valuable it can be for a poet to write a great deal. Not too much of that great deal, ever, is good poetry; but out of quantity can come practice, naturalness, accustomed mastery, adaptations and elaborations and reversals of old ways, new ways even – so that the poet can put into the poems, at the end of a lifetime, what the end of a lifetime brings him. Stevens has learned to write at will, for pleasure; his methods of writing, his ways of imagining, have made this possible for him as it is impossible for many living poets – Eliot, for instance. Anything can be looked at, felt about, meditated upon, so Stevens *can* write about anything; he does not demand of his poems the greatest concentration, intensity, dramatic immediacy, the shattering and inexplicable rightness the poet calls inspiration. (Often it is as if Stevens didn't want the poetic equivalent of sonata form, and had gone back to earlier polyphonic ways, days when the crescendo was still uninvented.) His good poems are as inspired as anybody else's – if you compare *The Auroras of Autumn* with 'The Rock,' you will decide that the last poems come from a whole period of the most marvelous inspiration; but Stevens does not think of inspiration (or whatever you want to call it) as a condition of composition. He too is waiting for the spark from heaven to fall – poets have no choice about this – but he waits writing; and this – other things being equal, when it's possible – is the best way for the poet to wait.

Stevens' rhetoric is at its worst, always, in the poems of other poets; just as great men are great disasters, overwhelmingly good poets are overwhelmingly bad influences. In Stevens the reign of the dramatic monologue – the necessity to present, present! in concentrated dramatic form – is over, and the motion of someone else's speech has been replaced by 'the motion of thought' of the poet himself. Ordinarily this poet's thought moves (until 'The Rock') in unrhymed iambic pentameter, in a marvelously accomplished Wordsworthian blank verse – or, sometimes, in something akin to Tennyson's bland lissome adaptation of it. If someone had predicted to Pound, when he was beginning his war on the iambic foot; to Eliot, when he was first casting a cold eye on post-Jacobean blank verse; to both, when they were first condemning generalization in poetry, that in forty or fifty years the chief – sometimes, I think in despair, the only – influence on younger American poets would be this generalizing, masterful, scannable verse of Stevens', wouldn't both have laughed in confident disbelief? And how many of the youngest English poets seem to want to write like Cowper! A great revolution is hardest of all on the great revolutionists.

At the bottom of Stevens' poetry there is wonder and delight, the child's or animal's or savage's – man's – joy in his own existence, and thankfulness for it. He is the poet of well-being: 'One might have thought of sight, but who could think / Of what it sees, for all the ill it sees?' This sigh of awe, of wondering pleasure, is underneath all the poems that show us the 'celestial possible,' everything that has not yet been transformed into the infernal impossibilities of our everyday earth. Stevens is full of the natural or Aristotelian virtues; he is, in the terms of Hopkins' poem, all windhover and no Jesuit. There is about him, under the translucent glazes, a Dutch solidity and weight, he sits surrounded by all the good things of this earth, with rosy cheeks and fresh clear blue eyes, eyes not going out to you but shining in their place, like fixed stars – or else moves off, like the bishop in his poem, 'globed in today and tomorrow.' If he were an animal he would be, without a doubt, that rational, magnanimous, voluminous animal, the elephant.

As John Stuart Mill read Wordsworth, to learn to feel, so any of a thousand logical positivists might read Stevens, to learn to imagine: 'That strange flower, the sun, / Is just what you say. / Have it your way. / The world is ugly, / And the people are sad. / That tuft of jungle feathers, / That animal eye, / Is just what you say. / That savage of fire, / That seed, / Have it your way. / The world is ugly, / And the people are sad.' But such a poem does more than imagine – it sees, it knows; so perhaps imagining is a part of seeing and knowing. Stevens finishes 'Tea at the Palaz of Hoon' by admitting that it has all been imaginary, that his ears have made the hymns they heard, that 'I was the world in which I walked, and what I saw / Or heard or felt came not but from myself; / And there I found myself more truly and more strange' – he has seen his own being, in truth and in strangeness, as he could never have seen it if he had looked at it directly.

When I read the first two lines of a poem, 'Place-bound and time-bound in evening rain / And bound by a sound which does not change'; or of something 'in which / We believe without belief, beyond belief; or of the people of the future beginning to 'avoid our stale perfections, seeking out / Their own, waiting until we go / To picnic in the ruins that we leave'; or that 'Time is a horse that runs in the heart, a horse / Without a rider on a road at night'; or of 'armies without / Either drums or trumpets, the commanders mute, the arms / On the ground, fixed fast in a profound defeat,' these low grave notes are more to me, almost, than any of the old bright ones. But then I remember that some of the old ones were as grave: 'The Snow Man' or 'The Death of a Soldier' or that haunting poem no one seems haunted by, 'Autumn Refrain':

> The skreak and skritter of evening gone
> And grackles gone and sorrows of the sun,
> The sorrows of sun, too, gone ... the moon and
>   moon,
> The yellow moon of words about the nightingale
> In measureless measures, not a bird for me
> But the name of a bird and the name of a nameless air
> I have never – shall never hear. And yet beneath
> The stillness of everything gone, and being still,
> Being and sitting still, something resides,
> Some skreaking and skrittering residuum,
> And grates these evasions of the nightingale
> Though I have never – shall never hear that bird.
> And the stillness is in the key, all of it is,
> The stillness is all in the key of that desolate sound.

But how charming Stevens' joke are, too! When he uses little cultural properties unexpectedly, with mocking elegiac humor; when we – so to speak – discover that the part of the collage we thought a washrag is really a reproduction of the Laocoön, we are pleased just as we are in Klee. 'This Dawn' *is* one of Klee's little watercolor-operas, isn't it?

> An opening of portals when night ends,
> A running forward, arms stretched out as drilled.
> Act I, Scene I, in a German Staats-Oper.

And when Stevens begins, 'O that this lashing wind was something more / Than the spirit of Ludwig Richter!'; when he thinks, looking out upon a prospect of the Alps, 'Claude has been dead a long time / And apostrophes are forbidden on the funicular'; when he says of 'Lions in Sweden' that he too was once

> A hunter of those sovereigns of the soul
> And savings banks, Fides, the sculptor's prize,
> All eyes and size, and galled Justitia,
> Trained to poise the tales of the law,
> Patientia, forever soothing wounds,
> And mighty Fortitudo, frantic bass ...

– when Stevens does all this, I am delighted; and I am more delighted with these souvenirs, these ambiguous survivals, because in other poems the other times and the other peoples, the old masters and the old masterpieces, exist in fresh and unambiguous magnificence.

Stevens does seem a citizen of the world. The other arts, the other continents, the other centuries are essential not merely to his well-being to his own idea of himself, his elementary identity. Yeats called Keats schoolboy with his nose pressed against the window of a sweetshop; we Americans stand with our noses pressed against the window of the world. How directly, in *The Cantos* and *The Waste Land,* Pound and Eliot appropriate that world! stones from the Coliseum, drops of water from the Jordan, glitter from the pages like a built mirage. (The only directer procedure would have been to go to Europe and stay there.) If Stevens could stay home, except for trips, it was because he had made for himself a Europe of his own, a past of his own, a whole sunlit, and, in the end, twilight – world of his own. It is an extremely large world, the world that an acute mind, varied interests and sympathies, and an enormous vocabulary can produce. (I know what an abject, basely material anticlimax that *enormous vocabulary* is; but the bigger a poet's effective natural vocabulary is, the larger his world will seem.) And Stevens has an extraordinarily original imagination, one that has created for us – so to speak – many new tastes and colors and sounds, many real, half-real, and nonexistent beings.

He has spoken, always, with the authority of someone who thinks of himself as a source of interest, of many interests. He has never felt it necessary to appeal to us, make a hit with us, nor does he try to sweep us away, to overawe us; he has written as if poems were certain to find, or make, their true readers. Throughout half this century of the common man, this age in which each is like his sibling, Stevens has celebrated the hero, the capacious, magnanimous, excelling man; has believed, with obstinacy and good humor, in all the heights which draw us toward them, make us like them, simply by existing. A few weeks ago I read, in Sacheverell Sitwell, two impressive sentences: 'It is my belief that I have informed myself of nearly all works of art in the known world .... I have heard most of the music of the world, and seen nearly all the paintings.' It was hard for me to believe these sentences, but I wanted Sitwell to be able to say them, liked him for having said them – I believed. While I was writing this essay the sentences kept coming back to me, since they seemed to me sentences Stevens would say if he could. In an age when almost everybody sold man and the world short, he never did, but acted as if joy *were* 'a world of our own,' as if nothing excellent were alien to us.

I should like, now, to give a list of eighteen or twenty of Stevens' best poems, and a list of twenty or thirty of his better. Reading the poems in these lists will give anyone a definite – dazzlingly definite – idea of the things I think exceptional about Stevens' poetry, and the lists can be of help to people just beginning to make, from this big *Collected Poems,* a 'Selected Poems' of their own. Some of his best poems are, I think: 'The Snow Man,' 'To an Old Philosopher in Rome, 'Esthétique du Mal,' 'The World as Meditation,' 'Peter Quince at the Clavier,' 'Autumn Refrain,' 'Angel Surrounded by Paysans,' 'Sunday Morning,' 'The Death of a Soldier,' 'Prologues to What Is Possible,' 'Madame La Fleurie,' 'Sea Surface Full of Clouds,' 'The Man on the Dump,' 'Some Friends from Pascagoula,' 'The Brave Man' – but now I begin to be very confused about where the best ends and the better begins – 'Dutch Graves in Bucks County,' 'Seventy Years Later,' 'The Comedian as the Letter C,' 'The Emperor of Ice-Cream,' 'Mrs. Alfred Uruguay,' 'Page from a Tale,' 'The Common Life,' 'Sailing After Lunch,' 'Le Monocle de Mon Oncle.' And now I begin, however uneasily, on my second list: 'To the One of Fictive Music,' 'St. Armorer's Church from the Outside,' 'Disillusionment of Ten O'Clock,' 'The Plain Sense of Things,' 'The Good Man has No Shape,' 'Lions in Sweden,' 'Gubbinal,' 'Sonatina to Hans Christian,' 'The American Sublime,' 'A Quiet Normal Life,' 'Tea at the Palaz of Hoon,' 'Bantams in Pine-Woods,' the first of 'Six Significant Landscapes,' Part IX of 'Credences of Summer,' 'A Lot of People Bathing in a Stream,' 'Metaphors of a Magnifico,' 'Cy Est Pourtraicte, Madame Ste Ursule, et Les Unze Mille Vierges,' 'The Idea of Order at Key West,' 'Anecdote of the Prince of Peacocks,'

'No Possum, No Sop, No Taters,' 'Martial Cadenza,' 'Anglais Mort à Florence,' 'Mozart, 1935,' 'A Rabbit as King of the Ghosts,' 'Poetry is a Destructive Force,' 'A Woman Sings a Song for a Soldier Come Home,' 'Less and Less Human, O Savage Spirit.'

Stevens has spoken with dignity and elegance and intelligence – with eloquence – of everything from pure sensation to pure reflection to pure imagination, from the 'elephant-colorings' of tires to the angel of reality, the 'necessary angel' in whose sight we 'see the earth again / Cleared of its stiff and stubborn, man-locked set' – the angel who asks as he departs:

> Am I not
> Myself, only half of a figure of a sort,
>
> A figure half seen, or seen for a moment, a man
> Of the mind, an apparition apparelled in
>
> Apparels of such lightest look that a turn
> Of my shoulder and quickly, too quickly, I am gone?

These lines, so pure and light and longing, remind me of the other figures which, in the second of the *Duino Elegies*, touch us lightly on the shoulder before they turn and go. 'A man / Of the mind': in this end of one line and beginning of another, and in the suspension between them, the angel has spoken an epitaph for Stevens.

107. G.S. Fraser, from 'The Aesthete and the Sensationalist', *Partisan Review*

Vol. 22, no. 2, Spring 1955, 265–72

Part of a review in which Stevens' work is contrasted with E.E. Cummings' *Poems 1923–54*, generally along the line of the classic dichotomy between 'paleface and redskin'. Two-thirds of the review deals with Cummings.

... We feel continually, in reading Mr. Stevens, that his actual *gifts* are comparable with those of the very greatest poets (we do not feel this, about Mr. Cummings, when reading him). Probably no modern poet has a more supple, rich, commanding, and evocative vocabulary; within certain limits – Mr. Stevens would be incapable of achieving the changes of pace, and the suddenings, slackenings and concentrations, of *The Waste Land* or 'Ash Wednesday' – few modern poets are more notable masters of rhythm; very few contemporary poets, again, combine as Mr. Stevens does the three apparently disparate gifts of evoking impressions with imagistic vividness, shaping long poems with musical care, and pursuing through a long poem a single, very abstruse, metaphysical argument. Yet in one's heart one does not quite think that he is a 'great' poet in the sense that, say, Yeats and Eliot are 'great' poets. What is it that one misses? Partly, or perhaps mainly, the whole area of life that lies between detached aesthetic perception and philosophical reflection on it; and, as a chief corollary to that, the urgency of ordinary human passion, the sense of commitment and the moment of final concentration. In one crude human sense,

Mr. Stevens's enormous talents are being exploited a little frivolously; in all'one's continuing pleasure and admiration, while reading him, there is the sense all the time of a lack of the highest tension....

108. Donald Davie, on Stevens' prolixity, conservatism and provincialism, *Shenandoah*

Vol. 6, no. 2, Spring 1955, 62–4

The amount of attention paid to Stevens' work towards the end of his career by British reviewers contrasts somewhat with the case of William Carlos Williams. The present review makes valuable points, but is equally notable for its mixture of condescension and reluctant admiration. Throughout Davie's distinguished criticism there is a curious and pervasive ambivalence in his appraisal of the American modernists.

American poetry has never at any time lacked for long a naive philosopher in verse, homespun, garrulous and strenuously hopeful; and reading in the 500 odd pages of this handsome volume (too much for any reviewer to cope with), the shocking thought occurred to me that Stevens is only the latest of these. The prolixity is there, and so is the optimism. 'Homespun' seems absurdly inappropriate to the sophistication that announces itself so loudly from all these pages, and from none so loudly as from the first dozen or so, with their list of titles. But isn't it just the loudness that makes the sophistication suspect? And isn't it just this that shows the naiveté is genuine? For of course it is precisely the genuinely naive who try hardest to seem urbane. The folksiness of the professionally homespun is too good to be true, and it is the folk-poet nowadays who struts on the highest stilts. Poetic diction at its most florid and overblown crops up in the ballad-singers of the nineteenth century. And so it is not absurd to regard Stevens as the real thing, for which a Carl Sandburg is only the fabricated substitute.

Of course, therefore, Stevens is *provincial*, as Housman is with less excuse. Of him one may say, as Hugh Kenner says of Housman, that he 'commits himself to statements about the way things are, that beg more questions than they allay, and exclude more experience than they evoke.' And from this point of view, the conspicuous 'elegance' (in the precious titles, for instance) is an awkward attempt to remove the provincialism, and to 'imply a recognition of other kinds of experience that are possible.' The addressees, for instance ('Swenson' in 'Lions in Sweden,' or 'Ramon' in 'The Idea of Order at Key West'), who make a fugitive appearance in pieces of otherwise pontifical statement, are a sketchy gesture towards embodying these statements in a dramatic situation which would make them less presumptuously inclusive. The same thing happens when the poetry drops every so often into a pastiche of Elizabethan dramatic blank verse.

To be sure, this does not apply to the poet of *Harmonium*. In that first volume, the self-conscious elegance can still exasperate, and it still testifies to the embarrassment of a speaker unsure of his audience; but it is not yet central to the poetic activity, and from the best of those early poems – 'The Death of a Soldier,' 'The Snow Man,' 'Nuances of a Theme by Williams,' 'Sunday Morning,' – it is absent altogether. To this early period belongs also Stevens's one technical discovery. If one means by this not just a new way of packaging or advertising, but a genuinely new mode of apprehension, thereafter made current for others, then to credit a poet with even one such is to say a great deal. And I can't see but that 'Thirteen Ways of Looking at a Blackbird' is just such an invention, one that Stevens has either chosen not to, or else has been unable to exploit.

The more one reviews Stevens's later career, the more one sees the point of Yvor Winters's verdict that from *Harmonium*, despite its technical variety, there could be no way forward. There was, in fact, one development that Winters did not foresee: the poetry could thereafter live on its own fat, gnaw its own vitals, conduct a running commentary on itself. This is what has happened, and all the variety has in the process been ironed out to one idiosyncratic, inimitable manner. Technically, this later style is extremely conservative. Indeed Stevens is for the most part a very conservative poet. His obscurity, for instance, comes not from his using any really new procedures, but from idiosyncrasies encrusted on thoroughly old ones. (And it is all the harder to deal with, just for that reason). When the later writing succeeds, it is with a sort of vulgar splendour, doing the obvious and accredited thing with rude force, as in decasyllabic lines that drum with Byronic vigour, or in opulent alliteration. (Alliteration is used with quite startling simplicity – Stevens can never resist it, however banal, however distracting). At the very end of the volume, the unexpected and beautiful recent poem, 'To an Old Philosopher in Rome,' only brings into relief and justifies our weariness with poems purged of all human action and passion, always in a major key, and with only one subject – themselves and the nature of their own operations. It is a pity – and yet it is significant – that poems often eloquent in themselves should come off so badly when read one after another.

109. John Holloway, 'Bravura adequate to this great hymn', *Spectator*

18 November 1955, 682–3

Holloway (b. 1920) is a poet, critic and wide-ranging scholar, whose books include *The Story of the Night* (1961), studies in Shakespearian tragedy.

... As late as 1937, Marianne Moore could still see fit to praise Stevens by calling him 'America's chief conjuror,' and to refute his harsher critics by referring to 'best of all, the bravura' of his work. Certainly, the bravura, the 'parachute-spinnaker of verbiage' is there. Virtuosity in words, in fact, is there twice over, for the early poems display one kind of it, and the later ones another, less obtrusive but much more impressive ....

Over and over again in this volume the reader will be struck with the measured austerity of this verse, with Stevens's limpid euphony. But in his later poems, it is the euphony of grave and lucid operations of the intellect, 'Inanimate in an inert savior,' as he writes himself. In that very line, there is a touch of the early polyglot bravura; but Marianne Moore, though she referred to this, did not mention how Stevens had indicated that it tried to serve a substantial purpose. 'Where shall I find / Bravura *adequate to this great hymn?*' he had written. As he went on, the purpose behind the hymn grew more explicit.

Geographically, the early poems draw most richly on Florida and Central America. They are full of brilliantly vivid descriptions, and the blue sea and blue sky of the Gulf of Mexico flood through them, helping to leave blue as a recurrent theme almost throughout his work. 'Helping,' because Picasso is also responsible, and Stevens is probably the

429

first major poet in English to have fully absorbed Impressionism and post-Impressionism into his work (music, of
course, also influenced it deeply). But later, this colourful
Southern influence was replaced by an austerer New England
one. The second volume was entitled *Ideas of Order*, and this
points the shift. The austere, hair-fine later work comes more
and more explicitly to the reason for writing the earlier
brilliant, colourful, fire-and-air-and-water poems ('the marriage of flesh and air'). The hurdy-gurdy was throwing off
fragments not of a shallow, but a deep harmony; 'God in the
object' not in a religious sense so much as of a supreme
felicitous completeness, realised so transiently that the poet
could well call it 'the giant of nothingness.' Thus the
technical mastery served a distinctive vision; and both of
these combine to produce lyrical masterpieces like 'Less and
Less Human O Savage Spirit,' 'The Beginning,' 'The Bird
with the Coppery, Keen Claws,' 'Angel Surrounded by
Paysans'; and his superb best-known poem, 'Anecdote of the
Jar.'

110. Alain Bosquet, from 'Deux poètes philosophes: Wallace Stevens et Conrad Aiken', *La Table Ronde*

Vol. 105, September 1956, 129–35

Bosquet (b. Anatole Bisk, in Russia, 1919) provided an
obituary of Stevens for the 1 October 1955 number of
Nouvelle Revue Française and made reference to his work
in 'Tendances Actuelles de la Poésie Américaine', in
L'Age Nouveau for March 1956.

Bosquet is a traveller, journalist, translator, memoirist,
novelist and essayist. His work reflects the grim

atmosphere of the atomic age. He shared a tendency of his period in believing that the world's uniqueness manifests itself when man can free himself from words. Bosquet's many books include *Solzhenitsyn pas d'accord* (1978).

...Fervent lecteur de Valéry, Wallace Stevens, après une période élégante où il s'est plu à assigner au poème ce rôle nuancé et agréable: faire le siège de l'objet à coup de définitions successives, à la manière de T. S. Eliot dans 'Prufrock', s'est résolument tourné vers le drame que constituait, à ses yeux, l'emploi de tout langage, quel qu'il fût. Ecrire, c'est-à-dire traduire en mots l'inexprimable, lui paraissait à la fois une absurdité et un délice irrésistible. Trop artiste – il est sans doute le plus parfait ciseleur de vers, en poésie américaine, depuis Poe – pour se laisser aller au désespoir de ne jamais écrire que la caricature de ce qu'il aimerait écrire, il donne à son scepticisme des allures de raffinement qui ont ce double pouvoir: le rendre délectable dans ses moindres manifestations d'*épicurien du doute*, et faire frémir le lecteur en lui prouvant, vers après vers, que le langage est un leurre immense et que la seule prérogative du poème est de chanter la précarité du poème. Ce cercle vicieux: dire pour prouver que dire est une dangereuse illusion, Stevens lui confere d'étranges séductions; il a du poids, de la lumière et de la mesure des choses un sens méditerranéen, et si tout, en fin de compte, ne doit servir qua'à une démonstration d'impuissance, il faut pour le moins que le chemin soit jonché de fleurs, de parfums et de choses vivantes. L'éternelle définition du poème ne doit point être abstraite, et la quête d'une lucidité à tout prix ne doit pas se faire aux dépens d'un univers palpable. Ceci dit, le verbe comme le cosmos, pour demeurer dignes d'eux-mêmes (mais c'est là encore une notion que Stevens se plaît á miner) doivent s'aborder pour mieux renaître de leurs contradictions foncières....

431

OPUS POSTHUMOUS

New York, 1957

The first run was of 4,800 copies.

---

111. William Carlos Williams, 'Poet of a Steadfast Pattern', *New York Times Book Review*

18 August 1957, 6

In *Opus Posthumous*, by Wallace Stevens (1879–1955), Samuel French Morse has edited a book – a bridge to Stevens' poetry – that is both authentic and delightful. Morse (literary adviser to Stevens' estate) deserves great credit for assembling and giving us a selection of the more or less unknown surviving poems, the prose, plays, essays and sayings of the late celebrated poet. Morse's preface makes several points of Stevens' genius fascinatingly clear and documents much else of his writing with wise comments carefully arranged as an introduction to a comprehensive final volume which must wait until a later time.

We observe the poet moving through a world which occupied him and with which he was only tangentially concerned. It is the picture of a devoted servant whose expert knowledge of financial and business affairs was accepted as the normal presences of his day and so demanded his attention, though his real business was the cultivation and care of the poem.

The book is eminently readable, even fascinating. You

wouldn't say that Stevens is particularly witty, though in his beginnings as the editor of the *Harvard Advocate* you would expect it of him. The man had too oblique an application to the whole field of knowledge for that. His knowledge and affection for Pascal, knowledge for its own sake, was disturbingly affected by the basic importance of the imagination that must govern a poet's affairs.

A glance at some of Stevens' titles (he used French as if it had been English) reveals him to be a lover of the French language as of the French people, so that if his style and the style of his thoughts reveal this love, it is not to be wondered at. He loved the French with their appreciation of the importance of style.

That Stevens could stand firm once he had established his ground is attested by the aspect of the poems themselves – full of a special whimsy permitted by the solidity of his reasoning. He permitted himself to go to the adventurous limits of his vocabulary, to stand on the point of a needle because he felt perfectly secure there, knowing the rest of the universe to be unstable. There were such vagaries as 'Le Monocle de mon Oncle' (ludicrous as the fantastic gestures of a clown), 'Peter Quince at the Clavier' (his first brilliant success), the 'Carlos Among the Candles,' 'The Comedian as the Letter C' and other extraordinary inventions.

In the 'Adagia' (I don't think it was Stevens' word) he has many of the poet's most pithy sayings, none better or truer than the statement 'One Must Sit Still to Discover the World.'

As good a summary of Stevens' situation facing the world is contained – as might be expected in a man at the same time so vocal and reticent as he was and prone to cover up his own traces – in the poem 'Architecture,' laying out when he was a young man a plan he was to follow during his entire life. He writes:

> What manner of building shall we build!
> Let us design a chastel de chasteté
> De pensée....
> Never cease to deploy the structure.
> Keep the laborers shouldering plinths.

Pass the whole of life hearing the clink of the
Chisels of the stone-cutters cutting the stones.

The poems from this beginning followed with amazing
fidelity this steadfast pattern. With this pattern fixed in his
mind, it is his genius that as a poet he kept wriggling as a
worm impaled on a hook, a simile which he would certainly
have applauded, wryly, violently, earthily his life long.

He is a sad but triumphant figure, showing in the end
above his frustrations a modern poet, whose final note is a
cock cry.

Mr. Morse while ending the book with some of Stevens'
best prose and the plays (of which 'Carlos Among the
Candles' is the only one showing any dramatic talent) gives
us a selection of his 'Adagia,' a wise decision, showing
Stevens the epigrammatist which Stevens the man has
bequeathed to us with a tolerant grin. Thus:

'The poet makes silk dresses out of worms.'

'Religion is dependent on faith. But esthetics is independent of faith. The relative position of the two might be
reversed. It is possible to establish esthetics in the individual
mind as immeasurably a greater thing than religion. Its
present state is the result of the difficulty of establishing it
except in the individual mind.'

'Realism is a corruption of reality.'

'It is necessary to any originality to have the courage to be
an amateur.'

'God is a symbol for something that can as well take other
forms, as, for example, the form of high poetry.'

'Ignorance is one of the sources of poetry.'

'All of our ideas come from the natural world: trees
equal umbrellas.'

'Sentimentality is a failure of feeling.'

112. Kenneth Rexroth, a glance at Stevens' influences from French, *Nation*

Vol. 185, no. 12, 19 October 1957, 268–9

An American poet, novelist, playwright, editor and essayist, Rexroth (1905–82) will possibly be best remembered as a translator, from Oriental languages and from Spanish and French. His publications include *The Collected Shorter Poems* (1966) and *The Collected Longer Poems* (1968). His dozen or so volumes of translation include *One Hundred French Poems*, and he is the author of 'The Influence of French Poetry on American' (*Assays*, 1961; originally written to introduce an anthology of American poets in French translation).

... He emphatically does not resemble Laforgue – an envious carbuncular tutor in an ill-fitting collar – but he does curiously resemble the only actual American Symbolist, the best American poet of the twenty-five years before the First War – Stuart Merrill, anarchist, good liver, skeptic and quiet dandy, who wrote only in French. However, if Stevens ever shared Merrill's desire to cut a swath (Merrill was a bit of a Stanford White), he disciplined it away. One thing he had above all else was good taste, the kind that is so good that nobody notices it. He too might have been happier, back in 1920 at least, writing in French. I am sure he never considered doing so, but if he had, I am sure he would have rejected the idea as too ostentatious, as bad form, all right for a Virginian like Merrill, but not done in Connecticut.

This collection contains some paraphrases of Leon Paul Fargue, another bon vivant with immense hidden reserves of power, and perhaps the only French poet since Jammes who is thoroughly likeable as a man. Had he not been a business man, Stevens might well have been very exactly the American Leon Paul Fargue. To anyone who loves Fargue as I do the kinship is an obvious and happy one. I think Fargue is the better poet, perhaps ultimately because he was poor and spent most of his time in hotel rooms and on café terraces. Fargue was a fat man, he looked and acted a little like a French Ford Madox Ford, but he was a sly and wily poet. Stevens weighed less, but there was always a trace of fat about his heart, a debilitating security, and in his later years his agility and mischievousness seemed a shade forced.

I guess it is true that compromise tells, even for one whose very philosophy of life, whose very aesthetics of creation, is based on the axiom that life, action, thought, are themselves compromise. Certainly Stevens never, in a long and very distinguished career, came up to the high point from which he started in his first book, *Harmonium*. That little book sold only a few copies, but it hit my generation with an unforgettable impact. *The Waste Land* may have made more noise, but when it was over, it left only a pose. *Harmonium* left wisdom, its own rather privileged kind of wisdom, but real nonetheless. I suppose the wisdom is riper in the late poems in this book, it is certainly very ripe, but the poetic excitement is a good deal less and sometimes is lacking altogether....

113. Irving Howe, on poetry as self-creation, 'Another Way of looking at the Blackbird', *New Republic*

Vol. 137, 4 November 1957, 16–19

Howe (b. 1920) is an American literary critic and writer on politics. His *World of Our Fathers* (1976) won him the National Book Award.

A perceptive, though lightly ballasted, overview, this article seems largely to have been overlooked in the general field of Stevens criticism.

What inmost allegiance, what ultimate religion, would be proper to a wholly free and disillusioned spirit? – George Santayana.

Gradually, under the pressure of time, the masks of Wallace Stevens are wearing away, and not because they have become obsolete or been proven deceptive but because they now seem to have figured mainly as preparations for a homelier reality. Gaudy mystifier, Crispin's pilot, flaunter of rare chromatic words, explorer of Yucatan, enemy of the day's routine, afficionado of strange hats, even the gamesman of epistemology – these roles yield to Steven's 'basic slate,' an American poet reflecting upon solitary lives in a lonely age and searching for that 'inmost allegiance' by which men might live out their years in thousands of Hartfords.

Stevens was the kind of poet who wrote methodically and a good deal, apparently without waiting for, though always delighted to receive, the blessings of inspiration. Writing verse seems to have become for him a means of wresting convictions of selfhood: the visible token of that which he insistently wrote about. His work is therefore very much of a piece, both in its success and failures. In *Opus Posthumous* – a collection of fugitive pieces, poems omitted from the *Collected Poems*, a few verse plays, a group of aphorisms on poetry, some critical essays and 30 late poems devoted to preparation for death – one can trace out something of the scheme and direction of Stevens' work, perhaps even a bit more easily than in the *Collected Poems*. For *Opus Posthumous* is a much less imposing book, and one therefore in which Stevens' intention juts out all the more sharply.

After the publication of *Harmonium* in 1923, the main job of his critics was to become familiar with his decor: the exotic places, the tropical language, the cheerful jibing at bourgeois norms, the apparent *fin-de-siècle* estheticism, the flip nose-thumbing of his titles. So luxuriant did the world of his poems seem, so free of traditional moral demands, that his early admirers could hardly avoid thinking of this world as primarily a sensuous landscape. It was a view that lingered into Marianne Moore's description of Stevens as 'a delicate apothecary of savors and precipitates' – though in that last word there is a hint that Miss Moore, as usual, saw more than she said.

While this was a way of reading Stevens that could yield genuine pleasures, it hardly went very far toward penetrating his deeper concerns, and even when confined to *Harmonium* it could be maintained only if one focused on the shorter poems and neglected 'Sunday Morning' and 'The Comedian as Letter C.' In an early study of Stevens, R.P. Blackmur quickly saw that the strange cries, hoots and words that ran through the poems, far from being mere exotica, were oblique and humorous tokens of a profoundly serious effort to grapple with the distinctively 'modern' in modern experience.

Later there was a tendency to read Stevens as if he were a versifying philosopher, a misfortune for which he was himself partly to blame, since at his prolific second-best he had a way of sounding like a versifying philosopher. Stevens' poetry, now in the hands of new exegetes, was said to be about the writing of poetry, and was regarded as a series of variations on the philosophical theme of the relation between reality and imagination. Both of these statements, while true and useful, were needlessly limiting as aids toward a fuller apprehension of the poetry: the first was too narrow, the second too academic, and from neither could one gain a sense of what might be urgent or particular in Stevens' work.

Poetry written mainly about the writing of poetry – could that be the ground for any large claim as to the interest Stevens might command from literate readers? Imagination and reality – did that not increase the peril of regarding Stevens as a shuffler of epistemological categories? Neither gambit is enough; another way is needed for looking at the blackbird: not the only or the best, but another.

As the base of Stevens' work, as a force barely acknowledged yet always felt, lies a pressing awareness of human disorder in our time – but an awareness radically different from that of most writers. Only rarely does it emerge in his poems as a dramatized instance or fiction; Stevens seldom tries and almost never manages to evoke the modern disorder through representations of moral conduct or social conflict. When in *Owl's Clover* he did write a poem with a relatively explicit politics, the result, as he later acknowledged, was unfortunate: rhetoric overrunning thought, an assault upon a subject which as a poet Stevens was not prepared to confront.

Lacking that 'novelistic' gift for portraiture-in-depth which is so valuable to a good many modern poets, Stevens does not examine society closely or even notice it directly for any length of time; he simply absorbs 'the idea' of it. A trained connoisseur in chaos, he sees no need to linger before the evidence: there is enough already. And that is why it seems neither a paradox nor a conceit to say that in Stevens' poetry the social world is but dimly apprehended while a perspective upon history is brilliantly maintained: history as it filters through his consciousness of living and writing at a given time. The disorder that occupies the foreground of so much modern literature is calmly accepted by Stevens, appearing in his work not as a dominant subject but as a pressure upon all subjects.

In a somewhat similar way, Stevens, though sharply responsive to the crisis of belief which has troubled so many sensitive persons in the twentieth century, is not himself directly or deeply involved in it. He knows and feels it, but has begun to move beyond it. When he writes that...

> The death of Satan was a tragedy
> For the imagination. A capital
> Negation destroyed him in his tenement
> And, with him, many blue phenomena...

the force of these lines is clearly secular, releasing an attitude of comic humaneness. Perhaps they are also a little blasphemous, since it is hard to imagine a religious writer making quite this complaint about the consequences of the death of Satan. Here, as elsewhere in Stevens, a secular imagination measures the loss that it suffers from the exhaustion of religious myths and symbols, and then hopes that emotional equivalents can be found in...

One's self and the mountains of one's land,

Without shadows, without magnificence,
The flesh, the bones, the dirt, the stone.

At times, it is true, Stevens can resemble the typical intellectual of his day (or the idea of the typical intellectual) and describes himself as 'A most inappropriate man / In a most unpropitious place.' He can appear to regret that 'The epic of disbelief / Blares oftener and soon, will soon be constant.' Yet if one compares him to Eliot and the later Auden, it becomes clear that Stevens is relatively free from religious or ideological nostalgia:

The truth is that there comes a time
When we can mourn no more over music
That is so much motionless sound.

There comes a time when the waltz
Is no longer a mode of desire, a mode
Of revealing desire and is empty of shadow.

Only occasionally does one find in Stevens that intense yearning for a real or imaginary past which has become so prevalent an attitude in our century. There is instead a recognition, both sensitive and stolid, of where we happen to be. And this, in Stevens' reckoning, imposes a new burden on the poet

... since in the absence of a belief in God, the mind turns to its own creations and examines them, not alone from the esthetic point of view, but for what they reveal, for what they validate and invalidate, for the support they give.

Stevens is not, I think, directly affected by the usual religious or intellectual uncertainties, at least not nearly so much as by the predicament – and possibilities – of the mind experiencing them, the mind that still moves within the orbit of some waning belief yet strives for a direction and momentum of its own. Even in those poems, such as 'Sunday Morning' and 'The Comedian as Letter C,' which do seem to deal explicitly with belief, one finds a recapitulation of a progress Stevens has already taken, not in freeing himself entirely from the crisis of belief or its emotional aftereffects (for to claim that would be impudent), but in learning to write as if in his poetic person he were a forerunner of post-crisis, post-ideological man. In 'The Man with the Blue Guitar,' where the guitar serves as the instrument of poetry, Stevens relates this role to an estimate, lovely in its comic modesty, of his own work:

> ... Poetry
>
> Exceeding music must take the place
> Of empty heaven and its hymns,
> Ourselves in poetry must take their place,
> Even in the chatter of your guitar.

Yet Stevens is too much of a realist, too aware (as in 'The Comedian as Letter C') of the sheer inertia of human existence, to suppose that the crisis of belief can be quickly overcome either by private decision or by public commitment.

Accepting the condition of uncertainty and solitariness as unavoidable to man once he has freed himself from the gods, Stevens poses as his ultimate question not, what shall we do about the crisis of belief, but rather, how shall we live with and perhaps beyond it? And one reason for thinking of Stevens as a comic poet is that he makes this choice of questions.

How shall we live with and then perhaps beyond the crisis of belief? – it is to confront this question that Stevens keeps returning to the theme of reality and imagination. Not merely because he is interested in epistemological forays as such – though he is; nor because he is fascinated with the creative process – though that too; but because his main concern is with discovering and, through his poetry, *enacting* the possibilities for human self-renewal in an impersonal and recalcitrant age.

How recalcitrant that age can be, Stevens knew very well. The fragmentation of personality, the loss of the self in its social roles, the problem of discovering one's identity amid a din of public claims – all this, so obsessively rehearsed in modern literature, is the premise from which Stevens moves to poetry. When Stevens does write directly about such topics, it is often with lightness and humor, taking easily on a tangent what other writers can hardly bear to face. An early little poem, 'Disillusionment of Ten O'Clock,' is about houses that are haunted by 'white night-gowns,' for Stevens the uniform of ordinariness and sober nights.

> None are green,
> Or purple with green rings,
> Or green with yellow rings,
> None of them are strange,
> With socks of lace,
> And beaded ceintures.

In this flat world 'People are not going / To dream of baboons and periwinkles.' Only here and there an old sailor, one who by age and trade stands outside the perimeter of busy dullness...

> Drunk and asleep in his boots,
> Catches tigers
> In red weather.

I hope it will not seem frivolous if I suggest that this drunken sailor embodies a central intention of Stevens' mind, and that when Stevens in his later poems turns to such formidable matters as inquiries into the nature of reality or the relation between the perceiving eye and the perceived object, he still keeps before him the figure of that old sailor dreaming in red weather.

The elaborate conceptual maneuvers of Stevens' longer poems have as their objective not any conclusion in the realm of thought but a revelation in the realm of experience. They are written to discover, and help us rediscover, the human gift for self-creation; they try to enlarge our margin of autonomy; they are incitements to intensifying our sense of what remains possible even today. Each nuance of perspective noted in a Stevens poem matters not merely in its own right, but as a comic prod to animation, a nudge to the man whose eye is almost dead. And in Stevens' poetry the eye is the central organ of consciousness.

When Stevens writes about the writing of poetry, he needs to be read not only on the level of explicit statement, but also as if the idea of poetry were a synecdoche for every creative potential of consciousness, as if poetry were that which can help liberate us from the tyranny of mechanical life and slow dying. In that sense, Stevens is a revolutionist of the imagination, neither exhorting nor needing to exhort but demonstrating through poetry the possibilities of consciousness. And he can do this, among other reasons, because in the background of his work loom the defeats and losses of the century.

Time and again Stevens turns to the clause, 'It is as if...', for that clause charts a characteristic turning or soaring of his mind, which then is followed by another opening of perception. And these, in turn, are openings to the drama of the mind as it reaches out toward new modes of awareness and thereby 'makes' its own life from moment to moment. There may be thirteen or three hundred and thirteen ways of looking at a blackbird, but what matters is that the eye, and the mind behind the eye, should encompass the life of these possible ways and the excitement of their variety. What also matters, as Mr. Richard Ellmann has remarked, is that the mind behind the eye should remember that the blackbird, no matter how it may be seen, is always there in its mysterious tangibility.

Putting it this way I may seem to be making Stevens into a moralist of sorts: which readers awed by his urbanity of style might well take to be implausible. But in his relaxed and unhurried way Stevens is, I think, a moralist – a moralist of seeing.

Like any other convention, Stevens' utilization of the theme of reality and imagination as a means of reaching to his deeper concerns, can slide into formula and habit. His extraordinary gifts as a stylist aggravate rather than lessen this danger, since they allow him to keep spinning radiant phrases long after his mind has stopped moving. The reader accustomed to Stevens' habits and devices may even respond *too* well to the poems, for their characteristic inflections and themes have a way of setting off emotions which are proper to Stevens' work as a whole but have not been earned by the particular poem. At other times Stevens' insistence upon human possibility can itself become mechanical, a ruthless-

ness in the demand for joy. And perhaps the greatest
weakness in his poems is a failure to extend the possibilities
of self-renewal beyond solitariness or solitary engagements
with the natural world and into the life of men living
together. (Yet Stevens, humorous with self-knowledge,
wrote some of his most poignant lines about this very
limitation: 'I cannot bring a world quite round, / Although I
patch it as I can. / I sing a hero's head, large eye / And bearded
bronze, but not a man, / Although I patch him as I can / And
reach through him almost to man.')

At his best, however, Stevens transforms each variant of
perception into a validation of the self. Sometimes the self is
to achieve renewal by a sympathetic merger with the outer
world:

> One must have a mind of winter
> To regard the frost and the boughs
> Of the pine trees crusted with snow...

At other times the self gains a kind of assurance from entire
withdrawal, as if to grant the outer world its own being. In
'Nuances on a Theme by Williams,' Stevens quotes William
Carlos Williams' lines, 'It's a strange courage / you give me,
ancient star' and then proceeds to tell the star:

> Lend no part to any humanity that suffuses
> You in its own light.
> Be no chimera of morning.
> Half-man, half-star.

The act of discovery by which sentience is regained can

> Be the finding of a satisfaction, and may
> Be of a man skating, a woman dancing, a woman
> Combing. The poem of the act of the mind.

It may be a sheer pleasure in the freshness of the physical
world:

> How should you walk in that space and know
> Nothing of the madness of space,
>
> Nothing of its jocular procreations?
> Throw the lights away. Nothing must stand

Between you and the shapes you take
When the crust of shape has been destroyed.

In the 'Idea of Order at Key West' the self 'takes over' the outer world by endowing it with a perceptual form:

She was the single artificer of the world
In which she sang. And when she sang, the sea,
Whatever self it had, became the self
That was her song, for she was the maker...

In 'Three Travellers Watch a Sunrise,' a play printed in *Opus Posthumous*, one of the voices says:

Sunrise is multiplied
Like the earth on which it shines,
By the eyes that open on it,
Even dead eyes,
As red is multiplied by the leaves of trees.

And finally in Stevens' last poems, which form the glory of *Opus Posthumous*, the cleared mind listens for solitary sounds in winter, waiting patiently for death. These astonishing poems, like Chinese paintings in their profound simplicity and rightness, are Stevens' last probings, the last quiet efforts to realize life through connecting with whatever is not human. The idea of the world, now as lucid as its single sounds, becomes the final objection of contemplation:

The palm at the end of the mind,
Beyond the last thought, rises
In the bronze distance,
A gold-feathered bird
Sings in the palm, without any human meaning,
Without human feeling, a foreign song.

Reading these last poems one encounters again the theme of discovery, the desire to transform and renew, that has given shape to all of Stevens' work. Here, if anywhere, is the answer to Santayana's question, the 'ultimate religion' of our secular comedy:

The honey of heaven may or may not come,
But that of earth both comes and goes at once.

114. Anthony Hecht, 'a sort of heroism', *Hudson Review*

Vol. 10, Winter 1957–8, 606–8

Anthony Hecht (b. 1923) is an American poet whose books include *The Hard Hours* (1968) and *The Venetian Vespers* (1979).

The present review also considers books by Robert Penn Warren, Richmond Lattimore and Eli Siegel.

...who else could have thought of writing a poem called 'Lytton Strachey, Also, Enters Into Heaven,' beginning,

> I care for neither fugues nor feathers.
> What interests me most is the people
> Who have always interested me most...

Sadly, most of the poems do not sustain their fun, or their level of feeling and language. But there is something else they *do* sustain, and the editor has very properly observed that the book 'is clearly held together by a "fixed point of view" apparent from the beginning and by an intention that reveals itself with equal clarity in the prose and poetry.' This binding force is Stevens' aesthetic doctrine, which is so obsessively present on almost every page that a reader is likely to feel badgered or wearied by the relentless declarations and adumbrations of a single idea. This idea is more complex than any summary statement of mine would do justice to, but it concerns the relationship of the 'real world' in its physical and changeable aspects to the imagination which orders and composes this material into a meaningful and harmonious whole. But it is with the act of imagination that Stevens is mainly concerned, with the very beauty of the abstract formulation of things, not unlike Paul Valéry's fascination with the Euclidian geometry. And after reading consistently through this book for a while, one feels like shouting for a little meat and potatoes. I suspect his qualifications as a philosopher, and some of the prose pieces are meant to be very philosophic indeed. They are in any case less convincing than even his most doctrinal poems. As for the plays, they are really to be classed among the doctrinal poems, and are plays only by a courteous extension of the word.

And yet, finally, the book represents a dedication so steady and determined and patient as to persuade you of a sort of heroism. Just what sort is hard to say, but I'd like to make a stab at it. William James, in his Gifford lectures, has a sentence that reads: ' "Thoughts are things," as one of the most vigorous mind-cure writers prints in bold type at the bottom of each of his pages.' Now while Stevens is specifically non-religious, or perhaps anti-religious (among the 'Adagia' we find, 'Poetry is a means of redemption,' 'It is the belief and not the god that counts,' 'There is no difference between god and his temple,') and though I leave it to others to dispute with James whether or not the mind-cure movement is truly the religious attitude he allows it to be, I think that not only might Stevens have put such a phrase at the bottom of his pages, or at least included it in the 'Adagia,' but he also bears in common with the exponents of this doctrine a steadfast confidence in and reliance upon the constructs of the mind. And under the pressure of experience, such a confidence may certainly become heroic. But if thoughts are things, there are still plenty of things that are not thoughts, and the world of Wallace Stevens is often thin for want of them. He certainly realized that his poetry was a particular kind of poetry, and there were qualities of experience beyond or apart from his literary sensibilities. His knowing this adds pathos to the heroic loneliness of his most serious poems.

115. Frank Kermode, 'The Gaiety of Language', *Spectator*

3 October 1958, 454–5

Kermode (b. 1919), King Edward VII Professor of Literature at Cambridge University, is an influential critic and editor. His many books include *The Romantic Image* (1957), a monograph, *Wallace Stevens* (1960) and several books of essays, most recently *The Genesis of Secrecy* (1979). He is editor of *Selected Prose of T.S. Eliot* (1975) and general editor of the Viking Press Modern Masters Series.

This article concludes with a note on Robert Pack's *Wallace Stevens: An Approach to his Poetry and Thought* (1958). In a confused comment on this review, Willard, in *Wallace Stevens: The Poet and His Critics*, p. 64, charges Kermode with 'a backhanded slap at Stevens' Whitmanian diction'. Kermode, in fact, praises the 'American gaiety' of Stevens' language and, in noticing the Pack book with some generosity, adds: 'To read the late poems of Stevens with a head full of Stevens is the richest experience offered us since the death of Yeats.' He also declares 'To an Old Philosopher in Rome' 'a great poem' and 'The Rock' 'a superb meditation'.

Granted, for an hour, the tongue of a critical angel, one could say of these books[1] nothing that could possibly be more extraordinary than this: they have not been published in this country. If the cause of this inexcusable default is a lack of public demand, how do we explain this lack? It is probably not so much the difficulty as the foreignness of Stevens that has delayed his full acceptance here. He is both familiar and strange. By rethinking the whole modern literary tradition in eccentric semi-solitude he found an odd way back to the

Romantic sources; and he owed much to certain French poetry which is a familiar part of the English tradition. Also, one of his two acknowledged masters was Mr. Eliot. But not quite *our* Mr. Eliot; and the other master, whom he does not name, must have been Whitman, whom we hardly recognise by Stevens's description:

> Nothing is final, he chants. No man shall see the end.
> His beard is of fire and his staff is a leaping flame.

Stevens himself remarked, in one of the 'Adagia', that 'nothing could be more inappropriate to American literature than its English source, since the Americans are not British in sensibility.' And since the poet must use the common language in order to speak a speech which is 'only a little of the tongue,' Stevens's various compoundings of 'the imagination's Latin' with vulgar eloquence are constantly surprising to us. The gaiety of that language is an American gaiety: here imagination and reality have married well 'because the marriage place / Was what they loved'. Stevens often insisted on the relevance of place to the nature of imaginative activity and objects.

This adds to our difficulties in that it adds to that element of the fortuitous which was, for Stevens, essential to poetry. Art is fortuitous because it deals in moments of unpredictable balance, because it works with anomalies and resemblances which can never in themselves be exact, though the product may be; and because the absolute rightness of language (which is its gaiety) bloods the man who feels it with a delight essentially unexpected. Over-reliance on the power of the fortuitous to signify is, in fact, one cause of Stevens's failure (though some poems that seem to me failures are much admired in America). The truth may be that some proportion of Stevens will always remain relatively inaccessible, though this proportion should become very small. The English reader even has the advantage that he can clearly see the greatness of the later poetry without having to get over the dazzle caused by over-long attention to the fireworks of *Harmonium*. But it is with much reading that the book of Stevens becomes true, and the English reader needs all the verse and the 300 or so pages of prose in which a great poet speaks greatly of poetry and the *materia poetica*.

The Necessary Angel (1951) consists of essays and lectures mostly of the Forties. It is worth saying, with the help of Mr. S.F. Morse – author of a forthcoming critical biography – how the book came by its title. In 1949 Stevens bought a still-life by Tal Coat; he admired it because 'for all its in-door light on in-door objects, the picture refreshes one with an out-door sense of things.' (This 'out-door sense' is nearly what he elsewhere calls 'major weather,' a discovery of the real by the 'in-door light' of imagination.) Soon he gave the picture the fanciful title of 'Angel surrounded by Peasants,' the angel being 'the Venetian glass bowl on the left' and the peasants the objects surrounding it. Then he described it in language exactly appropriate to his own poems, calling it 'an effort to attain a certain reality purely by way of the artist's own vitality.' The final poem in *The Auroras of Autumn* (1950) was entitled 'Angel Surrounded by Paysans.' In this masterpiece the angel who grew out of the Venetian glass represents the giant-poet's way of redeeming the earth. He tells the peasants that he has 'neither ashen wing nor wear of ore,' that he is one of them, yet 'the necessary angel of the earth.'

> Since in my sight you see the earth again
> Cleared of its stiff and stubborn man-locked set.

In 1951, persuaded at last to publish his prose, he called the collection *The Necessary Angel: Essays on Reality and the Imagination*.

There are two inferences from this. First, we may suppose that the best of the poetry – that which evades the dangers of mere epistemological doodling on one hand and the fall from ironic exaltation into flatulence on the other – will always derive its strength from hiding-places as deep as this. Second, Stevens came to write his major prose when he was already a doctor incomparably subtle, indeed angelic. When he comes from poetry, which discloses poetry, to prose, which discloses definitions of poetry, he will arrive at these definitions by strange routes. And, indeed, these essays are constructed like meditative poems, circling beautifully round central images, proceeding with a grave gaiety to repetitive but ever-changing statements about the imagination, 'the one reality in this imagined world', and about the poet, who must find 'what will suffice' to refresh an earth to which the God his predecessors created is no longer relevant. The imagination creates evil as well as good, political value as well as all other value; how important, then, is poetry as the supreme fiction, the sun of the mind, bringer of savour and health, slayer of the dragon of abstract philosophy, destroyer of our poverty?

'The Noble Rider and the Sound of Words' and 'Imagination as Value' are the most remarkable of the essays. Within their subtle yet monumental structures there is the quickness of the poet's mind, inventing the dialect of the angel whose joy redeems the world.

> Natives of poverty, children of malheur,
> The gaiety of language is our seigneur.

In the 'Adagia'—two or three hundred of them printed in the inaccessible *Opus Posthumous* – we may see, among much else, how this couplet grew from two observations: 'Poetry is a purging of the world's poverty and change and evil and death . . .'; 'Poetry is the gaiety (joy) of language.' Although the posthumous book necessarily contains some inferior material, it has some extremely important prose, notably a late essay called 'A Collect of Philosophy,' and, above all, the poems of Stevens's last year; one of them, 'As You Leave the Room,' is fit to stand beside 'The Circus Animal's Desertion,' its affirmations as emphatic, for all their calm, as the denunciations of Yeats. And this is characteristic, for Stevens's achievement is to have stripped of dead images and assumptions the myth that animates modern art and to have given it new and unforeseen reality. Mr. Morse, to whom we owe this fascinating collection, has also included the two early verse-plays, and some interesting early lyrics and drafts. There is almost nothing in the book that may safely be dispensed with by the reader undertaking the indispensable task of understanding the *mundo*, as he might put it, of Stevens. . . .

NOTE

1 *The Necessary Angel* and *Opus Posthumous*.

OPUS POSTHUMOUS

London, 1959

THE NECESSARY ANGEL

London, 1960

The English edition of each book was published by Faber in a run of 1,500 copies.

---

116. Ifor Evans, from 'The Insurance Man as a Poet', *Birmingham Post*

19 January 1960, 3

Evans (b. 1899) is the author of a number of studies of English literature, including *The Language of Shakespeare's Plays* (1959).

Like many British reviewers of the time, Evans refers to the fact that Stevens was an insurance executive and notes the possibility of a conflict between this career and a calling as a poet! This review deals only with *Opus Posthumous*.

... In poetic theory it was the French writers who most influenced him, and it may be thought that sometimes he turned over too easily the counters of philosophical criticism. It became at times, especially when his Hegelian studies intruded, over-elaborated without any compensating precision: 'a poem is a restricted creation of the imagination. The gods are the creation of the imagination at its utmost. Men are a part of reality.' Away from all this, in the lyric where he commanded such considerable success he could register many moods. Ultimately he was a romantic, and the coloured cohorts of words are often given ready access to his poems. This sweep of his romanticism sometimes allows rhetoric to enter into the verse and the lyrical element is diminished.

> A beautiful thing, milord, is beautiful
> Not only in itself but in the things
> Around it. Thus it has a large expanse,
> As the moon has in its moonlight, worlds away.
> As the sea has in its coastal clamorings.

When the lyrical quality is unalloyed the effect is impressive. So in his 'Blanche McCarthy,' now published for the first time:

> Look in the terrible mirror of the sky
> And not in this dead glass,
>   which can reflect
> Only the surfaces – the bending arm,
> The leaning shoulder and the searching eye.

> Look in the terrible mirror of the sky.
> Oh, bend against the invisible: and lean
> To symbols of descending night; and search
> The glare of revelations going by!

> Look in the terrible mirror of the sky.
> See how the absent moon waits in a glade.
> Of your dark self, and how the wings of stars,
> Upward, from unimagined coverts, fly.

England, and the English tradition he found less attractive than all France had to offer: Léon-Paul Fargue, Mallarmé and

Valéry, perhaps above all Valéry, it was to these that he turned. Some young critic should explore this whole problem. Why did American writers of Stevens's generation find so little in the English tradition in which their roots ultimately lay, and so much in France, which, let it be whispered, they never completely understood? Is it because of his neglect for us that English critics have treated him rather meanly? . . .

117. Austin Clarke, 'a naiveté which led to much complexity', from 'Business as Usual', *Irish Times*

5 March 1960, 6

An Irish poet, novelist, journalist and critic, Clarke (1896–1974) was educated at Belvedere College, where Joyce had been a student, and University College, Dublin. His work includes *Selected Poems* (1961) *Mnemosyne Lay in Dust* (1966) and several autobiographical and critical volumes.

. . . Wallace Stevens, like Amy Lowell and the early Imagists, belonged to the 'Gallic' School. Europe was still a far-off romance and no one dreamed of American military bases on our side of the Atlantic. The very first poem in this book is a naiveté which led eventually to much complexity.

> There's a little square in Paris,
> Waiting until we pass.
> They sit idly there,
> They sip the glass.

There's a cab-horse at the corner,
There's rain. The season grieves.
It was silver once,
And green with leaves.

Wallace Stevens quickly abandoned such simplicity of
rhyme for the delights of free verse, though he could never
resist adorning his poems with a Frenchified line.

What manner of building shall we build?
Let us design a chastel de chasteté. De penseé...

He had an amusing method of giving a large abstract title
to picturesque poems in which he mingled American detail.
'Reality is an Activity of the most August Imagination' is the
title of a poem which begins –

Last Friday, in the big light of last Friday night,
We drove home from Cornwall to Hartford, late.
It was not a night blown at a glassworks in Vienna
Or Venice, motionless, gathering time and dust.

'Presence of an External Master of Knowledge' is a poem
about Ulysses, but all that the great wanderer, 'symbol of the
seeker,' has to tell us is this:

Here I feel the human loneliness
And that, in space and solitude,
Which knowledge is: the world and fate.
The right within me and about me,
Joined in a triumphant vigor
Like a direction on which I depend...

In apposition, Stevens frequently used picturesque titles
for abstract poems. So 'Solitaire under the Oaks' begins –

In the oblivion of cards
One exists among pure principles.
Neither the cards nor the trees nor the air
Persist as facts.

Sometimes a plain title, such as 'In the Northwest,' leads
us to pretty affectations of colour.

All over Minnesota,
Cerise sopranos
Walking in the snow...

'Ice in the Mississippi' brings us, in the reflection, 'beautiful alliterations of shadows and of things shadowed.'

Wallace Stevens made two little experiments in dramatic
form. The first of these[1] is described rather hesitantly by Mr.
Morse as a piece of *chinoiserie,* but it is attractive and even the
colour scheme, as it were, of the actors, three Chinese, two
negroes, is unusual. 'Carlos among the Candles,' a brief
dramatic monologue, displaying symbolism in action,
would, I think, be effective on the stage, and it seems a pity
that Stevens did not persevere in these experiments because
verse-drama needs to become exotic again, if it is to be saved
from realism.

Stevens was influenced in his later years by Valéry. Much
of his mature work consists in subtle attempts to define the
undefinable. Not too wisely Mr. Morse has included a mixed
collection of apothegms, sententiae and other odd jottings
from the poet's notebooks[2]– some of them trite.

NOTES

1 'Three Travellers Watch a Sunrise', *CP,* pp. 127–43.
2 'Adagia', *CP,* pp. 157–80.

118. Unsigned review, 'Poet of Mind and Reality', *Times Literary Supplement*

18 March 1960, 179

Since the late 1930s a number of English poets and critics of
poetry, Mr. Julian Symons, Mr. Nicholas Moore, Mr. A.

Alvarez, and Professor Frank Kermode among them, have drawn attention to the excellence of Wallace Stevens's poetry, but he remains a poet very difficult for English readers to understand. He felt, himself, that the early English sources of American literature were irrelevant or a misfortune, since the American literary temperament was quite unlike the English; he drew on French models in a way that no leading English poet, of English birth, has been able in this century to do.

His fellow New Englander, Mr. Robert Frost, has a reticence and a dry humour and a particularized feeling for landscape, all of which appeal to English readers. Stevens is not reticent, but splendidly florid. His wit and gaiety, which can be extreme, belong to the choice of language, to the mode of presentation, rather than to the substance of what is presented. His landscape is not particularized but most typically an atmospheric landscape of light, colour, cloudscape, seascape, which lends itself to shaping, and reshaping, by his words. It is in a sense an interior landscape, a node of speculation. Though he is the kind of poet whom American critics describe as a Paleface rather than a Redskin, he is reminiscent, sometimes, of Whitman in his spaciousness, in his choice of highly coloured epithets, in his gift for using expansiveness, prolongation, repetition, as positive poetic qualities.

He sometimes seems to write nonsense verse, but it is always emotionally serious nonsense verse. His poetic passion is abstract rather than concrete. The great philosophical themes are, for him, also the great poetic themes, and he is a poet of mind and reality – vague, elusive concepts for many poets – rather than of human emotion, or even, in a Wordsworthian sense, of man and nature. His poems, in fact, seem to owe almost nothing to his more intimate personal emotional history. They are personal, but only in the sense that a style of speaking, an habitual gesture, a habit of recurring to favourite themes, is personal.

They are not at all dramatic, and the two little plays included in *Opus Posthumous* are pathetic failures. Yet, though concerned with atmospheres more than with persons or situations, and with the poet's mind even more than with

457

what impinges on it, they are not didactic or expository. They mime, it might be said, as art the great gestures of thought.

The finest prose piece in this collection by Mr. Morse is an essay which Stevens never published called 'A Collect of Philosophy'. He wanted to contribute it to a philosophical journal, and was told it would be more in place in a literary journal. It describes the kind of excitement he found not so much in strict philosophical method as in certain philosophical concepts, especially such concepts as those of infinity, or God, or Leibniz's world of monads, or Schopenhauer's World as Will. He felt that such concepts may occur to some philosophers not as the end-product of a long train of argument but, just as they occur to poets, in a sudden flash. Both poets and philosophers share 'the habit of probing for an integration,' which is part of 'the general will to order.' But the poet seeks integrations not so much for their own sakes as for

some quality that [an integration] possesses, such as its insight, its evocative power or its appearance in the eye of the imagination. The philosopher intends his integration to be fateful; the poet intends his to be effective.

If philosophy can be summed up, suggestively but inadequately, as 'the history of doctrines,' so, Stevens feels, if one says that 'poetry constantly requires a new station, it is a way, and an inadequate way, of saying what poetry is.' Elsewhere, Stevens speaks a great deal, and often rather bewilderingly, of the poet and reality. Reality is something different from the imagination and also from 'life,' it is something which the mind cannot manage and control, and poetry, like religion, makes a gesture of recognition towards reality. Stevens's aphoristic sentences are deceptively lucid. On the whole his view of life, or of reality, seems to combine something of the exaltation of the early New England Transcendentalist (he is very much in that American tradition) with that kind of post-Cartesian French thinking which makes a kind of God of the *pour-soi*, of mind or consciousness.

Perhaps all his poems might be seen as attempts to pierce

and penetrate, to illuminate from within, the *en-soi*; the human mind, as it were, irradiates, the outer world and gives it a certain godlikeness, and yet there is something real – in the depths of the mind, or in the outer world itself? – which resists this irradiation. And the point of the poetic process is in the end to make us aware of this reality, and that we have *not* grasped it: that may be why 'poetry constantly requires a new station.'

By the standards of modern linguistic analysis Stevens was not only a very amateur philosopher but a very confused one. But perhaps talking about philosophy was an indirect way, for him, of talking about religion. In his essay on philosophy he has such sentences as this:

The number of ways of passing between the traditional two fixed points of man's life, that is to say, of passing from the self to God, is fixed only by the limitations of space, which is limitless. The eternal philosopher is the eternal pilgrim on that road.... If the idea of God is the ultimate poetic idea, then the idea of the ascent into heaven is only a little below it.

But there is something disconcerting, from a religious point of view also, about God as 'the ultimate poetic idea,' as what Stevens elsewhere calls a 'supreme fiction.' In a sense, Stevens is perhaps ultimately a humanist, to whom religions and philosophies and poems are all ultimately valuable mainly as illustrations of the concept-forging fecundity of the human mind.

The sense of community, and the dramatic relations of men and women in a difficult and changing society, might seem to some critics to be as much 'fixed points of man's life' as 'the self' and 'God.' In so far as it is the humanism of the contemplative or fictive mind in isolation, Stevens's humanism seems oddly lacking in ordinary human warmth; and in so far as it aspires towards religion, towards a kind of religion in the teeth of what, for Stevens, were 'the facts,' does it move beyond the order of body and the order of mind to the order of charity? The great paradox of his poetic achievement is that, seeming to take in with so large a sweep so many ultimate concerns, he yet seems also to by-pass many of those things which for most men and women are the substance of life.

459

Stevens's basic attitudes are given a fuller and rounder statement in the little volume of six public addresses and one expository essay (about a poem by Miss Marianne Moore) which he brought out in his lifetime under the title *The Necessary Angel*. The reader of these poised and elegant pieces should not, however, expect from them the patient rigour, say, of Dr. I.A. Richards's or Collingwood's writings on aesthetic questions or, on the other hand, the intimate self-communion of Yeats. Stevens's thought tends to present itself in a series of more or less aphoristic, or at least self-contained, statements, some of which are striking, some rather obvious, and all carefully phrased. He does not argue, he states, and states very generally. In this, and also in a certain deliberate elevation of manner, his prose resembles Emerson's; it has a touch of the lay-sermon about it. He quotes a very elevated passage from Paul Klee, about the true artist establishing himself at 'the mind or heart of creation,' and comments (the comment would apply to much of his own writing): 'Conceding that this sounds a bit like sacerdotal jargon, that is not too much to allow to those that have helped to create a new reality, a modern reality, since what has been created is nothing less.' This 'modern reality' is a vision of the world which, divorcing itself from traditional religious belief, can still inspire a sense of awe and terror, directed now, however, towards the capacities of man's own mind:

Modern reality is a reality of decreation, in which our revelations are not the revelations of belief, but the precious portents of our own powers. The greatest truth we could hope to discover, in whatever field we discovered it, is that man's truth is the final resolution of everything.

Is there not something here of the arrogance of idealism which Santayana castigated in *Egotism in German Philosophy*? The phrase 'man's truth' certainly seems to have a much more subjective flavour about it than the word 'truth,' *tout court*. And is the ultimate attitude really religious or, perhaps, magical?

It would be tragic [Stevens writes] not to realize the extent of man's dependence on the arts. The kind of world that might result from too exclusive a dependence on them has been questioned, as if the discipline of the arts was in no sense a moral discipline. We have not to discuss that here.

It is a pity it is not discussed. But the general tone, certainly, is one of moral elevation: 'I am elevating this a little, because I am trying to generalize and because it is incredible that one should speak of the aspirations of the last two or three generations without a degree of elevation.' And in what tone should we speak of their blunders and crimes?

There is a slight but revealing little poem in *Opus Posthumous* which shows, perhaps as briefly as it can be shown, Stevens's fundamental state of creative puzzlement:

> Granted, we die for good.
> Life, then, is largely a thing
> Of happens to like, not should.
>
> And that, too, granted, why
> Do I happen to like red bush,
> Gray grass and green gray sky?
>
> What else remains? But red,
> Gray, green, why those of all?
> That is not what I said:
>
> Not those of all. But those.
> One likes what one happens to like,
> One likes the way red grows.
>
> It cannot matter at all.
> Happens to like is one
> Of the ways things happen to fall.

The gaiety there is all in the words and not at all in the resigned, sadly assenting substance. In a world, for him, without necessity Stevens tried to create a 'beauty of necessity' in poems like this which would salute the non-necessity which was one of the aspects for him of that ever-evasive concept, reality. 'In the long run,' says one of the most frightening of his aphorisms, 'the truth does not matter.' In the long run, does he mean, the human mind can treat the contingent as the necessary, can confer dignity on the accidental? Perhaps his thinking was basically a muddle; but his best poems rear a beautiful order on it.

461

119. Sam Hynes, 'Uncompromising Realist', *Time and Tide*

26 March 1960, 357

This review is on *The Necessary Angel* only. Hynes's works include *The Edwardian Turn of Mind* (1968) and *The Auden Generation* (1976).

Of the major modern American poets, Wallace Stevens has been the slowest to establish a reputation equal to his gifts. Perhaps one might explain this fact by saying that he is still, after his death at seventy-odd, too modern for most of us, and that his reputation will grow as we gradually catch up to him. Stevens' poems are the poems of a sensitive and supremely honest modern mind, meditating upon its own processes, and upon the nature of its knowledge, and steadfastly refusing the comforts of any beliefs – whether religious or political or philosophical – for which experience provided no evidence. He believed neither in God nor in Progress, the Liberal's substitute for God; his was a monism beyond belief and beyond scepticism, a poetry of things as they are.

Because he was an elegantly ironic and witty poet, and because he wrote poems about poetry, and about paintings and music, Stevens has sometimes been condemned as an aesthete, but in fact he was the most uncompromising of realists. The work of art was important to him, not because it was an aesthetic object, but because it demonstrated the way in which the imagination could give order to the chaos of reality. Poetry was for him 'the interdependence of the imagination and reality as equals'; and in fact this theme – the relation of the imagination and reality – was his only theme, though he found it of sufficient extent to encompass a whole philosophy of art and life.

Poems were, for Stevens, 'disclosures of poetry', but they were not 'disclosures of definitions of poetry'. For the definitions he turned to prose. He was, as one might expect, intensely interested in the theory of poetry, and regarded it as 'one of the great subjects of study'. He did not write, as he once meant to, an *Ars Poetica*, but he did use the occasional lectures which he gave as occasions for reflection on theory. These reflections have now been published as *The Necessary Angel: Essays on Reality and the Imagination*. They do not constitute a complete theory, but they do contain the most contemporary, perhaps the only rigorously contemporary approach to poetic theory that we have in English, and as such it would be difficult to exaggerate their importance for the future of poetry.

120. Henry Reed, 'an unexpected valuation of psychic health', *Listener*

Vol. 163, 14 April 1960, 675–6

Active as a critic, playwright and broadcaster, Henry Reed (b. 1914) has published little poetry, but established a reputation with *A Map of Verona* (1946).

These two books, so far as this country is concerned, may perhaps be regarded as books for which we are not yet ready, but which will probably have immense value and charm for us when we are. I would be the last to underestimate their value and charm even now: but over here we are in a peculiar position as regards Stevens. Most of us don't, quite simply, know him well enough. It is not our fault entirely; but it is possible to feel, with some resentment, that when Stevens was finally published in England a few years ago, it was because the event could no longer be decently delayed. For well over thirty years Stevens has been an accepted part of the American scene, even for younger readers there, the mere previous presence of his work in the world will have quickened appreciation and enjoyment. They will know what comes where and when in his work; and this is important for intelligent love of any poet.

Here, alas, there is the dangerous possibility that the 150 pages of verse in *Opus Posthumous* may be used as an introduction, though the real interest of these poems for the habituated reader lies in the fact that Stevens himself rejected them from his *Collected Poems*. They are indeed for the most part specialists' material. It is usually possible to see why Stevens pushed them aside. This is so even in the case of *Owl's Clover*, one of Stevens's longest poems, constantly referred to by American critics. The editor of *Opus Posthumous*, who contributes a valuable introduction, has seen fit to publish a version of this poem that restores 200 or more lines deleted by Stevens in previously published versions (here inaccessible). This is no way to edit anything; or if it is, Stevens's cuts should surely have been indicated by brackets. Much of the poem is powerfully moving in a way rather unusual in Stevens: in it he is often more like 'other' poets. He himself considered the poem 'rhetorical', and out it went. But it brings us strangely near to him personally – rather as *Stephen Hero* does to Joyce, or *Jean Santeuil* does to Proust.

Most of the other things in *Opus Posthumous,* and the whole of *The Necessary Angel* (assembled by Stevens himself, and published in America in 1951) consist of public statements about poetry and poets. Many of the pieces are lectures, and perhaps suffer a little because of this: a lecture has to be fitted unnaturally to a certain length of time. Stevens writes with alluring grace even when he is appallingly difficult to follow. One is glad to sense a certain reluctance about the perform-ance. Exhibitionism – that most damaging diversion for the creative man – is nowadays much encouraged in poets, both here and in America. Stevens resists this with fair nobility: but certainly the momentous statements we expect on such occasions are there; many of them have passed already into the reserve battery of useful quotes:

What is his [the poet's] function? Certainly it is not to lead people out of the confusion in which they find themselves. Nor is it, I think, to comfort them while they follow their leaders to and fro. I think that his function is to make his imagination theirs and that he fulfils himself only as he sees his imagination become the light in the mind of others. His role, in short, is to help people to live their lives. Time and again it has been said that he may not address himself to an élite. I think he may. There is not a poet whom we prize living today that does not address himself to an élite. The poet will continue to do this: to address himself to an élite even in a classless society, unless, perhaps, this exposes him to prison or exile.

This is the poet who has often been called a dandy and a hedonist: the terms have not always been consciously dismissive: but they do in fact belittle him, even if indulgently. For the idiosyncrasies of Stevens's thought and expression are not merely endearing perversities: a man who pleads his agnosticism so earnestly must be taken seriously even if he does so with elegance, humour and calm.

This is a theme of his prose as of his verse. Indeed it may be his passionate delight in what we can do with our own imagination, and in the sense of a happy power over our own lives and the things we are called on to contemplate ('reality'): all this may still disconcert us. We are so doggedly used to the idea that poetry springs from repeated bouts of torment, religious or erotic, or is a repeated conquest of despair, or a repeated act of autotherapy, that it is still strange to find a poet who eschews conflict and seems to believe that the autotherapy must be done before the pen is set to paper. Stevens extends the possible consciousness of future poets by an unexpected valuation of psychic health. It is poignant to think that but for the insularity of English culture we might have been enjoying Stevens's work in the years when he was still alive to be thanked for it.

121. Elizabeth Jennings, on Stevens as a visionary writer, *London Magazine*

Vol. 7, no. 5, May 1960, 85–7

Jennings (b. 1926) is a poet and writer on religion, whose recent work includes *After the Ark* (1978) and *Celebrations & Elegies* (1982).

... He is usually regarded as a metaphysician, a philosopher, whereas a truly accommodating reading of his work would, I am convinced, reveal him as essentially a *visionary* writer. He is a visionary poet, however, who has no belief in God and who searches for meaning and unity in an order both disclosed by and created in the human imagination. *Opus Posthumous* provides convincing evidence of the visionary character of Stevens's mind in the collection of aphorisms which are part of the contents of the book. Here are a few examples of what I mean: 'Reality is the spirit's true centre', 'The world of the poet depends on the world that he has contemplated', 'The man who asks questions seeks only to reach a point where it will no longer be necessary for him to ask questions.'

In such statements as these, as well as in his poems, Stevens shows himself to be a religious man who repudiated dogma, an agnostic who hungered for certainty. In his best-known and great poem, 'Sunday Morning', he discloses a world without God, a place where the senses are appeased but appeased only momentarily. Stevens's poems are, it is true, crammed with religious language and symbols but these things are removed from their proper contexts and employed by him for his own private purposes. Like the paintings, still lives and *objets d'art* which fill so much of his verse, these religious symbols are only springboards for Stevens's dominant preoccupation – his exploration of the limits of the imagination.

In all Stevens's best work there is a poignant sense of absence, together with a stoic determination to accept that absence. Against this poignancy, he sets a stylishness, a care for detail, a concern with subtleties and nuances. There is no full vision, only adumbrations. In the poems which Samuel French Morse has assembled in this book, the themes which constantly preoccupied Stevens are to be found in many forms and guises. If one predominant subject possessed Stevens all his life, he never ceased to examine that subject from different angles and in different lights. In 'A Mythology Reflects its Region', which may well be the last poem he wrote, we find the same obsession which appears so vividly, so concretely in 'Credences of Summer' and 'The Comedian as the Letter C'. In this late poem, however, imagery has been stripped down to its essence, simplified and laid bare:

> The image must be of the nature of its creator,
> It is the nature of its creator increased,
> Heightened. It is he, anew in a freshened youth
> And it is he in the substance of his region ...

The plays printed in this book are interesting only for their insights and images since Stevens was never a dramatic poet. Nor, on the other hand, was he a personal poet in the sense that he passionately explored his own motives, feelings and reactions; he was interested in feeling at its source rather than in its countless manifestations. When he turned inward to examine himself, it was always his own imagination which he tested and probed. His poetry presents the delicate adjustments of that imagination to exterior things, tangible and intangible. In an essay here called 'The Irrational Element in Poetry', Stevens declares, ' ... while it can lie in the temperament of very few of us to write poetry in order to find God, it is probably the purpose of each of us to write poetry to find the good which, in the Platonic sense, is synonymous with God'. This is an uncompromising affirmation and if *Opus Posthumous* contained nothing else but these essays in which Stevens makes himself wholly accessible to us, it would be of extreme value. But the poems and the aphorisms here are also useful and revealing; they are the products of a deeply reflective, subtle and dispassionate mind. There can surely be little doubt now that Wallace Stevens was a poet of extraordinary originality and splendid achievement.

LETTERS OF WALLACE STEVENS

New York, 1966
London, 1967

Knopf's first printing was 6,000 copies and this edition was reprinted in 1970. The Faber edition, printed from the American sheets, was in a first run of 1,455.

---

122. Unsigned review, 'The Two Lives of Wallace Stevens', *Times Literary Supplement*

30 March 1967, 266

This review was probably written by Roy Fuller (b. 1912), well-known British poet, novelist and critic.

Writing to the editor of the *Dial* in 1922 Wallace Stevens said: 'Do, please, excuse me from the biographical note. I am a lawyer and live in Hartford. But such facts are neither gay nor instructive.' However, the literary world has always found the facts enigmatic and fascinating, and his letters have long been anticipated in the expectation of their illuminating or explaining the supposed irreconcilability of his two modes of existence, as poet and successful man of affairs. What in fact comes out of them is the reverse of anything journalistically quirky or sensational; instead, the book draws a portrait sufficiently full and coherent to allay for ever the crude questionings, and one of far greater interest and subtlety than some no doubt imagined from the sparse lines previously available to view. Nothing from the archives of the Hartford insurance group of companies (which employed Stevens from 1916 until his death in 1955) is included here, but enough details emerge from Stevens's private correspondence to fix the routine of his life as a lawyer, his relations with his stenographer, the companies' coloured chauffeurs, and other colleagues, and his own attitude to his professional work. As might have been deduced – for Stevens, far from trying to escape from the Hartford, went on working for it five years beyond the compulsory retirement age – the tensions experienced by the poet were quite outside any mere clash of human types or division of time between office hours and art. The Hartford and its employees obviously held Stevens in respect and, when eventually his poetic reputation became public property, pride; on his side, there was no undue strain in his evolvement of a dignified and sometimes facetious affection, never false or condescending.

Nearly 3,300 of Stevens's letters were available for publication when his daughter compiled this book. Not many more than a quarter of this number have been printed here, and even from these some passages have been omitted. A critic in the *New York Review of Books* has hinted that Miss Stevens's unexpected purpose in this procedure was to remove evidence of some indiscretions and to spotlight her own filial devotion, but there is little indication of the former and none of the latter, and in reducing the enormous mass of material to reasonably saleable proportions and at so short a period from Stevens's death a modest degree of discretion can scarcely be complained of. In fact, Miss Stevens has included a number of letters which show the realities of her own marital affairs as well as some worn places in her relations with her father: besides, her omission of inessentials has almost certainly contributed to the book's compulsive readability and her footnotes and linking narrations are adequate and unobtrusive, quite admirably so.

Stevens was born in Pennsylvania in 1879, the son of a successful though not wealthy country town lawyer. The earliest letters here are a few he wrote to his mother from a summer camp at the age of fifteen. Amusing that the second letter actually contains one of those verbal imitations of non-human sounds that were such a persistent and curious feature of his verse; significant that they are full of observation; the syntax and vocabulary are already brilliant. He went to Harvard in 1897, but only one letter has survived from his years there. Miss Stevens has resourcefully filled the gap with extracts from a journal he began to keep in 1898 and with some letters from his father. The journal is full of observation, too, and of a Ruskinian precision: the letters from his father are quite remarkable. Both father and son grasp the issues of life that was to follow, and the opposition between them was far from simply conventional. The father is urging an orthodox career, though is in no doubt of his son's talent ('but for eccentricities in your genius you may be fitted for a Chair'). The son realizes that the father is holding him 'in check' but has few illusions about his own character or the realities of material existence. 'I am certainly a domestic creature, par excellence,' he writes; and

I should be quite content to work and be practical – but I hate the conflict whether it 'avails' or not. I want my powers to be put to their fullest use – to be exhausted when I am done with them. On the other hand I do not want to make a petty struggle for existence – physical or literary. I must try not to be dilettante – half dream, half deed. I must be all dream or all deed.

In a sense his life was aimed to disprove what his father puts in so forcible, so Stevensian a way:

One never thinks out a destiny – if a fellow takes Peach Pie – he often wishes he had chosen the Custard ... The only trouble is that since we cannot have both Pie and custard – it is oft too late to repent.

After Harvard, Stevens worked as a journalist for a short period, neither successfully nor congenially. He had the notion of resigning from his newspaper and devoting himself to writing, but quite soon he fell in with his father's urging and took up the law. In 1904 he had passed his bar examinations and was admitted to practice. In the same year he met and fell in love with his future wife. Following

Stevens's death she destroyed a number of his letters to her of this period (after first copying extracts she thought might be of interest), but this is probably no great loss. The letters of the long courtship are curiously pointless, a parallel to Stevens's career as a lawyer – and, indeed, as a writer – during the same epoch. He started a law firm but it was a failure, and then worked in several practices without apparently making any mark. Lone wolf business skill, the flair for acquiring clients, are not qualities possessed by shy men, and Stevens was certainly shy. He was big and (judging by the photographs here) at all stages of his life handsome, but the formidability noted by many arose almost certainly quite unconsciously from his brain-power, his lack of ease in direct personal contacts and, no doubt, his occasional exasperation at other men's disorder and importunity (what he characterized as his 'pretty well-developed mean streak'). His sexual desires were from the outset directed towards uxoriousness. And the *fin de siècle* literary tradition his adolescence inherited persisted with him for a very long time: as late as 1907 he is quoting Andrew Lang's Odyssey sonnet with approval.

But in 1908 he was freed from the antipathies of private practice by becoming employed as a lawyer by an insurance company. The following year he was earning enough to be able to marry. His father died in 1911 and his mother a year later (a sentence from his journal about his dying mother – 'the beating of her heart in the veins of her throat was as rapid as water running from a bottle' – is one of the few indications in his correspondence and journal of this time of his future literary power). And then quite out of the blue so far as the reader is concerned come the letters of November 6, 1914, and June 6, 1915 (which follow without intervening material), to the editor of *Poetry*, the first another laconic response to a request for a biographical note, the second discussing the order of the sections of 'Sunday Morning'. Somehow Stevens had become a modern poet.

Ex post facto it can be seen that apart from the change in and hardening of the bases of his personal life, Stevens was enabled to write the early poems of *Harmonium* by the liberation from explicit meaning arrived at through his reading of the French symbolists, a process similar to that undergone by Eliot. A large part of his initial powers resides in his extraordinary talent for iambic verse, his feeling for and interest in vocabulary; freed from the compulsion to narrate in any prose sense, these flourish in startling, evocative, exotic and disturbing style. Later in his life he was quite patient with correspondents who asked him to 'explain' passages in his poetry, particularly the famous pieces in *Harmonium*, and his further inexplicitness is often amusing. The 'nonsense' side of the modern movement in poetry – the arbitrary symbols, the private references, the unexplained personae and fragmentary plots – persisted with him, indeed, until the end and accounts for a large part of that growth sector of the American literary economy, the Stevens critical industry. But, of course, if there were no more to him than this he would merely share a place with a score of others. As it is, the conviction grows that he must be placed with the two or three greatest English-speaking poets of the twentieth century.

It is a sense uncontradicted by the letters, though the epochs they mainly record are unsensational indeed. Stevens moved to Hartford in 1916, having followed a former associate to join the Hartford group of insurance companies. His early years with them involved a fair amount of travel, including trips to Florida, which subsequently became a favourite vacation place, and this experience gave concreteness to the Americanness of his verse and in particular established the important polarity of rigorous New England and the lush tropics. He observed flora and fauna (in gardens and zoos as well as at large) with the old Ruskinian intensity. The first edition of *Harmonium* was published in 1923 and the following year his first and only child was born (about the possibility of a second child he characteristically said later: 'There is nothing I should have liked more, but I was afraid of it'). Between that time and the second, enlarged edition of *Harmonium* in 1931 he clearly worked harder at his professional career than at poetry. But once again a more settled background, the opportunity to become more comfortably 'a domestic creature', provided the conditions for a renewal of creativity. In 1932 he bought the spacious house he was to live in for the rest of his life (previously he had been a tenant in far from luxurious conditions) and, soon after, he was established in an impregnable position with his company, his travelling on business infrequent. From this time the typed letter becomes the rule rather than the exception as his office status enables him to use his stenographer to dictate his private correspondence, and a characteristic tone of voice emerges. There follows the larger part of his correspondence, and absorbing it is, even heroic. He sustains with a succession of correspondents an intercourse sometimes ironic, often subtly affectionate, always astonishingly polished and intelligent. Even what came to be the immutable routines of his existence are made continually fresh, and only in the last few years of his life did he himself seem to find them arduous: 'I begin to feel at the end of the day that I am through for that day', he wrote in his seventieth year. 'It is not that I grow tired but that my elan seems somewhat bent. I should much rather stroll home looking at the girls than anything else.' His continued response to nature and paintings, to new poets and periodicals and correspondents, is remarkable. 'I have never been bored in any general sense', he once observed, and we can unhesitatingly believe him.

This is not the place to try to give any account of what is the most important theme of his letters as it is of his verse – the relationship between poetry and reality. Nor to more than mention the interesting but less important question of how his devoting so much of his working time to an occupation and society removed from his art contributed to – or conceivably hindered – his working out of that theme. Almost from the outset he was seen to be a great master of language: increasingly he is being recognized as a poet of organic development and Rilkean penetration who had important things to say about the human condition of his time. How pathetic is the sparse evidence here of English interest in his work – for example, an appreciative letter in 1938 on being noticed in the little magazine *Twentieth Century Verse*, some negotiations with the Fortune Press, a comment on the notorious 'Stuffed Goldfinch' review in *New Verse* – 'What you say about the Pulitzer Prize is interesting. After all there are people who think that *Ideas of*

Order is not only bad but rotten' – a comment all the more ironical now because it can be seen to occur in a truly distinguished series of letters about poetry to Ronald Lane Latimer. Of course, wise after the event, we cannot begin to understand how the book that Stevens's more ribald business friends called *Ordeals of Ida* seemed to Geoffrey Grigson finicky, rhythmless, unreal, inhuman and to observe nothing –

> ... Children,
> Still weaving budded aureoles,
> Will speak our speech and never know,
>
> Will say of the mansion that it seems
> As if he that lived there left behind
> A spirit storming in blank walls,
>
> A dirty house in a gutted world,
> A tatter of shadows peaked to white,
> Smeared with the gold of the opulent
> > sun.

An operation Stevens underwent on April 26, 1955, showed that he was suffering from an inevitably fatal cancer. The fact was kept from him, and he made a sufficient recovery from the surgery to go to Yale to receive an honorary degree and actually return, at the end of June and into July, to his office for a few hours a day. Only a phrase from the last letter here, dated July 15, reveals any real slackening of his hold on the two preoccupations of his life – 'Considering my present condition, I can neither concentrate on poetry nor enjoy poetry'. These are harrowing words following the long years of asserting, in so many different ways, poetry to be life's only sanction, and of striving so elaborately to show in his art the nature of existence. But they come, after all, in a note written to try to help a young poet quite unknown to him. By August 2 he was dead.

123. V. S. Pritchett, 'Truffles in the Sky', *New Statesman*

Vol. 73, 31 March 1967, 439–40

A noted fiction-writer, memoirist and critic, Sir Victor Pritchett (b. 1900) published his *Selected Stories* in 1978. Recent work includes *On the Edge of the Cliff* and *The Tale Bearers* (both 1980).

I first read Wallace Stevens on a flight across the Atlantic. At the inhuman altitude of 40,000 feet, encased in one's ears, hung up in the blue ennui, over the silver tessellations of the tedious ocean – what a sentence! One catches the infection of 'The Comedian as the Letter C', as quick as measles:

> Portentous enunciation, syllable
> To blessed syllable affined, and sound
> Bubbling felicity in cantilene,
> Prolific and tormenting tenderness
> Of music, as it comes to unison,
> Forgather and bell boldly Crispin's last
> Deduction.
>
> Also the mood of Crispin's pilgrimage
> to drive away
>
> The shadow of his fellows from the skies,
> And from their stale intelligence released,
> To make a new intelligence prevail?

But resists it: one is not, as Wallace Stevens was, caught in the back-slapping insurance business, at every boozy convention between Chicago and Kansas. Then we come down on the runway with him and pick up what the aesthete said in his 'Journal' when he was barely 20:

We *must* come down, we must use tooth and nail, it is the law of nature: 'the survival of the fittest'; providing we maintain at the same time self-respect, integrity, fairness. I believe, as unhesitatingly as I believe anything, in the efficacy of fact meeting fact – with a background of the ideal. I am completely satisfied that behind every fact there is a divine force. Don't, therefore, look at facts, but through them.

Behind the mask of the pagan dandy, the quarterly period piece on the *New Yorker* cover of the joker of

> Chieftain Iffucan of Azcan in caftan
> Of tan with human hackles, halt!

is a man as drily homespun as Carlyle or Emerson. With all the blandness and competitive acumen of Dutch and German Pennsylvania, he is troubled by the question of imagination and reality. He is Rip Van Winkle, Harvard-trained and Paris-addled.

Stevens had a very few admirers when he published his first volume of poems *Harmonium* at the age of 44. In England there was Llewelyn Powys who liked his hedonism and his palette. There was a long silence in the uncongenial Thirties and then one or two American critics took Stevens up again – Blackmur, Marius Bewley – and he was thought by some the greatest American poet of the last 100 years. The punning ex-imagist who believed in the 'essential gaudiness of poetry' and who could amuse himself with jokes like

> He picked a bough to jog
> His single loathful cow

had a later phase, was spoken of as a thinking poet and compared to Whitman and even Wordsworth. My impression is that his reputation is now wobbling once more in America. Or rather – and this makes him very interesting as a man – he has reached what, in America, is the equivalent of canonisation: he has acquired the semi-sacredness of one of the established American Problems, an amendment to the Constitution. Such a process has, up to now, been unknown to English writers. We stand or fall on our own. In American literature, the fact or idea called Americans, or the American self-consciousness, are vital presences, whether explicitly or disguised by allegory or symbol. Just as in Russian literature, Russia itself always pervades as a nostalgia or a presence, so in the United States the idea of America also pervades, but as an energy perplexed by its direction.

The Letters of Wallace Stevens – a selection from his enormous correspondence made by his daughter – are all energy. He is even energetic when he is whimsical. He rarely abates or varies. For the most part they briskly concern his poetry or his reading. They are shrewd, decisive, sometimes sardonically sportive: he is, even when solemn, stylish. Here is the other Stevens, the top insurance executive, managing his business. Here – and how American this seems to us – is the sight of what Geoffrey Grigson wickedly called 'the stuffed goldfinch' openly on the job of being a stuffed goldfinch. There is the peculiar sight of a man who looks like a double. He is a fabricator of chinoiserie, lacquer work and ingenious metaphysic, yet he travels on his exacting legal work of one-night stands from conference to conference. His poems are filled with the bric-à-brac of medieval France and the France of the decadents; of Spanish Florida, Mexico, China, Ceylon, Japan and even of Ireland, but he was never out of America in his life and got home from the office to suburban Hartford to doze in esoteric weekends. Eliot found his Royalism in Europe: Stevens constructed an exotic and imaginary court in Connecticut.

How did he obtain these antiquities and these sensual nostalgias? By reading, by dreaming, and by writing to all those places for them; teas from China, figurines from Ceylon, pictures and special editions from France. The enterprise with which Stevens created his inner world of aristocratic bits and pieces, the efficiency with which he attempted to furnish a bare room in the American imagination, is commanding: one thinks of Henry James's earnestly and successfully pursued campaign to acquire London and European society as if it were up for sale at Sotheby's. The will and purpose throb. Although criticism has rightly called Stevens affected and liable, as the affected are, to vulgarity, he was obviously astonished by the accusation. Romantic, yes; and on principle. Reality is surrounded by our instant imaginings, but because fact must be met by fact, the ideal is concrete.

> You must become an ignorant man again
> And see the sun again with an ignorant eye
> And see it clearly in the idea of it.

'Poetry is the subject of the poem' – the line has shocked some critics.

If one is shocked one sees in Stevens one more representative of an American type who, however, effective and long-headed in his practical affairs, lives in a secret, artificial and reflected world and who seems to us to have the tetchiness and pathos of a sycophant. The paganism and the aestheticism are skin-deep and point to a lonely fear of life. The victim of Calvinism has put on gaudy disguise. With all the airs, these characters are lamed: they long for the plain life that mother gave them, but they either hate mother or they hate a vacancy in American life. They survive by striking attitudes: no one is as flippant, sardonic or monocled as the escaped Puritan. There is the suspicion (which we had of Eliot) that feeling was thin and that involutions of thought and imagination were strenuous attempts to conceal this: large talk of 'whores' but 'where's the bloody horse?' To talk of 'concupiscent curds' was an alternative to concupiscence or plain curds.

Such criticisms have been made of Wallace Stevens, particularly of his early work. Geoffrey Moore, writing appreciatively in the *Achievement* of the weakening part played by allegory and symbolism in the puritan culture, speaks of 'the lack of visceral quality', one misses 'the blood beat'. Not that Americans such as Stevens are bloodless, but

in American society there is a constant battle, none the less savage for being attenuated, between the regular guys and the eggheads, and it is savage and hysterical because in America the mass have so long and so palpably had the upper hand.

From the letters one gets an inside view. They show one how the critics are always straining to freeze a writer into an arbitrary shape, whereas his working life is full of guesses and changes. Stevens, being a secretive man, was ready for this. He hated being called 'decorative' in his early work, but has to admit that he liked the idea of images alone:

I am not sure that I don't think exactly the same thing now, but unquestionably I think at the same time that life is the essential part of literature.

News for criticism: a writer may hold two contradictory ideas at the same time! He can't remember what some images 'mean': must they mean?

People (he notes) very much prefer to take the solemn view of poetry. When severely pressed, Stevens was careful not to hand over his poetic processes to rational prose. Many of his letters will do the inventive thesis-writers out of their eloquent jobs. About his personal life one does not learn a great deal. There was a longish period of the conventional American research into genealogy and he was keen to get something out of being very Dutch or German; one suspects the results were not exotic enough. He got most out of his trips to Florida: the fine Key West poem, for example. He was not an escapist; he was a dedicated colonist, in the literal and imaginative senses of the term: that is to say, reality was being colonised by swarms of images. But, though he denies it, his life sounds dull. He was harassed by the insurance office; still he recommends poets to go into business because that is the best way of having a cache of money on which to write and of belonging to one's country. He claims to give all his energies to what he is doing, whether it is to insurance claims or poetry. There is no resentful split. His mind is always whole. The only difficulty is that spare time is harder to find as one rises to a responsible position and this means, in practical terms, that in poetry one is continuously starting again. This is a waste of time – a typical dislike of inefficiency. He was lazy-minded, and less perturbed about Communism than other writers of the Thirties and Forties. At one time he was pro-Mussolini, but took that back. He is a fair dealer. His general social view is ameliorative; he wants everyone – and in this he was a true American – to be well-furnished, well-fed and well-off; his idealism – so different from European idealism – believes in ripe, fragrant and solid material satisfactions. One has, from time to time, a sense of succulent glut and gourmandise in his interminable felicities and his *bonnes bouches*. And there are lines of greedy petulance. The inspired snout goes foraging for truffles – in the sky! There is also, once his Nineteen Twenties are over, a distinct effect of a great energy and wit that have created their own monotony. How, with so little time for poetry, could he have written so many expository and ceremonious letters?

BIBLIOGRAPHY

BIBLIOGRAPHICAL MATERIALS AND OTHER RELEVANT SOURCES

BROWN, ASHLEY, and ROBERT S. HALLER (eds), *The Achievement of Wallace Stevens* (Philadelphia: J.B. Lippincott, 1962).

BRYER, JACKSON R., and JOSEPH N. RIDDEL, *Twentieth-Century Literature*, VIII, nos 3–4, October 1962–January 1963, pp. 76–98.

EDELSTEIN, J.M. *Wallace Stevens: A Descriptive Bibliography* (University of Pittsburgh Press, 1974).

EHRENPREIS, IRVIN (ed.), *Wallace Stevens: A Critical Anthology*, (Harmondsworth, Middlesex: Penguin Books, 1972).

LENSING, GEORGE S., 'Wallace Stevens in England', in *Wallace Stevens: A Celebration*, edited by Frank Doggett and Robert Buttel (Princeton University Press, 1980), pp. 130–48.

MORSE, SAMUEL FRENCH, *Wallace Stevens: A Preliminary Checklist of His Published Writings* (New Haven, Connecticut: Yale University Press, 1954).

MORSE, SAMUEL FRENCH, JACKSON R. BRYER and JOSEPH N. RIDDEL, *Wallace Stevens: Checklist and Bibliography of Stevens Criticism* (Denver: Alan Swallow, 1963).

RIDDEL, JOSEPH N., 'Wallace Stevens', in *Fifteen Modern American Authors: A Survey of Research and Criticism*, edited by Jackson R. Bryer (Durham, North Carolina: Duke University Press, 1969), pp. 389–423.

STEVENS, HOLLY, *Souvenirs and Prophecies: The Young Wallace Stevens* (New York: Knopf, 1977).

WILLARD, ABBIE F. *Wallace Stevens: The Poet and His Critics* (Chicago: American Library Association, 1978).

Other sources are the half-yearly *Wallace Stevens Newsletter*, edited by W.T. Ford (Northwestern University), the annual *American Literary Scholarship* and the quarterly *American Literature*.

Listed alphabetically by author or editor, the following is a selection of books wholly, or centrally, concerned with Wallace Stevens:

BENAMOU, MICHEL, *Wallace Stevens and the Symbolist Imagination* (Princeton University Press, 1972).

BLOOM, HAROLD, *Poetry and Repression: Revisionism from Blake to Stevens* (New Haven, Connecticut: Yale University Press, 1976).

BLOOM, HAROLD, *Wallace Stevens: The Poems of Our Climate* (Ithaca, New York: Cornell University Press, 1977).

BORROFF, MARIE (ed.), *Wallace Stevens: A Collection of Critical Essays* (Englewood Cliffs, New Jersey: Prentice-Hall, 1963).

BUTTEL, ROBERT, *Wallace Stevens: The Making of Harmonium* (Princeton University Press, 1967).

DEMBO, L.S., *Conceptions of Reality in Modern American Poetry* (Berkeley, California: University of California Press, 1966).

DOGGETT, FRANK, *Stevens' Poetry of Thought* (Baltimore, Maryland; Johns Hopkins University Press, 1966).

DOGGETT, FRANK and ROBERT BUTTEL, *Wallace Stevens: A Celebration* (Princeton University Press, 1980).

DONOGHUE, DENIS, *Connoisseurs of Chaos: Ideas of Order in Modern American Poetry* (New York: Macmillan, 1965).

DONOGHUE, DENIS, *The Ordinary Universe* (London: Faber, 1968).

HILLIS MILLER, J., *Poets of Reality* (Cambridge, Massachusetts: Belknap Press of Harvard University, 1966).

HOFFMAN, FREDERICK J., *The Mortal No: Death and the Modern Imagination* (Princeton University Press, 1964).

KERMODE, FRANK, *Wallace Stevens* (Edinburgh: Oliver & Boyd, 1960).

LENTRICCHIA, FRANK, *The Gaiety of Language: An Essay on the Radical Poetics of W.B. Yeats and Wallace Stevens* (Berkeley, California: University of California Press, 1968).

LITZ, A. WALTON, *Introspective Voyageur: The Poetic Development of Wallace Stevens* (New York: Oxford University Press, 1972).

MARTZ, LOUIS L., *The Poem of the Mind* (New York: Oxford University Press, 1966).

MORSE, SAMUEL FRENCH *Wallace Stevens: Poetry as Life* (New York: Pegasus, 1970).

PEARCE, ROY HARVEY, and J. HILLIS MILLER, *The Act of the Mind: Essays on the Poetry of Wallace Stevens* (Baltimore, Maryland: Johns Hopkins University Press, 1963).

QUINN, SISTER M. BERNETTA, *The Metamorphic Tradition in Modern Poetry* (New Brunswick, New Jersey: Rutgers University Press, 1955; New York: Gordian Press, 1966).

REGUEIRO, HELEN, *The Limits of Imagination: Wordsworth, Yeats and Stevens* (Ithaca, New York: Cornell University Press, 1976).

RIDDEL, JOSEPH N., *The Clairvoyant Eye* (Baton Rouge: Louisiana State University Press, 1965).

VENDLER, HELEN HENNESSY, *On Extended Wings: Wallace Stevens' Longer Poems* (Cambridge, Massachusetts: Harvard University Press, 1969).

VENDLER, HELEN HENNESSY, *Part of Nature, Part of Us,* (Cambridge, Massachusetts: Harvard University Press, 1980).

REVIEWS AND PUBLISHED COMMENTS ON STEVENS' WORK 1926–67 NOT REPRINTED IN THE PRESENT COLLECTION

Harmonium (1923)

Bookman, LVIII, December 1923, p. 483; *Republican (Springfield, Massachusetts)* 23 October 1923, p. 7a; *Boston Evening Transcript,* 29 December 1923, part 6, p. 5; *Measure*, IV, March 1924, pp. 17–18; *Chicago Evening Post Literary Review*, 21 December 1923, p. 6; *New York World*, 28 October 1923, p. 7E.

Harmonium (1931)

Bookman, LXXIV, October 1931, pp. 207–8; *Boston Evening Transcript*, 2 September 1931, part 4, p. 3; Horace Gregory, *New York Herald Tribune Books*, 27 September 1931, p. 28; *Virginia Quarterly Review*, XII, April 1936, pp. 294–5

Ideas of Order (1935; 1936)

New Verse, no. 19, February – March 1936, pp 18–9; Boston Evening Transcript, 19 December 1936, sec. 6 p. 2; New York Times Book Review, 12 January 1936, p. 15; New York Herald Tribune Books, December 1936, p. 40; Isidor Schneider, New Masses, XXI, 27 October 1936, p. 24; Geoffrey Stone, American Review, , VIII, November 1936, pp. 120–5; Louis Untermeyer, American Mercury, XXXVI, November 1935, pp. 377–8; Eda Lou Walton, New York Times Book Review, 6 December 1936, p. 18.

Owl's Clover (1936)

William Rose Benét, Saturday Review of Literature, XV, 16 January 1937, p. 18.

The Man with the Blue Guitar (1937)

Ben Belitt, Nation, CXLV, 6 November 1937, p. 508–9; Boston Evening Transcript, 24 December 1937, sec. 4, p. 2; Morton Dauwen Zabel, Southern Review, V, Autumn 1939, pp. 603–5.

Parts of a World (1942)

American Mercury, LV, November 1942, p. 630; Time, XL, 2 November 1942, pp. 103–4; Laura Benét, Voices, no. 111, Autumn 1942, p. 54; R. P. Blackmur, Partisan Review, X, May–June 1943, pp. 297–301; Elizabeth Drew, Atlantic Monthly, CLXX, November 1942, p. 154; Library Journal, LXVII, 1 September 1942; Virginia Quarterly Review, XIX, Winter 1943, pp. 133–4; New York Herald Tribune Books, 8 November 1942, p. 26; Marianne Moore, Kenyon Review V, Winter 1943, pp. 144–7; William York Tindall, American Mercury, LVI, January 1943, pp. 119–20; T. Weiss, Quarterly Review of Literature, I, Summer 1944, pp. 326–7.

Notes Toward a Supreme Fiction (1942)

New York Herald Tribune Weekly Book Review, 28 February 1943, p. 14; Virginia Quarterly Review, XIX, Winter 1943, p. xiv; Harvey Breit, Poetry, LXII, April 1943, pp. 48–50; Horace Gregory, Sewanee Review, LII, Autumn 1944, p. 584;

Marianne Moore, *Kenyon Review*, V, Winter 1943, pp. 144–7; *Voices*, no. 113, Spring 1943, pp. 43–5; T. Weiss, *Quarterly Review of Literature*, I, Summer 1944, p. 328.

Esthétique du Mal (1944)

Keith Botsford, *Yale Poetry Review*, I, Spring 1946, pp. 34–7; Vivienne Koch, *Briarcliff Quarterly*, III, April 1946, pp. 7–9; *Voices*, no. 126, Summer 1946, pp. 55–7.

Transport to Summer (1947)

Christian Science Monitor, 24 May 1947, p. 17; *Kirkus Reviews*, XV, 15 March 1947, p. 187; *U.S. Quarterly Book List*, III, December 1947, pp. 345–6; R.P. Blackmur, *Poetry*, LXXI, February 1948, pp. 271–6; Babette Deutsch, *New York Herald Tribune Weekly Book Review*, 31 August 1947, p. 4; *Voices*, no. 131, Fall 1947, pp. 50–2; *Saturday Review of Literature*, XXX, 12 April 1947, p. 48; Allan Swallow, *New Mexico Quarterly Review*, XVIII, Winter 1948, pp. 460–1; Peter Viereck, *Kenyon Review*, X, Winter 1948, pp. 154–7.

The Auroras of Autumn (1950)

Booklist, XLVII, 1 October 1950, p. 58; *Cleveland Open Shelf*, October 1950, p. 19; *Kirkus Reviews*, XVIII, 15 July 1950, p. 411; *Time*, LVI, 25 September 1950, pp. 106, 108, 110; *U.S. Quarterly Book Review*, VI, December 1950, pp. 418–19; Joseph Bennett, *Hudson Review*, IV, Spring 1951, pp. 134–7; Babette Deutsch, *New York Herald Tribune Weekly Book Review*, 29 October 1950, p. 6; *Virginia Quarterly Review*, XXVII, Summer 1951, pp. 477–8; Lloyd Frankenberg, *New York Times Book Review*, 10 September 1950, p. 20; Rolfe Humphries, *Nation*, CLXXI, 30 September 1950, p. 293; *Voices*, no. 144, January–April 1951, pp. 52–3; *Library Journal*, LXXV, 1 October 1950, p. 1669; Marianne Moore, *Poetry–New York*, no. 4, 1951, pp. 7–9 Dachine Rainer, *Retort*, V, December 1951, p. 47; James M. Thompson, *Beloit Poetry Journal*, I, Spring 1951, p. 31.

The Necessary Angel (1951)

Booklist, XLVIII, 1 February 1952, p. 183; *Cincinnati Enquirer*, 2 December 1951, sec. 4, p. 19; *Kirkus Reviews*, XIX, 1

September 1951, p. 524; *New Yorker*, XXVIII, 23 February 1952, p. 111; *Perspectives USA*, no. 2, Winter 1953, p. 190; *Tulsa Daily World*, 8 July 1951, Sec. V, p. 9; *U.S. Quarterly Book Review*, VIII, June 1952, pp. 134–5; *Harvard Advocate*, CXXXV, March, 1962, pp. 23–4; *Hartford Courant*, 27 January 1952, mag. sec., p. 8; *Bridgeport Post*, 2 December 1951, sec. B., p. 4; *Christian Science Monitor*, 27 December 1951, p. 7;) Richard Eberhart, *Accent*, XII, Spring 1952, pp. 122 – 5; *San Francisco Chronicle*, 27 January 1952, mag., p. 11; *Hartford Times*, 17 November 1951, p. 16; *Virginia Pilot*, 9 December 1951, sec. V, p. 3; *Baltimore Evening Sun*, 28 November 1951, p. 40; *Saturday Review of Literature*, XXXIV, 29 December 1951, pp. 11–12; William Van O'Connor, *New York Times Book Review*, 2 December 1951, pp. 7, 22; *Dallas Times Herald*, 30 December 1951, sec. 3, p. 5; *Hartford Times*, 11 December 1951, p. 22; *Shenandoah*, III, Spring 1952, pp. 22–4; John Unterecker, *New Leader*, XXXIV, 17 December 1951, p. 25; Byron Vazakas, *New Mexico Quarterly Review*, XXII, Winter 1952, pp. 434–9; *Boston Herald*, 30 December 1951, book sec., p. 11; C. Roland Wagner, *Hudson Review*, V, Spring 1952, pp. 144–8; *St. Louis Post-Dispatch*, 3 January 1952, p. 2B; *Houston Post*, 3 June 1951, sec. V, p. 5.

Selected Poems (Fortune Press, 1952)

Austin Clarke, *Irish Times*, 14 February 1953, p. 6; *Tablet*, CCI, 25 April 1953, pp. 341–2.

Selected Poems (Faber, 1953)

British Book News, no. 152, April 1953, p. 246; *Times Literary Supplement*, 19 June 1953, p. 396; James Reeves, *Time and Tide*, XXXIV, 4 April 1953, p. 456; Stephen Spender, *Encounter*, I, October 1953, pp. 61–5.

Collected Poems (1954; 1955)

Booklist, LI, 1 January 1955, p. 197; *Bookmark*, XIV, February 1955, p. 110; *Kirkus Reviews*, XXII, 15 August 1954, p. 557; *Pasadena Star-News*, 20 February 1955, p. 27; *U.S. Quarterly Book Review*, XI, March 1955, p. 69; Louise Bogan, *New Yorker*, XXX, 11 December 1954, pp. 198–202; Thomas

Cole, *Imagi*, VI, no. 4, 1955, unpaged; Marcus Cunliffe, *Manchester Guardian*, 25 October 1955, p. 6; Babette Deutsch, *New York Herald Tribune Weekly Book Review*, 3 October 1954, p. 3; Paul Engle, *Chicago Sunday Tribune*, 24 October 1954, books, p. 2; *Coastlines*, I, Summer 1955, pp. 37–8; Edwin Honig, *Voices*, no. 157, May – August 1955, pp. 27–30; *Baltimore Evening Sun*, 14 December 1954, p. 30; *Library Journal*, LXXX, 1 January 1955, p. 80; *Saturday Review*, XXXVII, 4 December 1954, pp. 26–7; *Hartford Times*, 2 October 1954, p. 22; *Louisville Courier-Journal*, 10 October 1954, sec. 3, p. 11; *Dallas Times-Herald*, 28 November 1954, sec. 7, p. 3; *Providence Journal*, 10 October 1954, sec. 6, p. 8; *New York Times*, 3 February 1955, p. 21; *Christian Science Monitor*, 12 February 1955, p. 13; Karl Shapiro, *Chicago Sun-Times*, 28 November 1954, sec. 2 p. 4; Louis Simpson, *American Scholar*, XXIV, Spring 1955, p. 240; *New Leader*, XXXVIII, 2 May 1955, pp. 25 – 6.

Opus Posthumous (1957)

Booklist, LIV, 15 September 1957, p. 41; *Bridgeport Post*, 11 August 1957, Sec. B, p. 4; *Kirkus Reviews*, XXV, 1 June 1957, p. 408; *Los Angeles Mirror-News*, 23 September 1957, sec. II, p. 5; *New Yorker*, XXXIII, 7 December 1957, pp. 245–6; *Nashville Tennessean*, 15 September 1957, p. 7E; *Buffalo Evening News*, 17 August 1957, p. 8; *Indianapolis News*, 7 September 1957, sec. I p. 2; *Dallas Times-Herald*, 29 September 1957, books, p. 22; *Richmond Times-Dispatch*, 1 September 1957, p. L-5; *Commonweal*, LXVI, 20 September 1957, pp. 620 – 1; August Derleth, *Capital Times* (Madison, Wisconsin), 8 August 1957, p. 12; Babette Deutsch, *New York Herald Tribune Book Review*, 1 September 1957, p. 8; Barbara Gibbs, *Poetry*, XCII, April 1958, pp. 52–7; *San Francisco Examiner*, 27 October 1957, modern living, p. 8; *Progressive*, XXI, December 1957, p. 37; *Fort Wayne News-Sentinel*, 24 October 1957, p. 9; *Los Angeles Times*, 13 September 1957, sec. III, p. 5; *Library Journal*, LXXXII, 1 October 1957, p. 2460; *Richmond News-Leader,* 23 August 1957, p. 13; *Chicago Sunday Tribune*, 25 August 1957, Books, p. 4; *Cleveland News*, 21 August 1957, p. 13; *Houston Post,* 4 August 1957, mag., p. 19; *Christian Science Monitor*, 22

August 1957, p. 11; *Poetry Broadsides*, I, Winter 1957–8, p. 15; *New York Times*, 22 August 1957, p. 25; Karl Shapiro, *Prairie Schooner*, XXXII, Fall 1958, pp. 245–7; *Hartford Times*, 17 August 1957, mag., p. 13; *Dartmouth Alumni Magazine*, L, January 1958, pp. 6–7; *Critic*, XVI, October 1957, p. 36; *Louisville Courier-Journal*, 15 September 1957, see. 4, p. 6.

Opus Posthumous (1959) and *The Necessary Angel* (1960) (British editions)

The Times (London), 28 January 1960, p. 15; *Times Weekly Review*, 4 February 1960, p. 10; A. Alvarez, *Observer*, 14 February 1960, p. 21; Malcolm Bradbury, *Manchester Guardian*, 18 March 1960, p. 8; Martin Dodsworth, *Isis*, 27 January 1960, p. 32; *Oxford Times*, 19 February 1960, p. 22; G.S. Fraser, *New Statesman*, LIX, 9 January 1960, pp. 43–4; Frank Kermode, *Spectator*, 1 January 1960; Frank Kermode, *Spectator*, 26 February 1960; *Time and Tide,* XLI, 27 February 1960, p. 230; P. Le Brun, *Essays in Criticism*, XI, April 1961, pp. 226–32; *Poetry Review,* LI, April – June 1960, pp. 104–5; *Daily Telegraph*, 8 April 1960, p. 17.

Letters of Wallace Stevens (1966; 1967)

Critic, XXVI, October 1967, p. 86; Louise Bogan, *New Yorker*, XLIII, 4 March 1967, p.162; *Virginia Quarterly Review*, XLIII, Spring 1967, p. lxv; *Christian Science Monitor*, 15 December 1966, p. 11; *Book Week*, IV, 12 February 1967, pp. 15–6; *Choice*, IV, April 1967, pp. 164–5; Marie Borroff, *Yale Review*, LVI, Spring 1967, pp. 446–8; Cid Corman, *Caterpillar*, I, October 1967, pp. 103–30; Denis Donoghue, *New York Review of Books*, VII, 1 December 1966, p. 6; Ian Hamilton, *Listener*, LXXVII, 16 February 1967, p. 235; Richard Howard, *Poetry*, CXI, October 1967, pp. 39–40; Frank Kermode, *Encounter*, XXVIIII, May 1967, pp. 65–70; Hilton Kramer, *New Leader*, XLIX, 5 December 1966, p. 18; *Newsweek*, LXVIII, 28 November 1966, p. 114; Stanley Kunitz, *New Republic*, CLV, 12 November 1966, pp. 23–6 A. Walton Litz, *Nation,* CCIV, 16 January 1967, pp. 85–7; Helen McNeil, *Partisan Review,* XXXIV, Fall 1967, pp. 635–8; Norman Holmes Pearson, *New York Times Book*

Review, 6 November 1966, p. 4; Joseph N. Riddel, *American Literature*, XXXIX, November 1967, p. 421; M.L. Rosenthal, *Spectator*, CCXVIII, 24 March 1967, p. 340; Donald E. Stanford, *Southern Review*, III, Summer 1967, pp. 757–63; Tony Tanner, *London Magazine*, VII, April 1967, pp. 105–11; William York Tindall, *Saturday Review*, XLIX, 19 November 1966, pp. 42–3; *Library Journal*, XCI, 1 December 1966, p. 5972.

Index

The index is divided into four parts: I Wallace Stevens: Writings; II Characteristics of Stevens and His Work and Career; III Persons; IV Newspapers, Periodicals, Anthologies, Publishers, Works by Others.

I WALLACE STEVENS: WRITINGS

491

INDEX

INDEX

II CHARACTERISTICS OF STEVENS AND HIS WORK AND CAREER

INDEX

INDEX